THE ULTIMATE
BOOK OF KNITS

THE ULTIMATE
BOOK OF KNITS

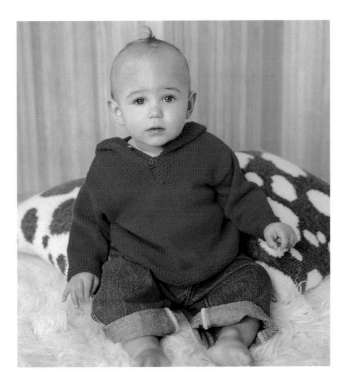

Edited by Stephen Sheard

COLLINS & BROWN

First published in Great Britain in 2002
by Collins & Brown Limited
64 Brewery Road
London N7 9NT

Copyright © Collins & Brown Limited 2002

A member of **Chrysalis** Books plc

Text copyright © Rowan Yarns 2002
Illustrations copyright © Collins & Brown Limited 2002
Photographs copyright © Rowan Yarns 2002

The right of Rowan Yarns to be identified as the author of this
work has been asserted by her in accordance with the Copyright,
Designs and Patents Act, 1988.

1 3 5 7 9 8 6 4 2

British Library Cataloguing-in-Publication Data:
A catalogue record for this book
is available from the British Library.

ISBN 1 85585 958 0

Conceived, edited and designed by
Collins & Brown Limited

EDITOR: Jane Ellis
INDEXER: Hilary Bird
PATTERN CHECKER: Eva Yates
PHOTOGRAPHY: Joey Toller
PROOF READER: Lydia Darbyshire

Reproduction by Classic Scan, Singapore
Printed and bound by Tat Wei, Singapore

contents

introduction

Over twenty years ago the fledgling Rowan Yarn Company started working with a number of designer knitters, both from the UK and the US. As a textile designer myself, I admired at a distance the brilliance and creativity of designers such as Kaffe Fassett, Sasha Keagan, Jean Moss and others. In the 1970s many young designers from the UK fashion and textile colleges idealistically wanted to live a rural life and work with circles of highly talented hand-knitters in a modern-day cottage industry. The pipeline from design concept through to knitting, then selling and marketing their garments around the world, was short and more in tune with the artisans of old than modern produced factory output. The consumers of the world responded and were willing to pay hundreds of pounds or dollars to own and wear a unique and individual garment.

As many of the designers/knitters were already using the large palettes of natural fibre yarns from Rowan, it was a short step to asking them if they would allow their designs to be photographed and translated into knitting patterns and to be made available to hand knitters around the world, who enjoyed knitting truly creative and fashionable designs as a hobby.

Now we have gathered together many of the best designs of the past twenty years from the most exciting designers in this special celebration of talent for you to enjoy.

Stephen Sheard
Rowan Yarns

spring

Welcome the spring by wearing these lightweight cardigans and pullovers, plain and patterned, in fresh shades of blue, lilac and pink.

queen of hearts by Kim Hargreaves

SIZES	1ST	2ND	3RD	4TH	5TH	6TH	7TH	
To fit	6mth	1 yr	2-3 yrs	4-5 yrs	6-7 yrs	7-8 yrs	9-10 yrs	
Actual width	29	34	37.5	42.5	46	51	55	cm
	11½	13½	14¾	16¾	18	20	21½	in
Length	30.5	37.5	42	47	51.5	57	61	cm
	12	14¾	16½	18½	20¼	22½	24	in
Sleeve length	19	21.5	25	29	33.5	38	40.5	cm
	7½	8½	9½	11½	13	15	16	in

YARN

Rowan Handknit DK Cotton 50gm (1¾oz) balls:

Gerba 223	5	6	7	9	11	13	15

NEEDLES
1 pair 3¼mm (US 3) needles
1 pair 4mm (US 6) needles

BUTTONS (1ST, 2ND, 3RD AND 4TH SIZES ONLY)
3

TENSION (GAUGE)
21 sts and 31 rows to 10cm (4in) measured over patterned stocking (stockinette) stitch using 4mm (US 6) needles

KEY
□ K on RS, P on WS
▣ P on RS, K on WS

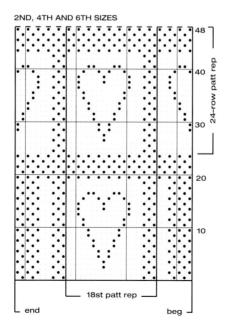

2ND, 4TH AND 6TH SIZES

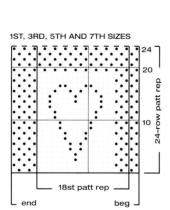

1ST, 3RD, 5TH AND 7TH SIZES

back

Cast on 61 (71: 79: 89: 97: 107: 115) sts using 3¼mm (US 3) needles.
Work in moss (seed) stitch as folls:
ROW 1 (RS): K1, (P1, K1) to end.
Rep this row 5 (5: 5: 5: 7: 7: 7) times more, ending with a WS row.
Change to 4mm (US 6) needles.

1st, 3rd, 5th & 7th sizes only
Work 24 rows in patt from appropriate chart, starting and ending as indicated, and rep the 18-st patt rep 3 (4: 5: 6) times across row.*

2nd, 4th & 6th sizes only
Work 48 rows in patt from appropriate chart, starting and ending as indicated, and rep the 18-st patt rep 3 (4: 5) times across row. *

All sizes
Cont rep the 24-row patt until work measures 25.5 (32.5: 37: 42: 51.5: 57: 61)cm (10 [12¾: 14½: 16½: 20¼: 22½: 24]in) from cast-on edge, ending with a WS row.

1st, 2nd, 3rd & 4th sizes only
DIVIDE FOR BACK NECK
NEXT ROW (RS): Patt 30 (35: 39: 44) sts, turn leaving rem sts on a holder, work each side of neck separately.

PATTERN NOTE
To give the back opening a neat edge, always K the edge, st on every row (RS or WS row).
Cont without shaping until work measures 30.5 (37.5: 42: 47)cm (12 [14¾: 16½: 18½]in) from cast-on edge, ending with a WS row.

SHAPE SHOULDER
Cast (bind) off 6 (7: 8: 9) sts at beg next row.
Cast (bind) off 7 (8: 9: 11) sts, patt to end.
Cast (bind) off 6 (8: 9: 10) sts, patt to end.
Cast (bind) off 4 sts, patt to end.

Cast (bind) off rem 7 (8: 9: 10) sts.
With RS facing rejoin yarn to rem sts, K2tog, patt to end. *30 (35: 39: 44) sts*
Complete to match first side, rev all shaping.

5th, 6th & 7th sizes only
SHAPE SHOULDERS AND BACK NECK
Cast (bind) off 10 (12: 13) sts at beg of next 2 rows.
Cast (bind) off 11 (12: 13) sts, patt 15 (16: 18) sts and turn, leaving rem sts on a holder.
Work each side of neck separately.
Cast (bind) off 4 sts, patt to end.
Cast (bind) off rem 11 (12: 14) sts.
With RS facing, rejoin yarn to rem sts, cast (bind) off center 25 (27: 27) sts, patt to end.
Complete as for first side, rev all shaping.

front
Work as for back to *.
All sizes
Cont rep the 24-row patt until front is 8 (10: 10: 10: 12: 12: 12) rows shorter then back to shoulder shaping, ending with a WS row.
SHAPE FRONT NECK
Patt 25 (30: 34: 37: 41: 46: 50)sts and turn, leaving rem sts on a holder.
Work each side of neck separately.
Dec 1 st at neck edge on next 6 (7: 8: 8: 9: 10: 10) rows. *19 (23: 26: 29: 32: 36: 40) sts*
Cont without further shaping until front matches back to shoulder shaping, ending with a WS row.
SHAPE SHOULDER
Cast (bind) off 6 (7: 8: 9: 10: 12: 13) sts at beg of next row and 6 (8: 9: 10: 11: 12: 13) sts at beg of foll alt row.
Work 1 row.
Cast (bind) off rem 7 (8: 9: 10: 11: 12: 14) sts.
With RS facing, rejoin yarn to rem sts, cast (bind) off center 11 (11: 11: 15: 15: 15: 15) sts and patt to end.
Complete as for first side, rev shaping.

sleeves (both alike)
Cast on 31 (35: 35: 39: 43: 47: 47) sts using 3¼mm (US 3) needles.
Work in moss (seed) st as folls:
ROW 1 (RS): P1, *K1, P1, rep from *, to end.
Rep this row 5 (5: 5: 5: 7: 7: 7) times more, ending with a WS row.

Change to 4mm (US 6) needles and work 24 rows in patt from chart for sleeve, inc each end of 3rd row and every foll 4th row.
Taking extra sts in patt, cont inc every 4th row to 53 (59: 67: 77: 87: 85: 85) sts and then for 6th and 7th sizes only, every foll 6th row to 91 (95) sts.
53 (59: 67: 77: 87: 91: 95) sts
Cont without further shaping until sleeve measures 19 (21.5: 25: 29: 33.5: 38: 40.5)cm (7½ [8½: 9½: 11½: 13: 15: 16]in) or length required from cast-on edge, ending with a WS row. Cast (bind) off loosely and evenly.

finishing
Press all pieces as described on the information page.
1st, 2nd, 3rd & 4th sizes only
Join both shoulder seams using back stitch.
NECKBAND
With RS facing, using 3¼mm (US 3) needles, and beg at left back neck opening, pick up and knit 12 (13: 14: 16) sts across back neck to shoulder, 12 (14: 14: 14) sts down left front neck, 11 (11: 11: 15) sts across center front, 12 (14: 14: 14) sts up right front neck and 12 (13: 14: 16) sts across right back neck. *59 (65: 67: 75) sts*
Work 4 (4: 5: 5) rows in moss (seed) st.
Cast (bind) off evenly in pattern.
Mark position of 3 buttons down left back opening, the first to come in the neckband and the others spaced evenly.
Work button loops to correspond down right back opening.
5th, 6th & 7th sizes only
Join right shoulder seam using back stitch.
NECKBAND
With RS facing and using 3¼mm (US 3) needles, pick up and knit 16 sts down left front neck, 15 sts across center front, 16 sts up right front neck and 33 (35: 35) sts across back neck. *80 (82: 82) sts*
Work 6 rows in moss (seed) st.
Cast (bind) off evenly in pattern.
See information page for finishing instructions, leaving 5 (5: 6: 6: 8: 8: 8)cm (2 [2: 2½: 2½: 3¼: 3¼: 3¼]in) open at side seam to form vents.
Press all seams.

SLEEVE (ALL SIZES)

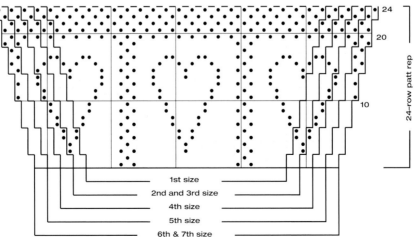

KEY
□ K on RS, P on WS
▪ P on RS, K on WS

1st size
2nd and 3rd size
4th size
5th size
6th & 7th size

24-row patt rep

sid by Kim Hargreaves

SIZES	CHILDREN'S					ADULTS'		
	1ST	2ND	3RD	4TH	5TH	M	L	
To fit chest	4–5 yrs	6–7 yrs	8–9 yrs	9–10 yrs	11–12yrs	–	–	
	–	–	–	–	–	102–107	107–112	cm
	–	–	–	–	–	38	40	in
Actual width	40.5	44.5	48.5	52.5	56.5	59	63	cm
	16	17½	19	20¾	22¼	23¼	25	in
Length	45	48	51	53	55	71	71	cm
	18	19	20	21	21¾	28	28	in
Sleeve length	27.5	30	33	35.5	38	50.5	50.5	cm
	11	12	13	14	15	20	20	in

(All measurements after washing)

YARN

Rowan Denim 50gm (1¾oz) balls:

Nashville 225	9	11	13	15	15	21	21

NEEDLES

1 pair 3¼mm (US 3) needles
1 pair 4mm (US 6) needles

TENSION (GAUGE) BEFORE WASHING

20 sts and 30 rows to 10cm (4in) measured over pattern using 4mm (US 6) needles

PATTERN NOTE

The pattern is written for the children's sizes followed by the adults' sizes in bold.

HORIZONTAL RIB PATTERN

ROWS 1, 3 & 5 (RS): Knit.
ROWS 2, 4 & 6: Purl.
ROWS 7 & 9: Purl.
ROWS 8 & 10: Knit.
ROWS 11, 13 & 15: Knit.
ROWS 12, 14 & 16: Purl.
ROW 17: Purl.
ROWS 18, 20 & 22: Purl.
ROWS 19, 21 & 23: Knit.
ROWS 24 & 26: Knit.
ROWS 25 & 27: Purl.
ROWS 28, 30 & 32: Purl.
ROWS 29, 31 & 33: Knit.
ROW 34 (WS): Knit.
These 34 rows form the pattern and are repeated throughout.

crewneck pullover
back

Cast on 81 (89: 97: 105: 113: **119: 127**) sts using 3¼mm (US 3) needles.
Work 6 (6: 6: 6: 6: **10: 10**) rows in garter st (knit every row).
Change to 4mm (US 6) needles.
Work 24 (24: 24: 24: 24: **40: 40**) rows in horizontal rib patt and AT THE SAME TIME work garter-st edgings to form side vents by knitting first and last 5 sts on every WS row.
This completes side vents.
Cont in patt, working across all sts until work measures 54 (58: 61: 63.5: 66: **85.5: 85.5**)cm (21¼ [22¾: 24: 25: 26: **33¾: 33¾**]in) from cast-on edge, ending with a WS row.

Children's sizes
SHAPE SHOULDERS AND BACK NECK
Patt 28 (32: 36: 40: 44) and turn, leaving rem sts on a holder.
Work each side of neck separately.
Cast (bind) off 3 sts, patt to end. Leave rem 25 (29: 33: 37: 41) sts on a holder. With RS facing, rejoin yarn to rem sts, cast (bind) off center 25 sts, patt to end.
Complete to match first side, rev shaping.

Adults' sizes
SHAPE SHOULDERS AND BACK NECK
Cast (bind) off **10 (11)** sts at beg of next 4 rows.
Cast (bind) off **10 (12)** sts, patt 16 and turn, leaving rem sts on a holder.
Work each side of neck separately.
Cast (bind) off **4** sts, patt to end.

Cast (bind) off rem **12 (12)** sts.

With RS facing, rejoin yarn to rem sts, cast (bind) off center 27 sts, patt to end.

Complete to match first side, rev shaping.

front

Work as given for back until front is 16 (16: 16: 18: 18: **22: 22**) rows shorter than back to shoulder shaping, ending with a WS row.

SHAPE FRONT NECK

Patt 36 (40: 44: 48: 52: **54: 58**) sts, turn and leave rem sts on a holder.

Work each side of neck separately.

Cast (bind) off 3 (3: 3: 3: 3: **4: 4**) sts, patt to end.

Dec 1 st at neck edge on next 5 rows and 3 foll alt rows. *25 (29: 33: 37: 41: 42: 46) sts*

Cont until front matches back to shoulder shaping, ending with a WS row.

Children's sizes only

Leave rem 25 (29: 33: 37: 41) sts on a holder.

With RS facing, rejoin yarn to rem sts, cast (bind) off center 9 sts, patt to end.

Complete to match first side.

Adults' sizes only

SHAPE SHOULDER

Cast (bind) off 10 (11) sts at beg of next row and foll alt row.

Work 1 row.

Cast (bind) off 10 (12) sts at beg of next row.

Work 1 row.

Cast (bind) off rem 12 sts.

With RS facing, rejoin yarn to rem sts, cast (bind) off center 11 sts, patt to end.

Complete to match first side, rev all shaping.

sleeves (both alike)

Cast on 35 (35: 43: 43: 43: **57: 57**) sts using 3¼mm (US 3) needles.

Work 6 (6: 6: 6: 6: **10: 10**) rows in garter st.

Change to 4mm (US 6) needles.

Cont in horizontal rib patt, rep the 34-row patt throughout and AT THE SAME TIME shape sides by inc 1 st at each end of 3rd row and every foll 4th (4th: 4th: 4th: 4th: **6th: 6th**) row to 57 (57: 65: 65: 75: **69: 69**) sts and then every foll 6th (6th: 6th: 6th: **8th: 8th**) row to 69 (73: 83: 87: 93: **101: 101**) sts.

Cont without further shaping until work measures 33 (35.5: 40.5: 43: 45.5: **60: 60**)cm (13 [14: 16: 17: 18: **23½: 23½**]in) from cast-on edge, ending with a WS row.

Cast (bind) off loosely and evenly.

v-neck pullover
(adults' sizes only)
back and sleeves

Work as given for crewneck pullover.

front

Work as for back until work measures 60cm (23½in) from cast-on edge, ending with a WS row.

SHAPE FRONT NECK

Patt 59 (63) sts and turn, leaving rem sts on a holder.

Work each side of neck separately.

Work 3 rows.

Dec 1 st at neck edge on next row and every foll 4th row to 42 (46) sts.

Cont without further shaping until front matches back to shoulder shaping, ending with a WS row.

SHAPE SHOULDER

Cast (bind) off 10 (11) sts at beg of next row and foll alt row.

Work 1 row.

Cast (bind) off 10 (12) sts, patt to end.

Work 1 row.

Cast (bind) off rem 12 sts.

Rejoin yarns to rem sts, K2tog, patt to end. *59 (63) sts*

Complete to match first side, rev all shaping.

finishing

Children's sizes

Join right shoulder seam by casting (binding) off sts together on RS.

Adults' sizes

Join right shoulder seam using back stitch.

Crewneck (all sizes)

NECKBAND

With RS facing and using 3¼mm (US 3) needles, pick up and knit 20 (20: 20: 22: 22: **30: 30**) sts down left front neck, 9 (9: 9: 9: 9: **11: 11**) sts across center front, 20 (20: 20: 22: 22: **30: 30**) sts up right front neck to shoulder and 31 (31: 31: 31: 31: **35: 35**) sts across back neck. *80 (80: 80: 84: 84: 106: 106) sts*

Work 8 (8: 8: 8: 8: **10: 10**) rows in garter st (knit every row), ending with a RS row.

Cast (bind) off evenly knitwise.

V-neck (adults' sizes only)

Join right shoulder seam using back stitch.

With RS facing and using 3¼mm (US 3) needles, pick up and knit 70 sts down left front neck, place marker at center front, pick up and knit 70 sts up right front neck and 35 sts across back neck. *175 sts*

NEXT ROW (WS): Knit to 2 sts before marker, P2tog, P2tog tbl, K to end.

NEXT ROW: Knit to 2 sts before marker, K2tog tbl, K2tog, K to end.

Rep these 2 rows 3 times more.

Cast off, dec each side of marker as before.

Both crewneck and V-neck pullovers

Join left shoulder as for right shoulder seam and neckband seam using an edge-to-edge stitch.

Wash all pieces before sewing tog (see ball band for washing instructions). See information page for finishing instructions.

shell by Louisa Harding

SIZE	S	M	
To fit bust	86–91	91–97	cm
	34–36	36–38	in
Actual width	48.5	56.5	cm
	19	22¼	in
Cropped pullover length			
DK Cotton	43.5	43.5	cm
	17	17	in
Denim	50	50	cm
	19¾	19¾	in
Tunic length			
DK Cotton	71	71	cm
	28	28	in
Denim	81.5	81.5	cm
	32	32	in
Sleeve length			
DK Cotton	48	45.5	cm
	19	18	in
Denim	55.5	52.5	cm
	22	20¾	in

(Denim measurements before washing)

YARNS
Rowan Handknit DK Cotton or Rowan Denim 50gm (1¾oz) balls:
Cropped Pullover (photographed in Nashville 225)

Denim	12	13
DK Cotton	12	13

Tunic (photographed in Ecru 251)

DK Cotton	17	17
Denim	19	19

NEEDLES
1 pair 3¼mm (US 3) needles
1 pair 4mm (US 6) needles

TENSION (GAUGE)
Handknit DK Cotton
22.5 sts and 28 rows to 10cm (4in) measured over shell stitch pattern using 4mm (US 6) needles
Denim (before washing)
22.5 sts and 26 rows to 10cm (4in) measured over shell stitch pattern using 4mm (US 6) needles

PATTERN NOTE
The Denim yarn shrinks in length by approximately one-fifth when washed for the first time, therefore lengths given for DK Cotton and Denim differ. It is essential the length is worked according to the yarn chosen. Where the instructions for length differ, the pattern is written for the DK Cotton, followed by the denim in bold.

SHELL PATTERN
ROW 1 (RS): Knit.
ROW 2: Knit.
ROW 3: K1, *(K2tog) 3 times, (yon, K1) 6 times, (K2tog) 3 times, rep from * to last st, K1.
ROW 4: K1, purl to last st, K1.
These 4 rows form the patt and are repeated throughout.
Note: When shaping sleeve, knit all extra stitches on patt row 3 until there are enough sts to complete a half patt (9 extra sts at each side), then work row 3 of patt rep as folls:
PATT ROW 3 (RS): K1, *(yo, K1) 3 times, (K2tog) 6 times, (yon, K1) 3 times, rep from * to last st, K1.
After another 9 sts increased at each side, revert to original pattern.

tunic
back
Cast on 110 (128) sts using 3¼mm (US 3) needles.
Work 6 rows in garter st (knit every row).
Change to 4mm (US 6) needles. *Cont in patt, rep the 4-row patt throughout, until work measures 71 (**81.5**)cm (28 [**32**]in) from cast-on edge, ending with row 4 of patt rep.
SHAPE BACK NECK
**Patt 28 (37) sts, turn and leave rem sts on a holder.
Work each side of neck separately.
Dec 1 st at neck edge on next 9 rows, ending with a WS row. *19 (28) sts*
SHAPE SHOULDERS
Cont in st st, beg with a K row.
Cast (bind) off 6 (9) sts at beg of next row and foll alt row.
Work 1 row. Cast (bind) off rem 7 (10) sts.
With RS facing, slip center 54 (54) sts onto a holder, rejoin yarn to rem sts, patt to end.
Complete to match first side, rev all shaping.

front
Work as given for back until front is 8 (**9.5**)cm (3¼ [**3¾**]in) shorter than back to shoulder, ending with a WS row.
SHAPE FRONT NECK
Patt 28 (37) sts, turn and leave rem sts on a holder.
Work each side of neck separately.
Keeping patt correct cast (bind) off 1 st at neck edge on next 4 rows and 5 foll alt rows. *19 (28) sts*

Cont in patt without further shaping until front matches back to shoulder, ending with a WS row.

SHAPE SHOULDERS
Complete as for back.

sleeves (both alike)

Note: The length of sleeve for smaller size is longer than medium size.

Cast on 56 (56) sts using 3¼mm (US 3) needles.
Work 6 rows in garter st.
Change to 4mm (US 6) needles.*
Cont in patt, rep the 4-row patt throughout, and AT THE SAME TIME shape sides by inc 1 st at each end of 4th (**5th**) row and every foll 4th (**5th**) row to 110 sts. Take the extra stitches into patt as described in the stitch note.
Cont without further shaping until work measures 48 (45.5: **55.5: 52.5)cm (18¾ [18: **21¾: 20¾**]in) from cast-on edge, ending with row 2 of patt rep. Work 3 rows in st st. Cast (bind) off knitwise.

cropped pullover
back

Work as for tunic back to *. Cont in patt, rep the 4-row patt throughout, until work measures 43.5 (**50**)cm (17 (**19¾**)in) from cast-on edge, ending with row 4 of patt rep.

SHAPE BACK NECK
Complete as for tunic back from **.

front

Work as for tunic front.

sleeves (both alike)

Work as for tunic sleeve to *.
Cont in patt, rep the 4-row patt throughout, and AT THE SAME TIME shape sides by inc 1 st at each end of 6th (**7th**) row and every foll 6th (**7th**) row to 94 sts. Take the extra stitches into patt as described in the stitch note. Complete as for tunic sleeve from **.

finishing

Handknit DK Cotton only
Press all pieces as described on the information page.
Handknit DK Cotton and Denim
TUNIC AND CROPPED PULLOVER
Join right shoulder using back stitch.
NECKBAND
With RS facing and using 3¼mm (US 3) needles, pick up and knit 16 sts down left front neck, 54 sts from holder, 16 sts up right front neck, 8 sts down back neck, 54 sts from holder and 8 sts up back neck. *156 sts*
Knit 1 row.
Small size
NEXT ROW (DEC): K21, [K2tog 4 times, K10] twice, K2tog 4 times, K34, [K2tog 4 times, K10] twice, K2tog 4 times, K13. Cast (bind) off knitwise.
Medium size
NEXT ROW (DEC): K16, *[K2tog twice, K10, K2tog twice] 3 times,* K24, rep from * to *, K8. Cast (bind) off knitwise.
Join left shoulder seam and neckband using back st. The Denim yarn pieces must be washed and dried before completing the garment (see ball band for washing instructions). See information page for finishing instructions.

lizzie by Kim Hargreaves

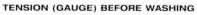

SIZES

	CHILDREN'S				LADIES'			
	6-8 YRS	8-9 YRS	9-11 YRS	12-14 YRS	S	M	L	
To fit chest	–	–	–	–	81–86	86–91	91–97	cm
	–	–	–	–	32–34	34–36	36–38	in
Actual width	47.5	51.5	53.5	56.5	58.5	61.5	63.1	cm
	19	20½	21	22	23	24	25	in
Length	53.5	57	60	63	68.5	71	71	cm
	21	22½	23½	25	27	28	28	in
Sleeve length	44.5	47	49.5	52	54	54	54	cm
	17½	18½	19½	20½	21½	21½	21½	in

(All measurements after washing)

YARN
Rowan Denim 50gm (1¾oz) balls:

	17	19	20	22	**25**	**26**	**26**

(child's photographed in Nashville 225, ladies' in Ecru 324)

NEEDLES
1 pair 3¼mm (US 3) needles
1 pair 4mm (US 6) needles
Cable needle

BUTTONS
5 buttons

TENSION (GAUGE) BEFORE WASHING
20 sts and 28 rows to 10cm (4in) measured over stocking (stockinette) stitch using 4mm (US 6) needles.

PATTERN NOTE
Denim will shrink in length when washed for the first time. Allowances have been made in this pattern for shrinkage.
The pattern is written for the four children's sizes, followed by the ladies' sizes in bold.

SPECIAL ABBREVIATIONS
C4F = Cable 4 front: Slip next 2 sts onto cable needle and hold at front, K2, then K2 from cable needle.
C4B = Cable 4 back: Slip next 2 sts onto cable needle and hold at back, K2, then K2 from cable needle.

back
Cast on 97 (103: 107: 113: **117: 123: 127**) sts using 3¼mm (US 3) needles.
Work 11 rows in garter st (knit every row).
NEXT ROW (WS) (INC): K2 (5: 7: 10: **12: 15: 17**), M1, K1, M1, K30, M1, K1, M1, K29, M1, K1, M1, K30, M1, K1, M1, K2 (5: 7: 10: **12: 15: 17**).

*105 (111: 115: 121: **125: 131: 135**) sts*
Change to 4mm (US 6) needles.
Beg and ending rows as indicated, work foll chart, rep the 24-row patt until back measures 39 (42: 44.5: 47: **53.5: 55: 55**)cm (15½ [16½: 17½: 18½: **21: 21½: 21½**]in), ending with a WS row.
SHAPE ARMHOLES
Children's sizes only
Cast (bind) off 5 sts at beg of next 2 rows.
95 (101: 105: 111) sts
Ladies' sizes only
Cast (bind) off 4 sts at beg of next 2 rows.
Dec 1 st at each end on next 7 rows, then on every foll alt row until (**95: 101: 105**) sts rem.
All sizes
Cont without further shaping until armhole measures 25 (26.5: 27.5: 29: **29: 30: 30**)cm (9½ (10½: 11: 11½: **11½: 12: 12**)in), ending with a RS row.
SHAPE SHOULDERS AND BACK NECK
Cast (bind) off 10 (11: 12: 12: **9: 10: 11**) sts at beg of next 2 rows.
NEXT ROW (RS): Cast (bind) off first 10 (11: 12: 12: **9: 10: 11**) sts, patt until there are 14 (15: 15: 17: **14: 15: 15**) sts on right needle and turn, leaving rem sts on a holder. Work each side of neck separately.
Cast (bind) off 4 sts at beg of next row.
Cast (bind) off rem 10 (11: 11: 13: **10: 11: 11**) sts.
With RS facing, rejoin yarn to rem sts, cast (bind) off center 27 (27: 27: 29: **31: 31: 31**) sts, patt to end.
Complete to match first side, rev shapings.

pocket linings (make two)

Cast on 21 (21: 23: 23: **25: 25: 25**) sts, using 4mm
(US 6) needles.
Beg with a K row, work 26 (26: 28: 28: **30: 30: 30**) rows
in st st.
Break yarn and leave sts on a holder.

left front

Cast on 53 (56: 60: 63: **65: 68: 70**) sts using 3¼mm
(US 3) needles.
Work 11 rows in garter st.
NEXT ROW (WS) (INC): K10 (10: 12: 12: **12: 12: 12**) and
slip these sts onto a holder for front band, K9, M1,
K1, M1, K30, M1, K1, M1, K2 (5: 7: 10: **12: 15: 17**).
*47 (50: 52: 55: **57: 60: 62**) sts*
Change to 4mm (US 6) needles.
Beg and ending rows as indicated, work 26 (26: 28:
28: **30: 30: 30**) rows, foll chart, rep the 24-row patt.
PLACE POCKET
NEXT ROW (RS): Patt 9 (12: 13: 16: **17: 20: 22**) sts, slip
next 21 (21: 23: 23: **25: 25: 25**) sts onto a holder and
patt across sts of first pocket lining, patt 17 (17: 16:
16: **15: 15: 15**) sts.
Cont in patt until left front matches back to start of
armhole shaping, ending with a WS row.
SHAPE ARMHOLE
Cast (bind) off 5 (5: 5: 5: **4: 4: 4**) sts at beg of next
row. *42 (45: 47: 50: **53: 56: 58**) sts*
Work 1 row, thus ending with a WS row.
SHAPE FRONT SLOPE
Children's sizes only
Dec 1 st at front opening edge of next and every foll
4th row until 36 (41: 45: 46) sts rem, then on every
foll 6th row (from previous dec) until 30 (33: 35: 37)
sts rem.
Ladies' sizes only
Dec 1 st at armhole edge on next 7 rows and AT
THE SAME TIME dec 1 st at front opening edge on
next and foll 4th row. *(**44: 47: 49**) sts.*
Work 1 row, thus ending with a WS row.
Dec 1 st at armhole edge on next and foll 3 alt rows
and AT THE SAME TIME dec 1 st at front opening
edge on next and foll 4th row. *(**38: 41: 43**) sts*
Now dec 1 st at front opening edge only on every
foll 4th row (from previous dec) until (**35: 40: 42**) sts
rem, then on every foll 6th row (from previous dec)
until (**28: 31: 33**) sts rem.
All sizes
Cont without further shaping until left front matches
back to start of shoulder shaping, ending with a WS row.
SHAPE SHOULDER
Cast (bind) off 10 (11: 12: 12: **9: 10: 11**) sts at beg of
next and foll alt row.
Work 1 row.
Cast (bind) off rem 10 (11: 11: 13: **10: 11: 11**) sts.

right front

Cast on 53 (56: 60: 63: **65: 68: 70**) sts using 3¼mm
(US 3) needles.
Work 11 rows in garter st.
NEXT ROW (WS) (INC): K2 (5: 7: 10: **12: 15: 17**), M1, K1,
M1, K9 and turn, leaving rem 10 (10: 12: 12: **12: 12:
12**) sts on a holder for front band.
*47 (50: 52: 55: **57: 60: 62**) sts*
Change to 4mm (US 6) needles.
Beg and ending rows as indicated, work 26 (26: 28:
28: **30: 30: 30**) rows, foll chart, rep the 24-row patt.

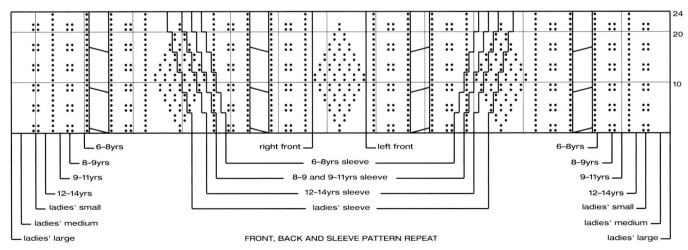

PLACE POCKET

NEXT ROW (RS): Patt 17 (17: 16: 16: **15: 15: 15**) sts, slip next 21 (21: 23: 23: **25: 25: 25**) sts onto a holder and patt across sts of second pocket lining, patt 9 (12: 13: 16: **17: 20: 22**) sts.

Complete as for left front, rev all shapings.

sleeves (both alike)

Cast on 43 (47: 47: 51: **57: 57: 57**) sts using 3¼mm (US 3) needles.

Work 16 (16: 16: 16: **20: 20: 20**)cm (6¼ [6¼: 6¼: 6¼: 7¾: 7¾: 7¾]in) in garter st, ending with a RS row.

NEXT ROW (WS) (INC): K6 (8: 8: 10: **13: 13: 13**), M1, K1, M1, K29, M1, K1, M1, K6 (8: 8: 10: **13: 13: 13**).

47 (51: 51: 55: 61: 61: 61) sts

Change to 4mm (US 6) needles.

Beg and ending rows as indicated, work foll chart, rep the 24-row patt, shaping sides by inc 1 st at each end of 5th and every foll 4th row until there are 81 (77: 81: 77: **69: 81: 81**) sts, then on every foll 6th row (from previous inc) until there are 89 (93: 97: 101: **101: 105: 105**) sts.

Cont without further shaping until sleeve measures 53.5 (56.5: 59.5: 62.5: **65: 65: 65**)cm (21 [22¼: 23½: 24¾: **25½: 25½: 25½**]in), ending with a WS row.

Children's sizes only

Cast (bind) off loosely and evenly.

Ladies' sizes only

Cast (bind) off 4 sts at beg of next 2 rows.

Dec 1 st at each end on next 7 rows, then on every foll alt row until (**71: 75: 75**) sts rem.

Work 1 row, thus ending with a WS row.

Cast (bind) off loosely and evenly.

finishing

DO NOT PRESS.

Join shoulder seams using back stitch.

BUTTON BAND AND COLLAR

Slip 10 (10: 12: 12: **12: 12: 12**) sts from left front holder onto 3¼mm (US 3) needles and rejoin yarn with RS facing.

Cont in garter st until band, when slightly stretched, fits up left front opening edge to start of front slope shaping, sewing in place as you go and ending at inner edge (edge where band is attached).

SHAPE COLLAR

Inc 1 st at beg (inner edge) of next row and at same edge on every foll 3rd row until there are 30 (30: 32: 32: **34: 34: 34**) sts, then on every foll 6th row until there are 32 (32: 34: 34: **38: 38: 38**) sts.

Cont without further shaping until collar fits up left front slope and across back neck to center, sewing in place as you go and ending at inner edge.

Cast (bind) off 8 (8: 9: 9: **10: 10: 10**) sts at beg of next and foll 2 alt rows. Work 1 row.

Cast (bind) off rem 8 (8: 7: 7: **8: 8: 8**) sts.

Mark positions for 5 buttons on this band, the first to be level with top of pocket, the last to be 2cm (¾in) below start of front slope shaping and the rem spaced evenly between.

BUTTONHOLE BAND AND COLLAR

Work as for button band and collar, rev all shapings and adding 5 buttonholes to correspond with positions marked for buttons.

TO MAKE A BUTTONHOLE (RS): K5, cast (bind) off 2 sts, K to end and back, casting on 2 sts over those cast (bound) off on previous row.

POCKET TOPS (BOTH ALIKE)

Slip 21 (21: 23: 23: **25: 25: 25**) sts from pocket holder onto 3¼mm (US 3) needles and rejoin yarn with RS facing.

Work 7 rows in garter st.

Cast (bind) off knitwise.

BELT (OPTIONAL)

Cast on 7 (7: 9: 9: **9: 9: 9**) sts using 3¼mm (US 3) needles.

Work 140 (150: 160: 170: **180: 180: 180**)cm (55 [59: 63: 67: **70¾: 70¾: 70¾**]in) in garter st.

Cast (bind) off.

Machine wash all pieces before sewing tog (see ball band for washing instructions). See information pages for finishing instructions.

KEY

☐ K on RS, P on WS

▣ P on RS, K on WS

⊏⊏⊏⊐ C4B

⊏⊏⊏⊐ C4F

6–8yrs
8–9yrs
9–11yrs
12–14yrs
ladies' small
ladies' medium
ladies' large

right front — — left front
6–8yrs sleeve
8–9 and 9–11yrs sleeve
12–14yrs sleeve
ladies' sleeve

6–8yrs
8–9yrs
9–11yrs
12–14yrs
ladies' small
ladies' medium
ladies' large

FRONT, BACK AND SLEEVE PATTERN REPEAT

24
20
10

jefferson by Kim Hargreaves

SIZES	LADIES'			MEN'S			
	S	**M**	**L**	**M**	**L**	**XL**	
To fit chest	81–86	86–91	91–97	**97–102**	**102–107**	**107–112**	cm
	32–34	34–36	36–38	**38–40**	**40–42**	**42–44**	in
Actual width	56.5	58.5	61.5	**63.5**	**66.5**	**68.5**	cm
	22	23	24	**25**	**26**	**27**	in
Length	57	58	59	**65**	**66**	**67**	cm
	22½	23	23	**25½**	**26**	**26½**	in
Sleeve length	41	41	42	**47**	**48**	**48**	cm
	16	16	16½	**18½**	**19**	**19**	in

(All measurements after washing)

YARN

Rowan Handknit DK Cotton 50gm (1¾oz) balls:

14	14	15	**17**	**18**	**19**

(ladies' photographed in Handknit DK Cotton, Carmen 201)

Rowan Handknit Denim 50gm (1¾oz) balls:

18	19	20	**23**	**24**	**25**

(men's photographed in Denim, Nashville 225)

NEEDLES
1 pair 3¼mm (US 3) needles
1 pair 4mm (US 6) needles

TENSION (GAUGE)
Handknit DK Cotton
20 sts and 28 rows to 10cm (4in) measured over stocking (stockinette) stitch using 4mm (US 6) needles

Denim (before washing)
20 sts and 28 rows to 10cm (4in) measured over stocking (stockinette) stitch using 4mm (US 6) needles.

PATTERN NOTE
Denim will shrink in length when washed for the first time. Allowances have been made in this pattern for shrinkage.
The pattern is written for the three ladies' sizes, followed by the men's sizes in bold.

back
Cast on 113 (117: 123: **127: 133: 137**) sts using 3¼mm (US 3) needles.
Beg with a RS row, work 8 rows in garter st (knit every row).
Change to 4mm (US 8) needles.

Starting and ending rows as indicated and rep the 74-row rep throughout, cont in patt from body chart as folls:
Handknit DK Cotton version
Cont straight until back measures 33 (34: 34: **38: 38: 39**)cm (13 [13½: 13½: **15: 15: 15½**]in) from cast-on edge, ending with a WS row.
Denim version
Cont straight until back measures 38.5 (39.5: 39.5: **44.5: 44.5: 45.5**)cm (15¼ [15½: 15½: **17½: 17½: 17½**]in) from cast-on edge, ending with a WS row.
Both versions
SHAPE ARMHOLES
Keeping patt correct, cast (bind) off 4 sts at beg of next 2 rows. *105 (109: 115: **119: 125: 129**) sts*
Dec 1 st at each end of next 6 rows.
*93 (97: 103: **107: 113: 117**) sts*
Handknit DK Cotton version
Cont straight until armhole measures 24 (24: 25: **27: 28: 28**)cm, (9½ [9½: 9¾: **10¾: 11¼: 11¼**]in), ending with a WS row.
Denim version
Cont straight until armhole measures 28 (28: 29: **31.5: 32.5: 32.5**)cm, (11¼ [11¼: 11½: **12½: 12¾: 12¾**]in), ending with a WS row.
Both versions
SHAPE SHOULDERS AND BACK NECK
Keeping patt correct, cast (bind) off 10 (10: 11: **12:**

12: 13) sts at beg of next 2 rows.
*73 (77: 81: **83: 89: 91**) sts*
NEXT ROW (RS): Cast (bind) off 10 (10: 11: **12: 12: 13**) sts, patt until there are 14 (15: 16: **15: 17: 17**) sts on right needle and turn, leaving rem sts on a holder.
Work each side of neck separately.
Cast (bind) off 4 sts at beg of next row.
Cast (bind) off rem 10 (11: 12: **11: 13: 13**) sts.
With RS facing, rejoin yarn to rem sts, cast (bind) off center 25 (27: 27: **29: 31: 31**) sts, patt to end.
Work to match first side, rev shaping.

front
Handknit DK Cotton version
Work as for back until armhole measures 7 (**10**)cm (2¾ [**4**]in), ending with a WS row.
Denim version
Work as for back until armhole measures 8 (**11.5**)cm (3¼ [**4½**]in), ending with a WS row.
Both versions
SHAPE NECK
NEXT ROW (RS): Patt 46 (48: 51: **53: 56: 58**) sts and turn, leaving rem sts on a holder.
Work each side of neck separately.
Work 1 row.
Handknit DK Cotton version
Keeping patt correct, dec 1 st at neck edge on next and foll 12 (13: 13: **16: 16: 16**) alt rows, then on every foll 4th row until 30 (31: 34: **35: 37: 39**) sts rem.

Denim version
Keeping patt correct, dec 1 st at neck edge on next and foll 7 (9: 9: **12: 13: 13**) alt rows, then on every foll 4th row until 30 (31: 34: **35: 37: 39**) sts rem.
Both versions
Cont straight until front matches back to start of shoulder shaping, ending with a WS row.
SHAPE SHOULDER
Keeping patt correct, cast (bind) off 10 (10: 11: **12: 12: 13**) sts at beg of next and foll alt row.
Work 1 row.
Cast (bind) off rem 10 (11: 12: **11: 13: 13**) sts.
With RS facing, rejoin yarn to rem sts, slip center st onto a safety pin, patt to end.
Work to match first side, rev shaping.

sleeves (both alike)
Cast on 57 (57: 57: **61: 61: 61**) sts using 3¼mm (US 3) needles.
Beg with a RS row, work 8 rows in garter st.
Change to 4mm (US 8) needles.
Starting and ending rows as indicated and rep the 50-row rep throughout, cont in patt from sleeve chart as folls:
Handknit DK Cotton version
Inc 1 st at each end of 7th and every foll 6th row to 73 (73: 67: **77: 71: 71**) sts, then on every foll 4th row until there are 97 (97: 101: **109: 113: 113**) sts, taking inc sts into patt.

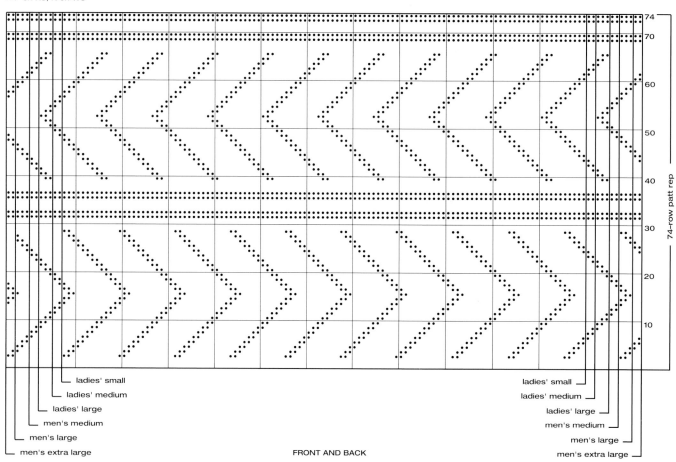

ladies' small
ladies' medium
ladies' large
men's medium
men's large
men's extra large

ladies' small
ladies' medium
ladies' large
men's medium
men's large
men's extra large

FRONT AND BACK

74-row patt rep

Cont straight until sleeve measures 41 (41: 42:
47: 48: 48)cm (16¼ [16¼: 16½: **18½: 18¾: 18¾**]in)
from cast-on edge, ending with a WS row.

Denim version
Inc 1 st at each end of 7th and every foll 6th row to
91 (91: 87: **99: 95: 95**) sts, then on every foll 4th row
until there are 97 (97: 101: **109: 113: 113**) sts, taking
inc sts into patt.
Cont straight until sleeve measures 48 (48: 49:
55: 56: 56)cm (18¾ [18¾: 19¼: **21½: 22: 22**]in) from
cast-on edge, ending with a WS row.

Both versions
SHAPE TOP
Cast (bind) off 4 sts at beg of next 2 rows.
*89 (89: 93: **101: 105: 105**) sts*

Handknit DK Cotton version
Dec 1 st at each end of next and foll 4 alt rows.
*79 (79: 83: **91: 95: 95**) sts*

Denim version
Dec 1 st at each end of next and foll 6 alt rows.
*75 (75: 79: **87: 91: 91**) sts*

Both versions
Purl 1 row. Cast (bind) off.

finishing
Handknit DK Cotton version
Press all pieces as described on the information page.
Denim version
DO NOT PRESS.
Both versions
Join right shoulder seam using back stitch.
NECKBAND
With RS facing and 3¼mm (US 3) needles, pick up
and knit 40 (**42**) sts down left side of neck, K st from
safety pin, pick up and K 40 (**42**) sts up right side of
neck, then 33 (35: 35: **37: 39: 39**) sts across back neck.
*114 (116: 116: **122: 124: 124**) sts.*
Handknit DK Cotton version
Beg with a purl row, work 5 rows in st st.
Denim version
Beg with a purl row, work 7 rows in st st.
Both versions
Cast (bind) off evenly.
After all knitting is completed, machine wash all
Denim pieces as described on the ball band before
sewing pieces together. See information page for
finishing instructions.

KEY
☐ K on RS, P on WS
▣ P on RS, K on WS

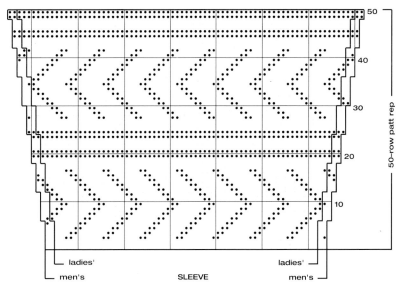

ladies' ladies'
men's   SLEEVE   men's

50-row patt rep

fitted rib bodice pullover by Kim Hargreaves

SIZE

To fit bust	86	91	97	cm
	34	36	38	in
Actual width	46.5	49	52	cm
	18¼	19¼	20½	in
Length	66	67.5	69	cm
	26¼	26¾	27¼	in
Sleeve length	41.5	43.5	45.5	cm
	16¼	17¼	18	in

YARN

Rowan Wool Cotton–50gm (1¾oz) balls:

Violet	933	10	10	11

NEEDLES

1 pair 3¼mm (US 3)
1 pair 4mm (US 6)

TENSION (GAUGE)

22 sts and 30 rows to 10cm (4in) measured over
stocking (stockinette) stitch using 4mm (US 6) needles

back

Cast on 110 (116: 122) sts using 3¼mm (US 3)
needles and set rib patt as folls:

Small size only

ROW 1 (RS): P2, *K3, P4, K3, P2, rep from * to end.
ROW 2: K2, *P2, K1, P1, K2, P1, K1, P2, K2, rep from
* to end.
ROW 3: P2, *K1, P1, K2, P2, K2, P1, KI, P2, rep from
* to end.
ROW 4: K2, *K1, P3, K2, P3, K3, rep from * to end.

Medium size only

ROW 1 (RS): K3, P2, *K3, P4, K3, P2, rep from * to last
3 sts, K3.
ROW 2: K1, P2, K2, *P2, KI, P1, K2, P1, K1, P2, K2,
rep from * to last 3 sts, P2, KI.
ROW 3: K1, P1, K1, P2, *K1, P1, K2, P2, K2, P1, K.1,
P2, rep from * to last 3 sts, K1, P1, K1.
ROW 4: P2, K3, *K1, P3, K2, P3, K3, rep from * to last
3 sts, K1, P2.

Large size only

ROW 1 (RS): P3, K3, P2, *K3, P4, K3,P2, rep from * to
last 6 sts, K3, P3.
ROW 2: K2, P1, K1, P2, K2, *P2, K1, P1, K2, P1, K1,
P2, K2, rep from * to last 6 sts, P27, K1, P1, K2.
ROW 3: P2, K2, P1, K1, P2, *K1, P1, K2, P2, K2, P1,
K1, P2, rep from * to last 6 sts, KI, P1, K2, P2.
ROW 4: K2, P3, K3, *K1, P3, K2, P3, K3, rep from *
to last 6 sts, K1, P3, K2.

These 4 rows form the patt rep.
Work 6 more rows in patt.

SHAPE SIDES

Keeping patt correct, dec 1 st at each end of next row
and every foll 4th row until there are 78 (84: 90) sts.
Work 19 rows without further shaping, thus ending
with a WS row.
Keeping patt correct, inc 1 st at each end of next row
and every foll 5th row until there are 94 (100: 106)
sts. Work 2 rows without further shaping, thus ending
with a 4th-patt row.
Change to 4mm (US 6) needles and st st, beg with a
K row. AT THE SAME TIME, shape sides by inc 1 st
at each end of 3rd row and every foll 5th row until
there are 102 (108: 114) sts.
Cont without further shaping until work measures
44.5 (46: 47.5)cm (17½ [18: 18¾]in) from beg, ending
with a WS row.

SHAPE ARMHOLES

Cast (bind) off 4 sts at beg of next 2 rows.
Dec 1 st at each end of next row and 3 foll alt rows.
86 (92: 98) sts *
Cont without further shaping until work measures 66
(67.5: 69)cm (26 [26½: 27]in) from beg, ending with a
WS row.

DIVIDE FOR NECK AND SHAPE SHOULDERS

Cast (bind) off 10 (11: 11) sts, K22 (23: 25) sts, turn
and leave rem sts on a holder.
Work each side of neck separately.
NEXT ROW: P2tog, P to end.
NEXT ROW: Cast (bind) off 10 (10: 11) sts, K to last 2 sts,
K2tog.
NEXT ROW: P2tog, P to end.
Cast (bind) off rem 9 (10: 11) sts.
With RS facing, rejoin yarn to sts left on holder, cast
(bind) off center 24 (24: 26) sts, K to end.
Complete to match first side, rev all shaping.

front

Work as given for back to *.
Cont without further shaping until work measures
49.5 (50: 51)cm (19½ [19¾: 20]in) from beg, ending
with a WS row.

DIVIDE FOR NECK

K 41 (44: 47) sts, K2tog, turn and leave rem sts on a
holder.
Work each side of neck separately.
Work 2 rows without further shaping.
Dec 1 st at neck edge on next row and at same edge
on every foll 3rd row until 29 (31: 33) sts rem.

Cont without further shaping until front matches
back to shoulder, ending with a WS row.

SHAPE SHOULDER

Cast (bind) off 10 (11: 11) sts at beg of next row and
10 (11: 11) sts at beg of foll alt row. Work 1 row.
Cast (bind) off rem 9 (10: 11) sts.
With RS facing, rejoin yarn to sts left on holder,
K2tog, K to end.
Complete to match first side, rev all shaping.

sleeves (both alike)

Cast on 50 sts using 3¼mm (US 3) needles and set
rib patt as for small-size back.
Cont until 30 rows of patt have been completed, then
shape sides by inc 1 st at each end of next row and
every foll 4th row until there are 60 sts.
Work one row, thus ending with a 4th-patt row.
Change to 4mm (US 6) needles and st st, beg with a
K row. AT THE SAME TIME, shape sides by inc 1 st
at each end of 3rd row and every foll 4th row until
there are 96 sts.
Cont without further shaping until work measures
41.5 (43.5: 45.5)cm (16¼ [17: 17½]in) from beg,
ending with a WS row.

SHAPE SLEEVE TOP

Cast (bind) off 4 sts at beg of next 2 rows.
Dec 1 st at each end of next row and foll 2 alt rows. *82 sts*
Work 1 row.
Cast (bind) off loosely and evenly.

collar

Cast on 75 sts using 3¼mm (US 3) needles.
Work in moss (seed) stitch as folls:
ROW 1: KI, *P1, K1, rep from * to end.
ROW 2: K1, *P1, K1, rep from * to end.
Rep these 2 rows once more, dec 1 st at center of last
row. *74 sts*
Then cont in rib patt, setting sts as folls:
ROW 1 (RS): K1, P1, K1, P2, *K3, P4, K3, P2, rep from
* to last 9 sts, K3, P3, K1, P1, K1.
ROW 2: K1, P1, K3, P1, KI, P2, K2, *P2, K1, P1, K2,
P1, K1, P2, K2, rep from * to last 3 sts, K1, P1, K1.
ROW 3: K1, P1, K1, P2, *K1, P1, K2, P2, K2, P1, K1, P2,
rep from * to last 9 sts, K1, P1, K2, P2, K1, P1, K1.
ROW 4: K1, P1, K3, P3, K3, *K1, P3, K2, P3, K3, rep
from * to last 3 sts, KI, P1, K1.
Keeping continuity of moss (seed) stitch edge and rib
patt, work in patt until collar measures 13.5cm (5¼in)
from beg, ending with a WS row.

DIVIDE FOR FRONTS

Patt 26 sts, cast (bind) off 22 sts, patt to end.
Work each side of collar separately.
Keeping moss (seed) stitch edge and rib patt correct,
dec 1 st at inside neck edge on next 5 rows. *21 sts*
Patt 14 (16: 18) rows without shaping.
Dec 1 st at inside neck edge on next row and every
foll alt row until 1 st remains. Fasten off.
With WS facing, rejoin yarn to rem sts, patt to end.
Complete to match first side rev all shaping.

finishing

Press all pieces (except ribbing) on WS, using a warm
iron over a damp cloth. Join both shoulder seams
using back stitch. Slipstitch collar to neck edge,
matching center back of collar to center back neck
and having the two points meeting at start of front
neck shaping. Sew sleeve top into armhole. Join side
and sleeve seams. Press seams.

shadow by Kim Hargreaves

SIZE	XS	S	M	L	
To fit bust	81	86	91	97	cm
	32	34	36	38	in
Actual width	39	42	45	48	cm
	15½	16½	18	19	in
Length	33	35.5	38	40.5	cm
	13	14	15	16	in
Sleeve length	43	43	43	43	cm
	17	17	17	17	in

YARNS

Rowan Cotton Glacé 50gm (1¾oz) balls

Cardigan

Mint xxx	10	10	11	11

Vest

Delft 782	5	5	6	6

(Shade no longer available)

NEEDLES

1 pair 2¾mm (US 2) needles
1 pair 3¼mm (US 3) needles

BUTTONS

8

TENSION (GAUGE)

28 sts and 32 rows to 10cm (4in) measured over rib patt using 3¼mm (US 3) needles

cardigan
back

Cast on 96 (104: 112: 120) sts using 3¼mm (US 3) needles.
ROW 1 (RS): P1, *K2, P2, rep from * to last 3 sts, K2, P1.
ROW 2: K1, *P2, K2, rep from * to last 3 sts, P2, K1.
These 2 rows form the rib patt and are repeated throughout. Work 4 more rows.
Keeping patt correct, inc 1 st at each end of next row and every foll 5th (6th: 6th: 6th) row to 110 (118: 126: 134) sts, taking extra sts into patt as they occur.
Cont without further shaping until work measures 13 (15.5: 18: 20.5)cm (5 [6: 7: 8]in) from cast-on edge, ending with a WS row.

SHAPE ARMHOLES

Cast (bind) off 6 sts at beg of next 2 rows.
98 (106: 114: 122) sts
NEXT ROW (RS) (DEC): P2, K2, P3tog, rib to last 7 sts, P3tog, K2, P2.
Work 1 row. Dec as before on next row, 2 foll alt rows and 4 foll 4th rows. *66 (74: 82: 90) sts*
Cont without shaping until work measures 20cm (7¾in) from beg of armhole shaping ending, with a WS row.

SHAPE SHOULDERS AND BACK NECK

Cast (bind) off 4 (6: 7: 8) sts at beg of next 2 rows.
Cast (bind) off 5 (6: 7: 9) sts, rib 9 (10: 12: 13), turn and leave rem sts on a holder.
Work each side of neck separately.
Cast (bind) off 4 sts, rib to end. Cast (bind) off rem 5 (6: 8: 9) sts.
With RS facing, rejoin yarn to rem sts, cast (bind) off center 30 sts, patt to end.
Complete to match first side, rev shaping.

left front

Cast on 49 (53: 57: 61) sts using 3¼mm (US 3) needles.
ROW 1 (RS): P1, *K2, P2, rep from * to end.
ROW 2: *K2, P2, rep from * to last st, K1.
These 2 rows form the rib patt and are repeated throughout. Work 4 more rows.
Keeping patt correct, inc 1 st at side edge on next row and every foll 5th (6th: 6th: 6th) row to 56 (60: 64: 68) sts.
Work without shaping until front matches back to armhole shaping, ending with a WS row.

SHAPE ARMHOLE AND FRONT NECK

Cast (bind) off 6 sts at beg of next row. Work 1 row.
Dec 2 sts at armhole edge as given for back on next row, 3 foll alt rows and 2 foll 4th rows, ending with a RS row. *38 (42: 46: 50) sts*
Work 3 rows.
NEXT ROW (RS) (DEC): P2, K2, P3tog, rib to last 7 sts, P3tog, K2, P2. *34 (38: 42: 46) sts*
Rep last 4 rows once more. *30 (34: 38: 42) sts*
This completes armhole shaping. Work 3 rows.
Cont dec as before at neck edge on next row and every foll 4th row to 14 (18: 22: 26) sts.
Cont without further shaping until front matches back to shoulder shaping, ending with a WS row.

SHAPE SHOULDER

Cast (bind) off 4 (6: 7: 8) sts at beg of next row and 5 (6: 7: 9) sts at beg of foll alt row.
Work 1 row. Cast (bind) off rem 5 (6: 8: 9) sts.

right front

Cast on 49 (53: 57: 61) sts using 3¼mm (US 3) needles.
ROW 1 (RS): *P2, K2, rep from * to last st, P1.
ROW 2: K1, *P2, K2, rep from * to end.
These 2 rows form the rib patt and are repeated throughout.
Complete to match first side, rev all shaping.

sleeves (both alike)

Cast on 54 sts using 3¼mm (US 3) needles.

ROW 1 (RS): P2, *K2, P2, rep from * to end.

ROW 2: K2, *P2, K2, rep from * to end.

These 2 rows form the rib patt and are repeated throughout. Keeping rib patt correct, inc 1 st at each end of next row and every foll 6th row to 66 sts and then every foll 8th row to 90 sts.

Cont without further shaping until sleeve measures 43cm from cast-on edge, ending with a WS row.

SHAPE SLEEVEHEAD

Cast (bind) off 6 sts at beg of next 2 rows.

NEXT ROW (RS) (DEC): P2, K2, P3tog, rib to last 7 sts, P3tog, K2, P2.

Work 1 row.

Dec as before on next row and foll alt row. *66 sts*

Work 3 rows.

Dec as before on next row, 2 foll alt rows and 1 foll 6th row. *50 sts*

Work 3 rows.

Dec as before on next row, 1 foll 4th row and 4 foll alt rows. *26 sts*

Work 1 row.

Cast (bind) off 6 sts at beg of next 2 rows.

Cast (bind) off rem 14 sts.

Vest

back and fronts

Work as given for cardigan.

finishing

Press all pieces as described on the information page (the rib needs to be opened out).

Join both shoulder seams using back stitch.

Cardigan and vest

LACE EDGING

Cast on 12 sts using 3¼mm (US 3) needles and work lace edging as folls:

ROW 1 (WS): Sl1, K3, yon, K2tog, K2, yon, K2tog, yon, K2. *13 sts*

ROW 2: Yon, K2tog, K11.

ROW 3: Sl1, K2, (yon, K2tog) twice, K2, yon, K2tog, yon, K2. *14 sts*

ROW 4: Yon, K2tog, K12.

ROW 5: Sl1, K3, (yon, K2tog) twice, K2, yon, K2tog, yon, K2. *15 sts*

ROW 6: Yon, K2tog, K13.

ROW 7: Sl1, K2, (yon, K2tog) 3 times, K2, yon, K2tog, yon, K2. *16 sts*

ROW 8: Yon, K2tog, K14.

ROW 9: Sl1, K2, (K2tog, yon) twice, K2, K2tog, (yon, K2tog) twice, K1. *15 sts*

ROW 10: Yon, K2tog, K13.

ROW 11: Sl1, K1, (K2tog, yon) twice, K2, K2tog, (yon, K2tog) twice, K1. *14 sts*

ROW 12: Yon, K2tog, K12.

ROW 13: Sl1, K2, K2tog, yon, K2, K2tog, (yon, K2tog) twice, K1. *13 sts*

ROW 14: Yon, K2tog, K11.

ROW 15: Sl1, K1, K2tog, yon, K2, K2tog, (yon, K2tog) twice, K1. *12 sts*

ROW 16: Yon, K2tog, K10.

Rep rows 1–16 until edging is long enough to fit around bottom edge of garment, leave sts on a holder. Slipstitch into place, adjust length, cast (bind) off.

BUTTONHOLE BAND

With RS of right front facing and using 2¾mm

(US 2) needles, pick up and knit 63 (70: 77: 84) sts from lower edge of lace to beg of neck shaping, 46 sts up to shoulder and 20 sts to center back neck. *129 (136: 143: 150) sts*

NEXT ROW (WS) (BUTTONHOLES): Knit to last 61 (68: 75: 82) sts, cast (bind) off 2, K6 (7: 8: 9) 7 times, cast (bind) off 2, knit to end.

NEXT ROW: Knit across row, casting on sts over those cast (bound) off on previous row. Cast (bind) off knitwise.

BUTTON BAND

Work as for buttonhole band, omitting buttonholes. Join bands at center back neck.

ARMHOLE EDGINGS (VEST ONLY)

With RS facing and using 2¾mm (US 2) needles, pick up and knit 110 sts around armhole edge. Knit 2 rows. Cast (bind) off knitwise.

See information page for finishing instructions.

hatty by Kim Hargreaves

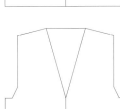

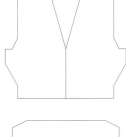

SIZE	S	M	
To fit bust	81–86	91–97	cm
	32–34	36–38	in
Actual width	45.5	48	cm
	18	19	in
Longer version length	64	68	cm
	25	26½	in
Cropped version length	41	44	cm
	16	17	in
Sleeve length	12	12	cm
	4¾	4¾	in

YARNS

Rowan Glacé Cotton 50gm (1¾oz) balls:

Longer version	9	10

(Photographed in Crushed Rose 793)

Cropped version	6	7

(Photographed in Lilac Wine 440; no longer available)

BUTTONS

Longer version 8 Rowan 75008
Cropped version 5 Rowan 75235

NEEDLES

1 pair 2¾mm (US 2) needles
1 pair 3¼mm (US 3) needles

TENSION (GUAGE)

23 sts and 32 rows to 10cm (4in) measured over stocking (stockinette) stitch using 3¼mm (US 3) needles

longer version
back

Cast on 105 (111) sts using 2¾mm (US 2) needles and work 8 rows in moss (seed) st.
Change to 3¼mm (US 3) needles and work 12 (14) rows st st, beg with a K row.
NEXT ROW (RS) (DEC): K2, K2tog, K25 (27), K2tog, K43 (45), K2tog tbl, K25 (27), K2tog tbl, K2. *101 (107) sts*
Work 15 rows without shaping.
NEXT ROW (RS) (DEC): K2, K2tog, K24 (26), K2tog, K41 (43), K2tog tbl, K24 (26), K2tog tbl, K2. *97 (103) sts*
Work 15 rows without shaping.
NEXT ROW (RS) (DEC): K2, K2tog, K23 (25), K2tog, K39 (41), K2tog tbl, K23 (25), K2tog tbl, K2. *93 (99) sts*
Work 15 rows without shaping.
NEXT ROW (RS) (DEC): K2, K2tog, K22 (24), K2tog, K37 (39), K2tog tbl, K22 (24), K2tog tbl, K2. *89 (95) sts*

Work 17 (19) rows without shaping.
* NEXT ROW (RS) (INC): K2, M1, K22 (24), M1, K41 (43), M1, K22 (24), M1, K2. *93 (99) sts*
Work 9 rows without shaping.
NEXT ROW (RS) (INC): K2, M1, K23 (25), M1, K43 (45), M1, K23 (25), M1, K2. *97 (103) sts*
Work 9 rows without shaping.
NEXT ROW (RS) (INC): K2, M1, K24 (26), M1, K45 (47), M1, K24 (26), M1, K2. *101 (107) sts*
Work 9 rows without shaping.
NEXT ROW (RS) (INC): K2, M1, K25 (27), M1, K47 (49), M1, 5 (27), M1, K2. *105 (111) sts* **
Cont without further shaping until work measures 43.5 (46)cm (17 (18)in) from cast-on edge, ending with a WS row.
***SHAPE ARMHOLES
Cast (bind) off 6 (7) sts, at beg of next 2 rows.
Work 2 rows st st.
NEXT ROW (DEC): K2, K3tog, K to last 5 sts, K3tog tbl, K2.
Work 3 rows st st.
Rep last 4 rows once more, then work dec row again. *81 (85) sts*
Cont without further shaping until work measures 20.5 (22)cm (8 [8½]in) from beg of armhole shaping.
SHAPE SHOULDER AND BACK NECK
Cast (bind) off 7 (8) sts at beg of next 2 rows.
NEXT ROW: Cast (bind) off 7 sts, K18 sts, turn and leave rem sts on a holder.
Work each side of neck separately.
Cast (bind) off 4 sts, patt to end.
Cast (bind) off 6 sts, patt to end.
Cast (bind) off 2 sts, patt to end.
Cast (bind) off rem 6 sts.
With RS facing, rejoin yarn to rem sts and cast (bind) off center 17 (19) sts, patt to end.
Complete to match first side, rev all shaping.

left front

Cast on 52 (55) sts using 2¾mm (US 2) needles and work 8 rows in moss (seed) st.
Change to 3¼mm (US 3) needles and work 12 (14) rows in st st, beg with a K row.
NEXT ROW (RS) (DEC): K2, K2tog, K25 (27) sts, K2tog, K to end. *50 (53) sts*
Work 15 rows without shaping.
NEXT ROW (RS) (DEC): K2, K2tog, K24 (26) sts, K2tog, K to end. *48 (51) sts*
Work 15 rows without shaping.
NEXT ROW (RS) (DEC): K2, K2tog, K23 (25) sts, K2tog, K to end. *46 (49) sts*

Work 15 rows without shaping.

NEXT ROW (RS) (DEC): K2, K2tog, K22 (24) sts, K2tog, K to end. *44 (47) sts*

Work 17 (19) rows without shaping.

**** NEXT ROW (RS) (INC): K2, M1, K22 (24), M1, K to end. *46 (49) sts*

Work 9 rows without shaping.

NEXT ROW (RS) (INC): K2, M1, K23 (25), M1, K to end. *48 (51) sts*

Work 9 rows without shaping.

NEXT ROW (RS) (INC): K2, M1, K24 (26), M1, K to end. *50 (54) sts*

Work 9 rows without shaping.

NEXT ROW (RS) (INC): K2, M1, K25 (27), M1, K to end. *52 (55) sts*

Work 1 row.

SHAPE FRONT NECK

NEXT ROW (RS) (DEC): Knit to the last 4 sts, K2tog tbl, K2.

Work 3 rows.

Dec 1 st at neck edge, as before, on next row and 4 foll 4th rows and then every foll 6th row until 26 (27) sts on needle and AT THE SAME TIME, when front matches back to beg of armhole shaping, shape armhole as folls:

SHAPE ARMHOLE

Cast (bind) off 6 (7) sts at beg of next row.

Work 3 rows.

NEXT ROW (DEC): K2, K3tog, K to end.

Rep the last 4 rows twice more.

Cont without further shaping until work matches back to beg shoulder shaping.

SHAPE SHOULDER

Cast (bind) off 7 (8) sts at beg of next row and 7 sts at beg of foll alt row.

Work 1 row.

Cast (bind) off 6 sts, patt to end.

Work 1 row. Cast (bind) off rem 6 sts.

right front

Work as for left front, rev all shaping.

sleeves (both alike)

Cast on 58 (64) sts using 2¾mm (US 2) needles.

Work 8 rows in moss (seed) st.

Change to 3¼mm (US 3) needles and work 2 rows in st st, beg with a K row.

NEXT ROW (RS) (INC): K2, MI , K1 to last 2 sts, MI, K2.

Work 1 row.

Inc 1 st as before at each end of next row and every foll alt row until 82 (88) sts on needle, ending with a RS row.

Work 7 rows.

SHAPE SLEEVE HEAD

Cast (bind) off 6 (7) sts at beg of next 2 rows.

NEXT ROW (DEC): K2, K3tog, K to last 5 sts, K3tog tbl, K2.

Work 1 row.

Rep these last 2 rows 4 times more.

NEXT ROW (DEC): K2, K2tog, K to last 4 sts, K2tog tbl, K2.

Work 1 row.

Rep these last 2 rows until 30 sts rem on needle.

Cast (bind) off 2 sts at beg of next 6 rows.

Cast (bind) off 4 sts at beg of next 2 rows.

Cast (bind) off rem 10 sts.

cropped version
back

Cast on 89 (95) sts using 2¾mm (US 2) needles and work 8 rows in moss (seed) st.

Change to 3¼mm (US 3) needles and work 12 (14) rows in st st, beg with a K row.

Cont as for longer version from * to **.

Cont without further shaping until work measures 20.5 (22)cm (8 (8½)in) from cast-on edge, ending with a WS row.

Complete as for back of longer version, working from ***.

left front

Cast on 44 (47) sts using 2¾mm (US 2) needles and work 8 rows in moss (seed) st.

Change to 3¼mm (US 3) needles and work 12 (14) rows in st st, beg with a K row.

Complete as for left front of longer version, working from ****.

right front

Work as for left front, rev all shaping.

sleeves (both alike)

Work as for sleeves for longer version.

finishing
Both versions

Press pieces as described on information page.

Join both shoulder seams, with a fine back stitch seam.

BUTTON BAND AND COLLAR

Cast on 7 st using 2¾mm (US 2) needles and work in moss (seed) st until band fits neatly up left front to 1.5cm (¾in) below front neck shaping when slightly stretched.

SHAPE COLLAR

Inc 1 st at beg of next row and at same edge on every foll 4th row until 20 (22) sts on needle, ending at the straight edge of work.

Cast (bind) off 7 (8) sts, and now cast on 7 (8) sts using the cable method as folls: replace st on RH needle onto LH needle, * insert point of RH needle between 1st and 2nd st on LH needle, yon, bring loop through and place loop on LH needle, thus one st cast on, rep from * 6 (8) times more. *20 (22) sts*

Cont without further shaping until collar fits neatly up left front to shoulder seam and across to center back neck, ending at the shaped edge.

Slipstitch shaped edge of band neatly into place, adjusting length if necessary and ending at shaped edge.

NEXT ROW: Cast (bind) off 5 sts at beg of next row and next 2 alt rows.

Work 1 row.

Cast (bind) off rem 5 (7) sts.

Mark positions of 8 buttons on longer version or 5 buttons on cropped version, the first to come 1.5cm (¾in) from cast-on edge, the last to come 1cm (½in) from beg of collar shaping and others spaced evenly between.

BUTTONHOLE BAND AND COLLAR

Work as for button band adding 8(5) buttonholes to correspond with button markers as folls:

BUTTONHOLE ROW: Patt 2, cast (bind) off 3, patt 2.

NEXT ROW: Patt across row, casting on 3 sts to replace those cast (bound) off on previous row.

See information page for finishing instructions.

lime by Kim Hargreaves

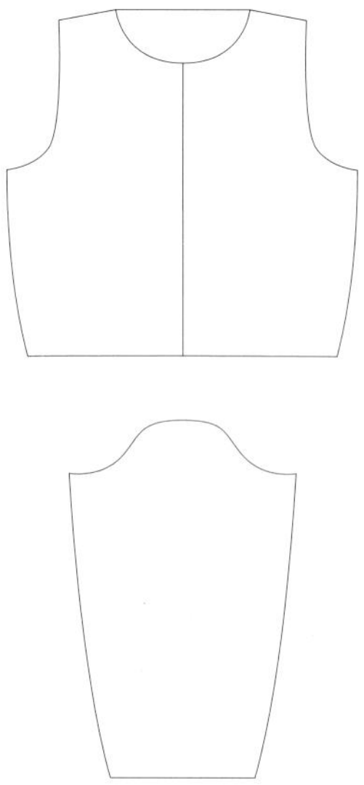

SIZE

	XS	S	M	L	XL	
To fit bust	81	86	91	97	102	cm
	32	34	36	38	40	in
Actual width	43	45.5	48.5	51	53.5	cm
	17	18	19	20	21	in
Length	44	45	46	47	48	cm
	17½	17½	18	18½	19	in
Sleeve length	41	41	42	42	43	cm
	16	16	16½	16½	17	in

YARN

Rowan 4 ply Cotton and Fine Cotton Chenille 50gm (1¾oz) balls:

A Marine	102	1	1	1	1	1
B Ch. Cornflower	412	5	6	6	6	7

NEEDLES

1 pair 2¼mm (US 1) needles
1 pair 3¼mm (US 3) needles

BUTTONS

7

TENSION (GAUGE)

23 sts and 36 rows to 10cm (4in) measured over pattern using 3¼mm (US 3) needles and yarn B.

back

Cast on 171 (183: 195: 207: 219) sts using 2¼mm (US 1) needles and yarn A.

ROW 1 (RS) (DEC): K3, *cast (bind) off next 3 sts, K until there are 3 sts on right needle after cast (bind) off, rep from * to end. *87 (93: 99: 105: 111) sts*
Knit 1 row.

Change to 3¼mm (US 3) needles and yarn B.
Cont in lace patt from chart, setting sts as folls:

ROW 1 (RS): Knit.

ROW 2 AND EVERY ALT ROW: Purl.

ROW 3: K3 (6: 9: 4: 7), *yfwd, sl1, K1, psso, K6, rep from * to last 4 (7: 10: 5: 8) sts, yfwd, sl1, K1, psso, K2 (5: 8: 3: 6).

ROW 5: K1 (4: 7: 2: 5), *K2tog, yfwd, K1, yfwd, sl1, K1, psso, K3, rep from * to last 6 (9: 12: 7: 10) sts, K2tog, yfwd, K1, yfwd, sl1, K1, psso, K1 (4: 7: 2: 5).

ROW 7: As row 3.

ROW 9: Knit.

ROW 11: K7 (2: 5: 8: 3), *yfwd, sl1, K1, psso, K6, rep from * to last 8 (3: 6: 9: 4) sts, yfwd, sl1, K1, psso, K6 (1: 4: 7: 2).

ROW 13: K5 (0: 3: 6: 1), *K2tog, yfwd, K1, yfwd, sl1, K1, psso, K3, rep from * to last 10 (5: 8: 11: 6) sts, K2tog, yfwd, K1, yfwd, sl1, K1, psso, K5 (0: 3: 6: 1).

ROW 15: As row 11.

ROW 16: Purl.

Rows 1 to 16 form patt.
Cont in patt, shaping side seams by inc 1 st at each end of next and every foll 12th row until there are 99 (105: 111: 117: 123) sts, taking inc sts into patt.
Cont straight until back measures 24 (25: 25: 26: 26)cm (9½ [9¾: 9¾: 10¼: 10¼]in), from cast-on edge, ending with a WS row.

SHAPE ARMHOLES

Keeping patt correct, cast (bind) off 3 (4: 4: 5: 5) sts at beg of next 2 rows. *93 (97: 103: 107: 113) sts*
Dec 1 st at each end of next 7 (7: 9: 9: 11) rows, then on every foll alt row until 67 (69: 71: 73: 75) sts rem.
Cont straight until armhole measures 20 (20: 21: 21: 22)cm, (7¾ [7¾: 8¼: 8¼: 8½]in), ending with a WS row.

KEY

☐ K on RS, P on WS
▣ yfwd
▨ K2tog
▧ Sl1, K1, psso

FRONTS, BACK AND SLEEVE PATTERN REPEAT

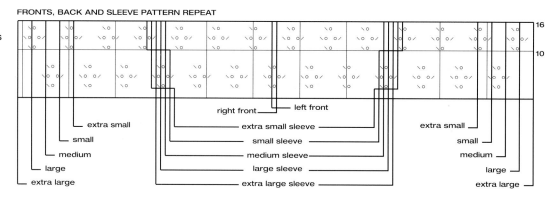

SHAPE SHOULDERS AND BACK NECK

Cast (bind) off 5 (6: 6: 6: 6) sts at beg of next 2 rows.
57 (57: 59: 61: 63) sts

NEXT ROW (RS): Cast (bind) off 5 (6: 6: 6: 6) sts, patt
until there are 10 (9: 9: 10: 11) sts on right needle and
turn, leaving rem sts on a holder.
Work each side of neck separately.
Cast (bind) off 4 sts at beg of next row.
Work 1 row.
Cast (bind) off rem 6 (5: 5: 6: 7) sts.
With RS facing, rejoin yarn to rem sts, cast (bind) off
center 27 (27: 29: 29: 29) sts, patt to end.
Work to match first side, rev shapings.

left front

Cast on 87 (93: 99: 105: 111) sts using 2¼mm
(US 1) needles and yarn A.
ROW 1 (RS) (DEC): K3, *cast (bind) off next 3 sts, K
until there are 3 sts on right needle after cast (bind)
off, rep from * to end. *45 (48: 51: 54: 57) sts.*
Knit 1 row, dec 1 st at center. *44 (47: 50: 53: 56) sts.*
Change to 3¼mm (US 3) needles and yarn B.**
Cont in lace patt from chart, setting sts as folls:
ROW 1 (RS): Knit.
ROW 2 AND EVERY ALT ROW: Purl.
ROW 3: K3 (6: 9: 4: 7), *yfwd, sl1, K1, psso, K6, rep
from * to last st, K1.
ROW 5: K1 (4: 7: 2: 5), *K2tog, yfwd, K1, yfwd, sl1,
K1, psso, K3, rep from * to last 3 sts, K3.
ROW 7: As row 3.
ROW 9: Knit.
ROW 11: K7 (2: 5: 8: 3), *yfwd, sl1, K1, psso, K6, rep
from * to last 5 sts, yfwd, sl1, K1, psso, K3.
ROW 13: K5 (0: 3: 6: 1), *K2tog, yfwd, K1, yfwd,
sl1, K1, psso, K3, rep from * to last 7 sts, K2tog, yfwd,
K1, yfwd, sl1, K1, psso, K2.
ROW 15: As row 11.
ROW 16: Purl.
Rows 1 to 16 form patt.
Cont in patt, shaping side seam by inc 1 st at beg of
next and every foll 12th row until there are 50 (53:
56: 59: 62) sts, taking inc sts into patt. Cont straight
until left front matches back to beg of armhole
shaping, ending with a WS row.

SHAPE ARMHOLE

Keeping patt correct, cast (bind) off 3 (4: 4: 5: 5) sts at
beg of next row. *47 (49: 52: 54: 57) sts*
Work 1 row.
Dec 1 st at armhole edge of next 7 (7: 9: 9: 11) rows,
then on every foll alt row until 34 (35: 36: 37: 38) sts
rem.
Cont straight until left front is 29 (29: 31: 31: 31)
rows shorter than back to start of shoulder shaping,
ending with a RS row.

SHAPE NECK

Keeping patt correct, cast (bind) off 7 sts at beg of
next row, then 4 sts at beg of foll alt row.
23 (24: 25: 26: 27) sts.
Dec 1 st at neck edge on next 3 rows, then on foll
2 (2: 3: 3: 3) alt rows. *18 (19: 19: 20: 21) sts*
Work 3 rows.
Dec 1 st at neck edge on next and foll 4th row.
16 (17: 17: 18: 19) sts
Work 11 rows, ending with a WS row.

SHAPE SHOULDER

Cast (bind) off 5 (6: 6: 6: 6) sts at beg of next and foll
alt row.
Work 1 row. Cast (bind) off rem 6 (5: 5: 6: 7) sts.

right front

Work as given for left front to **.
Cont in lace patt from chart, setting sts as folls:

ROW 1 (RS): Knit.

ROW 2 AND EVERY ALT ROW: Purl.

ROW 3: K8, *yfwd, sl1, K1, psso, K6, rep from * to last 4 (7: 10: 5: 8) sts, yfwd, sl1, K1, psso, K2 (5: 8: 3: 6).

ROW 5: K6, *K2tog, yfwd, K1, yfwd, sl1, K1, psso, K3, rep from * to last 6 (9: 12: 7: 10) sts, K2tog, yfwd, K1, yfwd, sl1, K1, psso, K1 (4: 7: 2: 5).

ROW 7: As row 3.

ROW 9: Knit.

ROW 11: K4, *yfwd, sl1, K1, psso, K6, rep from * to last 8 (3: 6: 9: 4) sts, yfwd, sl1, K1, psso, K6 (1: 4: 7: 2).

ROW 13: K2, *K2tog, yfwd, K1, yfwd, sl1, K1, psso, K3, rep from * to last 10 (5: 8: 11: 6) sts, K2tog, yfwd, K1, yfwd, sl1, K1, psso, K5 (0: 3: 6: 1).

ROW 15: As row 11.

ROW 16: Purl.

Rows 1 to 16 form patt.
Complete to match left front, rev shapings.

sleeves (both alike)

Cast on 87 (87: 93: 99: 99) sts using 2¼mm (US 1) needles and yarn A.

ROW 1 (RS) (DEC): K3, *cast (bind) off next 3 sts, K until there are 3 sts on right needle after cast (bind) off, rep from * to end. *45 (45: 48: 51: 51) sts*

Knit 1 row, dec 2 (0: 1: 2: 0) sts evenly across row. *43 (45: 47: 49: 51) sts*

Change to 3¼mm (US 3) needles and yarn B.
Cont in lace patt from chart, setting sts as folls:

ROW 1 (RS): Knit.

ROW 2 AND EVERY ALT ROW: Purl.

ROW 3: Inc in first st, K4 (5: 6: 7: 8), *yfwd, sl1, K1, psso, K6, rep from * to last 6 (7: 8: 9: 10) sts, yfwd, sl1, K1, psso, K3 (4: 5: 6: 7), inc in last st. *45 (47: 49: 51: 53) sts*

ROW 5: K4 (5: 6: 7: 8), *K2tog, yfwd, K1, yfwd, sl1, K1, psso, K3, rep from * to last 1 (2: 3: 4: 5) sts, K1 (2: 3: 4: 5).

ROW 7: K6 (7: 8: 9: 10), *yfwd, sl1, K1, psso, K6, rep from * to last 7 (8: 9: 10: 11) sts, yfwd, sl1, K1, psso, K5 (6: 7: 8: 9).

ROW 9: Knit.

ROW 11: Inc in first st, K1 (2: 3: 4: 5), *yfwd, sl1, K1, psso, K6, rep from * to last 3 (4: 5: 6: 7) sts, yfwd, sl1, K1, psso, K0 (1: 2: 3: 4), inc in last st.

ROW 13: K1 (2: 3: 4: 5), *K2tog, yfwd, K1, yfwd, sl1, K1, psso, K3, rep from * to last 6 (7: 8: 9: 10) sts, K2tog, yfwd, K1, yfwd, sl1, K1, psso, K1 (2: 3: 4: 5).

ROW 15: K3 (4: 5: 6: 7), *yfwd, sl1, K1, psso, K6, rep from * to last 4 (5: 6: 7: 8) sts, yfwd, sl1, K1, psso, K2 (3: 4: 5: 6).

ROW 16: Purl.

Rows 1 to 16 set patt and sleeve shaping.
Keeping patt correct, inc 1 st at each end of every 8th row until there are 75 (77: 79: 81: 83) sts, taking inc sts into patt.
Cont straight until sleeve measures 41 (41: 42: 42: 43)cm (16¼ [16¼: 16½: 16½: 17]in) from cast-on edge, ending with a WS row.

SHAPE TOP

Keeping patt correct, cast (bind) off 3 (4: 4: 5: 5) sts at beg of next 2 rows. *69 (69: 71: 71: 73) sts*
Dec 1 st at each end of next 5 rows, then on foll 4 (4: 5: 4: 5) alt rows. *51 (51: 51: 53: 53) sts*
Work 3 rows, ending with a WS row.
Dec 1 st at each end of next and every foll 4th row until 37 sts rem.
Work 1 row.
Dec 1 st at each end on next 4 rows. *29 sts*
Cast (bind) off 4 sts at beg of next 2 rows.
Cast (bind) off rem 21 sts.

finishing

Press all pieces as described on the information page.
Join shoulder seams using back stitch.

BUTTONHOLE BORDER

With RS facing, 2¼mm (US 1) needles and yarn A, pick up and knit 97 (97: 97: 103: 103) sts along right front opening edge.

ROW 1: Knit.

ROW 2 (RS) (BUTTONHOLE ROW): K3, *yfwd, K2tog, K13 (13: 13: 14: 14), rep from * to last 4 sts, yfwd, K2tog, K2.

Cast (bind) off knitwise (on WS).

BUTTON BORDER

With RS facing, 2¼mm (US 1) needles and yarn A, pick up and knit 97 (97: 97: 103: 103) sts along left front opening edge.

ROWS 1 AND 2: Knit.

Cast (bind) off knitwise (on WS).

NECKBAND

With RS facing, 2¼mm (US 1) needles and yarn A, pick up and knit 32 (32: 34: 34: 34) sts up right side of neck, 35 (35: 37: 37: 37) sts from back, and 33 (33: 35: 35: 35) sts down left side of neck. *100 (100: 106: 106: 106) sts*

ROWS 1 AND 2: Knit.

Work picot cast (bind) off as folls: cast (bind) off 2 sts, *slip st on right needle back onto left needle, cast on 2 sts, cast (bind) off 4 sts, rep from * to end.
Fasten off.
See information page for finishing instructions.

henrietta by Helen Dawson

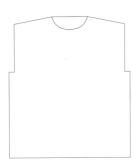

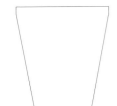

SIZES	CHILDREN'S			LADIES'					
	4-6 YRS	6-8 YRS	8-9 YRS	1ST	2ND	3RD	4TH	5TH	
To fit chest	–	–	–	81	86	91	97	102	cm
	–	–	–	32	34	36	38	40	in
Actual width	44.5	47	50	57	60	63	66	67.5	cm
	17½	18½	20	22½	23½	24½	26	26½	in
Length	49.5	54	57	70	71	72	73	74	cm
	19½	21	22½	27½	28	28½	29	29½	in
Sleeve length	33	38	41.5	48	48	48	48	48	cm
	13	15	16½	19	19	19	19	19	in

YARN
Rowan Handknit DK Cotton 50gm (1¾oz) balls:

11	12	14	18	19	20	21	22

(child's photographed in Sugar 303, ladies' in Raindrop 206)

NEEDLES
1 pair 3¼ mm (US 3) needles
1 pair 4mm (US 6) needles

TENSION (GAUGE)
21 sts and 28 rows to 10cm (4in) measured over patterned stocking (stockinette) stitch using 4mm (US 6) needles

PATTERN NOTE
The ladies' garments has three vents on back and front and one on each sleeve. The child's garment has only two vents on back and front and none on the sleeve. The pattern is written for the three children's sizes followed by the five ladies' sizes in bold.

back
1st panel
Cast on 31 (34: 37: **29: 32: 35: 38: 40**) sts using 3¼mm (US 3) needles and work from appropriate chart as folls:
Working between markers for 1st panel, knit 4 rows.
Change to 4mm (US 6) needles, cont from chart until chart row 12 (**18**) completed, ending with a WS row.
Break yarn and leave sts on a holder.
2nd panel
Cast on 31 sts using 3¼ mm (US 3) needles.
Working between markers for 2nd panel, knit 4 rows.
Change to 4mm (US 6) needles, cont from chart until chart row 12 (**18**) completed, ending with a WS row.
Break yarn and leave sts on a holder.
3rd panel
Cast on 31 (34: 37: **31: 31: 31: 31: 31**) sts using

3¼mm (US 3) needles.
Working between markers for 3rd panel, knit 4 rows.
Change to 4mm (US 6) needles, cont from chart until chart row 12 (**18**) completed, ending with a WS row.
Children's sizes only
Do not break yarn.
Ladies' sizes only
Break yarn and leave sts on a holder.
4th panel
Cast on **29 (32: 35: 38: 40)** sts using 3¼ mm (US 3) needles.
Working between markers for 4th panel, knit 4 rows.
Change to 4mm (US 6) needles and cont until chart row 18 completed, ending with a WS row.
Join the 4 panels together:
CHART ROW 19 (RS): Working from chart, patt across **29 (32: 35: 38: 40)** sts of 4th panel, patt across 31 sts of 3rd panel, patt across 31 sts of 2nd panel, patt across **29 (32: 35: 38: 40)** sts of 1st panel.
120 (126: 132: 138: 142) sts
Children's sizes only
Join the 3 panels together:
CHART ROW 13 (RS): Working from chart, patt across 31 (34: 37) sts of 3rd panel, patt across 31 sts of 2nd panel, patt across 31 (34: 37) sts of 1st panel. *93 (99: 105) sts*
All sizes
Cont from chart until chart row 42 completed, ending with a WS row.
Now rep the 24-row patt rep until work measures 29.5 (33: 35: **47: 47: 47: 47: 47**)cm (11¾ [13: 13¾: **18½: 18½: 18½: 18½: 18½**]in) from cast-on edge, ending with a WS row.

SHAPE ARMHOLE

Cast (bind) off 5 (6) sts at beg of next 2 rows.
*83 (89: 95: **108: 114: 120: 126: 130**) sts*
Keeping patt correct, cont until work measures
20 (21: 22: **23: 24: 25: 26: 27**)cm (7¾ [8¼: 8½: **9: 9½: 9¾: 10¼: 10¾**]in) from beg of armhole shaping ending with a WS row.

SHAPE SHOULDERS AND BACK NECK

Cast (bind) off 8 (8: 9: **11: 12: 13: 14: 14**) sts at beg of next 2 rows.
Cast (bind) off 8 (9: 9: **11: 12: 13: 14: 15**) sts, patt 12 (13: 14: **15: 16: 17: 18: 19**) sts, turn and leave rem sts on a holder.
Work each side of neck separately.
Cast (bind) off 4 sts, patt to end.
Cast (bind) off rem 8 (9: 10: **11: 12: 13: 14: 15**) sts.
With RS facing, rejoin yarn to rem sts, cast (bind) off center 27 (29: 31: **34: 34: 34: 34: 34**) sts, patt to end.
Complete to match first side, rev shaping.

front

Work as given for back until front is 12 (12: 14: **18: 18: 18: 18: 18**) rows shorter than back to shoulder shaping, ending with a WS row.

SHAPE FRONT NECK

Patt 35 (37: 39: **44: 47: 50: 53: 55**) sts, turn and leave rem sts on a holder.
Work each side of neck separately.
Cast (bind) off 4 sts, patt to end.
Dec 1 st at neck edge on next 6 (6: 6: **3: 3: 3: 3: 3**) rows, 1 (1: 1: **3: 3: 3: 3: 3**) foll alt rows and for ladies' only 1 foll 4th row. *24 (26: 28: **33: 36: 39: 42: 44**) sts*
Cont until front matches back to shoulder shaping, ending with a WS row.

SHAPE SHOULDER

Cast (bind) off 8 (8: 9: **11: 12: 13: 14: 14**) sts at beg of next row and 8 (9: 9: **11: 12: 13: 14: 15**) sts at beg of foll alt row.
Work 1 row.
Cast (bind) off rem 8 (9: 10: **11: 12: 13: 14: 15**) sts.
With RS facing, rejoin yarn to rem sts, cast (bind) off center 13 (15: 17: **20: 20: 20: 20: 20**) sts, patt to end.
Complete to match first side, rev shaping.

KEY

☐ K on RS,
P on WS

▣ P on RS,
K on WS

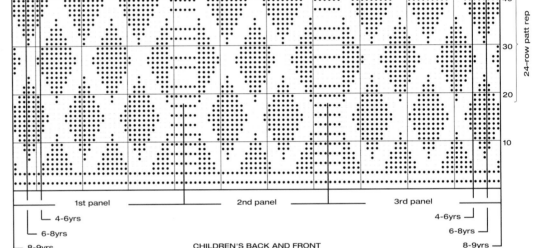

CHILDREN'S BACK AND FRONT

1st panel   2nd panel   3rd panel

4-6yrs
6-8yrs
8-9yrs

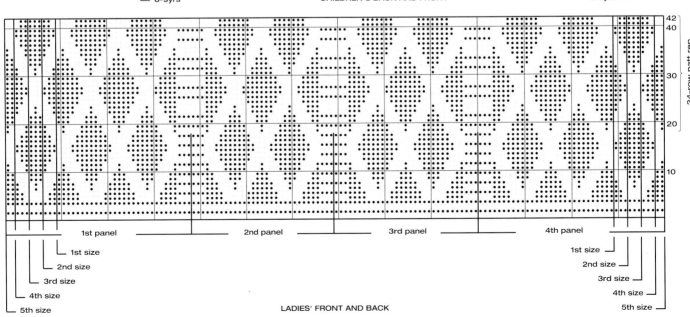

1st panel   2nd panel   3rd panel   4th panel

1st size
2nd size
3rd size
4th size
5th size

LADIES' FRONT AND BACK

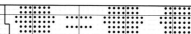

CHILDREN'S SLEEVE

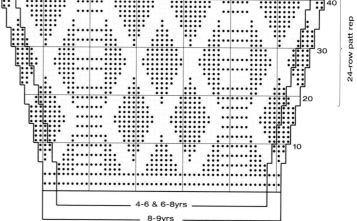

42
40

30

24-row patt rep

20

10

4-6 & 6-8yrs
8-9yrs

LADIES' SLEEVE

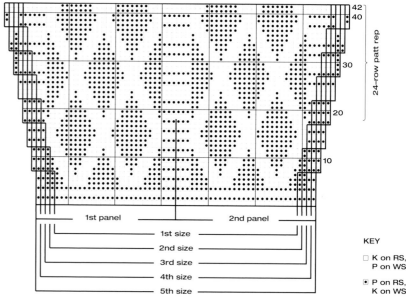

42
40

30

24-row patt rep

20

10

1st panel   2nd panel

1st size
2nd size
3rd size
4th size
5th size

KEY

☐ K on RS,
   P on WS

▣ P on RS,
   K on WS

sleeves (both alike)

Ladies' only

1st panel

Cast on 26 (27: 28: 29: 30) sts using 3¼mm (US 3)
needles and work from appropriate chart as folls:
Working between markers for 1st panel, knit 4 rows.
Change to 4mm (US 6) needles and cont from chart
until chart row 18 completed, inc 1 st at side edge of
chart row 8 and 2 foll 5th rows, ending with a WS
row. *29 (30: 31: 32: 33) sts*
Break yarn and leave sts on a holder.

2nd panel

Cast on 26 (27: 28: 29: 30) sts using 3¼mm (US 3)
needles.
Working between markers for 2nd panel, knit 3 rows.
Change to 4mm (US 6) needles and cont until chart
row 18 completed, inc 1 st at side edge of chart row 8
and 2 foll 5th rows, ending with a WS row.
29 (30: 31: 32: 33) sts
Join panels together:
CHART ROW 19 (RS): Working from chart, patt across
29 (30: 31: 32: 33) sts of 2nd panel, patt across 29 (30:
31: 32: 33) sts of 1st panel. *58 (60: 62: 64: 66) sts*
Cont until chart row 42 completed, inc at each end
of every 5th row as indicated and ending with a
WS row. *66 (68: 70: 72: 74) sts*

Children's sizes only

Cast on 45 (45: 51) sts using 3¼mm (US 3) needles
and work from chart as folls:
Knit 3 rows.
Change to 4mm (US 6) needles and cont from chart
until chart row 42 completed, shaping sides by inc
1 st at each end of chart row 7 and every foll 4th row
as indicated. *63 (63: 69) sts*

All sizes

Cont in patt, rep the 24-row patt rep throughout, and
AT THE SAME TIME inc each end of next row and
every foll 4th (5th) row to 85 (81: 81: **96: 102: 100:
90: 84**) sts and then for 2 large children's sizes and
3 large ladies' sizes only every foll 5th (4th) row to
89 (93: 106: 110: 114) sts, taking the extra stitches

into the patt as they occur.
85 (89: 93: 96: 102: 106: 110: 114) sts
Cont without further shaping until sleeve measures
33 (38: 41.5 **48: 48: 48: 48: 48**)cm (13 [15: 16¼: **18¾:
18¾: 18¾: 18¾: 18¾**]in) from cast-on edge, ending
with a WS row.
Cast (bind) off loosely and evenly.

finishing

Press all pieces as described on the information page.
Join right shoulder seam using back stitch.

NECKBAND

With RS facing and using 3¼mm (US 3) needles,
pick up and knit 18 (18: 20: **25: 25: 25: 25: 25**) sts
down left front neck, 13 (15: 17: **20: 20: 20: 20: 20**) sts
across front neck, 18 (18: 20: **25: 25: 25: 25: 25**) sts up
right front neck and 35 (37: 39: **42: 42: 42: 42: 42**) sts
across back neck.
84 (88: 96: 112: 112: 112: 112: 112) sts
Knit 4 rows. Cast (bind) off.
See information page for finishing instructions.

weekender by Martin Storey

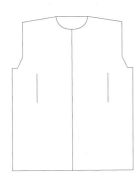

SIZES

	CHILDREN'S (YRS)					ADULTS'				
	4–6	6–8	8–9	9–11	12–14	S	M	L	XL	
To fit chest	–	–	–	–	–	81–86	91–97	102–107	107–112	cm
	–	–	–	–	–	32–34	36–38	40–42	42–44	in
Actual width	44.5	47.5	51.5	53.5	56.5	58.5	61.5	64.5	66.5	cm
	17½	18¾	20	21	22	23	24	25	26	in
Length	49	53.5	57	60	63	68	70.5	73	73	cm
	19	21	22½	23½	24½	27	28	29	29	in
Sleeve length	33	38	40.5	43	45.5	45.5	45.5	45.5	53	cm
	13	15	16	17	18	18	18	18	21	in

YARN

Rowan Handknit DK Cotton 50gm (1¾oz) balls

14	15	16	18	20	22	24	25	26

(child's photographed in Gooseberry 219, adults' in Bleached 263)

NEEDLES
1 pair 3mm (US 2/3) needles
1 pair 4mm (US 6) needles
2 double-pointed 3mm (US 2/3) needles

BUTTONS
7

TENSION (GAUGE)
20 sts and 28 rows to 10cm (4in) measured over pattern using 4mm (US 6) needles

back

Cast on 89 (95: 103: 107: 113: **117: 123: 129: 133**) sts using 3mm (US 3) needles.
Work in moss (seed) st as foll:
ROW 1 (RS): K1, *P1, K1, rep from * to end.
Rep this row until 8 (8: 8: 8: 8: **16: 16: 16: 16**) rows in all are complete.
Change to 4mm (US 6) needles and cont working side vents as folls:
NEXT ROW (RS): Moss (seed) st 6, K to last 6 sts, moss (seed) st 6.
NEXT ROW: Moss (seed) st 6, P to last 6 sts, moss (seed) st 6.
Rep these last 2 rows 5 (6: 7: 8: 9: **12: 12: 14: 14**) times more, ending with a WS row.
Cont in st st across all sts, beg with a K row, until work measures 20 (22.5: 25: 26: 27: **30: 32: 34: 34**)cm (7¾ [8¾: 9¾: 10¼: 10¾: **12: 12½: 13½: 13½**]in) from cast-on edge, ending with a WS row.

WORK YOKE PATTERN
Working from appropriate chart, cont in patt until row 26 (28: 28: 32: 32: **32: 34: 36: 36**) is complete, ending with a WS row.

SHAPE ARMHOLE
Cast (bind) off 5 (5: 5: 5: 5: **8: 8: 8: 8**) sts at beg of every 2 rows.

Adults' sizes only
Dec 1 st at each end of next row and 4 foll alt rows. *91 (**97: 103: 107**) sts*

All sizes
Cont from chart until row 82 (86: 90: 96: 100: **106: 108: 110: 110**) is complete ending with a WS row.

SHAPE SHOULDER

Children's sizes only
Cast (bind) off 8 (8: 9: 10: 11) sts at beg of next 2 rows and 8 (9: 10: 10: 11) sts at beg of foll 2 rows. Work 1 row.
Cast (bind) off 9 (9: 10: 11: 12) sts at beg of next 2 rows. *29 (33: 35: 35: 35) sts*
Leave rem sts on a holder for hood.

Adults' sizes only
Cast (bind) off 4 sts at beg of next 10 (**10: 12: 12**) rows. *51 (**57: 55: 59**) sts*
Cast (bind) off 4 (**7: 5: 7**) sts at beg of next 2 rows.
Leave rem 43 (**43: 45: 45**) sts on a holder.

left front

Cast on 48 (51: 55: 57: 60: **63: 66: 69: 71**) sts using 3mm (US 3) needles.
Work in moss (seed) st as folls:
ROW 1 (RS): K0 (1: 1: 1: 0: **1: 0: 1: 1**), *P1, K1, rep from * to end.
ROW 2: *K1, P1, rep from * to last 0 (1: 1: 1: 0: **1: 0: 1: 1**), K0 (1: 1: 1: 0: **1: 0: 1: 1**).

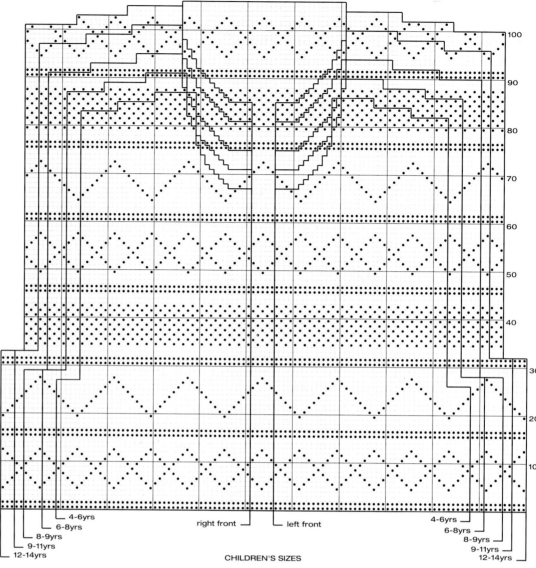

KEY

☐ K on RS, P on WS

☒ P on RS, K on WS

4-6yrs
6-8yrs
8-9yrs
9-11yrs
12-14yrs

right front ⎤   ⎡ left front

4-6yrs
6-8yrs
8-9yrs
9-11yrs
12-14yrs

CHILDREN'S SIZES

Work until 7 (7: 7: 7: 7: **15: 15: 15: 15**) rows in all are complete, ending with a RS row.

ROW 8 (16) (WS): Patt 6 (6: 6: 6: 6: **9: 9: 9: 9**) sts and leave these on a holder for front band, patt to end. *42 (45: 49: 51: 54: **54: 57: 60: 62**) sts*

Change to 4mm (US 6) needles and cont working side vent as folls:

NEXT ROW (RS): Moss (seed) st 6 sts, K to end.

NEXT ROW: Purl to last 6 sts, moss (seed) st 6.

Rep these last 2 rows 5 (6: 7: 8: 9: **12: 12: 14: 14**) times more, ending with a WS row.

Beg with a K row, cont in st st across all sts until front matches back to beg of yoke pattern, ending with a WS row.

Children's sizes only

WORK YOKE PATTERN

Working from appropriate chart, cont in patt until row 26 (28: 28: 32: 32) is complete, ending with a WS row.

SHAPE ARMHOLE

Cast (bind) off 5 sts at beg of next row. *37 (40: 44: 46: 49) sts*

Cont from chart until row 67 (71: 75: 81: 85) is complete, ending with a RS row.

Adults' sizes only

Work yoke pattern and divide for side pockets.

POCKET FRONT

CHART ROW 1 (RS): Patt 26 (28: 30: 32) sts and leave these sts on a holder for pocket side, patt to end. *28 (29: 30: 30) sts*

Keeping patt correct, cont from chart until row **48 (48: 50: 50)** is complete, ending with a WS row. Break yarn, leave sts on a holder.

WORK SIDE PANEL AND POCKET LINING

Using a spare 4mm (US 6) needle, cast on 28 (29: 30: 30) sts, then with WS facing, patt across 26 (28: 30: 32) sts of side panel. *54 (57: 60: 62) sts*

Now working extra sts cast on in st st and 26 (28: 30: 32) side panel sts in patt, cont until chart row 32 (34: 36: 36) is complete, ending with a WS row.

SHAPE ARMHOLE

Cast (bind) off 8 sts at beg of next row. Work 1 row. Dec 1 st at armhole edge on next row and 4 foll alt rows. *41 (44: 47: 49) sts*

Cont until chart row 47 (47: 49: 49) is complete, ending with a RS row.

ROW 48 (50) (WS): Cast (bind) off 28 (29: 30: 30) sts, patt to end. *13 (15: 17: 19) sts*

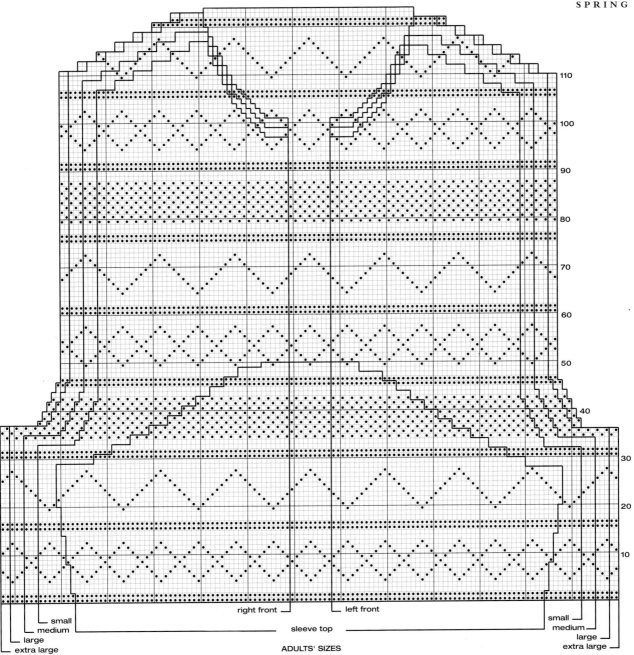

small
medium
large
extra large

right front ⌐   ⌐ left front

sleeve top

small
medium
large
extra large

ADULTS' SIZES

KEY

☐ K on RS, P on WS

▣ P on RS, K on WS

JOIN SIDE PANEL AND POCKET FRONT

CHART ROW 49 (51) (RS): Patt across **13 (15: 17: 19)** sts of side panel, then patt across **28 (29: 30: 30)** sts of pocket front. *41 (44: 47: 49) sts*

Cont from chart until row **97 (99: 101: 101)** is complete, ending with a RS row.

All sizes

SHAPE FRONT NECK AND SHOULDER

Patt 5 sts and leave these on a holder, patt to end. Dec 1 st at neck edge on next 5 (7: 7: 7: 7: **7: 7: 7: 7**) rows and 2 (2: 3: 3: 3: **5: 5: 6: 6**) sts on foll alt rows. AT THE SAME TIME, when chart row 82 (86: 90: 96: 100: **106: 108: 110: 110**) is complete, shape shoulder as for back and as indicated on chart.

right front

Cast on 48 (51: 55: 57: 60: **63: 66: 69: 71**) sts using 3mm (US 3) needles.

Work in moss (seed) st as folls:

ROW 1 (RS): K0 (1: 1: 1: 0: **1: 0: 1: 1**), *P1, K1, rep from * to end.

ROW 2: *K1, P1, rep from * to last 0 (1: 1: 1: 0: **1: 0: 1: 1**) sts, K0 (1: 1: 1: 0: **1: 0: 1: 1**).

Work until 7 (7: 7: 7: 7: **15: 15: 15: 15**) rows in all are complete, ending with a RS row.

ROW 8 (16) (WS): Patt to last 6 (6: 6: 6: 6: **9: 9: 9: 9**) sts, turn and leave these on a holder for front band. *42 (45: 49: 51: 54: 54: 57: 60: 62) sts*

Change to 4mm (US 6) needles and cont working side vent as folls:

NEXT ROW (RS): Knit to last 6 sts, moss (seed) st to end.

NEXT ROW: Moss st 6 sts, purl to end.

Rep these last 2 rows 5 (6: 7: 8: 9: 12: 12: 14: 14) times more, ending with a WS row.

Beg with a K row, cont in st st across all sts until front matches back to beg of yoke pattern, ending with a WS row.

Children's sizes only

Complete as for left front, working from chart for right front and rev shaping.

Adults' sizes only

Work yoke pattern and divide for side pockets.

WORK SIDE PANEL AND POCKET LINING

CHART ROW 1 (RS): Patt **28 (29: 30: 30)** sts and leave these sts on a holder for pocket front, patt to end. *26 (28: 30: 32)* sts

CHART ROW 2: Patt **26 (28: 30: 32)** sts, turn and cast on **28 (29: 30: 30)** sts. *54 (57: 60: 62)* sts

Now working extra cast on in st st and **26 (28: 30: 32)** side panel sts in patt, cont until chart row **33 (35: 37: 37)** is complete, ending with a RS row.

SHAPE ARMHOLE

Cast (bind) off 8 sts at beg of next row.

Dec 1 st at armhole edge on next row and 4 foll alt rows. **41 (44: 47: 49)** *sts*

Cont until chart row **47 (47: 49: 49)** is complete, ending with a RS row.

ROW 48 (50) (WS): Patt **13 (15: 17: 19)**, cast (bind) off rem **28 (29: 30: 30)** sts.

Leave rem **13 (15: 17: 19)** sts on a spare needle. Break yarn, leave sts on a holder.

POCKET FRONT

With WS facing, rejoin yarn to rem **28 (29: 30: 30)** sts on holder for pocket front, and cont in patt until chart row **48 (48: 50: 50)** is complete, ending with a WS row.

JOIN SIDE PANEL AND POCKET FRONT

CHART ROW 49 (51) (RS): Patt across **28 (29: 30: 30)** sts of pocket front, then patt across **13 (15: 17: 19)** sts of side panel. *41 (44: 47: 49)* sts

Complete as for left front, rev shaping.

sleeves (both alike)

Children's sizes only

Cast on 43 (43: 49: 49: 49) sts using 3mm (US 3) needles and work 8 rows in moss (seed) st as for back.

Change to 4mm (US 6) needles and, beg with a K row, work in st st, shaping sides by inc as folls:

1st & 2nd sizes only

Inc 1 st at each end of 3rd row, 2 foll 3rd rows and then every foll 4th row to 81 (85) sts.

Cont without shaping until work measures 33 (38)cm (13 [15]in) or length required from cast-on edge, ending with a WS row.

Cast (bind) off loosely and evenly.

3rd, 4th & 5th child's sizes only

Inc 1 st at each end of 3rd row, every foll 4th row to 81 (81: 85) sts and then every foll 6th row to 89 (93: 97) sts.

Cont without further shaping until work measures 40.5 (43: 45.5)cm (16 [17: 18]in) or length required from cast-on edge, ending with a WS row.

Cast (bind) off loosely and evenly.

Adults' sizes only

Note: The ladies' sleeve differs from the men's. The pattern is written for the ladies' sleeves, followed by the men's sleeves in bold.

Cast on 51 (**57**) sts using 3mm (US 3) needles and work 20 rows in moss (seed) st as for back.

Change to 4mm (US 6) needles and, beg with a K row, work in st st, inc 1 st at each end of 3rd row and every foll 3rd (**4th**) row to 93 (**91**) sts and then every foll 4th (**6th**) row to 101 sts.

Work 1 (**3**) rows, ending with a WS row.

Now work 28 rows in patt from chart, working between markers for sleeve and inc each end of row 3 and every foll 6th row to 109 sts.

SHAPE SLEEVEHEAD

CHART ROW 29 (RS): Cast (bind) off 8 sts at beg of next 2 rows.

Cast (bind) off 4 sts at beg of next 8 rows and 3 sts at beg of foll 10 rows. *31 sts*

Cast (bind) off 5 sts at beg of next 2 rows.

Cast (bind) off rem 21 sts.

finishing

Press all pieces as described on the information page. Join both shoulder seams using back stitch.

BUTTON BAND

With RS facing, slip the 6 (6: 6: 6: 6: 9: 9: 9: 9) sts from holder on right front for boy/man or left front for girl/woman onto a 3mm (US 3) needle.

Keeping patt correct, work 1 row in moss (seed) st, inc 1 st in inside edge. 7 (7: 7: 7: 7: **10: 10: 10: 10**) sts

Cont in moss (seed) st until band fits neatly, when slightly stretched, up front to beg of neck shaping. Slipstitch into place, leave sts on a holder.

Mark position of 7 buttons, the first to come 5 (5: 5: 5: 5: **7.5: 7.5: 7.5: 7.5**)cm (2 [2: 2: 2: 2: **3: 3: 3: 3**]in) from cast-on edge, the 7th to be worked in hood approx 1cm (½in) above neck edge and the rem spaced evenly between.

BUTTONHOLE BAND

Work as given for button band, adding 6 buttonholes to correspond with marker as foll:

Child's only

BUTTONHOLE ROW (RS): Patt 3, yon, K2tog, patt 2.

Adults' only

BUTTONHOLE ROW (RS): Patt 4, cast (bind) off 2, patt 4.

NEXT ROW: Patt across row, casting on 2 sts over those cast (bound) off on previous row.

HOOD

With RS facing and using 3mm (US 3) needles, work across 7 (7: 7: 7: 7: **10: 10: 10: 10**) sts from holder on right front band as foll: patt 5 (5: 5: 5: 5: **8: 8: 8: 8**) sts, K2tog, K 5 sts from holder on right front, pick up and knit 19 (20: 21: 22: 23: **24: 25: 26: 27**) sts up right front neck, 29 (33: 35: 35: 35: **43: 43: 45: 45**) sts from holder at back neck, 19 (20: 21: 22: 23: **24: 25: 26: 27**) sts down left front and 5 sts from holder on left front.

Work across 7 (7: 7: 7: 7: **10: 10: 10: 10**) sts from holder on left front band as folls: K2tog, patt 5 (5: 5: 5: 5: **8: 8: 8: 8**).

*89 (95: 99: 101: 103: **119: 121: 125: 127**) sts*

Work 2 rows in moss (seed) st.

Girls'/ladies' only

NEXT ROW (WS) (BUTTONHOLE ROW): Patt to last 5 (5: 5: 5: 5: **6: 6: 6: 6**) sts, cast (bind) off 2 sts, patt to end.

Boys'/men's only

NEXT ROW (WS) (BUTTONHOLE ROW): Patt 3 (3: 3: 3: 3: **4: 4: 4: 4**) sts, cast (bind) off 2 sts, patt to end.

All versions

NEXT ROW: Patt across row, casting on 2 sts over those cast (bound) off on previous row.

Work 2 (2: 2: 2: 2: **4: 4: 4: 4**) rows in moss (seed) st.

Cast (bind) off 6 (6: 6: 6: 6: **9: 9: 9: 9**) sts at beg of next 2 rows. *77 (83: 87: 89: 91: **101: 103: 107: 109**) sts*

NEXT ROW (WS) (INC): P38 (41: 43: 44: 45: **50: 51: 53: 54**), inc in next st, P to end.

*78 (84: 88: 90: 92: **102: 104: 108: 110**) sts*

Change to 4mm (US 6) needles and beg with a K row, work 30 (32: 34: 36: 38: **40: 42: 44: 46**) rows in st st, ending with a WS row.

SHAPE CROWN

NEXT ROW (RS): K39 (42: 44: 45: 46: **51: 52: 54: 55**) sts, turn and leave rem sts on a holder.

Work each side separately.

NEXT ROW: P2tog, P to end.

Work 5 (5: 5: 5: 5: **7: 7: 7: 7**) rows.

Dec at same edge as before on next row, 2 foll 5th (5th: 5th: 5th: 5th: **7th: 7th: 7th: 7th**) rows, and then every foll alt row to 26 (26: 26: 26: 26: **42: 42: 42: 42**) sts.

Dec 1 st at the same edge as before on every foll row to 23 (23: 23: 23: 23: **37: 37: 37: 37**) sts.

Cast (bind) off.

With RS facing, rejoin yarn to rem sts, K to end.

NEXT ROW (WS): P to last 2 sts, P2tog.

Cont to match first side, rev all shaping.

HOOD EDGING

With RS together, join shaped crown of hood in a smooth curve, using a neat back stitch.

With RS of hood facing and using 3mm (US 3) needles, pick up and knit 109 (111: 113: 115: 117: **135: 137: 139: 141**) sts evenly around edge of hood.

Work 4 (6) rows in moss (seed) st.

ROW 7: Patt 5 sts, cast (bind) off 2 sts, patt to last 7 sts, cast (bind) off 2 sts, patt 5 sts.

ROW 8: Patt across row, casting on 2 sts over those cast (bound) off on previous row.

Cont in moss (seed) st until 15 (15: 15: 15: 15: **19: 19: 19: 19**) rows in all are complete.

Cast (bind) off.

Fold moss (seed) st edging in half to WS of hood to form casing and slipstitch the cast- (bound-) off edge neatly over the cast-on edge.

Starting halfway across front bands, slipstitch ends of casing to top of front band.

CORD

Using two 3mm (US 3) double-pointed needles, cast on 3 sts and work as folls:

K3, *slide sts to other end of needle and without turning work, K3; rep from * until cord measures 90 (90: 90: 100: 100: **110: 110: 110: 110**)cm (35½ [35½: 35½: 39: 39: **43: 43: 43: 43**]in)

Cast (bind) off.

Thread the cord through hood casing and knot ends.

Adults' only

SIDE POCKET EDGINGS

With RS facing and using 3mm (US 3) needles, pick up and knit 39 sts evenly along edge of pocket opening.

Work 10 rows in moss (seed) st.

Cast (bind) off.

Slipstitch edges into place on RS.

See information page for finishing instructions.

native by Kim Hargreaves

Childrens' pullover

SIZES	4-6 YRS	6-8 YRS	8-10YRS	
Actual width	45	49.5	54	cm
	17½	19½	21½	in
Length	45	50	54	cm
	17½	19½	21½	in
Sleeve length	39	41	43	cm
	15½	16	17	in

YARN
Rowan Handknit DK Cotton 50gm (1¾oz) balls:

A	Flame	254	2	2	2
B	Oasis	202	2	2	2
C	Raindrop	206	3	3	3
D	Linen	205	2	3	3
E	Artichoke	209	2	2	2
F	Tope	253	2	2	2
G	Popcorn	229	2	2	2

Ladies' pullover

SIZES	S	M	L	
To fit bust	86	91	97	cm
	34	36	38	in
Actual width	58.5	61.5	64.5	cm
	23	24	25½	in
Length	70	72	74	cm
	27½	28½	29	in
Sleeve length	45	45	45	cm
	17½	17½	17½	in

YARN
Rowan Handknit DK Cotton 50gm (1¾oz) balls:

A	Gerba	223	3	3	3
B	Artichoke	209	3	3	3
C	Zing	300	4	4	4
D	Chime	204	4	4	4
E	Linen	205	3	4	4
F	Muddy	302	4	4	4
G	Carmen	201	3	3	3

Men's pullover

SIZES	M	L	XL	
To fit chest	102	107	112	cm
	40	42	44	in
Actual width	67.5	70.5	73.5	cm
	26½	28	29	in
Length	65	67	69	cm
	25½	26½	27	in
Sleeve length	49	49	49	cm
	19½	19½	19½	in

YARN
Rowan Handknit DK Cotton 50gm (1¾oz) balls:

A	Soft Green	228	3	3	3
B	Ice Water	239	3	3	3
C	Rainwater	206	4	4	5
D	Linen	205	4	4	4
E	Tope	253	3	4	4
F	Artichoke	209	4	4	4
G	Zing	300	3	3	3

NEEDLES
1 pair 3¼mm (US 3) needles
1 pair 4mm (US 6) needles

TENSION (GAUGE)
20 sts and 28 rows to 10cm (4in) measured over stocking (stockinette) stitch using 4mm (US 6) needles

PATTERN NOTE
The pattern is written for the three children's sizes, followed by the three ladies' sizes in bold, followed by the men's sizes.

back
Using 3¼mm (US 3) needles, cast on as folls:
30 (33: 36: **39: 41: 43:** 45: 47: 49) sts using yarn D,
30 (33: 36: **39: 41: 43:** 45: 47: 49) sts using yarn C and
30 (33: 36: **39: 41: 43:** 45: 47: 49) sts using yarn F.
*90 (99: 108: **117: 123: 129:** 135: 141: 147) sts*
Using the intarsia technique described on the information page, cont in striped st st from chart as folls:
ROW 1 (RS): Work first 30 (33: 36: **39: 41: 43:** 45: 47: 49) sts using left panel color, work next 30 (33: 36: **39: 41: 43:** 45: 47: 49) sts using center panel color, work last 30 (33: 36: **39: 41: 43:** 45: 47: 49) sts using right panel color.
ROW 2: Work first 30 (33: 36: **39: 41:** 43: 45: 47: 49) sts using right panel color, work next 30 (33: 36: **39: 41:**

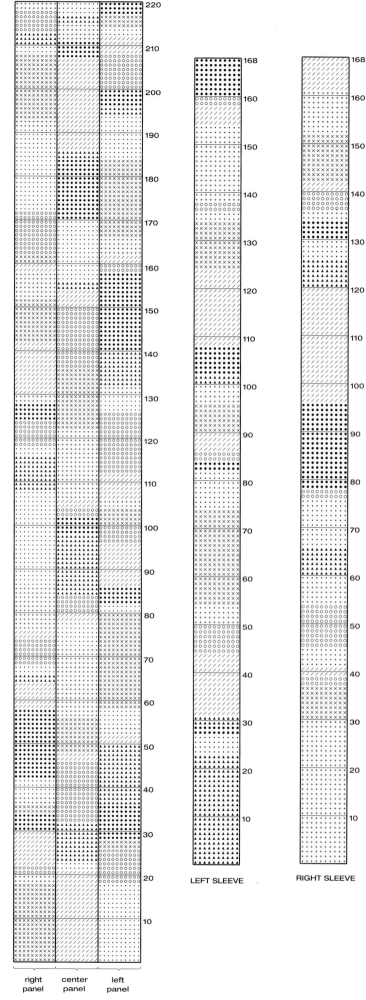

KEY

- ▪ A
- ⊙ B
- ▨ C
- ⊠ D
- ⊞ E
- ⊡ F
- ▲ G

43: 45: 47: 49) sts using center panel color, work last 30 (33: 36: **39: 41: 43:** 45: 47: 49) sts using left panel color.

These 2 rows set position of colors as on chart.

Keeping chart correct, cont as folls:

Work 8 rows.

Change to 4mm (US 6) needles.

Cont straight until back measures 25 (28: 31: **46: 47: 48:** 40: 41: 42)cm (9¾ [11¼: 12¼: **18: 18½: 18¾:** 15¾: 16¼: 16½]in), ending with a WS row.

SHAPE ARMHOLES

Cast (bind) off 4 sts at beg of next 2 rows.
*82 (91: 100: **109: 115: 121:** 127: 133: 139) sts*

Dec 1 st at each end of next 4 (6: 6) rows.
*74 (83: 92: **97: 103: 109:** 115: 121: 127) sts*

Cont straight until armhole measures 20 (22: 23: **24: 25: 26:** 25: 26: 27)cm (7¾ [8½: 9: **9½: 9¾: 10¼:** 9¾: 10¼: 10¾]in), ending with a WS row.

SHAPE SHOULDERS AND BACK NECK

Cast (bind) off 7 (9: 10: **10: 10: 11:** 12: 12: 13) sts at beg of next 2 rows. *60 (65: 72: **77: 83: 87:** 91: 97: 101) sts*

NEXT ROW (RS): Cast (bind) off 7 (9: 10: **10: 10: 11:** 12: 12: 13) sts, K until there are 12 (12: 14: **13: 15: 15:** 15: 17: 18) sts on right needle and turn, leaving rem sts on a holder.

Work each side of neck separately.

Cast (bind) off 4 sts at beg of next row.

Cast (bind) off rem 8 (8: 10: **9: 11: 11:** 11: 13: 14) sts.

With RS facing, rejoin yarn to rem sts, cast (bind) off center 22 (23: 24: **31: 33: 35:** 37: 39: 39) sts, K to end.

Work to match first side, rev shaping.

right panel   center panel   left panel

BACK AND FRONT

LEFT SLEEVE   **RIGHT SLEEVE**

front

Work as given for back until there are 12 (**12**: 14) rows fewer than on back to start of shoulder shaping, ending with a WS row.

SHAPE NECK

NEXT ROW (RS): K31 (35: 39: **38: 40: 42:** 45: 47: 50) and turn, leaving rem sts on a holder.

Work each side of neck separately.

Cast (bind) off 4 sts at beg of next row.

27 (31: 35: 34: 36: 38: 41: 43: 46) sts

Dec 1 st at neck edge of next 3 rows, then on foll 2 (**2**: 3) alt rows. *22 (26: 30: 29: 31: 33: 35: 37: 40) sts*

Work 3 rows, ending with a WS row.

SHAPE SHOULDER

Cast (bind) off 7 (9: 10: **10: 10: 11:** 12: 12: 13) sts at beg of next and foll alt row.

Work 1 row.

Cast (bind) off rem 8 (8: 10: **9: 11: 11:** 11: 13: 14) sts.

With RS facing, rejoin yarn to rem sts, cast (bind) off center 12 (13: 14: **21: 23: 25:** 25: 27: 27) sts, K to end.

Work to match first side, rev all shaping.

left sleeve

Cast on 44 (46: 48: **56:** 62) sts using 3¼mm (US 3) needles and yarn G.

Cont in color sequence from chart for left sleeve as folls:

Work 8 (**10**: 10) rows.

Change to 4mm (US 6) needles.

Inc 1 st at each end of next and every foll 6th row until there are 70 (64: 64: **76:** 98) sts, then on every foll 4th row until there are 80 (88: 94: **96: 100: 104:** 100: 104: 108) sts.

Cont straight until sleeve measures 39 (41: 43: **45:** 49)cm (15½ [16¼: 17: **17¾:** 19¼]in), ending with a WS row.

SHAPE TOP

Cast (bind) off 4 sts at beg of next 2 rows.

72 (80: 86: 88: 92: 96: 92: 96: 100) sts

Dec 1 st at each end of next and foll 4 (**4:** 5) alt rows.

Work 1 row, ending with a WS row.

Cast (bind) off rem 62 (70: 76: **78: 82: 86:** 80: 84: 88) sts.

right sleeve

Work as given for left sleeve, casting on with yarn E and foll chart for right sleeve.

finishing

Press all pieces as described on the information page. Join right shoulder seam using back stitch or mattress stitch if preferred.

NECKBAND

With RS facing and using 3¼mm (US 3) needles and yarn C (**F:** E), pick up and knit 19 (**19:** 21) sts down left side of neck, 12 (13: 14: **21: 23: 25:** 25: 27: 27) sts from front, 19 (**19:** 21) sts up right side of neck and 30 (31: 32: **39: 41: 43:** 45: 47: 47) sts from back.

80 (82: 84: 98: 102: 106: 112: 116: 116) sts

Beg with a P row, work in st st for 6 (**8:** 8) rows.

Cast (bind) off.

See information page for finishing instructions, setting in sleeves using the shallow set-in method.

pittsburg by Kim Hargreaves

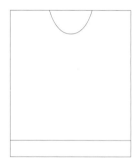

SIZES

	S	M	L	
To fit bust	86	91	97	cm
	34	36	38	in
Actual width	57.5	60	62.5	cm
	22¾	23¾	24¾	in
Length	69.5	71.5	73.5	cm
	27½	28¼	29	in
Sleeve length	48	48	48	cm
	19	19	19	in

(All measurements after washing)

YARN

Rowan Denim–50gm (1¾oz) balls:

Nashville 225	21	22	23	

NEEDLES

1 pair 3¼mm (US 3) needles
1 pair 4mmn (US 6) needles
Cable needle

PATTERN NOTE

The Denim yarn shrinks in length when washed by approximately one-fifth; lengths given in pattern are before washing.

TENSION (GAUGE)

26 sts (1 patt rep) measures 11.5cm (4½in) before and after washing; 24 rows (1 patt rep) measures 9cm (3½in) before washing or about 7.5cm (3in) after washing using 4mm (US 6) needles.

SPECIAL ABBREVIATIONS

BKC = Back knit cross: Slip next st onto cable needle hold at back, K2, then K1 from cable needle.
FKC = Front knit cross: Slip next 2 sts onto cable needle hold at front, K1, then K2 from cable needle.
BPC = Back purl cross: Slip next st onto cable needle, hold at back, K2, then P1 from cable needle.
FPC = Front purl cross: Slip next 2 sts onto cable needle, hold in front, P1, then K2 from cable needle.

back

Cast on 110 (116: 122) sts using 3¼mm, (US 3) needles.
ROW 1: K0 (0: 1), P0 (0: 2), K0 (2:2), P0 (1:1), * P1, (K2, P2) twice, K4, (P2, K2) twice, P1, rep from * to last 0 (3: 6) sts, P0 (1: 1), K0 (2: 2), P0 (0: 2), K0 (0: 1).
ROW 2: P0 (0: 1), K0 (0: 2), P0 (2: 2), K0 (1: 1), * K1, (P2, K2) twice, P4, (K2, P2) twice, K1, rep from * to last 0 (3: 6) sts, K0 (1: 1), P0 (2: 2), K0 (0: 2), P0 (0: 1).

Rep these 2 rows 10 times more, then rep first row again.
ROW 24 (INC): P0 (01), K0 (0: 2), P0 (2: 2), K0 (1: 1), * K1, P2, K2, P2, inc into each of next 2 sts, P4, inc into each of next 2 sts, P2, K2, P2, K1, rep from * to last 0 (3: 6) sts, K0 (1: 1), P0 (2: 2), K0 (0: 2), P0 (0: 1). *130 (136: 142) sts*
Change to 4mm (US 6) needles and work in patt as folls:
ROW 1: K0 (0: 2), P0 (3: 4), (P4, BKC, K12, FKC, P4) 5 times, P0 (3: 4), K0 (0: 2).
ROW 2 & ALL (WS) ROWS: Knit all knit sts and purl all purl sts as they face you.
ROW 3: FKC 0 (0: 1) time, P0 (3: 3), (P3, BKC, K4, BPC, FPC, K4, FKC, P3) 5 times, P0 (3: 3), BKC 0 (0: 1) time.
ROW 5: K0 (1 1), FKC 0 (0: 1) time, P0 (2: 2), (P2, BKC, K4, BPC, P2, FPC, K4, FKC, P2) 5 times, P0 (2: 2), BKC 0 (0: 1) time, K0 (1: 1).
ROW 7: K0 (2: 2), FKC 0 (0: 1) time, P0 (1: 1), (P1, BKC, K4, BPC, P4, FPC, K4, FKC, P1) 5 times, P0 (1: 1), BKC 0 (0: 1) time, K0 (22).
ROW 9: K0 (0: 3), FKC 0 (1: 1) time, (BKC, K4, BPC, P6, FPC, K4, FKC) 5 times, BKC 0 (1: 1) time, K0 (0: 3).
ROW 11: K0 (3: 6), (K6, BPC, P8, FPC, K6) 5 times, K0 (3: 6).
ROW 13: K0 (3: 6), (K6, FKC, P8, BKC, K6) 5 times, K0 (3: 6).
ROW 15: K0 (0: 3), BPC 0 (1: 1) time, (FPC, K4, FKC, P6, BKC, K4, BPC) 5 times, FPC 0 (1 1) time, K0 (0, 3).
ROW 17: K0 (2: 2), BPC 0 (0: 1) time, (P1, FPC, K4, FKC, P4, BKC, K4, BPC, P1) 5 times, FPC 0 (1: 1) time, K0 (2: 2).
ROW 19: K0 (1: 1), BPC 0 (0: 1) time. P0 (2: 2), (P2, FKC, K4. FKC, P2, BKC, K4, BPC, P2) 5 times, P0 (2: 2), FPC 0 (0: 1) time, K0 (1: 1).
ROW 21: BPC 0 (0: 1) time, P0 (3: 3), (P3, FPC, K4, FKC, BKC, K4, BPC, P3) 5 times, P0 (3: 3), FPC 0 (0: 1) time.
ROW 23: K0 (0: 2), P0 (3: 4), (P4, FPC, K12, BPC, P4) 5 times. P0 (3: 4), K0 (0: 2).
ROW 24: Work as for row 2.
Rep these 24 rows until work measures 77.5 (80: 82.5)cm (30½ [31½: 32½]in) from top of rib—work will shrink by 15.5 (16: 16.5)cm (6 [6¼: 6½]in) during washing—or length required, ending with WS row.
SHAPE SHOULDERS AND BACK NECK
Patt 49 (52: 55) sts, turn, leaving rem sts on a holder.

With RS facing, rejoin yarn to rem sts, cast (bind) off center 14 sts, patt to end.

Complete to match first side, rev all shaping.

COMPLETE RIGHT SHOULDER SEAM.

Cast (bind) off sts of right back and right front shoulder tog as folls:

With the 2 sets of sts on spare needle, hold the 2 needles tog with WS of work tog, then working on the RS, K tog 1 st from each needle to give 1 st on RH needle, * K tog the next 2 sts (now 2 sts on RH needle), pass the first of these 2 sts over the second. Rep from * to end.

NECKBAND

With RS facing and using 3¼mm (US 3) needles, pick up and knit 32 sts down left front neck, 14 sts across center front, 32 sts up right front neck and 40 sts across back neck. *118 sts*

Work 6.25cm (2½in) in K2, P2 rib.

Cast (bind) off loosely and evenly.

Cast (bind) off sts for left shoulder tog as given for right shoulder.

Join neckband using an edge-to-edge stitch.

sleeves (both alike)

Cast on 50 sts using 3¼mm (US 3) needles.

ROW 1: * P1, K4, (P2, K2) 4 times, P1, rep from * once more, P1, K4, P1.

ROW 2: * K1, P4, (K2, P2) 4 times, K1 rep from * once more, K1, P4, K1.

Rep these 2 rows 10 times more, then rep first row once more.

ROW 24 (INC): K1, P2, * P2, inc into each of next 2 sts, (P2, K2) 3 times, P2, inc into each of next 2 sts, P2, rep from * once more, P2, K1. *58 sts*

Change to 4mm (US 6) needles and work in patt, setting sts as folls:

ROW 1: P3, (P4, BKC, K1 2, FKC, P4) twice, P3.

ROW 2 & ALL (WS) ROWS: Knit all knit sts and purl all purl sts as they face you.

ROW 3: Inc into first st, P2, (P3, BKC, K4, BPC, FPC, K4, FKC, P3) twice, P2, inc into last st.

Cont in patt as for back and AT THE SAME TIME inc 1 st at each end of every foll 4th row until there are 114 sts, taking extra sts into patt as they occur.

Cont without further shaping until work measures 48.75cm (19¼in) from top of rib (this will shrink to about 40.5cm [16in] during washing) or length required.

Cast (bind) off loosely and evenly.

finishing

See information page for finishing instructions. Leave ribs open at side seams to form vents.

Note: The Denim yarn and pieces must be washed and dried before sewing up the garment as specified on the ball bands to allow garment to shrink.

Work each side separately.

Cast (bind) off 4 sts, patt to end.

Leave rem 45 (48: 51) sts on a holder.

With RS facing, rejoin yarn to rem sts, cast (bind) off center 32 sts, patt to end.

Complete to match first side.

front

Work as for back until front is 28 rows shorter than back to beg of shoulder shaping, ending with a WS row.

SHAPE FRONT NECK

Patt 58 (61: 64) sts and turn, leaving rem sts on a holder.

Work each side of neck separately.

Dec 1 st at neck edge on next 6 rows and foll 5 alt rows. Work 3 rows.

Dec at neck edge on next row and foll 4th row. *45 (48: 51) sts*

Cont without further shaping until front matches back to shoulder shaping.

SHAPE SHOULDER

Leave rem sts on a holder.

moira by Fiona McTague

SIZE	XS	S	M	L	XL	
To fit bust	81	86	91	97	102	cm
	32	34	36	38	40	in
Actual width	48.5	50.5	53	55	57.5	cm
	19	20	21	21.5	22.5	in
Length	57	58	59	60	61	cm
	22	23	23	23½	24	in
Sleeve length	40	40	41	41	41	cm
	15½	15½	16	16	16	in

YARN

Rowan Cotton Glacé—50gm (1¾oz) balls:

A	Mint	748	9	9	10	10	10
B	Bubbles	724	3	3	4	4	4
C	Pear	780	3	3	3	3	4
D	Oyster	730	3	3	3	3	3
E	Hyacinth	787	1	1	1	2	2

NEEDLES

1 pair 2¾mm (US 2) needles
1 pair 3¼mm (US 3) needles

BUTTONS

8

TENSION (GAUGE)

27 sts and 30 rows to 10cm (4in) measured over patterned stocking (stockinette) stitch using 3¼mm (US 3) needles

back

Cast on 125 (131: 137: 143: 149) sts using 2¾mm (US 2) needles and yarn A.
Beg with a RS row, work 6 rows in garter st (knit every row).
Change to 3¼mm (US 3) needles.
Using the Fair Isle technique described on the information page, starting and ending rows as indicated and rep the 62-row rep throughout, cont in patt from chart, which is worked entirely in st st, as folls:
Patt 12 (14: 14: 16: 16) rows.
Dec 1 st at each end of next and every foll 4th row until 111 (117: 123: 129: 135) sts rem.
Work 9 rows.
Inc 1 st at each end of next and every foll 6th row to 121 (127: 133: 139: 145) sts, then on every foll 4th row to 131 (137: 143: 149: 155) sts, taking inc sts into patt.
Cont in patt until back measures 37 (38: 38: 39: 39)cm (14½ [15: 15: 15½: 15½]in), ending with a WS row.

SHAPE ARMHOLES

Keeping patt correct, cast (bind) off 3 (4: 4: 5: 5) sts at beg of next 2 rows. *125 (129: 135: 139: 145) sts*
Dec 1 st at each end of next 7 (7: 9: 9: 11) rows, then on every foll alt row until 95 (97: 99: 101: 103) sts rem.
Cont straight until armhole measures 20 (20: 21: 21: 22)cm (7¾ [7¾: 8¼: 8¼: 8½]in), ending with a WS row.

SHAPE SHOULDERS AND BACK NECK

Keeping patt correct, cast (bind) off 8 (9: 9: 9: 9) sts at beg of next 2 rows. *79 (79: 81: 83: 85) sts*
NEXT ROW (RS): Cast (bind) off 8 (9: 9: 9: 9) sts, patt until there are 13 (12: 12: 13: 14) sts on right needle and turn, leaving rem sts on a holder.
Work each side of neck separately.
Cast (bind) off 4 sts at beg of next row.
Cast (bind) off rem 9 (8: 8: 9: 10) sts.
With RS facing, rejoin yarn to rem sts, cast (bind) off center 37 (37: 39: 39: 39) sts, patt to end.
Work to match first side, rev shaping.

left front

Cast on 63 (66: 69: 72: 75) sts using 2¾mm (US 2) needles and yarn A.
Beg with a RS row, work 6 rows in garter st.
Change to 3¼mm (US 3) needles.
Cont in patt from chart as folls:
Patt 12 (14: 14: 16: 16) rows.
Dec 1 st at beg of next and every foll 4th row until 56 (59: 62: 65: 68) sts rem.
Work 9 rows.
Inc 1 st at beg of next and every foll 6th row to 61 (64: 67: 70: 73) sts, then on every foll 4th row to 66 (69: 72: 75: 78) sts, taking inc sts into patt.
Cont in patt until left front matches back to beg of armhole shaping, ending with a WS row.

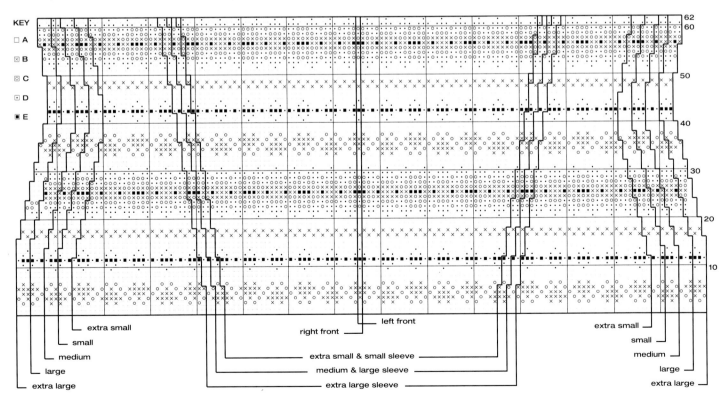

RIGHT AND LEFT FRONTS, BACK AND SLEEVE

SHAPE ARMHOLE

Keeping patt correct, cast (bind) off 3 (4: 4: 5: 5) sts at beg of next row. *63 (65: 68: 70: 73) sts*
Work 1 row.
Dec 1 st at armhole edge of next 7 (7: 9: 9: 11) rows, then on every foll alt row until 48 (49: 50: 51: 52) sts rem.
Cont straight until front is 17 (17: 19: 19: 19) rows shorter than back to start of shoulder shaping, ending with a RS row.

SHAPE NECK

Keeping patt correct, cast (bind) off 13 sts at beg of next row, then 4 sts at beg of foll alt row.
31 (32: 33: 34: 35) sts
Dec 1 st at neck edge on next 3 rows, then on foll 3 (3: 4: 4: 4) alt rows. *25 (26: 26: 27: 28) sts*
Work 5 rows, ending with a WS row.

SHAPE SHOULDER

Keeping patt correct, cast (bind) off 8 (9: 9: 9: 9) sts at beg of next and foll alt row.
Cast (bind) off rem 9 (8: 8: 9: 10) sts.

right front

Cast on 63 (66: 69: 72: 75) sts using 2¾mm (US 2) needles and yarn A.
Beg with a RS row, work 6 rows in garter st.
Change to 3¼mm (US 3) needles.
Cont in patt from chart as folls:
Patt 12 (14: 14: 16: 16) rows.
Dec 1 st at end of next and every foll 4th row until 56 (59: 62: 65: 68) sts rem.
Complete to match left front, rev shaping.

sleeves

Cast on 59 (59: 63: 63: 67) sts using 2¾mm (US 2) needles and yarn A.
Beg with a RS row, work 6 rows in garter st.
Change to 3¼mm (US 3) needles and cont in patt from chart as folls:
Inc 1 st at each end of 7th and every foll 6th row to 83 (91: 91: 97: 101) sts, then on every foll 8th row to 91 (93: 97: 99: 103) sts, taking inc sts into patt.
Cont straight until sleeve measures 40 (40: 41: 41: 41)cm 15¾ [15¾: 16¼: 16¼: 16¼]in), ending with a WS row.

SHAPE TOP

Keeping patt correct, cast (bind) off 3 (4: 4: 5: 5) sts at beg of next 2 rows. *85 (85: 89: 89: 93) sts*
Dec 1 st at each end of next 5 rows, then on foll 3 alt rows. *69 (69: 73: 73: 77) sts*
Work 3 rows, ending with a WS row.
Dec 1 st at each end of next and every foll 4th row until 61 (61: 67: 67: 73) sts rem, then on every foll alt row until 59 sts rem.
Work 1 row.
Dec 1 st at each end on next 6 rows. *47 sts*
Cast (bind) off 4 sts at beg of next 4 rows.
Cast (bind) off rem 31 sts.

left hood

Cast on 12 sts using 3¼mm (US 3) needles and yarn A.
Work in patt from chart for left hood as folls:
Work 2 rows.
Cast on 6 sts at beg of next and foll 2 alt rows. *30 sts*
Work 1 row.
Cast on 6 sts at beg and dec 1 st at end of next row.
35 sts
Work 1 row.

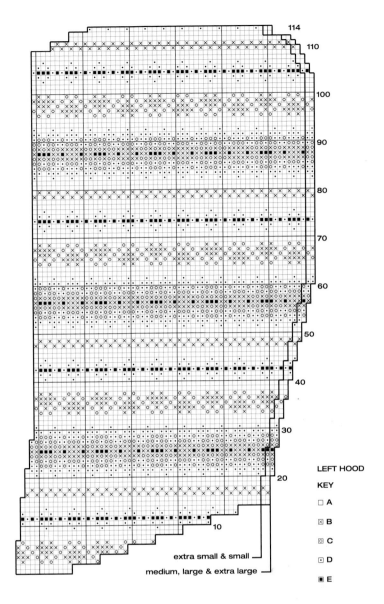

LEFT HOOD

KEY

□ A
⊠ B
⊡ C
⊡ D
■ E

extra small & small ⎤
medium, large & extra large ⎦

Cast on 6 sts at beg of next and foll alt row, then 5 (5: 7: 7: 7) sts at beg of foll alt row.
52 (52: 54: 54: 54) sts.
Work 1 row.
Dec 1 st at end of next row. *51 (51: 53: 53: 53) sts*
Work 3 rows.
Inc 1 st at beg of next row. *52 (52: 54: 54: 54) sts*
Work 1 row.
Rep last 6 rows twice more.
Work 2 rows.
Inc 1 st at beg of next and every foll 4th row until there are 59 (59: 61: 61: 61) sts.
Cont straight until chart row 104 is complete or hood measures 34.5cm (13½in) from cast-on edge, ending with a WS row.
Dec 1 st at beg of next and foll 2 alt rows.
56 (56: 58: 58: 58) sts
NEXT ROW (WS): Cast (bind) off 4 sts at beg of next row. *52 (52: 54: 54: 54) sts*
Dec 1 st at beg of next row. *51 (51: 53: 53: 53) sts*
Cast (bind) off 4 sts at beg and dec 1 st at end of next row. *46 (46: 48: 48: 48) sts*
Cast (bind) off 4 sts at beg of next 2 rows.
Cast (bind) off rem 38 (38: 40: 40: 40) sts.

right hood

Cast on 12 sts using 3¼mm (US 3) needles and yarn A. Working odd-numbered rows as purl rows, reading rows from right to left, and even-numbered rows as knit rows, reading rows from left to right (and therefore rev patt), work in patt from chart for left hood as folls:

Work 2 rows.

Cast on 6 sts at beg of next and foll 2 alt rows. *30 sts*

Work 1 row.

Cast on 6 sts at beg and dec 1 st at end of next row. *35 sts*

Work 1 row.

Cast on 6 sts at beg of next and foll alt row, then 5 (5: 7: 7: 7) sts at beg of foll alt row. *52 (52: 54: 54: 54) sts*

Work 1 row.

Dec 1 st at end of next row. *51 (51: 53: 53: 53) sts*

Work 3 rows.

Complete to match left hood, rev shaping.

finishing

Press all pieces as described on the information page. Join shoulder seams using back stitch. Join back and crown seams of hood using back stitch. Sew hood to neck edge using back stitch.

FRONT OPENING AND HOOD BORDER

Cast on 6 sts using 2¾mm (US 2) needles and yarn A. Beg with a RS row, work in garter st until border, when slightly stretched, fits up left front opening edge to hood seam, ending with a RS row.

Mark positions for 8 buttons on this section of border, the lowest button 1cm (½in) up from lower edge, the top button 1.5cm (¾in) below neck edge and the rem 6 buttons evenly spaced between.

Cast on 6 sts at beg of next row. *12 sts*

Work 4 rows.

NEXT ROW (RS) (CORD EYELET ROW): K2, cast (bind) off 2 sts, K to end.

NEXT ROW: Knit, casting on 2 sts over those cast (bound) off on previous row.

Cont in garter st until this wider section, when slightly stretched, fits up left front hood and down right front hood to a point 1cm (½in) above neck seam, ending with a WS row.

NEXT ROW (RS) (CORD EYELET ROW): K2, cast (bind) off 2 sts, K to end.

NEXT ROW: Knit, casting on 2 sts over those cast (bound) off on previous row.

Work 3 rows.

Cast (bind) off 6 sts at beg of next row. *6 sts*

Cont in garter st until this section of border, when slightly stretched, fits down right front opening edge to lower edge, ending with a WS row and adding 8 buttonholes to correspond with positions marked for buttons as folls:

BUTTONHOLE ROW (RS): K2, yfwd, K2tog, K2.

Cast (bind) off.

Slipstitch border in position.

Fold border in half around edge of hood to form casing and slipstitch in place. Make 150cm (59in) cord using yarn A and knot ends. Thread cord through hood casing using eyelet holes.

See information page for finishing instructions.

bella by Kim Hargreaves

SIZE

	S	M	L	
To fit bust	81–86	86–91	91–97	cm
	32–34	34–36	36–38	in
Actual width	43.5	46	48	cm
	17	18	19	in
Length	48	48	48	cm
	19	19	19	in
Sleeve length	43	43	43	cm
	17	17	17	in

YARNS

Rowan 4-ply Cotton 50gm (1¾oz) balls and
Cotton Glacé 50gm (1¾oz) balls:

				S	M	L
A	4-ply	Magenta	106	7	8	8
B	4-ply	Monsoon	109	2	2	2
C	Glacé	Lagoon	797	1	1	1
D	4-ply	Vine	103	1	1	1
E	4-ply	Racey	107	1	1	1

NEEDLES

1 pair 2¼mm (US 1) needles
1 pair 3mm (US 2/3) needles
2¼mm (US 1) circular needle

BUTTONS

6

TENSION (GAUGE)

28 sts and 38 rows to 10cm (4in) measured over
stocking (stockinette) stitch using 3mm (US 2/3)
needles

back

Cast on 122 (128: 134) sts using 2¼mm (US 1)
needles and yarn D.
Work 4 rows in garter st (knit every row).
Break yarn D and join yarn A.
ROW 1 (RS): K4, K2tog, K2 (5: 8), yfwd, K1, *yfwd,
K5, K2tog tbl, K2tog, K5, yfwd, K1, rep from * to last
8 (11: 14) sts, yfwd, K2 (5: 8), K2tog tbl, K4.
ROW 2: K8 (11: 14), *P1, K14, rep from * to last
9 (12: 15) sts, P1, K8 (11: 14).
ROW 3: As row 1.
ROW 4: Purl.
ROW 5: K3, K3tog, K2 (5: 8), yfwd, K1, *yfwd, K5,
K2tog tbl, K2tog, K5, yfwd, K1*, **yfwd, K4, K3tog
tbl, K3tog, K4, yfwd, K1**, rep from * to * 3 times
more, rep from ** to ** once more, rep from * to *
once more, yfwd, K2 (5: 8), K3tog tbl, K3.
116 (122: 128) sts

ROW 6: K7 (10: 13), P1, K14, P1, K12, (P1, K14) 3 times,
P1, K12, P1, K14, P1, K7 (10: 13).
ROW 7: K3, K2tog, K2 (5: 8), yfwd, K1, *yfwd, K5,
K2tog tbl, K2tog, K5, yfwd, K1*, **yfwd, K4,
K2tog tbl, K2tog, K4, yfwd, K1**, rep from * to *
3 times more, rep from ** to ** once more, rep from
* to * once more, yfwd, K2 (5: 8), K2tog tbl, K3.
ROW 8: Purl.
ROW 9: K3, K2tog, K2 (5: 8), yfwd, K1, *yfwd, K5,
K2tog tbl, K2tog, K5, yfwd, K1*, **yfwd, K3, K3tog
tbl, K3tog, K3, yfwd, K1**, rep from * to * 3 times
more, rep from ** to ** once more, rep from * to *
once more, yfwd, K2 (5: 8), K2tog tbl, K3.
112 (118: 124) sts
ROW 10: K7 (10: 13), P1, K14, P1, K10, (P1, K14) 3
times, P1, K10, P1, K14, P1, K7 (10: 13).
ROW 11: K2, K2tog, K2 (5: 8), yfwd, K1, *yfwd, K5,
K2tog tbl, K2tog, K5, yfwd, K1*, **yfwd, K3, K2tog
tbl, K2tog, K3, yfwd, K1**, rep from * to * 3 times
more, rep from ** to ** once more, rep from * to *
once more, yfwd, K2 (5: 8), K3tog tbl, K2.
110 (116: 122) sts
ROW 12: Purl.
ROW 13: K2, K2tog, K2 (5: 8), yfwd, K1, *yfwd, K5,
K2tog tbl, K2tog, K5, yfwd, K1*, **yfwd, K2, K3tog
tbl, K3tog, K2, yfwd, K1**, rep from * to * 3 times
more, rep from ** to ** once more, rep from * to *
once more, yfwd, K2 (5: 8), K2tog tbl, K2.
106 (112: 118) sts
ROW 14: K6 (9: 12), P1, K14, P1, K8, (P1, K14) 3 times,
P1, K8, P1, K14, P1, K6 (9: 12).
ROW 15: K2, K2tog, K2 (5: 8), yfwd, K1, *yfwd, K5,
K2tog tbl, K2tog, K5, yfwd, K1*, **yfwd, K2, K2tog
tbl, K2tog, K2, yfwd, K1**, rep from * to * 3 times
more, rep from ** to ** once more, rep from * to *
once more, yfwd, K2 (5: 8), K2tog tbl, K2.
Beg with a P row, work 5 rows in st st, thus ending
with a WS row.
Change to 3mm (US 2/3) needles.
Beg with a K row, work 8 rows in st st, inc 1 st at
each end of 7th row. *108 (114: 120) sts*
Using the intarsia technique described on the
information page, beg and ending rows as indicated,
work in patt from chart. Rep the 38-row patt, which is
worked entirely in st st, beg with a K row and shaping
sides by inc 1 st at each end of every foll 8th row from
previous inc until there are 122 (128: 134) sts.
Cont without further shaping until all 38 chart rows
have been worked twice in all, thus ending with
a WS row.

SHAPE ARMHOLES

Keeping chart correct, cast (bind) off 5 (6: 7) sts at beg of next 2 rows. *112 (116: 120) sts*

Dec 1 st at each end of next 5 rows, then on every foll alt row until 92 (96: 100) sts rem.

Cont without further shaping until 38 chart rows have been worked 4 times in all, thus ending with a WS row.

SHAPE SHOULDERS AND BACK NECK

Working in st st using yarn A only, proceed as folls:

Cast (bind) off 9 (9: 10) sts at beg of next 2 rows. *74 (78: 80) sts*

NEXT ROW (RS): Cast (bind) off 9 (9: 10) sts, K until there are 12 (14: 14) sts on right needle and turn, leaving rem sts on a holder.

Work each side of neck separately.

Cast (bind) off 4 sts at beg of next row.

Cast (bind) off rem 8 (10: 10) sts.

With RS facing, rejoin yarn to rem sts, cast (bind) off center 32 sts, K to end.

Work to match first side, rev shaping.

left front

Cast on 62 (65: 68) sts using 2¼mm (US 1) needles and yarn D.

Work 4 rows in garter st.

Break yarn D and join yarn A.

ROW 1 (RS): K4, K2tog, K2 (5: 8), yfwd, K1, *yfwd, K5, K2tog tbl, K2tog, K5, yfwd, K1, rep from * to last 8 sts, yfwd, K5, K2tog tbl, K1.

ROW 2: K8, *P1, K14, rep from * to last 9 (12: 15) sts, P1, K8 (11: 14).

ROW 3: As row 1.

ROW 4: Purl.

ROW 5: K3, K3tog, K2 (5: 8), yfwd, K1, *yfwd, K5, K2tog tbl, K2tog, K5, yfwd, K1*, yfwd, K4, K3tog tbl, K3tog, K4, yfwd, K1, rep from * to * once more, yfwd, K5, K2tog tbl, K1. *59 (62: 65) sts*

ROW 6: K8, P1, K14, P1, K12, P1, K14, P1, K7 (10: 13).

ROW 7: K3, K2tog, K2 (5: 8), yfwd, K1, *yfwd, K5, K2tog tbl, K2tog, K5, yfwd, K1*, yfwd, K4, K2tog tbl, K2tog, K4, yfwd, K1, rep from * to * once more, yfwd, K5, K2tog tbl, K1.

ROW 8: Purl.

ROW 9: K3, K2tog, K2 (5: 8), yfwd, K1, *yfwd, K5, K2tog tbl, K2tog, K5, yfwd, K1*, yfwd, K3, K3tog tbl, K3tog, K3, yfwd, K1, rep from * to * once more, yfwd, K5, K2tog tbl, K1. *57 (60: 63) sts*

ROW 10: K8, P1, K14, P1, K10, P1, K14, P1, K7 (10: 13).

ROW 11: K2, K3tog, K2 (5: 8), yfwd, K1, *yfwd, K5, K2tog tbl, K2tog, K5, yfwd, K1*, yfwd, K3, K2tog tbl, K2tog, K3, yfwd, K1, rep from * to * once more, yfwd, K5, K2tog tbl, K1. *56 (59: 62) sts*

ROW 12: Purl.

ROW 13: K2, K2tog, K2 (5: 8), yfwd, K1, *yfwd, K5, K2tog tbl, K2tog, K5, yfwd, K1*, yfwd, K2, K3tog tbl, K3tog, K2, yfwd, K1, rep from * to * once more, yfwd, K5, K2tog tbl, K1. *54 (57: 60) sts*

ROW 14: (K8, P1, K14, P1) twice, K6 (9: 12).

ROW 15: K2, K2tog, K2 (5: 8), yfwd, K1, *yfwd, K5, K2tog tbl, K2tog, K5, yfwd, K1*, yfwd, K2, K2tog tbl, K2tog, K2, yfwd, K1, rep from * to * once more, yfwd, K5, K2tog tbl, K1.

Place marker at end of last row.

Beg with a P row, work 5 rows in st st, thus ending with a WS row.

Change to 3mm (US 2/3) needles.

Beg with a K row, work 8 rows in st st, inc 1 st at beg of 7th row. *55 (58: 61) sts*

Beg and ending rows as indicated, work in patt from chart, rep the 38-row patt, beg with a K row and shaping sides by inc 1 st at beg of every foll 8th row from previous inc until there are 62 (65: 68) sts.

Cont in patt until all 38 chart rows have been worked twice in all, thus ending with a WS row.

SHAPE ARMHOLE

Keeping chart correct, cast (bind) off 5 (6: 7) sts at beg of next row. *57 (59: 61) sts*

Work 1 row, thus ending with a WS row.

SHAPE FRONT SLOPE

Dec 1 st at armhole edge on next 4 rows and AT THE SAME TIME dec 1 st at front slope edge on next and foll alt row, thus ending with a WS row. *51 (53: 55) sts*

Dec 1 st at each end of next and foll 5 alt rows. *39 (41: 43) sts*

Dec 1 st at front slope edge only on every foll 4th row from previous dec until 26 (28: 30) sts rem.

Cont without further shaping until 38 chart rows have been worked 4 times in all, thus ending with a WS row.

SHAPE SHOULDER

Working in st st and using yarn A only, proceed as folls:

Cast (bind) off 9 (9: 10) sts at beg of next and foll alt row.

Work 1 row. Cast (bind) off rem 8 (10: 10) sts.

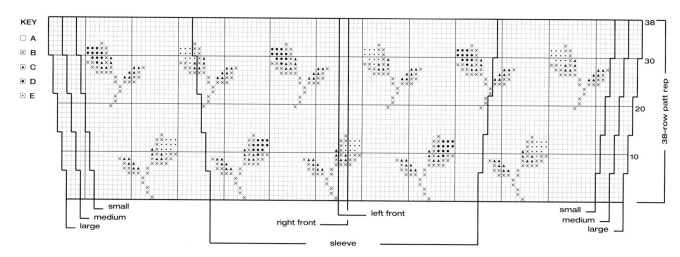

KEY

□ A
⊠ B
▲ C
● D
⊡ E

small
medium
large

right front
left front

small
medium
large

38-row patt rep

sleeve

RIGHT AND LEFT FRONTS, BACK AND SLEEVE

ROW 13: K1, K2tog, K5, yfwd, K1, *yfwd, K5, K2tog tbl, K2tog, K5, yfwd, K1*, yfwd, K2, K3tog tbl, K3tog, K2, yfwd, K1, rep from * to * once more, yfwd, K2 (5: 8), K2tog tbl, K2. *54 (57: 60) sts*

ROW 14: K6 (9: 12), (P1, K14, P1, K8) twice.

ROW 15: K1, K2tog, K5, yfwd, K1, *yfwd, K5, K2tog tbl, K2tog, K5, yfwd, K1*, yfwd, K2, K2tog tbl, K2tog, K2, yfwd, K1, rep from * to * once more, yfwd, K2 (5: 8), K2tog tbl, K2.

Place marker at beg of last row.

Complete to match left front, rev all shaping.

sleeves (both alike)

Cast on 56 sts using 2¼mm (US 1) needles and yarn A.

Work 4 rows in garter st.

Change to 3mm (US 2/3) needles.

Beg with a K row, work 4 rows in st st, inc 1 st at both ends of 3rd of these rows. *58 sts*

Now work in patt from chart, rep the 38-row patt, beg with a K row and shaping sides by inc 1 st at each end of every foll 8th row (from previous inc) to 84 sts, then on every foll 10th row until there are 92 sts, taking inc sts into patt.

Work another 13 rows without further shaping, thus ending with chart row 4 and a WS row.

SHAPE TOP

Keeping chart correct, cast (bind) off 6 sts at beg of next 2 rows. *80 sts*

Dec 1 st at each end of next 5 rows, then on every foll alt row until 58 sts rem.

Work 3 rows, thus ending with a WS row.

Dec 1 st at each end of next and every foll 4th row until 50 sts rem.

Work 1 row, thus ending with a WS row.

Dec 1 st at each end of next and foll 3 alt rows. *42 sts*

Dec 1 st at each end of next 7 rows, thus ending with a WS row. *28 sts*

Cast (bind) off 4 sts at beg of next 4 rows.

Cast (bind) off rem 12 sts.

finishing

Press all pieces as described on the information page.

Join both shoulder seams using back stitch.

FRONT BORDER

With RS facing and using 2¼mm (US 1) circular needle and yarn A, pick up and K 14 sts beg at right front cast-on edge to marker, 66 sts up right front opening edge to start of front slope shaping, 67 sts up front slope to shoulder, 40 sts across back neck, 67 sts down left front slope to start of front slope shaping, 66 sts down left front opening edge to marker and 14 sts to left front cast-on edge. *334 sts*

Working backward and forward in rows, not rounds, proceed as folls:

K 1 row.

BUTTONHOLE ROW (RS): K16, cast (bind) off 2 sts, K until there are 10 sts on right needle after cast (bind) off) 5 times, cast (bind) off 2 sts, K to end.

NEXT ROW: K to end, casting on 2 sts over those cast (bound) off on previous row.

K 1 row.

Cast (bind) off knitwise.

See information page for finishing instructions.

right front

Cast on 62 (65: 68) sts using 2¼mm (US 1) needles and yarn D.

Work 4 rows in garter st.

Break yarn D and join yarn A.

ROW 1 (RS): K1, K2tog, K5, yfwd, K1, *yfwd, K5, K2tog tbl, K2tog, K5, yfwd, K1, rep from * to last 8 (11: 14) sts, yfwd, K2 (5: 8), K2tog tbl, K4.

ROW 2: K8 (11: 14), *P1, K14, rep from * to last 9 sts, P1, K8.

ROW 3: As row 1.

ROW 4: Purl.

ROW 5: K1, K2tog, K5, yfwd, K1, *yfwd, K5, K2tog tbl, K2tog, K5, yfwd, K1*, yfwd, K4, K3tog tbl, K3tog, K4, yfwd, K1, rep from * to * once more, yfwd, K2 (5: 8), K3tog tbl, K3. *59 (62: 65) sts*

ROW 6: K7 (10: 13), P1, K14, P1, K12, P1, K14, P1, K8.

ROW 7: K1, K2tog, K5, yfwd, K1, *yfwd, K5, K2tog tbl, K2tog, K5, yfwd, K1*, yfwd, K4, K2tog tbl, K2tog, K4, yfwd, K1, rep from * to * once more, yfwd, K2 (5: 8), K2tog tbl, K3.

ROW 8: Purl.

ROW 9: K1, K2tog, K5, yfwd, K1, *yfwd, K5, K2tog tbl, K2tog, K5, yfwd, K1*, yfwd, K3, K3tog tbl, K3tog, K3, yfwd, K1, rep from * to * once more, yfwd, K2 (5: 8), K2tog tbl, K3. *57 (60: 63) sts*

ROW 10: K7 (10: 13), P1, K14, P1, K10, P1, K14, P1, K8.

ROW 11: K1, K2tog, K5, yfwd, K1, *yfwd, K5, K2tog tbl, K2tog, K5, yfwd, K1*, yfwd, K3, K2tog tbl, K2tog, K3, yfwd, K1, rep from * to * once more, yfwd, K2 (5: 8), K3tog tbl, K2. *56 (59: 62) sts*

ROW 12: Purl.

peaches by Kim Hargreaves

SIZE	S	M	
To fit bust	81–86	91–97	cm
	32–34	36–38	in
Actual width	45.5	48	cm
	18	19	in
Length	43	45.5	cm
	17	18	in
Sleeve length	34	36	cm
	13½	14	in

YARN
Rowan Glacé Cotton 50gm (1¾oz) balls:
Cardigan

Oyster 730	9	9

Vest

Butter 795	5	5

(Shade no longer available)

NEEDLES
1 pair 2¾mm (US 2) needles
1 pair 3¼mm (US 3) needles

BUTTONS
Cardigan: 9
Vest: 6

TENSION (GAUGE)
23 sts and 34 rows to 10cm (4in) measured over lace pattern using 3¼mm (US 3) needles

cardigan
back
Cast on 89 (95) sts using 2¾mm (US 2) needles and work 4 rows in garter st (knit every row).
Change to 3¼mm (US 3) needles and cont in leaf pattern as follows:

LEAF PATTERN
ROW 1 (RS): K1 (4), *yon, K2, sl1, K2tog, psso, K2, yon, K1, rep from * to last 0 (3) sts, K0 (3).
ROW 2 & ALL WS ROWS: Purl.
ROW 3: K1 (4), *K1, yon, K1, sl1, K2tog, psso, K1 yon, K2, rep from * to last 0 (3) sts, K0 (3).
ROW 5: K1 (4), *K2, yon, sl1, K2tog, psso, yon, K3, rep from * to last 0 (3) sts, K0 (3).
ROW 7: K0 (3), K2tog, *K2, yon, K1, yon, K2, sl1, K2tog, psso, rep from * to last 7 (10) sts, K2, yon, K1, yon, K2 sl1, K1, psso, K0 (3).
ROW 9: K0 (3), K2tog, *K1, yon, K3, yon, K1, sl1, K2tog, psso, rep from * to last 7 (10) sts, K1, yon, K3, yon, K1, sl1, K1, psso, K0 (3).
ROW 11: K0 (3), K2tog, *yon, K5, yon, sl1, K2tog, psso, rep from * to last 7 (10) sts, yon, K5, yon, sl1, K1, psso, K0 (3).
ROW 12: Purl.
These 12 rows form the patt and are rep throughout.
Keeping patt correct throughout, inc 1 st at each end of next row and every foll 8th row to 105 (111) sts, working extra sts either into st st or patt.
Cont without further shaping until work measures 23 (25.5)cm (9 [10]in) from cast-on edge, ending with a WS row.

SHAPE ARMHOLES
Cast (bind) off 6 (7) sts at beg of next 2 rows.
Dec 1 st at each end of next 5 rows and 5 (6) foll alt rows. *73 (75) sts*
Cont without further shaping until work measures 20cm (7¾in) from beg of armhole shaping, ending with a WS row.

SHAPE SHOULDERS AND BACK NECK
Cast (bind) off 6 (7) sts at beg of next 2 rows.
Cast (bind) off 7 sts, patt 11, turn and leave rem sts on a holder.
Work each side of neck separately.
Cast (bind) off 4 sts, patt to end.
Cast (bind) off rem 7 sts.
With RS facing, rejoin yarn to rem sts, cast (bind) off center 25 sts, patt to end.
Complete to match first side, rev shaping.

left front
Cast on 45 (48) sts using 2¾mm (US 2) needles and work 4 rows in garter st.
Change to 3¼mm (US 3) needles and cont in leaf pattern as folls:

LEAF PATTERN
ROW 1 (RS): K1 (4), *yon, K2, sl1, K2tog, psso, K2, yon, K1, rep from * to last 4 sts, yon, K2, sl1, K1, psso.
ROW 2 & ALL WS ROWS: Purl.
ROW 3: K1 (4), *K1, yon, K1, sl1, K2tog, psso, K1 yon, K2, rep from * to last 4 sts, K1, yon, K1, sl1, K1, psso.
ROW 5: K1 (4), *K2, yon, sl1, K2tog, psso, yon, K3, rep from * to last 4 sts, K2, yon, sl1, K1, psso.
ROW 7: K0 (3), K2tog, *K2, yon, K1, yon, K2, sl1, K2tog, psso, rep from * to last 3 sts, K2, yon, K1.
ROW 9: K0 (3), K2tog, *K1, yon, K3, yon, K1, sl1, K2tog, psso, rep from * to last 3 sts, K1, yon, K2.
ROW 11: K0 (3), K2tog, *yon, K5, yon, sl1, K2tog, psso, rep from * to last 3 sts, yon, K3.

ROW 12: Purl.

These 12 rows form the patt and are repeated throughout. Keeping patt correct throughout, inc 1 st at beg of next row and every foll 8th row to 53 (56) sts, working extra sts in st st until it is possible to take them into patt.
Cont without further shaping until work matches back to armhole shaping, ending with a WS row. **

SHAPE ARMHOLE

Cast (bind) off 6 (7) sts at beg of next row. Work 1 row.
Dec 1 st at armhole edge on next 5 rows and 5 (6) foll alt rows. *37 (38) sts*
Keeping patt correct, cont until front measures 14.5cm (5¾in) from beg of armhole shaping, ending with a RS row.

SHAPE FRONT NECK

Cast (bind) off 5 sts at beg of next row and 4 sts at beg of foll alt row.
Dec 1 st at neck edge on next 5 rows, 2 foll alt rows and 1 foll 4th row. *20 (21) sts*
Cont without further shaping until front matches back to shoulder shaping, ending with a WS row.

SHAPE SHOULDER

Cast (bind) off 6 (7) sts at beg of next row and 7 sts at beg of foll alt row.
Work 1 row. Cast (bind) off rem 7 sts.

right front

Cast on 45 (48) sts using 2¾mm (US 2) needles and work 4 rows in garter st.
Change to 3¼mm (US 3) needles and cont in leaf pattern as folls:

LEAF PATTERN

ROW 1 (RS): K2tog, K2, yon, K1, *yon, K2, sl1, K2tog, psso, K2, yon, K1, rep from * to last 0 (3) sts, K0 (3).
ROW 2 AND ALL WS ROWS: Purl.
ROW 3: K2tog, K1, yon, K2, *K1, yon, K1, sl1, K2tog,

psso, K1, yon, K2, rep from * to last 0 (3) sts, K0 (3).
ROW 5: K2tog yon, K3, *K2, yon, sl1, K2tog, psso, yon, K3, rep from * to last 0 (3) sts, K0 (3).
ROW 7: K1, yon, K2, sl1, K2tog, psso, *K2, yon, K1, yon, K2, sl1, K2tog, psso, rep from * to last 7 (10) sts, K2, yon, K1, yon, K2, sl1, K1, psso, K0 (3).
ROW 9: K2, yon, K1, sl1, K2tog, psso, *K1, yon, K3, yon, K1, sl1, K2tog, psso, rep from * to last 7 (10) sts, K1, yon, K3, yon, K1, sl1, K1, psso, K0 (3).
ROW 11: K3, yon, sl1, K2tog, psso, *yon, K5, yon, sl1, K2tog, psso, rep from * to last 7 (10) sts, yon, K5, yon, sl1, K1, psso, K0 (3).
ROW 12: Purl. *
Keeping patt correct throughout, complete as given for left front, rev shaping.

sleeves (both alike)

Cast on 49 sts using 2¾mm (US 2) needles and work 4 rows in garter st.
Change to 3¼mm (US 3) needles and work 12 rows in leaf pattern as given for first size of back.
Keeping patt correct throughout, inc 1 st at each end of next row and every foll 8th row to 67 (75) sts and then, for 1st size only, every foll 10th row to 73 sts, taking extra sts into st st until it is possible to take them into patt.
Cont without further shaping until sleeve measures 34 (36)cm (13½ [14½]in) or length required from cast-on edge, ending with a WS row.

SHAPE SLEEVEHEAD

Cast (bind) off 6 (7) sts at beg of next 2 rows.
Dec 1 st at each end of next 3 rows and 2 foll alt rows. *51 sts*
Work 3 rows.
Dec 1 st at each end of next row and 6 foll 4th rows. *37 sts*
Dec 1 st at each end of next 7 rows and 2 foll alt rows. *19 sts*
Cast (bind) off 4 sts at beg of next 2 rows.
Cast (bind) off rem 11 sts.

vest
back

Work as given for cardigan back.

left front

Work as given for left front of cardigan to **.

SHAPE ARMHOLE AND FRONT NECK

Cast (bind) off 6 (7) sts at beg of next row.
Work 1 row.
Dec 1 st at armhole edge on next 5 rows and 1 foll alt row. *41 (43) sts*
Work 1 row.
Cont dec 1 st at armhole edge on next row and 3 (4) foll alt rows and AT THE SAME TIME dec 1 st at neck edge on next row and every foll 3rd row to 24 (25) sts and then every foll 4th row to 20 (21) sts.
Cont without further shaping, until front matches back to shoulder shaping, ending with a WS row.

SHAPE SHOULDER

Cast (bind) off 6 (7) sts at beg of next row and 7 sts at beg of foll alt row. Work 1 row.
Cast (bind) off rem 7 sts.

right front

Work as given for right front of cardigan to *.
Complete as given for left front of vest, rev all shaping.

finishing

Press all pieces as described on the information page. Join both shoulder seams using back stitch.

Cardigan only

BUTTON BAND

With RS of left front facing and using 2¾mm (US 2) needles, pick up and K 95 (103) sts from neck edge down to cast-on edge.

Knit 2 rows.

Cast (bind) off knitwise.

BUTTONHOLE BAND

With RS of right front facing and using 2¾mm (US 2) needles, pick up and K 95 (103) sts from cast-on edge to neck shaping.

1ST ROW (WS) (BUTTONHOLES): K2, [cast (bind) off 3, K8 (9)] 8 times, cast (bind) off 3, K2.

2ND ROW: Knit across row, casting on 3 sts over those cast (bound) off on previous row.

Cast (bind) off knitwise.

COLLAR

Cast on 105 sts using 2¾mm (US 2) needles.

Knit 2 rows.

NEXT ROW (INC): K2, M1, K to last 2 sts, M1, K2.

Knit 3 rows.

Rep these last 4 rows 6 times.

Cont inc on next and every foll 4th row AT THE SAME TIME shape collar as folls:

*NEXT ROW: K25, including inc st, wrap next st (sl1 st, bring yarn to front of work, put sl st back onto LH needle), turn, K to end.

NEXT ROW: K18, wrap next st, turn, K to end.

NEXT ROW: K11, including inc st, wrap next st, turn, K to end.

NEXT ROW: K8, wrap next st, turn, K to end.

NEXT ROW: K6, including inc st, wrap next st, turn, K to end.

NEXT ROW: K5, wrap next st, turn, K to end.

NEXT ROW: K3, including inc st, wrap next st, turn, K to end.

NEXT ROW: K2, wrap next st, turn, K to end.

Knit 1 row across all stitches, knitting loop and wrapped st tog as you go. *

Rep from * to *.

Cast (bind) off evenly.

Vest only

BUTTON BAND

With RS of center back neck facing and using 2¾mm (US 2) needles, pick up and K 16 sts from center back neck to left shoulder seam, 49 sts down to beg of front neck shaping, 55 sts down to cast-on edge. *120 sts*

Knit 2 rows.

Cast (bind) off knitwise.

BUTTONHOLE BAND

With RS of right front facing and using 2¾mm (US 2) needles, pick up and K 55 sts from cast-on edge to beg of front neck shaping, 49 sts to shoulder seam and 16 sts to center back neck. *120 sts*

1ST ROW (WS) (BUTTONHOLE): K to last 55 sts, [cast (bind) off 3, K7] 5 times, cast (bind) off 3, K2.

2ND ROW: Knit across row, casting on 3 sts over those cast (bound) off on previous row.

Cast (bind) off knitwise.

ARMHOLE EDGING

With RS facing and using 2¾mm (US 2) needles, pick up and knit 100 sts around armhole edge.

Knit 2 rows.

Cast (bind) off knitwise.

See information page for finishing instructions.

patchwork heart by Zoë Mellor

SIZE	XS	S	M	L	XL	
To fit bust	81	86	91	97	102	cm
	32	34	36	38	40	in
Actual width	48	50.5	52.5	56	58	cm
	19	20	20½	22	23	in
Length	48	49	50	51	52	cm
	19	19½	19½	20	20½	in
Sleeve length	43	43	44	44	44	cm
	17	17	17½	17½	17½	in

YARN

Rowan Handknit DK Cotton 50gm (1¾oz) balls:

A	Raindrop	206	4	4	4	4	4
B	Icewater	239	8	8	8	9	9
C	Softgreen	228	6	6	6	6	7

NEEDLES

1 pair 3¼mm (US 3) needles
1 pair 4mm (US 6) needles

BUTTONS

5

TENSION (GAUGE)

20 sts and 28 rows to 10cm (4in) measured over patterned stocking (stockinette) stitch using 4mm (US 6) needles

back

Cast on 96 (100: 106: 110: 116) sts using 3¼mm (US 3) needles and yarn C.
ROW 1: K1 (1: 0: 0: 1), *P1, K1, rep from * to last 1 (1: 0: 0: 1) st, P1 (1: 0: 0: 1).
ROW 2: P1 (1: 0: 0: 1), *K1, P1, rep from * to last 1 (1: 0: 0: 1) st, K1 (1: 0: 0: 1).
Rows 1 and 2 form moss (seed) st.
Work another 8 rows in moss (seed) st.
Change to 4mm (US 6) needles.
Using the intarsia technique described on the information page and joining and breaking colors as required, work in patt from body chart, which is worked in blocks of st st and moss (seed) st, as folls:
Patt 2 rows.
Inc 1 st at each end of next and every foll 12th row to 106 (110: 116: 120: 126) sts, taking inc sts into patt.
Cont straight until chart row 82 (84: 84: 86: 86) has been completed, ending with a WS row.

SHAPE ARMHOLES

Keeping chart correct, cast (bind) off 4 sts at beg of next 2 rows. *98 (102: 108: 112: 118) sts*

Dec 1 st at each end of next 4 rows.
90 (94: 100: 104: 110) sts
Cont straight until chart row 146 (148: 152: 154: 156) has been completed, ending with a WS row.

SHAPE SHOULDERS AND BACK NECK

Keeping chart correct, cast (bind) off 10 (10: 11: 12: 13) sts at beg of next 2 rows. *70 (74: 78: 80: 84) sts*
NEXT ROW (RS): Cast (bind) off 10 (10: 11: 12: 13) sts, patt until there are 13 (15: 15: 15: 16) sts on right needle and turn, leaving rem sts on a holder.
Work each side of neck separately.
Cast (bind) off 4 sts at beg of next row.
Cast (bind) off rem 9 (11: 11: 11: 12) sts.
With RS facing, rejoin yarn to rem sts, cast (bind) off center 24 (24: 26: 26: 26) sts, patt to end.
Work to match first side, rev shaping.

left front

Cast on 55 (57: 60: 62: 65) sts using 3¼mm (US 3) needles and yarn C.
ROW 1: K1 (1: 0: 0: 1), *P1, K1, rep from * to end.
ROW 2: *K1, P1, rep from * to last 1 (1: 0: 0: 1) st, K1 (1: 0: 0: 1).
Rows 1 and 2 form moss (seed) st.
Work another 7 rows in moss (seed) st.
ROW 10 (WS): Patt 8 sts and slip these sts onto a holder, M1, patt to end. *48 (50: 53: 55: 58) sts*
Change to 4mm (US 6) needles and work in patt from body chart as folls:
Patt 2 rows.
Inc 1 st at beg of next and every foll 12th row to 53 (55: 58: 60: 63) sts, taking inc sts into patt.
Cont straight until chart row 82 (84: 84: 86: 86) has been completed, ending with a WS row.

SHAPE ARMHOLE

Keeping chart correct, cast (bind) off 4 sts at beg of next row. *49 (51: 54: 56: 59) sts*
Work 1 row.
Dec 1 st at armhole edge of next 4 rows.
45 (47: 50: 52: 55) sts
Cont straight until chart row 129 (131: 133: 135: 137) has been completed, ending with a RS row.

SHAPE NECK

Keeping chart correct, cast (bind) off 7 sts at beg of next row, then 4 sts at beg of foll alt row.
34 (36: 39: 41: 44) sts
Dec 1 st at neck edge on next 3 rows, then on every foll alt row until 29 (31: 33: 35: 38) sts rem.
Work 7 rows, ending with chart row 146 (148: 152: 154: 156).

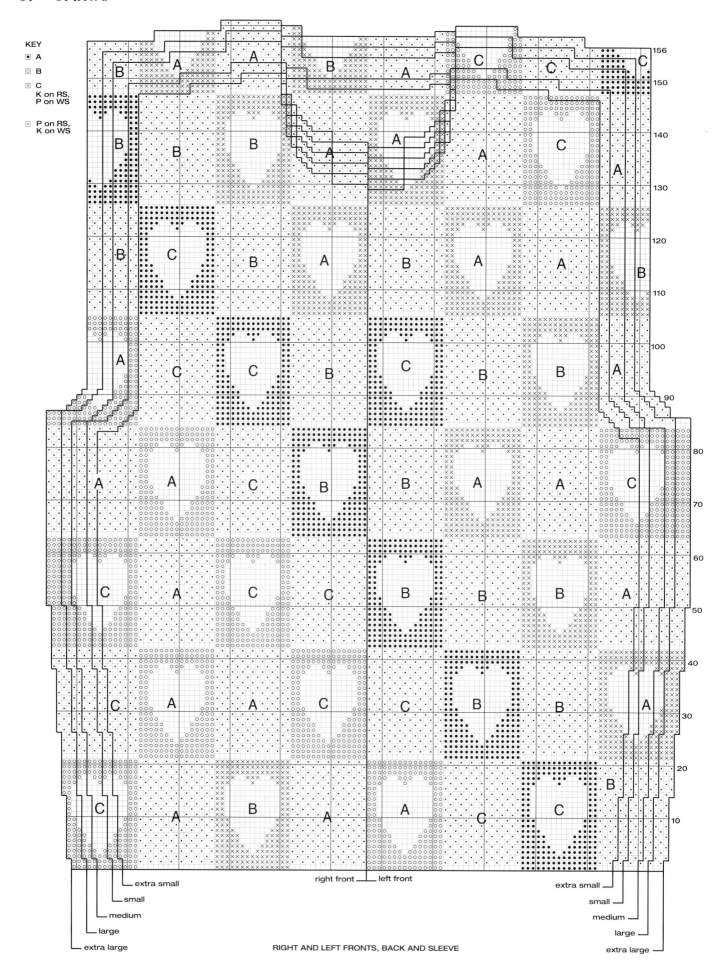

KEY
▪ A
▨ B
⊠ C
K on RS,
P on WS

▫ P on RS,
K on WS

RIGHT AND LEFT FRONTS, BACK AND SLEEVE

SHAPE SHOULDER

Keeping chart correct, cast (bind) off 10 (10: 11: 12: 13) sts at beg of next and foll alt row.
Work 1 row. Cast (bind) off rem 9 (11: 11: 11: 12) sts.

right front

Cast on 55 (57: 60: 62: 65) sts using 3¼mm (US 3) needles and yarn C.
ROW 1: *P1, K1, rep from * to last 1 (1: 0: 0: 1) st, P1 (1: 0: 0: 1).
ROW 2: P1 (1: 0: 0: 1), *K1, P1, rep from * to end.
Rows 1 and 2 form moss (seed) st.
Work another 4 rows in moss (seed) st.
ROW 7 (RS) (BUTTONHOLE ROW): P1, K1, P2tog, yrn, patt to end.
Work another 2 rows in moss (seed) st.
ROW 10 (WS): Patt to last 8 sts, M1 and turn, leaving last 8 sts on a holder. *48 (50: 53: 55: 58) sts*
Change to 4mm (US 6) needles and complete to match left front, rev shaping.

sleeves (both alike)

Cast on 45 (47: 49: 51: 53) sts using 3¼mm (US 3) needles and yarn C.
ROW 1: K1, *P1, K1, rep from * to end.
ROW 2: As row 1.
These 2 rows form moss (seed) st.
Work another 8 rows in moss (seed) st.
Change to 4mm (US 6) needles and yarn B.
Beg with a K row, cont in st st as folls:
Inc 1 st at each end of 5th and every foll 4th row until there are 65 (67: 69: 71: 73) sts.
Work 1 row, ending with a WS row.

PLACE HEART MOTIF

NEXT ROW (RS): K18 (19: 20: 21: 22), work next 29 sts as row 1 of heart motif chart, K18 (19: 20: 21: 22).
NEXT ROW: P18 (19: 20: 21: 22), work next 29 sts as row 2 of heart motif chart, P18 (19: 20: 21: 22).
These 2 rows set position of heart motif chart.
Keeping chart correct as set, cont until all 38 rows of chart have been completed, inc 1 st at each end of next and every foll 4th row. *83 (85: 87: 89: 91) sts*
Now working all sts in st st, inc 1 st at each end of next and every foll 4th row to 91 (87: 93: 89: 97) sts, then on every foll 6th row to 93 (93: 97: 97: 101) sts.
Cont straight until sleeve measures 43 (43: 44: 44: 44)cm, (17 [17: 17¼: 17¼: 17¼]in), ending with a WS row.

SHAPE TOP

Cast (bind) off 4 sts at beg of next 2 rows.
85 (85: 89: 89: 93) sts
Dec 1 st at each end of next and foll 5 alt rows.
Work 1 row, ending with a WS row.
Cast (bind) off rem 73 (73: 77: 77: 81) sts.

finishing

Press all pieces as described on the information page.
Join shoulder seams using back stitch.

BUTTON BORDER

Slip 8 sts from left front holder onto 3¼mm (US 3) needles and rejoin yarn C with RS facing.
Cont in moss (seed) st as set until border, when slightly stretched, fits up left front opening edge to neck shaping, ending with a WS row.
Cast (bind) off.
Slipstitch border in place.
Mark positions for 5 buttons on this border, the lowest button level with buttonhole already worked in right front, the top button 1cm (½in) below the start of neck shaping and rem 3 buttons evenly spaced between.

BUTTONHOLE BORDER

Work as for button border, rejoining yarn with WS facing and adding another 4 buttonholes to correspond with positions marked for buttons as folls:
BUTTONHOLE ROW (RS): P1, K1, P2tog, yrn, (P1, K1) twice.
Slipstitch border in place.

COLLAR

With RS facing, using 3¼mm (US 3) needles and yarn C, starting and ending midway across top of borders, pick up and knit 32 (32: 33: 33: 33) sts up right front neck, 33 (33: 35: 35: 35) sts across back neck, and 32 (32: 33: 33: 33) sts down left front neck.
97 (97: 101: 101: 101) sts
Work 8cm (3¾in) in moss (seed) st as for sleeves.
Cast (bind) off in patt.
See information page for finishing instructions.

KEY
- ▣ A
- ▢ B
- ⊠ C
- K on RS, P on WS
- ⊡ P on RS, K on WS

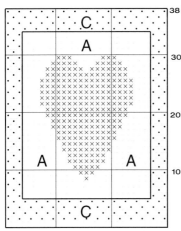

HEART MOTIF CHART FOR SLEEVE

shaker by Kim Hargreaves

SIZE	1ST	2ND	3RD	4TH	
To fit bust	81–86	86–91	91–97	97–102	cm
	32–34	34–36	36–38	38–40	in
Actual width	44.5	48	52	56	cm
	17½	19	20½	22	in
Length	43	45.5	48	50	cm
	17	18	19	20	in
Sleeve length	40.5	40.5	42	43	cm
	16	16	16½	17	in

YARN
Rowan 4-ply Cotton 50gm (1¾oz) balls:
Bleached 113   6   6   7   7

NEEDLES
1 pair 2¼ mm (US 1) needles
1 pair 3mm (US 2/3) needles

BUTTONS
5

TENSION (GAUGE)
25 sts and 38 rows to 10cm (4in) measured over lace pattern using 3mm (US 2/3) needles

LACE PATTERN
Pattern A (1 full patt rep, worked over 10 sts plus 1)
ROW 1 (RS): K1, *(yf, sl1, K1, psso) twice, K1, (K2tog, yf) twice, K1; rep from * to end.
ROW 2: Purl.
ROW 3: K2, *yf, sl1, K1, psso, yf, sl1, K2tog, psso, yf, K2tog, yf, K3; rep from * to last 9 sts, yf, sl1, K1, psso, yf, sl1, K2tog, psso, yf, K2tog, yf, K2.
ROW 4: Purl.
These 4 rows form the patt and are repeated throughout.

Pattern B (one full patt rep plus half a patt rep on left side, worked over 10 plus 6)
ROW 1 (RS): K1, *(yf, sl1, K1, psso) twice, K1, (K2tog, yf) twice, K1; rep from * to last 5 sts, (yf, sl1, K1, psso) twice, K1.
ROW 2: Purl.
ROW 3: K2, *yf, sl1, K1, psso, yf, sl1, K2tog, psso, yf, K2tog, yf, K3; rep from * to last 4 sts, yf, sl1, K1, psso, yf, K2tog tbl.
ROW 4: Purl.
These 4 rows form the patt and are repeated throughout.

Pattern C (1 full patt rep plus half a patt rep on right side, worked over 10 plus 6)
ROW 1 (RS): K1, (K2tog, yf) twice, K1,*(yf, sl1, K1, psso) twice, K1, (K2tog, yf) twice, K1; rep from * to end.
ROW 2: Purl.
ROW 3: (K2tog, yf) twice, K3, *yf, sl1, K1, psso, yf, sl1, K2tog, psso, yf, K2tog, yf, K3; rep from * to last 9 sts, yf, sl1, K1, psso, yf, sl1, K2tog, psso, yf, K2tog, yf, K2.
ROW 4: Purl.

back
Cast on 91 (101: 111: 121) sts using 2¼mm (US 1) needles.
Work 6 rows in garter st (knit every row).
Change to 3mm (US 2/3) needles and, working from pattern A for all sizes, cont as folls:
Work 2 (8: 8: 8: 8) rows in lace patt, ending with a WS row.
Keeping patt correct, shape sides by inc 1 st at each end of next row and every foll 8th row to 111 (121: 131: 141) sts, taking the extra sts into patt when possible.
Cont without shaping until work measures 23 (25.5: 26.5: 27)cm (9 [10: 10¼: 10¾:]in) from cast-on edge, ending with a WS row.
SHAPE ARMHOLE
Cast (bind) off 6 sts at beg of next 2 rows.
Dec 1 st at each end of next 7 rows and 7 foll alt rows. *71 (81: 91: 101) sts*
Cont without shaping until work measures 20 (20: 21.5: 23)cm (7¾ [7¾: 8½: 9]in) from beg of armhole shaping, ending with a WS row.
SHAPE SHOULDERS AND BACK NECK
Cast (bind) off 5 (7: 8: 10) sts at beg of next 2 rows.
Cast (bind) off 6 (7: 9: 10) sts, patt 10 (12: 13: 14) sts, turn and leave rem sts on a holder.
Work each side of neck separately.
Cast (bind) off 4 sts, patt to end. Cast (bind) off rem 6 (8: 9: 10) sts.
With RS facing, rejoin yarn to rem sts, cast (bind) off center 29 (29: 31: 33) sts, patt to end.
Complete to match first side, rev shaping.

left front
Cast on 52 (57: 62: 67) sts using 2¼ mm (US 1) needles.
Work 5 rows in garter st.
ROW 6 (WS): K6 and leave these sts on a holder for front band, K to end. *(46 (51: 56: 61) sts*
Change to 3mm (US 2/3) needles and, working from pattern B for first and 3rd sizes or pattern A for 2nd and 4th sizes, cont as folls:

Work 2 (8: 8: 8) rows in lace patt from appropriate patt, ending with a WS row.

Keeping patt correct, shape side by inc 1 st at beg of next row and every foll 8th row to 56 (61: 66: 71) sts, taking extra stitches into patt where possible.

Cont without shaping until front matches back to armhole shaping, ending with a WS row.

SHAPE ARMHOLE

Cast (bind) off 6 sts at beg of next row.

Work 1 row.

Dec 1 st at armhole edge on next 7 rows and 7 foll alt rows. *36 (41: 46: 51) sts*

Cont without further shaping until work measures 13 (13: 14.5: 16)cm (5 [5: 5¾: 6¼]in) from beg of armhole shaping, ending with a RS row.

SHAPE FRONT NECK

NEXT ROW (WS): Cast (bind) off 5 sts at beg of next row and foll alt row. *26 (31: 36: 41) sts*

Dec 1 st at neck edge on next 3 (3: 4: 5) rows, 4 foll alt rows and 2 foll 4th rows. *17 (22: 26: 30) sts*

Cont until front matches back to shoulder shaping, ending with a WS row.

SHAPE SHOULDER

Cast (bind) off 5 (7: 8: 10) sts at beg of next row and 6 (7: 9: 10) sts at beg of foll alt row.

Work 1 row.

Cast (bind) off rem 6 (8: 9: 10) sts.

right front

Cast on 52 (57: 62: 67) sts using 2¼mm (US 1) needles.

Work 5 rows in garter st.

NEXT ROW (WS): K to last 6 sts, turn and leave rem sts on a holder for front band. *46 (51: 56: 61) sts*

Change to 3mm (US 2/3) needles and, working from pattern C for 1st and 3rd sizes or pattern A for 2nd and 4th sizes, complete as for left front, rev shaping.

sleeves (both alike)

Cast on 61 sts using 2¼ mm (US 1) needles.

Work 6 rows in garter st.

Change to 3mm (US 2/3) needles and working from pattern A for all sizes, cont as folls:

Work 8 rows in lace pattern, ending with a WS row.

Keeping patt correct, shape sides by inc 1 st at each end of next row and every foll 12th row to 75 (75: 83: 85) sts and then, for 1st and 2nd sizes only, every foll 16th row to 81 st. *81 (81: 83: 85) sts*

Cont without shaping until work measures 40.5 (40.5: 42: 43)cm (16 [16: 16½: 17]in) from cast-on edge, ending with a WS row.

SHAPE SLEEVEHEAD

Cast (bind) off 6 sts at beg of next 2 rows.

Dec 1 st at each end of next 3 rows and 3 foll alt rows. *57 (57: 59: 61) sts*

Work 3 rows.

Dec 1 st at each end of next row and 6 (6: 7: 8) foll 4th rows. *43 sts*

Work 1 row.

Dec 1 st at each end of next row and 3 foll alt rows. *35 sts*

Dec 1 st at each end of next 3 rows.

Cast (bind) off 4 sts at beg of next 4 rows. Cast (bind) off rem 13 sts.

finishing

Press all pieces as described on the information page. Join both shoulder seams using back stitch.

BUTTON BAND

With RS facing, slip sts from holder on left front onto a 2¼ mm (US 1) needle and cont in garter st until band fits neatly, when slightly stretched, up to cast (bind) off for neck shaping, ending with a WS row. Slipstitch neatly into place, break yarn but leave sts on a holder for neckband.

Mark position of 5 buttons, the first to come at top of lower edging, the 5th to come 1cm (½in) above neck edge in neckband and the rem spaced evenly between.

BUTTONHOLE BAND

Work as for button band, adding 4 buttonholes to correspond with markers as folls:

BUTTONHOLE ROW (RS): K1, K2tog, yon twice, K2tog, K1.

Slipstitch into place, but do not break yarn.

NECKBAND

With RS facing and using 2¼ mm (US 1) needles, knit across 6 sts of buttonhole band, pick up and knit 39 sts up right front neck to shoulder, 37 (37: 39: 41) sts across back neck and 39 sts down left front neck, K across 6 sts of button band. *127 (127: 129: 131) sts*

Knit 3 rows.

NEXT ROW (RS) (BUTTONHOLE): K1, K2tog, yon twice, K2tog, K to end.

Knit 2 more rows. Cast (bind) off knitwise.

See information page for finishing instructions.

nancy by Debbie Bliss

SIZE	XS	S	M	L	XL	
To fit bust	81	86	91	97	102	cm
	32	34	36	38	40	in
Actual width	44.5	47	50	53	55.5	cm
	17½	18½	19½	21	22	in
Length	54	55	56	57	58	cm
	21½	21½	22	22½	23	in
Sleeve length	42	42	43	43	43	cm
	16½	16½	17	17	17	in

YARN

Rowan Wool Cotton 50gm (1¾oz) balls:

Multi-color version

A Riviera	930	12	12	13	14	14	
B Gypsy	910	1	1	1	1	1	
C Tulip	944	1	1	1	1	1	
D Deepest Olive	907	1	1	1	1	1	

One-color version

Clear	941	12	12	13	14	14	

NEEDLES

1 pair 3¼mm (US 3) needles
1 pair 4mm (US 6) needles

BUTTONS

7

TENSION (GAUGE)

21 sts and 33 rows to 10cm (4in) measured over pattern using 4mm (US 6) needles

Special note: For one-color version, work as given for floral version, using same color throughout.

back

Cast on 93 (99: 105: 111: 117) sts using 3¼mm (US 3) needles and yarn A.
ROW 1 (RS): P1 (0: 1: 0: 1), *K1, P1, rep from * to last 0 (1: 0: 1: 0) st, K0 (1: 0: 1: 0).
ROW 2: As row 1.
These 2 rows form moss (seed) st.
Work in moss (seed) st for another 4 rows, ending with a WS row.
Change to 4mm (US 6) needles.
Using the intarsia technique described on the information page, starting and ending rows as indicated and rep the 28-row repeat throughout, cont in patt, foll chart as folls:
Work 4 (6: 6: 8: 8) rows.

Dec 1 st at each end of next and every foll 6th row until 79 (85: 91: 97: 103) sts rem.
Work 11 rows.
Inc 1 st at each end of next and every foll 6th row until there are 93 (99: 105: 111: 117) sts.
Cont straight until back measures 32 (33: 33: 34: 34)cm (12½ [13: 13: 13½: 13½]in), ending with a WS row.
SHAPE ARMHOLES
Keeping chart correct, cast (bind) off 3 (4: 5: 6: 7) sts at beg of next 2 rows. *87 (91: 95: 99: 103) sts*
Dec 1 st at each end of next 7 rows, then on every foll alt row until 71 (73: 75: 77: 79) sts rem.
Cont straight until armhole measures 22 (22: 23: 23: 24)cm (8½ [8½: 9: 9: 9½]in), ending with a WS row.
SHAPE SHOULDERS AND BACK NECK
Cast (bind) off 6 (6: 7: 7: 7) sts at beg of next 2 rows. *59 (61: 61: 63: 65) sts*
NEXT ROW (RS): Cast (bind) off 6 (6: 7: 7: 7) sts, patt until there are 11 (11: 10: 10: 11) sts on right needle and turn, leaving rem sts on a holder.
Work each side of neck separately.
Cast (bind) off 4 sts at beg of next row.
Cast (bind) off rem 7 (7: 6: 6: 7) sts.
With RS facing, rejoin yarn to rem sts, cast (bind) off center 25 (27: 27: 29: 29) sts, patt to end.
Work to match first side, rev shaping.

left front

Cast on 52 (55: 58: 61: 64) sts using 3¼mm (US 3) needles and yarn A.
ROW 1 (RS): K0 (1: 0: 1: 0), *P1, K1, rep from * to end.
ROW 2: *K1, P1, rep from * to last 0 (1: 0: 1: 0) st, K0 (1: 0: 1: 0).
These 2 rows form moss (seed) st.
Work in moss (seed) st for another 3 rows, ending with a RS row.
ROW 6 (WS): Moss (seed) st 6 and slip these 6 sts onto a holder for button band, M1, moss (seed) st to end. *47 (50: 53: 56: 59) sts*
Change to 4mm (US 6) needles.
Cont in patt, foll chart as folls:
Work 4 (6: 6: 8: 8) rows.
Dec 1 st at beg of next and every foll 6th row until 40 (43: 46: 49: 52) sts rem.
Work 11 rows. Inc 1 st at beg of next and every foll 6th row until there are 47 (50: 53: 56: 59) sts.
Cont straight until left front matches back to beg of armhole shaping, ending with a WS row.
SHAPE ARMHOLE
Keeping chart correct, cast (bind) off 3 (4: 5: 6: 7) sts

at beg of next row. *44 (46: 48: 50: 52) sts*
Work 1 row.
Dec 1 st at armhole edge of next 7 rows, then on
every foll alt row until 36 (37: 38: 39: 40) sts rem.
Cont straight until there are 25 (25: 25: 27: 27) rows
less than on back to start of shoulder shaping, ending
with a RS row.

SHAPE NECK
Keeping chart correct, cast (bind) off 4 (5: 5: 5: 5) sts
at beg of next row, then 4 sts at beg of foll alt row.
28 (28: 29: 30: 31) sts
Dec 1 st at neck edge of next 3 rows, then on foll
4 (4: 4: 5: 5) alt rows, then on every foll 4th row until
19 (19: 20: 20: 21) sts rem.
Work 3 rows, ending with a WS row.

SHAPE SHOULDER
Cast (bind) off 6 (6: 7: 7: 7) sts at beg of next and foll
alt row.
Work 1 row.
Cast (bind) off rem 7 (7: 6: 6: 7) sts.

right front

Cast on 52 (55: 58: 61: 64) sts using 3¼mm (US 3)
needles and yarn A.
ROW 1 (RS): *K1, P1, rep from * to last 0 (1: 0: 1: 0) st,
K0 (1: 0: 1: 0).
ROW 2: K0 (1: 0: 1: 0), *P1, K1, rep from * to end.
These 2 rows form moss (seed) st.
Work in moss (seed) st for another 3 rows, ending
with a RS row.
ROW 6 (WS): Moss (seed) st to last 6 sts, M1 and turn,
leaving last 6 sts on a holder for buttonhole band.
47 (50: 53: 56: 59) sts
Change to 4mm (US 6) needles.
Cont in patt, foll chart as folls:
Work 4 (6: 6: 8: 8) rows.
Dec 1 st at end of next and every foll 6th row until
40 (43: 46: 49: 52) sts rem.
Complete to match left front, rev shaping.

KEY
☐ A - K on RS, P on WS
⊡ A - P on RS, K on WS
⊠ B
⊡ C
◎ D

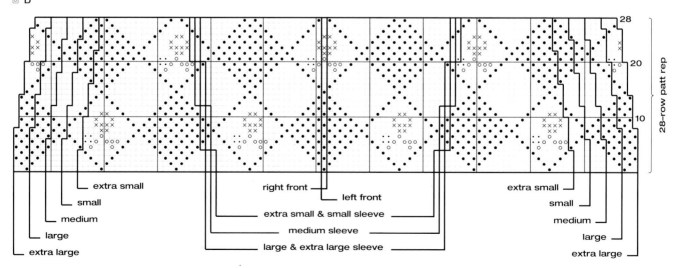

extra small
small
medium
large
extra large

right front
left front
extra small & small sleeve
medium sleeve
large & extra large sleeve

extra small
small
medium
large
extra large

28
20
10
28-row patt rep

RIGHT AND LEFT FRONTS, BACK AND SLEEVE

sleeves (both alike)

Cast on 41 (41: 43: 45: 45) sts using 3¼mm (US 3) needles and yarn A.

ROW 1 (RS): P1 (1: 0: 1: 1), *K1, P1, rep from * to last 0 (0: 1: 0: 0) st, K0 (0: 1: 0: 0).

ROW 2: As row 1.

These 2 rows form moss (seed) st. Work in moss (seed) st for another 4 rows, ending with a WS row.

Change to 4mm (US 6) needles.

Cont in patt, foll chart as folls:

Work 4 rows. Inc 1 st at each end of next and every foll 8th row until there are 49 (59: 57: 59: 69) sts, then on every foll 10th row until there are 67 (69: 71: 73: 75) sts, taking inc sts into patt.

Cont straight until sleeve measures 42 (42: 43: 43: 43)cm (16½ [16½: 17: 17: 17]in), ending with a WS row.

SHAPE TOP

Keeping chart correct, cast (bind) off 3 (4: 5: 6: 7) sts at beg of next 2 rows. *61 sts*

Dec 1 st at each end of next 3 rows, then on foll 3 (3: 3: 3: 2) alt rows, then on every foll 4th row until 35 (35: 33: 33: 33) sts rem.

Work 1 row, ending with a WS row.

Dec 1 st at each end of next and foll 1 (1: 0: 0: 0) alt rows, then on foll 3 rows, ending with a WS row. *25 sts*

Cast (bind) off 4 sts at beg of next 2 rows.

Cast (bind) off rem 17 sts.

finishing

Press all pieces as described on the information page.

Join both shoulder seams using back stitch, or mattress stitch if preferred.

Slip the 6 sts from holder for button band onto 3¼mm (US 3) needles and rejoin yarn A with RS facing.

Cont in moss (seed) st as set until band, when slightly stretched, fits up left front to neck shaping, ending with a WS row.

Cast (bind) off.

Slipstitch band in place.

Mark positions for 7 buttons on this band, the lowest button 10cm (4in) up from cast-on edge, the top button 1.2cm (½in) below neck shaping and the rem 5 buttons evenly spaced between.

BUTTONHOLE BAND

Work as given for button band, rejoining yarn A with WS facing and adding 7 buttonholes to correspond with positions marked for buttons as folls:

BUTTONHOLE ROW (RS): K1, P1, yrn, P2tog, K1, P1.

Slipstitch band in place.

COLLAR

Cast on 81 (85: 85: 93: 93) sts using 3¼mm (US 3) needles and yarn A.

ROW 1 (RS): K1, *P1, K1, rep from * to end.

ROW 2: As row 1.

These 2 rows form moss (seed) st.

Cont in moss (seed) st until collar measures 10cm (4in), ending with a WS row.

Cast (bind) off in moss (seed) st.

Sew cast-on edge of collar to neck edge, positioning the ends of collar halfway across top of bands.

See information page for finishing instructions, setting in sleeves using the set-in method.

daisy by Kim Hargreaves

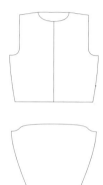

SIZE

	1ST	2ND	3RD	4TH	5TH	6TH	
To fit	2–3	3–4	4–5	6–7	8–9	9–10	yrs
Chest size	56	58	61	66	71	76	cm
	22	23	24	26	28	30	in
Actual width	31	32.5	35	38	43	45.5	cm
	12	13	14	15	17	18	in
Length	31.5	33	35	37.5	40	42.5	cm
	12½	13	14	15	15½	16½	in
Sleeve length	23	25.5	29	33	36.5	40	cm
	9	10	11½	13	14½	15½	in

YARN

Rowan Cotton Glacé 50gm (1¾oz) balls:

		1ST	2ND	3RD	4TH	5TH	6TH
A	Candy Floss 747	4	5	5	6	7	8
B	Bubbles 724	2	2	2	2	2	3
C	Butter 795	1	1	1	1	1	1

NEEDLES

1 pair 2¾mm (US 2) needles
1 pair 3¼mm (US 3) needles

BUTTONS

5

TENSION (GAUGE)

23 sts and 32 rows to 10cm (4in) measured over patterned stocking (stockinette) stitch using 3¼mm (US 3) needles.

back

Cast on 67 (71: 77: 83: 93: 97) sts using 2¾mm (US 2) needles and yarn A.
Knit 3 rows.
ROW 4 (WS): K0 (0: 1: 0: 1: 1), *P1, K1, rep from * to last 1 (1: 0: 1: 0: 0) st, P1 (1: 0: 1: 0: 0).
ROW 5: As row 4.
Last 2 rows form moss (seed) st.
Work another 3 rows in moss (seed) st.
Change to 3¼mm (US 3) needles.
Using the intarsia technique described on the information page, starting and ending rows as indicated and beg with a K row, work in patt from chart for back, which is worked mainly in st st, as folls:
Inc 1 st at each end of chart row 9 (9: 9: 7: 7: 5) and every foll 16th (16th: 16th: 14th: 14th: 12th) row until there are 71 (75: 81: 89: 99: 105) sts, taking inc sts into patt.
Cont straight until chart row 44 (48: 50: 56: 62: 66) has been completed, ending with a WS row.

SHAPE ARMHOLES

Keeping chart correct, cast (bind) off 3 (3: 3: 4: 4: 4) sts at beg of next 2 rows. *65 (69: 75: 81: 91: 97) sts*
Dec 1 st at each end of next 3 rows.
59 (63: 69: 75: 85: 91) sts
Cont straight until chart row 94 (100: 106: 114: 122: 130) has been completed, ending with a WS row.

SHAPE SHOULDERS AND BACK NECK

Cast (bind) off 6 (6: 7: 7: 9: 9) sts at beg of next 2 rows. *47 (51: 55: 61: 67: 73) sts.*
NEXT ROW (RS): Cast (bind) off 6 (6: 7: 7: 9: 9) sts, patt until there are 9 (10: 10: 12: 12: 14) sts on right needle and turn, leaving rem sts on a holder.
Work each side of neck separately.
Cast (bind) off 4 sts at beg of next row.
Cast (bind) off rem 5 (6: 6: 8: 8: 10) sts.
With RS facing, rejoin yarn to rem sts, cast (bind) off center 17 (19: 21: 23: 25: 27) sts, patt to end.
Work to match first side, rev all shaping.

left front

Cast on 39 (41: 44: 47: 52: 54) sts using 2¾mm (US 2) needles and yarn A.
Knit 3 rows.
ROW 4 (WS): *P1, K1, rep from * to last 1 (1: 0: 1: 0: 0) st, P1 (1: 0: 1: 0: 0).
ROW 5: P1 (1: 0: 1: 0: 0), *K1, P1, rep from * to end.
Last 2 rows form moss (seed) st.
Work a further 3 rows in moss (seed) st.
Change to 3¼mm (US 3) needles.
Work in patt from chart for front as folls:
Cont in patt foll chart, inc 1 st at beg of chart row 9 (9: 9: 7: 7: 5) and every foll 16th (16th: 16th: 14th: 14th: 12th) row until there are 41 (43: 46: 50: 55: 58) sts, taking inc sts into patt.
Cont straight until chart row 44 (48: 50: 56: 62: 66) has been completed, ending with a WS row.

SHAPE ARMHOLE

Keeping chart correct, cast (bind) off 3 (3: 3: 4: 4: 4) sts at beg of next row. *38 (40: 43: 46: 51: 54) sts*
Work 1 row.
Dec 1 st at armhole edge of next 3 rows.
35 (37: 40: 43: 48: 51) sts
Cont straight until chart row 82 (86: 90: 96: 102: 108) has been completed, ending with a WS row.

SHAPE NECK

NEXT ROW (RS): Patt to last 12 sts and turn, leaving last 12 sts on a holder. *23 (25: 28: 31: 36: 39) sts*
Dec 1 st at neck edge of next 3 rows, then on every foll alt row until 17 (18: 20: 22: 26: 28) sts rem.

KEY

☐ A
☒ B
⊡ C

134
130
120
110
100
90
80
70
66
60
50
40
30
20
10

1st size

2nd size

3rd size

4th size

5th size

6th size

1st & 2nd sleeve

3rd & 4th sleeve

5th & 6th sleeve

1st size

2nd size

3rd size

4th size

5th size

6th size

BACK AND SLEEVE

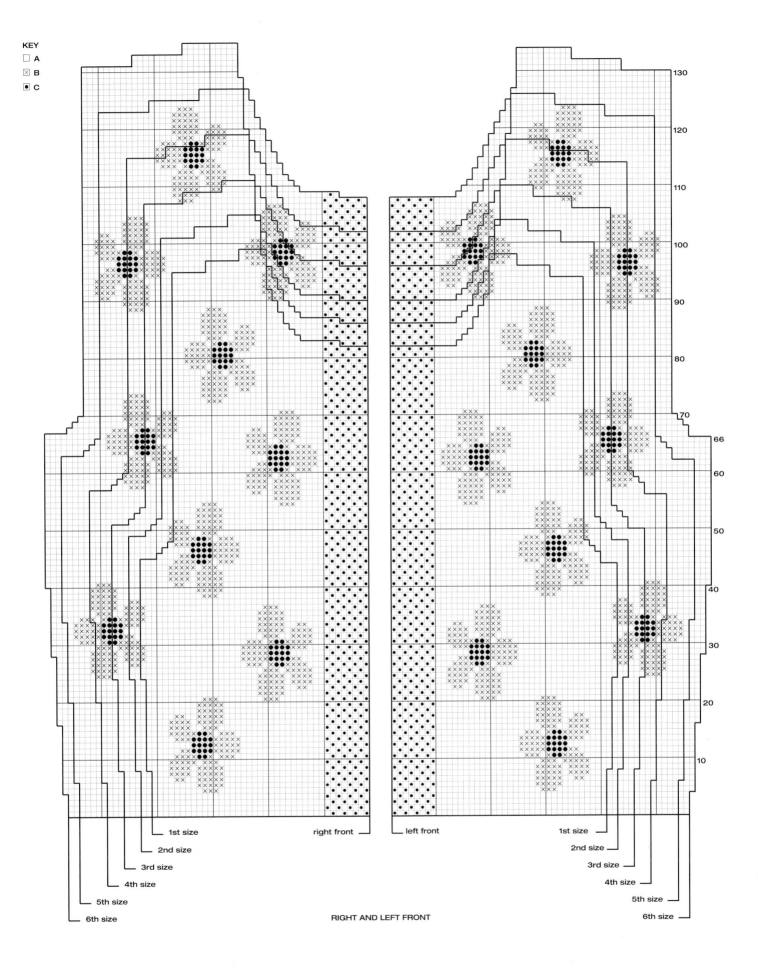

KEY
□ A
⊠ B
● C

130
120
110
100
90
80
70
66
60
50
40
30
20
10

1st size
2nd size
3rd size
4th size
5th size
6th size

right front

left front

1st size
2nd size
3rd size
4th size
5th size
6th size

RIGHT AND LEFT FRONT

Cont straight until chart row 94 (100: 106: 114: 122: 130) has been completed, ending with a WS row.

SHAPE SHOULDER

Cast (bind) off 6 (6: 7: 7: 9: 9) sts at beg of next and foll alt row.

Work 1 row.

Cast (bind) off rem 5 (6: 6: 8: 8: 10) sts.

right front

Cast on 39 (41: 44: 47: 52: 54) sts using 2¾mm (US 2) needles and yarn A.

Knit 3 rows.

ROW 4 (WS): P1 (1: 0: 1: 0: 0), *K1, P1, rep from * to end.

ROW 5: P1, K1, P1, cast (bind) off 2 sts [1 st on right needle after cast (bind) off], *P1, K1, rep from * to last 1 (1: 0: 1: 0: 0) st, P1 (1: 0: 1: 0: 0).

Last 2 rows form moss (seed) st.

ROWS 6: Moss (seed) st to end, casting on 2 sts over those cast (bound) off on previous row.

Work another 2 rows in moss (seed) st.

Change to 3¼mm (US 3) needles.

Work in patt from chart for front as folls:

Making another 4 buttonholes in every foll 20th (22nd: 22nd: 24th: 26th: 26th) row from previous buttonhole, cont as folls:

Inc 1 st at end of chart row 9 (9: 9: 7: 7: 5) and every foll 16th (16th: 16th: 14th: 14th: 12th) row until there are 41 (43: 46: 50: 55: 58) sts, taking inc sts into patt.

Cont straight until chart row 45 (49: 51: 57: 63: 67) has been completed, ending with a RS row.

SHAPE ARMHOLE

Keeping chart correct, cast (bind) off 3 (3: 3: 4: 4: 4) sts at beg of next row. *38 (40: 43: 46: 51: 54) sts*

Dec 1 st at armhole edge of next 3 rows. *35 (37: 40: 43: 48: 51) sts*

Cont straight until chart row 82 (86: 90: 96: 102: 108) has been completed, ending with a WS row.

SHAPE NECK

NEXT ROW (RS): Cast (bind) off 5 sts, patt until there are 7 sts on right needle and slip these sts onto a holder, patt to end. *23 (25: 28: 31: 36: 39) sts*

Dec 1 st at neck edge of next 3 rows, then on every foll alt row until 17 (18: 20: 22: 26: 28) sts rem.

Cont straight until chart row 95 (101: 107: 115: 123: 131) has been completed, ending with a RS row.

SHAPE SHOULDER

Cast (bind) off 6 (6: 7: 7: 9: 9) sts at beg of next and foll alt row.

Work 1 row.

Cast (bind) off rem 5 (6: 6: 8: 8: 10) sts.

sleeves (both alike)

Cast on 37 (37: 41: 41: 45: 45) sts using 2¾mm (US 2) needles and yarn A.

Knit 3 rows.

ROW 4 (WS): K0 (0: 1: 0: 1: 1), *P1, K1, rep from * to last 1 (1: 0: 1: 0: 0) st, P1 (1: 0: 1: 0: 0).

ROW 5: As row 4.

Last 2 rows form moss (seed) st.

Work another 3 rows in moss (seed) st, inc 1 st at each end of 2nd of these rows. *39 (39: 43: 43: 47: 47) sts*

Change to 3¼mm (US 3) needles.

Noting that sleeves are shown on chart only to row 40 and thereafter referring back to motifs below row 40 as markers and working incs and sleevehead from instructions, work in patt from chart for sleeve as folls:

Inc 1 st at each end of chart row 3 and every foll 4th

row until there are 69 (73: 75: 75: 77: 77) sts, taking inc sts into patt.

3rd, 4th, 5th and 6th sizes only

Inc 1 st at each end of every foll 6th row until there are (79: 83: 87: 93) sts.

All sizes

Cont straight until chart row 68 (76: 86: 100: 110: 122) has been completed, ending with a WS row.

SHAPE TOP

Keeping chart correct, cast (bind) off 3 (3: 3: 4: 4: 4) sts at beg of next 2 rows. *63 (67: 73: 75: 79: 85) sts*

Dec 1 st at each end of next and foll 2 alt rows.

Work 1 row.

Cast (bind) off rem 57 (61: 67: 69: 73: 79) sts.

finishing

Press all pieces as described on the information page.

Join shoulder seams using back stitch.

NECK BORDER

With RS facing, yarn A and 2¾mm (US 2) needles, slip 7 sts from right front holder onto RH needle, rejoin yarn and pick up and knit 15 (17: 19: 21: 23: 25) sts up right side of neck, 25 (27: 29: 31: 33: 35) sts from back neck, 15 (17: 19: 21: 23: 25) sts down left side of neck, then patt across 12 sts from left front holder. *74 (80: 86: 92: 98: 104) sts*

Keeping moss (seed) st correct as set by front opening borders, cont as folls:

Cast (bind) off 5 sts at beg of next row. *69 (75: 81: 87: 93: 99) sts*

Work 4 rows in moss (seed) st.

Knit 3 rows.

Cast (bind) off knitwise (on WS).

See information page for finishing instructions, setting in sleeves using the shallow set-in method.

folklore by Kim Hargreaves

SIZE	S	M	L	
To fit bust	81–86	91–97	102–107	cm
	32–34	36–38	40–42	in
Actual width	58.5	61	63.5	cm
	23	24	25	in
Length	69.5	72	74.5	cm
	27½	28½	29½	in
Sleeve length	46	46	46	cm
	18	18	18	in

(All measurements after washing)

YARNS

Rowan Denim 50gm (1¾oz) balls:
Shorter neckband with roll

	24	25	26

Polo

	25	26	27

(Both photographed in Ecru 324)

NEEDLES

1 pair 3¼mm (US 3) needles
1 pair 4mm (US 6) needles

TENSION (GAUGE) BEFORE WASHING

20 sts and 28 rows to 10cm (4in) measured over stocking (stockinette) stitch using 4mm (US 6) needles

PATTERN NOTE

Denim will shrink in length when washed for the first time. Allowances have been made in this pattern for shrinkage (see size diagram for after-washing measurements).

SPECIAL ABBREVIATIONS

K1B = Knit through back of stitch.
MB = *Make bobble:* (K1, P1, K1, P1, K1) into next st, turn, K5, turn, K5, then slip 2nd, 3rd, 4th and 5th st over first.
RT = *Right twist:* On right-side rows: K2tog leaving sts on left needle, then insert right needle from the front between the 2 sts just knitted tog and knit the first st again, then slip both sts from needle tog. On wrong-side rows: with right needle in front of left needle, skip one st and purl the second st in front of loop, then insert right needle into fronts of both sts (the skipped st and the second st) and P2tog.
LT = *Left twist:* On right-side rows: with right needle behind left needle, skip one st and knit the second st in back of loop, then insert right needle into backs of both sts (the skipped st and the second st) and K2tog

tbl. On wrong side rows: P2tog tbl leaving sts on left needle, then purl the first st again, then slip both sts from needle tog.
4-ST BOBBLE = On next 4 sts make bobble as folls: (K4, turn, P4, turn) 3 times, then pick up loop from the first row of bobble and knit it tog with first st on left needle, K2, then pick up a loop from first row of bobble and knit it tog with next st, completing bobble.

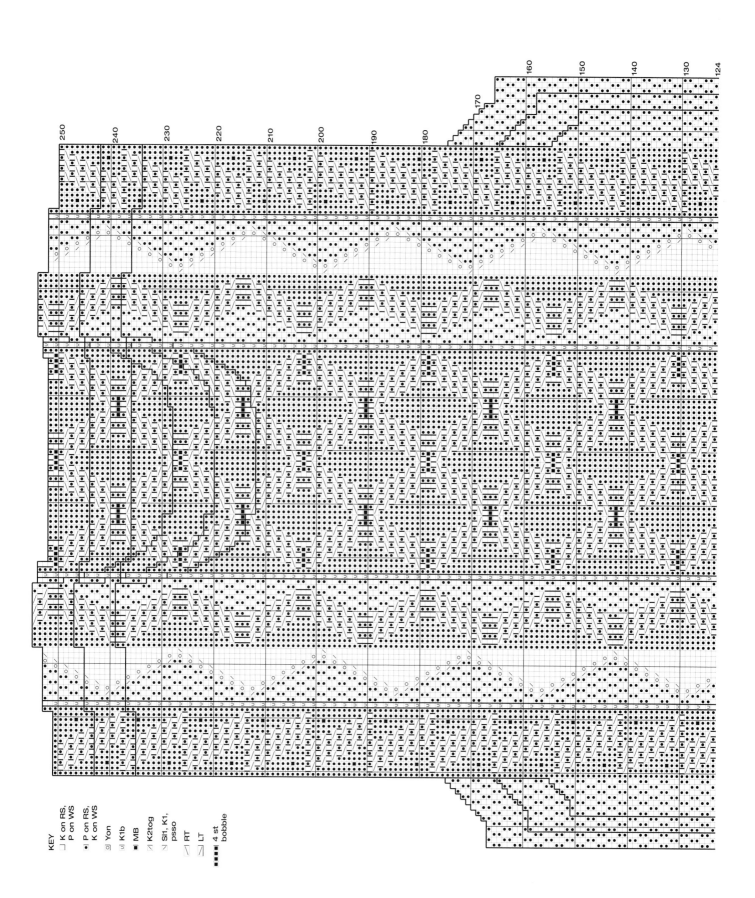

KEY

☐ K on RS,
   P on WS

• P on RS,
   K on WS

⊙ Yon

∪ K1b

■ MB

⁄ K2tog

⁄ Sl1, K1,
   psso

⁄ RT

⁄ LT

▪▪▪ 4 st
    bobble

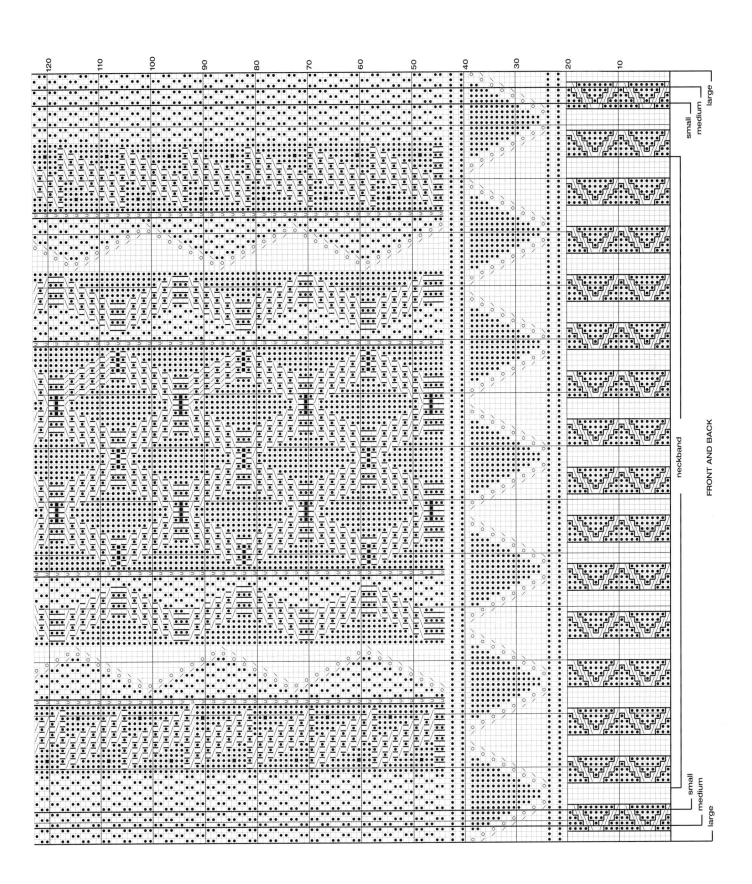

back

Cast on 132 (138: 144) sts using 3¼mm (US 3) needles.
Beg and ending rows as indicated, work rows 1 to 20, foll chart for back.
Change to 4mm (US 6) needles.
Cont foll chart until row 150 (158: 166) is complete.

SHAPE ARMHOLES
Cast (bind) off 3 (4: 5) sts at beg of next 2 rows.
Dec 1 st at each end on next 4 (6: 8) rows. *118 sts*
Cont without further shaping until chart row 234 (242: 250) is complete.

SHAPE SHOULDERS AND BACK NECK
Cast (bind) off 12 sts at beg of next 2 rows.
NEXT ROW (RS): Cast (bind) off 12 sts, patt 16 and turn, leaving rem sts on a holder.
Work each side of neck separately.
Cast (bind) off 4 sts at beg of next row.
Cast (bind) off rem 12 sts.
With RS facing, rejoin yarn to rem sts, cast (bind) off center 38 sts, patt to end.
Complete to match first side, rev all shaping.

front

Work as given for back until chart row 212 (220: 228) is complete.

SHAPE NECK
NEXT ROW (RS): Patt 49 and turn, leaving rem sts on a holder.
Work each side of neck separately.
Cast (bind) off 4 sts at beg of next row.
Dec 1 st at neck edge on next 3 rows, then on every foll alt row until 38 sts rem.
Dec 1 st at neck edge on every foll 4th row (from previous dec) until 36 sts rem.
Work 1 row, thus ending with a WS row.

SHAPE SHOULDER
Cast (bind) off 12 sts at beg of next and foll alt row.
Work 1 row.
Cast (bind) off rem 12 sts.
With RS facing, rejoin yarn to rem sts, cast (bind) off center 20 sts, patt to end.
Complete to match first side, rev all shaping.

sleeves (both alike)

Cast on 56 sts using 3¼mm (US 3) needles.
Work rows 1–20 foll chart for sleeve.
Change to 4mm (US 6) needles.
Cont foll chart, shaping sides by inc 1 st at each end of chart rows 21 and 23, then every foll 4th row until there are 100 sts.
Inc 1 st at each end on every foll 6th row (from previous inc) until there are 114 sts.
Cont without further shaping until chart row 154 is complete.

SHAPE SLEEVEHEAD
Cast (bind) off 3 (4: 5) sts at beg of next 2 rows.
Dec 1 st at each end on next 4 (6: 8) rows.
Cast (bind) off rem 100 (94: 88) sts loosely and evenly.

finishing

DO NOT PRESS.
Join right shoulder seam using back stitch.

Shorter neckband with roll
With RS facing and 3¼mm (US 3) needles, pick up and knit 25 sts down left front neck, 20 sts across center front, 25 sts up right front neck, 4 sts down right back neck, 40 sts across center back, and 4 sts up left back neck. *118 sts*
NEXT ROW (WS): P1, (K3, P6) 13 times.
Beg and ending rows as indicated, work rows 1–20 foll chart for back.
Beg with a K row, work 8 rows in st st.
Cast (bind) off loosely and evenly.

Polo neck
With RS facing and 3¼mm (US 3) needles, pick up and knit 25 sts down left front neck, 20 sts across center front, 25 sts up right front neck, 4 sts down right back neck, 40 sts across center back and 4 sts up left back neck. *118 sts*
Beg and ending rows as indicated, work rows 1–20 foll chart for back.
Change to 4mm (US 6) needles and rep rows 1–20.
Now rep rows 1–10 again, making bobbles on first of this row as folls:
NEXT ROW (RS OF POLO NECK, WS OF PULLOVER):
*Make 4-st bobble, patt 5, rep from * to last st, patt 1.
Cast (bind) off loosely and evenly.
Machine wash all pieces before sewing tog (see ball band for washing instructions).
See information page for finishing instructions.

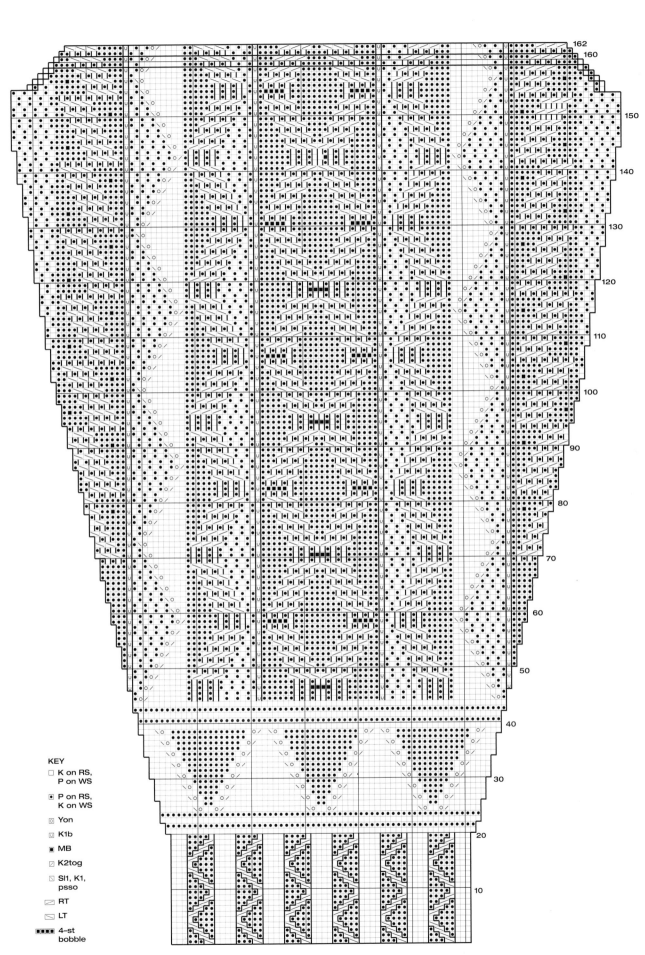

KEY

☐ K on RS,
   P on WS

▣ P on RS,
   K on WS

▣ Yon

Ⓤ K1b

■ MB

◪ K2tog

◩ Sl1, K1,
   psso

▨ RT

▧ LT

▰▰▰ 4-st
      bobble

SLEEVE

summer

Crisp cotton pullovers and fine knitted vests in white and neutrals are the perfect choice for balmy summer days and nights.

archie by Kim Hargreaves

SIZE	1ST	2ND	3RD	4TH	5TH	6TH	
To fit	2–3	3–4	4–5	6–7	8–9	9–10	yrs
Chest size	56	58	61	66	71	76	cm
	22	23	24	26	28	30	in
Actual width	37	40.5	43	46.5	51	56	cm
	14½	16	17	18½	20	22	in
Length	35	40	44	47.5	54	58	cm
	14	15½	17½	18½	21½	23	in
Sleeve length	21.5	23	26	30.5	33	35.5	cm
	8½	9	10	12	13	14	in

YARN

Rowan Cotton Glacé 50gm (1¾oz) balls:

Steel 798	7	9	10	12	14	16

NEEDLES

1 pair 2¼mm (US 1) needles
1 pair 2¾mm (US 2) needles
1 pair 3¼mm (US 3) needles

BUTTONS

2

TENSION (GAUGE)

23 sts and 32 rows to 10cm (4in) measured over stocking (stockinette) stitch using 3¼mm (US 3) needles

back

Cast on 85 (93: 99: 107: 117: 129) sts using 2¼mm (US 1) needles.
Beg with a K row, work 8 rows in st st.
NEXT ROW (RS): Purl (to form fold line).
NEXT ROW: Purl.
Change to 2¾mm (US 2) needles and work in moss (seed) st as folls:
ROW 1 (RS): K1, *P1, K1, rep from * to end.
ROW 2: As row 1.
Work another 5 rows in moss (seed) st, ending with a RS row.
NEXT ROW (WS): Purl.
Change to 3¼mm (US 3) needles and, beg with a K row, cont in st st as folls:
Cont straight until back measures 18.5 (22.5: 25: 27.5: 32.5: 35)cm (7¼ [8¾: 9¾: 11: 12¾: 13¾]in) from fold line-row, ending with a WS row.

SHAPE ARMHOLES

Cast (bind) off 3 sts at beg of next 2 rows.
79 (87: 93: 101: 111: 123) sts
Dec 1 st at each end of next 3 (3: 3: 4: 4: 4) rows.
73 (81: 87: 93: 103: 115) sts

Cont straight until armhole measures 16.5 (17.5: 19: 20: 21.5: 23)cm (6½ [6¾: 7½: 7¾: 8½: 9]in), ending with a WS row.

SHAPE SHOULDERS AND BACK NECK

Cast (bind) off 8 (9: 9: 10: 11: 13) sts at beg of next 2 rows. *57 (63: 69: 73: 81: 89) sts*
NEXT ROW (RS): Cast (bind) off 8 (9: 9: 10: 11: 13) sts, K until there are 11 (13: 14: 14: 16: 17) sts on right needle and turn, leaving rem sts on a holder.
Work each side of neck separately.
Cast (bind) off 4 sts at beg of next row.
Cast (bind) off rem 7 (9: 10: 10: 12: 13) sts.
With RS facing, rejoin yarn to rem sts, cast (bind) off center 19 (19: 23: 25: 27: 29) sts, K to end.
Work to match first side, rev shaping.

front pocket linings (make 2)

Cast on 25 (27: 27: 29: 29: 31) sts using 3¼mm (US 3) needles.
Beg with a K row, work 31 (33: 35: 37: 39: 41) rows in st st, ending with a RS row.
Break yarn and leave sts on a holder.

front pocket flaps (make 2)

Cast on 27 (29: 29: 31: 31: 33) sts using 3¼mm (US 3) needles.
Work 14 (14: 14: 16: 16: 16) rows in moss (seed) st as given for back, ending with a WS row.
Break yarn and leave sts on a holder.

front

Cast on 85 (93: 99: 107: 117: 129) sts using 2¼mm (US 1) needles.
Beg with a K row, work 8 rows in st st.
NEXT ROW (RS): Purl (to form fold line).
NEXT ROW: Purl.
Change to 2¾mm (US 2) needles and work 3 rows in moss (seed) st as given for back, ending with a WS row.
NEXT ROW (RS): Moss (seed) st 41 (45: 48: 52: 57: 63), cast (bind) off 3 sts, moss (seed) st to end.
NEXT ROW: Moss (seed) st to end, casting on 2 sts over those cast (bound) off on previous row.
Work another 2 rows in moss (seed) st, ending with a RS row.
NEXT ROW (WS): Purl.
Change to 3¼mm (US 3) needles.
Beg with a K row, work 6 rows in st st.

PLACE POCKETS

ROW 1 (RS): K11 (12: 14: 16: 19: 21), moss (seed) st 25 (27: 27: 29: 29: 31), K13 (15: 17: 17: 21: 25), moss (seed) st 25 (27: 27: 29: 29: 31), K11 (12: 14: 16: 19: 21).

ROW 2: P11 (12: 14: 16: 19: 21), moss (seed) st 25 (27: 27: 29: 29: 31), P13 (15: 17: 17: 21: 25), moss (seed) st 25 (27: 27: 29: 29: 31), P11 (12: 14: 16: 19: 21).

Rep last 2 rows 14 (15: 16: 17: 18: 19) times more.

NEXT ROW (RS): K11 (12: 14: 16: 19: 21), cast (bind) off next 25 (27: 27: 29: 29: 31) sts in moss (seed) st, K until there are 13 (15: 17: 17: 21: 25) sts on right needle after cast off, cast (bind) off next 25 (27: 27: 29: 29: 31) sts in moss (seed) st, K to end.

NEXT ROW: P11 (12: 14: 16: 19: 21), P across 25 (27: 27: 29: 29: 31) sts of first pocket lining, P13 (15: 17: 17: 21: 25), P across 25 (27: 27: 29: 29: 31) sts of second pocket lining, P to end.

JOIN POCKET FLAPS

NEXT ROW (RS): K10 (11: 13: 15: 18: 20), holding WS of first pocket flap against RS of front, K tog first st of pocket flap and next st of front, K tog rem 26 (28: 28: 30: 30: 32) sts of pocket flap with next 26 (28: 28: 30: 30: 32) sts of front in same way, K11 (13: 15: 15: 19: 23), holding WS of second pocket flap against RS of front, K tog first st of pocket flap tog with next st of front, K tog rem 26 (28: 28: 30: 30: 32) sts of pocket flap with next 26 (28: 28: 30: 30: 32) sts of front in same way, K to end.

Beg with a P row, cont in st st as folls:

Cont straight until front matches back to beg of armhole shaping, ending with a WS row.

SHAPE ARMHOLES

Cast (bind) off 3 sts at beg of next 2 rows.
79 (87: 93: 101: 111: 123) sts

Dec 1 st at each end of next 3 (3: 3: 4: 4: 4) rows.
73 (81: 87: 93: 103: 115) sts

Cont straight until armhole measures 6 (7: 8: 9: 10: 11) cm (2½ [2¾: 3¼: 3½: 4: 4¼]in), ending with a WS row.

SHAPE FRONT OPENING BORDERS

ROW 1 (RS): K31 (35: 38: 41: 46: 52), (P1, K1) 5 times, P1, K31 (35: 38: 41: 46: 52).

ROW 2: P30 (34: 37: 40: 45: 51), (K1, P1) 6 times, K1, P30 (34: 37: 40: 45: 51).

ROW 3: K29 (33: 36: 39: 44: 50), (P1, K1) 7 times, P1, K29 (33: 36: 39: 44: 50).

ROW 4: P28 (32: 35: 38: 43: 49), (K1, P1) 8 times, K1, P28 (32: 35: 38: 43: 49).

ROW 5: K27 (31: 34: 37: 42: 48), (P1, K1) 9 times, P1, K27 (31: 34: 37: 42: 48).

ROW 6: P26 (30: 33: 36: 41: 47), (K1, P1) 10 times, K1, P26 (30: 33: 36: 41: 47).

DIVIDE FOR FRONT OPENING

NEXT ROW (RS): K25 (29: 32: 35: 40: 46), (P1, K1) 5 times, P1 and turn, leaving rem sts on a holder.
36 (40: 43: 46: 51: 57) sts

Work each side of neck separately.

NEXT ROW: (P1, K1) 6 times, P to end.

NEXT ROW: K to last 13 sts, (P1, K1) 6 times, P1.

NEXT ROW: (P1, K1) 7 times, P to end.

Rep last 2 rows until front matches back to start of shoulder shaping, ending with a WS row.

SHAPE SHOULDER

Cast (bind) off 8 (9: 9: 10: 11: 13) sts at beg of next and foll alt row, then 7 (9: 10: 10: 12: 13) sts at beg of foll alt row.

Work 1 row. Break yarn and leave rem 13 (13: 15: 16: 17: 18) sts on a holder.

With RS facing, rejoin yarn to rem sts and cont as folls:

NEXT ROW (RS): P2tog, (K1, P1) 5 times, K to end.
36 (40: 43: 46: 51: 57) sts

NEXT ROW: P to last 12 sts, (K1, P1) 6 times.
NEXT ROW: P1, (K1, P1) 6 times, K to end.
NEXT ROW: P to last 14 sts, (K1, P1) 7 times.
Rep last 2 rows until front matches back to start of shoulder shaping, ending with a RS row.

SHAPE SHOULDER
Cast (bind) off 8 (9: 9: 10: 11: 13) sts at beg of next and foll alt row, then 7 (9: 10: 10: 12: 13) sts at beg of foll alt row.
Do NOT break yarn.
Leave rem 13 (13: 15: 16: 17: 18) sts on a holder and set aside ball of yarn; this will be used for hood.

right sleeve

Cast on 45 (47: 49: 53: 55: 59) sts using 2¾mm (US 2) needles.
Work 6 rows in moss (seed) st as given for back, ending with a WS row.
Change to 3¼mm (US 3) needles and, beg with a K row, cont in st st, shaping sides by inc 1 st at each end of 3rd (3rd: 3rd: 5th: 5th: 5th) and every foll 4th row until there are 65 (71: 79: 93: 99: 107) sts.

4th, 5th and 6th sizes only
Inc 1 st at each end of every foll alt row until there are 77 (81: 87) sts.

All sizes
Cont straight until sleeve measures 21.5 (23: 26: 30.5: 33: 35.5)cm (8½ [9: 10¼: 12: 13: 14]in), ending with a WS row.

SHAPE TOP
Cast (bind) off 3 sts at beg of next 2 rows.
71 (75: 81: 87: 93: 101) sts
Dec 1 st at each end of next and foll 2 (2: 2: 3: 3: 3) alt rows.
Work 1 row, ending with a WS row.
Cast (bind) off rem 65 (69: 75: 79: 85: 93) sts.

sleeve pocket lining

Cast on 19 (19: 21: 21: 23: 23) sts using 3¼mm (US 3) needles.
Beg with a K row, work 21 (21: 23: 23: 25: 25) rows in st st, ending with a RS row.
Break yarn and leave sts on a holder.

sleeve pocket flap (make 1)

Cast on 21 (21: 23: 23: 25: 25) sts using 3¼mm (US 3) needles.
Work 10 (10: 10: 12: 12: 12) rows in moss (seed) st as given for back, ending with a WS row.
Break yarn and leave sts on a holder.

left sleeve

Work as for right sleeve until sleeve measures 11 (12: 13: 15: 17: 18)cm (4¼ [4¾: 5: 6: 6½: 7]in), ending with a WS row.
Place markers on either side of center 19 (19: 21: 21: 23: 23) sts.
Keeping increases correct as set, cont as folls:
NEXT ROW (RS): K to first marker (working inc if appropriate), (P1, K1) 9 (9: 10: 10: 11: 11) times, P1, K to end (working inc if appropriate).
This row sets position of moss (seed) st worked over center 19 (19: 21: 21: 23: 23) sts between markers.
Working increases as for right sleeve, work another 19 (19: 21: 21: 23: 23) rows in st st, with center sts between markers in moss (seed) st, ending with a WS row.
NEXT ROW (RS): K to first marker (working inc if appropriate), cast (bind) off center 19 (19: 21: 21: 23: 23) sts in moss (seed) st, K to end (working inc if appropriate).
NEXT ROW: P to first marker, P across 19 (19: 21: 21: 23: 23) sts of pocket lining, P to end.

JOIN POCKET FLAP
NEXT ROW (RS): K to within 1 st of first marker (working inc if appropriate), holding WS of pocket flap against RS of sleeve, K tog first st of pocket flap and next st of sleeve, K tog rem 20 (20: 22: 22: 24: 24) sts of pocket flap and next 20 (20: 22: 22: 24: 24) sts of sleeve in same way, K to end (working inc if appropriate).
Beg with a P row, cont in st st and complete as for right sleeve.

finishing

Press all pieces as described on the information page.
Join shoulder seams using back stitch.

HOOD
With RS facing, using ball of yarn left at right front neck edge and 3¼mm (US 3) needles, patt across 13 (13: 15: 16: 17: 18) sts of right front, pick up and knit 27 (27: 31: 33: 35: 37) sts across back neck, placing marker on center st, then patt across 13 (13: 15: 16: 17: 18) sts of left front. *53 (53: 61: 65: 69: 73) sts*
Now work in moss (seed) st as set by front opening edge sts as folls:
Work 1 row.
NEXT ROW (RS) (INC): Moss (seed) st to marked st, M1, K1, M1, moss (seed) st to end.
Rep last 2 rows 10 times more. *75 (75: 83: 87: 91: 95) sts*
Work 3 rows.
NEXT ROW (RS) (INC): Moss (seed) st to marked st, M1, K1, M1, moss (seed) st to end.
Rep last 4 rows 5 times more. *87 (87: 95: 99: 103: 107) sts*
Cont straight until hood measures 23 (24: 25: 26: 27: 28)cm (9 [9½: 9¾: 10¼: 10¾: 11¼]in), ending with a WS row.
NEXT ROW (RS) (DEC): Moss (seed) st to within 2 sts of marked center st, work 2 tog, K1, work 2 tog tbl, moss (seed) st to end.
Work 1 row.
Rep last 2 rows twice more, dec 1 st at center of last row. *80 (80: 88: 92: 96: 100) sts*
NEXT ROW (RS): Moss (seed) st 40 (40: 44: 46: 48: 50) and turn.
Fold hood in half with WS facing and, using a spare needle, cast (bind) off sts from each needle tog to form hood seam.

BUTTON LOOPS (MAKE 2)
Cast on 14 sts using 3¼mm (US 3) needles.
Cast (bind) off.
Fold button loops in half and sew to inside of front opening edge as in photograph. Attach buttons to correspond.

Fold first 8 rows of front and back to inside along fold line and slipstitch in place. Make a twisted cord approx 150cm (60 in) long and knot ends. Thread cord through hem casing and tie ends at front.
See information page for finishing instructions, setting in sleeves using the shallow set-in method.

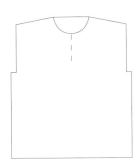

boata by Kim Hargreaves

SIZES	CHILDREN'S (YRS)					ADULTS'				
	4-6	6-8	8-9	9-11	12-14	S	M	L	XL	
To fit chest	–	–	–	–	–	91.5–96.5	96.5–102	102–107	107–112	cm
	–	–	–	–	–	36–38	38–40	40–42	42–44	in
Actual width	44.5	47.5	51.5	53.5	56.5	58.5	61.5	63.5	66.5	cm
	17½	18½	20	21	22	23	24	25	26	in
Length	49.5	53.5	57	60	63	69	71.5	73.5	73.5	cm
	19½	21	22½	23½	25	27	28	29	29	in
Sleeve length	33	38	40.5	43	45.5	45.5 (53)	45.5 (53)	45.5 (53)	45.5 (53)	cm
	13	15	16	17	18	18 (21)	18 (21)	18 (21)	18 (21)	in

Adult sleeve lengths show the ladies' version first, followed by the men's version in brackets.
(All measurements after washing)

YARN
Rowan Handknit DK Cotton or Rowan Denim 50gm (1¾oz) balls:

Handknit DK Cotton
Striped version

A	10	10	10	11	12	13	14	15	16
B	3	4	4	4	4	5	5	5	6

One-color version

	11	11.	12	13	17	19	20	21	22

Denim
Striped version

A	12	14	15	16	17	17	18	19	19
B	3	4	5	5	6	6	6	7	7

(Men's photographed in Ecru 324 and Nashville 225)
One-color version

	11	13	15	17	19	23	23	24	25

(Children's photographed in Nashville 225)

NEEDLES
1 pair 3¼mm (US 3) needles
1 pair 4mm (US 6) needles

TENSION (GAUGE)
Handknit DK cotton
20 sts and 28 rows to 10cm (4in) measured over patterned stocking (stockinette) stitch using 4mm (US 6) needles
Denim (before washing)
20 sts and 28 rows to 10cm (4in) measured over patterned stocking (stockinette) stitch using 4mm (US 6) needles

PATTERN NOTE
Denim will shrink in length when washed for the first time. Allowances have been made in this pattern for shrinkage. Where the pattern differs, the instructions are written for the Handknit Cotton

version first, followed by the Denim version **in bold**. One set of figures refers to both versions. The pattern is written for the striped version. For the one-color version, ignore all color changes.

back
Cast on 89 (95: 103: 107: 113: 117: 123: 127: 133) sts using 3¼mm (US 3) needles.
Work 6 (6: 8: 8: 8: 10: 10: 10: 10) rows in garter st (knit every row).
Change to 4mm (US 6) needles and cont in striped patt, which is worked entirely in st st beg with a K row. Take yarn not in use loosely up side of work.
Work 4 rows in A.
Work 2 rows in B.
These 6 rows form the striped patt for the lower part of the back and are repeated throughout. *
Cont in patt until work measures 30.5 (33.5: 36: 38: 40: 43.5: 46: 48: 48)cm (12 [13: 14¼: 15: 15¾: 17: 18:

18¾: 18¾]in), **35.5 (39: 42: 44: 46.5: 51: 53.5: 56: 56)cm (14 [15½: 16½: 17¼: 18¼: 20: 21: 22: 22]in)** from cast-on edge, ending with a WS row.

SHAPE ARMHOLE
Cast (bind) off 5 sts at beg of next 2 rows.
79 (85: 93: 97: 103: 107: 113: 117: 123) sts
Work 6 (6: 8: 8: 10: 12: 12: 12: 12) rows, ending with a WS row.
Using yarn A throughout, work in ridge pattern as folls:

ROW 1 (RS): Purl.
ROW 2: Knit.
ROW 3: Purl.
ROWS 4 AND 6: Purl.
ROWS 5 AND 7: Knit.
ROW 8: Purl.

These 8 rows form the ridge pattern and are repeated throughout.**
Keeping patt correct, cont until work measures 19 (20: 21: 22: 23: 25.5: 25.5: 25.5 25.5)cm (7½ [7¾: 8¼: 8½: 9: 10: 10: 10: 10]in), **22 (23: 24.5: 25.5: 27: 30: 30: 30: 30)cm (8½ [9: 9¾: 10: 10¾: 12: 12: 12: 12]in)** from beg of armhole shaping, ending with a WS row.

SHAPE SHOULDERS AND BACK NECK
Boat neck (all sizes)
Cast (bind) off 5 (6: 7: 7: 8: 9: 10: 10: 11) sts at beg of next 2 rows and 6 (6: 7: 8: 8: 9: 10: 10: 11) sts at beg of foll 2 rows.
Cast (bind) off 6 (7: 8: 8: 9: 9: 10: 11: 12) st at beg of next 2 rows.
Cast (bind) off rem 45 (47: 49: 51: 53: 53: 53: 55: 55) sts.

Polo collar (adults' sizes only)
Cast (bind) off 12 (13: 13: 14) sts at beg of next 2 rows.
Cast (bind) off 12 (13: 13: 14) sts, patt 16 (17: 18: 19) sts, turn and leave rem sts on a holder.
Work each side of neck separately.
Cast (bind) off 4 sts, patt to end. Cast (bind) off rem 12 (13: 14: 15) sts.
With RS facing, rejoin yarn to rem sts, cast (bind) off center 27 (27: 29: 29) sts, patt to end.
Complete to match first side, rev shaping.

pocket lining
(4-6, 6-8 & 8-9 yrs only)
Cast on 49 (51: 55) sts.
Work 10 (12: 14) rows in st st, beg with a K row.
Leave sts on a spare needle.

front
Boat neck
9-11, 12-14 yrs & four adults' sizes
Work as given for back.
4-6, 6-8 & 8-9 yrs only
Work as given for back to *.
Work 4 (6: 8) more rows in stripe pattern, ending with a WS row.

DIVIDE FOR POCKET
NEXT ROW (RS): K20 (22: 24), slip next 49 (51: 55) sts onto a holder for pocket front, K across sts for pocket lining, K to end. *89 (95: 103) sts*

WORK SIDES AND POCKET LINING
Keeping patt correct, work 31 (33: 35) rows, ending with a WS row.
Leave sts on a spare needle but do not break yarn.

WORK POCKET FRONT
Return to sts on holder for pocket front, with RS facing rejoin appropriate yarn and work 32 (34: 36) rows in stripe pattern.

JOIN PIECES TOGETHER
With RS facing, return to sts for sides and pocket lining, K20 (22: 24) sts, now with needle for pocket front held parallel and in front of needle for pocket lining, Ktog 1 st from each needle, rep until all 49 (51: 55) pocket front sts are joined, K to end.
89 (95: 103) sts
Complete as given for back.

Polo collar version (adults' sizes only)
Work as given for back to **.

DIVIDE FOR FRONT NECK
NEXT ROW (RS): Keeping patt correct, work 51 (54: 56: 59) sts, turn and leave rem sts on a holder.
Work each side of neck separately.
Cont in patt until front is 20 (**22**) rows shorter than back to beg of neck shaping, ending with a WS row.

SHAPE FRONT NECK
Work to last 4 sts, turn and leave rem sts on a holder.
NEXT ROW (WS): Work 4 sts and leave these on the first holder, patt to end. *43 (46: 48: 51) sts*
Dec 1 st at neck edge on next 3 (3: 5: 5) rows and 4 (4: 3: 3) foll alt rows. *36 (39: 40: 43) sts*
Cont until front matches back to shoulder, ending with a WS row.

SHAPE SHOULDER
Cast (bind) off 12 (13: 13: 14) sts at beg of next and foll alt row.
Work 1 row.
Cast (bind) off rem 12 (13: 14: 15) sts.
Return to sts on a holder, thread a colored marker through the center 5 sts and slip these onto a holder, rejoin yarn and patt to end.
Complete to match first side, rev shaping.

sleeves (both alike)
The sleeve patt is written for the 5 children's sizes, followed by the ladies' and men's.
Cast on 45 (49: 49: 53: 53) (57: 63) sts using 3¼mm (US 3) needles.
Work 6 (6: 8: 8: 8) (10: 10) rows in garter st (knit every row).
Change to 4mm (US 6) needles.
Work in 6-row striped patt as given for back, inc 1 st at each end of next row and every foll 6th (6th: 6th: 6th: 6th) (6th: 8th) row to 63 (75: 75: 85: 85) (79: 77) sts and then every foll 4th (4th: 4th: 4th: 4th) (4th: 6th) row to 75 (81: 85: 89: 93) (101: 101) sts.
Cont without further shaping until sleeve measures 33 (38: 40.5: 43: 45.5) (45.5: 53)cm (13 [15: 16: 17: 18] (18: 21)in), **38.5 (44: 47: 50: 53) (53: 61.5)cm (15¼ [17¼: 18½: 19¾: 21] (21: 24¼)in)** from cast-on edge, ending with a WS row.
Cast (bind) off loosely and evenly.

finishing
Handknit cotton version
Press all pieces as described on the information page.
Denim version
DO NOT PRESS.
Boat neck
Join right shoulder seam using back stitch.
With RS facing and using 3¼mm (US 3) needles, beg at left front and pick up and knit 90 (94: 98: 102: 106: 106: 106: 110: 110) sts around neck edge.
Beg with a K row, work 4 (4: 4: 4: 6: 6: 6: 6: 6) rows in st st, ending with a RS row.
Cast (bind) off knitwise.

Polo collar

LEFT FRONT BAND

With RS facing, slip a 3¼mm (US 3) needle through 5 sts on thread (from left to right) but leave marker through sts, rejoin yarn and work as folls, inc 1 st at inside edge, K5. *6 sts*

Cont in garter st until band fits neatly when slightly stretched up front to beg of neck shaping.

Leave sts on a holder, break yarn and slipstich into place up left front edge.

RIGHT FRONT BAND

Working behind first band for men's and in front of first band for ladies', slip a 3¼mm (US 3) needle through the same 5 sts on thread and work to match first side, but do not break yarn.

COLLAR

With RS facing, K across 6 sts of front band, K 8 sts from holder, pick up and K 21 sts up right front neck to shoulder, 41 sts across back neck and 21 sts down left front neck, K 8 sts from first holder, K 6 sts of left band. *111 sts*

Note: WS of garment now becomes RS of collar.

NEXT ROW (RS): K6, (K3, P3) to last 9 sts, K9.

NEXT ROW: K6, (P3, K3) to last 9 sts, P3, K6.

NEXT ROW (INC): K9, M1, patt to last 9 sts, M1, K9.

Work 3 rows on sts as set.

NEXT ROW (INC): K9, M1, patt to last 9 sts, M1, K9.

Work 3 rows on sts as set.

NEXT ROW (INC): K9, M1, patt to last 9 sts, M1, K9.

Work 3 rows on sts as set.

Inc as before on next row and 2 foll 4th rows. *123 sts*

Cont until collar measures 10cm (4in), **11.5cm (4½in)** from cast-on edge, ending with a WS row.

Cast (bind) off in patt.

4-6, 6-8 & 8-9 yrs only

POCKET EDGING (BOTH ALIKE)

With RS facing and using 3¼ mm (US 3) needles and yarn A, pick up and knit 24 (26: 28) sts along pocket edge.

Knit 5 rows.

Cast (bind) off knitwise.

After all knitting is completed, machine wash all Denim pieces as described on the ball band before sewing together.

See information page for finishing instructions.

guernsey frock by Kim Hargreaves

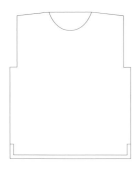

SIZES

	CHILDREN'S (YRS)				ADULTS'			
	1	4	10	12	S	M	L	
To fit chest	45.5	56	71	76	81–86	91–97	102–107	cm
	18	22	28	30	32–34	36–38	40–42	in
Actual width	28.5	32.5	50.5	55.5	60.5	63.5	66.5	cm
	11¼	12¾	20	21¾	24	25	26¼	in
Length	28	33	54	59	61.5	63.5	66.5	cm
	11	13	21¼	23¼	24¼	25	26¼	in
Sleeve length	12	16	28.5	32	41	41	41	cm
	4¾	6¼	11¼	12½	16	16	16	in

YARN
Rowan Hand Knit Cotton 50gm (1¾oz) balls:

Bleached 263	4	6	16	17	19	19	20

NEEDLES
1 pair 3¼mm (US 3) needles
1 pair 4mm (US 6) needles

TENSION (GAUGE)
20 sts and 28 rows to 10cm (4in) measured over stocking (stockinette) stitch using 4mm (US6) needles

back
Cast on 57 (65: 101: 111: 121: 127: 133) sts using 3¼mm (US 3) needles.
Work 4 (4: 6: 6: 6: 6: 6) rows in garter st (K every row).
Change to 4mm (US 6) needles and work border and side vents as folls:
1 and 4 years only
ROW 1: Knit.
ROW 2: K3, P to last 3 sts, K3.
Rep these 2 rows twice more.
5 larger sizes only
Work 28 rows in patt from Chart A and AT THE SAME TIME work first 5 and the last 5 sts in garter st (knit every row). (These 5 sts form the side-vent border.)
All sizes
Work another 28 (28: 30: 44: 44: 50: 58) rows in st st only, ending with a WS row.
CONT FROM CHART B
5 larger sizes only
Work in pattern from Chart B until chart row 30 has been completed.
SHAPE ARMHOLES
Cast (bind) off 4 (4: 6: 6: 6) sts at beg of next 2 rows *.
All sizes
Cont working in patt from Chart B until chart row

42 (56: 94: 94: 100: 100: 100) has been completed.
SHAPE SHOULDERS AND BACK NECK
Cast (bind) off 0 (0: 10: 12: 12: 13: 14) sts at beg of next 2 rows.
Cast (bind) off 0 (0: 10: 12: 12: 13: 14) sts, patt 17 (21: 14: 15: 17: 18: 19) sts, turn and leave rem sts on a holder. Work each side separately.
Cast (bind) off 3 (3: 4: 4: 4: 4: 4) sts at beg of next row.
Cast (bind) off rem 14 (18: 10: 11: 13: 14: 15) sts.
Rejoin yarn to rem sts and cast (bind) off center 23 (23: 25: 25: 27: 27: 27) sts, patt to end.
Complete to match first side.

front
Work as for back to *.
Cont working in patt from Chart B until chart row 34 (48: 68: 68: 72: 72: 72) has been completed, ending with a WS row.
SHAPE FRONT NECK
Patt 23 (27: 42: 47: 50: 53: 56) sts, turn and leave rem sts on a holder.
Work each side of neck separately.
Cast (bind) off 3 (3: 0: 0: 0: 0: 0) sts at beg of next row.
Dec 1 st at neck edge on next 6 (6: 6: 6: 8: 8: 8) rows and foll 0 (0: 6: 6: 2: 2: 2) alt rows.
3 largest sizes only
Work 3 rows, dec 1 st at neck edge on next row and foll two 4th rows. *14 (18: 30: 35: 37: 40: 43) sts*
Work until front matches back to shoulder shaping.
SHAPE SHOULDER
Cast (bind) off 0 (0: 10: 12: 12: 13: 14) sts at beg of next row.
Cast (bind) off 0 (0: 10: 12: 12: 13: 14) sts at beg of next row.

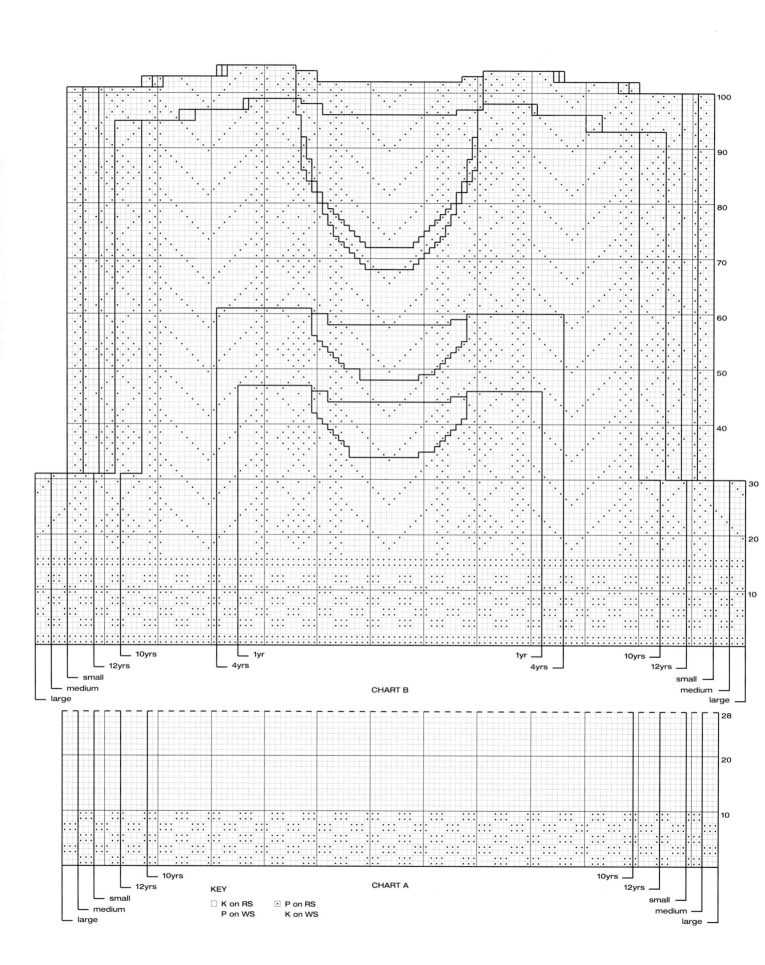

CHART B

10yrs
12yrs
1yr
4yrs
small
medium
large

1yr
4yrs
10yrs
12yrs
small
medium
large

CHART A

10yrs
12yrs
small
medium
large

10yrs
12yrs
small
medium
large

KEY

☐ K on RS
P on WS

⊡ P on RS
K on WS

100
90
80
70
60
50
40
30
20
10

28
20
10

Work 0 (0: 1: 1: 1: 1: 1) row.
Cast (bind) off rem sts.
Rejoin yarn to rem sts and cast (bind) off center 11
(11: 9: 9: 9: 9: 9) sts, patt to end of row.
Work 1 row.
Complete to match first side.

sleeves (both alike)

Cast on 28 (32: 46: 46: 54: 54: 54) sts using 3¼mm
(US 3) needles.
Work 6 rows in st st, beg with a knit row.
NEXT ROW RS: (K2, P2) to last 0 (0: 2: 2: 2: 2: 2) sts, K2.
Work in rib as set until rib measures 2.5 (2.5: 5: 5: 5:
5: 5)cm (1 [1: 2: 2: 2: 2: 2]in), ending with a WS row,
and inc 1 st at end of last row.
29 (33: 47: 47: 55: 55: 55) sts
Change to 4mm (US 6) needles and work 34 (44:
82: 92: 116: 116: 116) rows from chart, noting that
the sleeves start on chart rows 1 (1: 30: 20: 1: 1: 1)
respectively, and AT THE SAME TIME shape sides
by inc 1 st at both ends of 3rd row and then every
2nd (2nd: 3rd: 3rd: 4th: 4th: 4th) row until there are

57 (61: 93: 93: 95: 95: 95) sts and then for 3 larger
sizes only every 6th row to 101 (101: 101) sts.
Cast (bind) off loosely and evenly.

finishing

Press all pieces as described on information page.
Join right shoulder seam.
NECKBAND
With RS facing and 3¼mm (US 3) needles, pick
up and knit 14 (14: 28: 28: 30: 30: 30) sts down
left front neck, 11 (11: 9: 9: 9: 9: 9) sts across center
front, 14 (14: 28: 28: 30: 30: 30) sts up right front
neck and 25 (25: 33: 33: 35: 35: 35) sts across back
neck. *64 (64: 98: 98: 104: 104: 104) sts*
ROW 1 (WS): (K2, P2) to last 0 (0: 2: 2: 0: 0: 0) sts, K2.
Keeping rib correct, work until band measures 2 (2:
2.5: 2.5: 2.5: 2.5: 2.5)cm (¾ [¾: 1: 1: 1: 1: 1]in),
ending with a WS row.
Now beg with a knit row, work 6 rows in st st.
Cast (bind) off loosely and evenly.
See information page for finishing instructions.

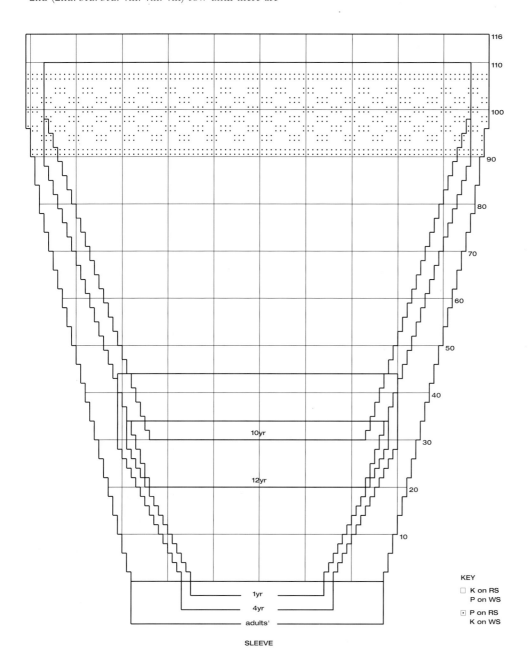

SLEEVE

KEY
☐ K on RS
P on WS

⊡ P on RS
K on WS

breaker by Kim Hargreaves

SIZE

	S	M	L	
To fit bust	81–86	91–97	102–107	cm
	32–34	36–38	40–42	in
Actual width	63.5	66.5	68.5	cm
	25	26	27	in
Length	69	71.5	73.5	cm
	27½	28	29	in
Sleeve length	41.5	41.5	41.5	cm
	16½	16½	16½	in

YARN

Rowan Designer DK 50gm (1¾oz) balls:
Bleached 263	18	19	20

BUTTONS

1

NEEDLES

1 pair 3¾mm (US 5) needles
1 pair 4mm (US 6) needles

TENSION (GAUGE)

20 sts and 28 rows to 10cm (4in) measured over stocking (stockinette) stitch using 4mm (US 6) needles

back

Cast on 127 (133: 137) sts using 3¾mm (US 5) needles.
ROW 1 (RS): K1, (P1, K1) to end.
This row forms moss (seed) st. Work 6 rows in all.
Change to 4mm (US 6) needles and work side vents, setting rib patt as folls:
ROW 1 (RS): Moss (seed) st 5, K3 (3: 2), (P3, K3) to last 5 (5: 10) sts, P0 (0: 3), K0 (0: 2), moss (seed) st 5.
ROW 2: Moss (seed) st 5, P3 (3: 2), (K3, P3) to last 5 (5: 10) sts, K0 (0: 3), P0 (0: 2), moss (seed) st 5.
Rep these 2 rows 11 times more, ending with a WS row.
Side vents completed.*
Cont in st st, beg with a K row, until work measures 43.5 (46: 48)cm (17 [18: 18¾]in) from cast-on edge, ending with a WS row.

SHAPE ARMHOLES

Cast (bind) off 4 sts at beg of next 2 rows.
NEXT ROW (RS) (DEC): K3, K3tog, K to last 6 sts, K3tog tbl, K3. Work 1 row.
Dec as before on next row and 3 foll alt rows.
99 (105: 109) sts
Cont without further shaping until work measures 25.5cm (10in) from beg of armhole shaping, ending with a WS row.

SHAPE SHOULDERS AND BACK NECK

Cast (bind) off 10 (11: 12) sts at beg of next 2 rows.
Cast (bind) off 11 (12: 12) sts, K15 (16: 17), turn and leave rem sts on a holder.
Work each side of neck separately.
Cast (bind) off 4 sts, P to end.
Cast (bind) off rem 11 (12: 13) sts.
With RS facing, rejoin yarn to rem sts, cast (bind) off center 27 sts, K to end.
Complete to match first side, rev shaping.

front

Work as given for back to *.
Cont in st st beg with a K row, until work measures 29 (30: 32)cm (11½ [12: 12½]in) from cast-on edge, ending with a WS row.

DIVIDE FOR FRONT NECK

NEXT ROW (RS): K56 (59: 61) sts, place a colored marker through the next 15 sts on LH needle, then using a 3¾mm (US 5) needle, work across these 15 sts as folls: (P3, K3) twice, K1, P1, K1, turn and leave rem 56 (59: 61) sts on a holder. *71 (74: 76) sts*
NEXT ROW (WS): Using a 3¾mm (US 5) needle, K1, P1, K1, (P3, K3) twice, using a 4mm (US 6) needle, P to end.
These 2 rows set the stitches. Keeping stitches correct and working 15 sts at center front on the 3¾mm (US 5) needle and the rem on 4mm (US 6) needles, cont until front matches back to armhole shaping, ending with a WS row.

SHAPE ARMHOLE

Cast (bind) off 4 sts at beg of next row. Work 1 row.
NEXT ROW (RS) (DEC): K3, K3tog, work to end.
Work 1 row.
Dec as before on next row and 3 foll alt rows.
57 (60: 62) sts
Cont without shaping until front is 19 rows shorter than back to shape shoulder, ending with RS row.
NEXT ROW (WS): Patt 15 sts and leave these on a holder for collar, P to end. *42 (45: 47) sts*
NEXT ROW (RS): K to last 3 sts, turn and leave these 3 sts on the holder for collar, P to end. *39 (42: 44) sts*
Dec 1 st at neck edge on next 3 rows, 3 foll alt rows and 1 foll 4th row. *32 (35: 37) sts*
Cont until front matches back to shoulder shaping, ending with a WS row.

SHAPE SHOULDER

Cast (bind) off 10 (11: 12) sts at beg of next row and 11 (12: 12) sts at beg of foll alt row. Work 1 row.
Cast (bind) off rem 11 (12: 13) sts.
Return to rem sts and with RS facing, pick up a loop from the front of each of the 15 sts on the colored

marker and place these onto a LH 3¾mm (US 5) needle. Rejoin yarn and work as folls across these 15 sts:
Using a 3¾mm (US 5) needle, K1, P1, K1, (K3, P3) twice, then using a 4mm (US 6) needle, K across rem 56 (59: 61) sts on holder. *71 (74: 76) sts*
NEXT ROW (WS): Using a 4mm (US 6) needle, P to last 15 sts, then using a 3¼mm (US 5) needle, (K3, P3) twice, K1, P1, K1.
These 2 rows set the stitches.
Complete to match first side, rev shaping.

sleeves (both alike)

Cast on 67 sts using 3¾mm (US 5) needles and work 6 rows in moss (seed) st as given for back.
Change to 4mm (US 6) needles and work in rib patt as folls:
ROW 1 (RS): K5, (P3, K3) to last 2 sts, K2.
ROW 2: P5, (K3. P3) to last 2 sts, P2.
Rep these last 2 rows 6 times more, ending with a WS row.
NEXT ROW (RS) (INC): K3, M1, patt to last 3 sts, M1, K3. *69 sts*
Work 5 rows.
NEXT ROW (RS) (INC): K3, M1, patt to last 3 sts, M1, K3. *71 sts*
Work 3 rows in rib patt.
Work 2 rows in st st, beg with a K row.
NEXT ROW (RS) (INC): K3, M1, K to last 3 sts, M1, K3.
Work 5 rows.
Inc as before on next row and every foll 6th row to 89 sts and then every foll 4th row to 101 sts.
Cont without further shaping until sleeve measures 41.5cm (16¼in) or length required from cast-on edge, ending with a WS row.
SHAPE SLEEVEHEAD
Cast (bind) off 4 sts at beg of next 2 rows.
NEXT ROW (RS) (DEC): K3, K3tog, K to last 6 sts, K3tog tbl, K3. Work 1 row.
Rep the last 2 rows until 73 sts rem, ending with a WS row. Cast (bind) off evenly.

finishing

Press all pieces, including ribs, as described on the information page.
Join both shoulder seams using back stitch.
COLLAR
With RS facing, rejoin yarn and using 3¾mm (US 5) needles, patt across 15 sts on first holder on right front, K3 from 2nd holder, pick up and knit 23 sts up right front neck to shoulder, 35 sts across back neck and 23 sts down left front, K 3 sts from first holder, patt across 15 sts on second holder. *117 sts*
Note: WS of garment now becomes RS of collar.
NEXT ROW (RS): Moss (seed) st 3, P3, (K3, P3) to last 3 sts, moss (seed) st 3.
NEXT ROW: Moss (seed) st 3, K3, (P3, K3) to last 3 sts, moss (seed) st 3.
Rep these 2 rows until collar measures 10cm (4in) from cast-on edge, ending with a WS row.
Cast (bind) off in patt.
BUTTON LOOP
Cast on 10 sts using 3¾mm (US 5) needles.
Cast (bind) off.
Fold in half lengthways to form a loop and sew neatly into place on the inside edge of the right front, 10cm (4in) below start of neck shaping as in photograph.
Sew button into place on left front to match.
See information page for finishing instructions, leaving 10cm (4in) open at side seams to form vents.

core by Kim Hargreaves

SIZE

SIZE	XS	S	M	L	XL	
To fit bust	81	86	91	97	102	cm
	32	34	36	38	40	in
Actual width	48.5	50.5	53.5	55.5	58.5	cm
	19	20	21	22	23	in
Length	49	50	51	52	53	cm
	19½	19½	20	20½	21	in
Sleeve length	45	45	46	46	46	cm
	17½	17½	18	18	18	in

YARN

Rowan Handknit DK Cotton 50gm (1¾oz) balls:

Sugar 303	12	13	13	14	14

Rowan Denim 50gm (1¾oz) balls:

Memphis 229	13	14	15	15	16

NEEDLES

1 pair 3¼mm (US 3) needles
1 pair 4mm (US 6) needles

BUTTONS

9

TENSION (GAUGE)

Handknit DK Cotton
20 sts and 28 rows to 10cm (4in) measured over stocking (stockinette) stitch using 4mm (US 6) needles.
Denim (before washing)
20 sts and 28 rows to 10cm (4in) measured over stocking (stockinette) stitch using 4mm (US 6) needles

PATTERN NOTE

Denim will shrink in length when washed for the first time. Allowances have been made in this pattern for shrinkage.
The pattern is written for Handknit DK Cotton with alterations for Denim given in **bold** afterwards in brackets. Where no bold figures are given, instructions are the same for both yarns unless stated otherwise.

back

Cast on 81 (85: 91: 95: 101) sts using 3¼mm (US 3) needles.
ROW 1 (RS): K1, *P1, K1, rep from * to end.
ROW 2: As row 1.
These 2 rows form moss (seed) st.
Work another 8 rows in moss (seed) st, ending with a WS row.

Change to 4mm (US 6) needles.
NEXT ROW (RS): P21 (22: 24: 25: 27), K2, P1, K33 (35: 37: 39: 41), P1, K2, P21 (22: 24: 25: 27).
NEXT ROW: K21 (22: 24: 25: 27), P2, K1, P33 (35: 37: 39: 41), K1, P2, K21 (22: 24: 25: 27).
These 2 rows set the sts.
Keeping patt correct as set, cont as folls:
Work another 4 (6: 6: 6: 6) rows for Handknit DK Cotton or **6 (8: 8: 8: 8)** rows for Denim.
NEXT ROW (RS) (INC): P21 (22: 24: 25: 27), K2, P1, M1, K33 (35: 37: 39: 41), M1, P1, K2, P21 (22: 24: 25: 27). *83 (87: 93: 97: 103) sts*
NEXT ROW: K21 (22: 24: 25: 27), P2, K1, P35 (37: 39: 41: 43), K1, P2, K21 (22: 24: 25: 27).
Working all increases as set by last 2 rows, inc 1 st at either side of center panel on every foll 8th (**10th**) row until there are 97 (101: 107: 111: 117) sts, taking inc sts into st st.
Cont straight until back measures 28 (29: 29: 30: 30) cm (11¼ [11½: 11½: 12: 12]in) for Handknit DK Cotton or **32.5 (34: 34: 35: 35)cm (12¾ [13½: 13½: 13¾: 13¾]in)** for Denim, ending with a WS row.

SHAPE ARMHOLES

Keeping patt correct, cast (bind) off 4 sts at beg of next 2 rows. *89 (93: 99: 103: 109) sts*
Dec 1 st at each end of next 7 (7: 9: 9: 11) rows, then on foll alt row. *73 (77: 79: 83: 85) sts*
Work 1 row, ending with a WS row.
NEXT ROW (RS): P2tog, P to last 2 sts, P2tog.
NEXT ROW: Knit.
Beg with a K row, now cont in st st as folls:
Dec 1 st at each end of next and foll 1 (2: 2: 3: 3) alt rows. *67 (69: 71: 73: 75) sts*
Cont straight until armhole measures 21 (21: 22: 22: 23)cm (8¼ [8¼: 8½: 8½: 9]in) for Handknit DK Cotton or **24.5 (24.5: 25.5: 25.5: 27)cm (9¾ [9¾: 10: 10: 10¾]in)** for Denim, ending with a WS row.

SHAPE SHOULDERS AND BACK NECK

Cast (bind) off 6 (6: 7: 7: 7) sts at beg of next 2 rows. *55 (57: 57: 59: 61) sts*
NEXT ROW (RS): Cast (bind) off 6 (6: 7: 7: 7) sts, K until there are 11 (11: 10: 10: 11) sts on right needle and turn, leaving rem sts on a holder.
Work each side of neck separately.
Cast (bind) off 4 sts at beg of next row.
Cast (bind) off rem 7 (7: 6: 6: 7) sts.
With RS facing, rejoin yarn to rem sts, cast (bind) off center 21 (23: 23: 25: 25) sts, K to end.
Work to match first side, rev shapings.

left front

Cast on 47 (49: 52: 54: 57) sts using 3¼mm (US 3) needles.

ROW 1 (RS): *K1, P1, rep from * to last 1 (1: 0: 0: 1) st, K1 (1: 0: 0: 1).

ROW 2: K1 (1: 0: 0: 1), *P1, K1, rep from * to end.
These 2 rows form moss (seed) st.
Work another 7 rows in moss (seed) st, ending with a RS row.

ROW 10 (WS): Moss (seed) st 7 and slip these 7 sts onto a holder for button band, M1, moss (seed) st to end.
41 (43: 46: 48: 51) sts
Change to 4mm (US 6) needles.

NEXT ROW (RS): P21 (22: 24: 25: 27), K2, P1, moss (seed) st 7, P1, K2, P7 (8: 9: 10: 11).

NEXT ROW: K7 (8: 9: 10: 11), P2, K1, moss (seed) st 7, K1, P2, K21 (22: 24: 25: 27).
These 2 rows set the sts.
Keeping sts correct as now set, cont as folls:
Work another 12 (14: 14: 14: 14) rows for Handknit DK Cotton or **16 (18: 18: 18: 18)** rows for Denim.

NEXT ROW (RS) (INC): P21 (22: 24: 25: 27), K2, P1, M1, moss (seed) st 7, M1, P1, K2, P7 (8: 9: 10: 11).

NEXT ROW: K7 (8: 9: 10: 11), P2, K1, moss (seed) st 9, K1, P2, K21 (22: 24: 25: 27).
Working all increases as set by last 2 rows, inc 1 st at either side of moss (seed) st panel on every foll 16th (**20th**) row until there are 49 (51: 54: 56: 59) sts, taking inc sts into moss (seed) st.
Cont straight until left front matches back to beg of armhole shaping, ending with a WS row.

SHAPE ARMHOLE

Keeping patt correct, cast (bind) off 4 sts at beg of next row. *45 (47: 50: 52: 55) sts*
Work 1 row.
Dec 1 st at armhole edge of next 7 (7: 9: 9: 11) rows, then on foll alt row. *37 (39: 40: 42: 43) sts*
Work 1 row, ending with a WS row.

NEXT ROW (RS): P2tog, P to end.

NEXT ROW: Knit.
Beg with a K row, now cont in st st as folls:
Dec 1 st at armhole edge of next and foll 1 (2: 2: 3: 3) alt rows. *34 (35: 36: 37: 38) sts*
Cont straight until there are 21 (21: 21: 23: 23) fewer rows for Handknit DK Cotton or **25 (25: 25: 27: 27)** fewer rows for Denim, than on back to start of shoulder shaping, ending with a RS row.

SHAPE NECK

Cast (bind) off 5 (6: 6: 6: 6) sts at beg of next row.
29 (29: 30: 31: 32) sts
Dec 1 st at neck edge of next 5 rows, then on foll 4 (4: 4: 5: 5) alt rows for Handknit DK Cotton or **3 (3: 3: 4: 4)** alt rows for Denim, then every foll 4th row until 19 (19: 20: 20: 21) sts rem.
Work 3 (**5**) rows, ending with a WS row.

SHAPE SHOULDER

Cast (bind) off 6 (6: 7: 7: 7) sts at beg of next and foll alt row.
Work 1 row.
Cast (bind) off rem 7 (7: 6: 6: 7) sts.

right front

Cast on 47 (49: 52: 54: 57) sts using 3¼mm (US 3) needles.

ROW 1 (RS): K1 (1: 0: 0: 1), *P1, K1, rep from * to end.

ROW 2: *K1, P1, rep from * to last 1 (1: 0: 0: 1) st, K1 (1: 0: 0: 1).
These 2 rows form moss (seed) st.

Work another 7 rows in moss (seed) st, ending with a RS row.

ROW 10 (WS): Moss (seed) st to last 7 sts, M1 and turn, leaving last 7 sts on a holder for buttonhole band.
41 (43: 46: 48: 51) sts
Change to 4mm (US 6) needles.

NEXT ROW (RS): P7 (8: 9: 10: 11), K2, P1, moss (seed) st 7, P1, K2, P21 (22: 24: 25: 27).

NEXT ROW: K21 (22: 24: 25: 27), P2, K1, moss (seed) st 7, K1, P2, K7 (8: 9: 10: 11).
These 2 rows set the sts.
Complete to match left front, rev shaping.

left sleeve

SLEEVE FRONT

Cast on 38 (38: 39: 40: 40) sts using 4mm (US 6) needles.

ROW 1 (RS): (K1, P1) twice, K to end.

ROW 2: P to last 5 sts, K1, (P1, K1) twice.
Rep last 2 rows 9 times more, inc 1 st at end of 9th (**11th**) of these rows. *39 (39: 40: 41: 41) sts*
Break yarn and leave sts on a holder.

SLEEVE BACK

Cast on 14 (14: 15: 16: 16) sts using 4mm (US 6) needles.

ROW 1 (RS): K to last 4 sts, (P1, K1) twice.

ROW 2: K1, (P1, K1) twice, P to end.
Rep last 2 rows 9 times more, inc 1 st at beg of 9th (**11th**) of these rows. *15 (15: 16: 17: 17) sts*

JOIN SECTIONS

Handknit DK Cotton version

NEXT ROW (RS): Inc in first st of sleeve back, K to last 5 sts of this section, then with WS of sleeve front against RS of sleeve back, K tog first st of sleeve front with next st of sleeve back, K tog next 4 sts of sleeve front with rem 4 sts of sleeve back, K to last st of sleeve front, inc in last st. *51 (51: 53: 55: 55) sts*

Denim version

NEXT ROW (RS): K to last 5 sts of sleeve back then, with WS of sleeve front against RS of sleeve back, K tog first st of sleeve front with next st of sleeve back, K tog next 4 sts of sleeve front with rem 4 sts of sleeve back, K to end of sleeve front. *49 (49: 51: 53: 53) sts*

Both versions

Beg with a P row, cont in st st, inc 1 st at each end of every foll 10th (**12th**) row from previous inc until there are 55 (67: 67: 69: 65) sts for Handknit DK Cotton or **53 (67: 67: 69: 63)** sts for Denim, then on every foll 12th (0: 12th: 12th: 8th) row for Handknit DK Cotton or **14th (0: 14th: 14th: 10th)** row for Denim until there are 65 (67: 69: 71: 73) sts.
Cont straight until sleeve measures 40 (40: 41: 41: 41)cm (15¾ [15¾: 16¼: 16¼: 16¼]in) for Handknit DK Cotton, or **46.5 (46.5: 48: 48: 48)cm (18¼ [18¼: 18¾: 18¾: 18¾]in)** for Denim, ending with a WS row.

SHAPE TOP

Cast (bind) off 4 sts at beg of next 2 rows.
57 (59: 61: 63: 65) sts
Dec 1 st at each end of next 5 rows, then on foll 3 alt rows.
Work 3 rows.
Dec 1 st at each end of next and every foll 4th row until 33 (37: 39: 43: 45) sts rem for Handknit DK Cotton or **29 (31: 33: 35: 37)** sts rem for Denim.
Work 1 row.
Dec 1 st at each end of next and foll alt row until 27 sts rem.
Dec 1 st at each end of next 3 rows, ending with a

WS row. *21 sts.*
Cast (bind) off 4 sts at beg of next 2 rows.
Cast (bind) off rem 13 sts.

right sleeve

SLEEVE BACK

Cast on 14 (14: 15: 16: 16) sts using 4mm (US 6) needles.
ROW 1 (RS): (K1, P1) twice, K to end.
ROW 2: P to last 5 sts, K1, (P1, K1) twice.
Rep last 2 rows 9 times more, inc 1 st at end of
9th (**11th**) of these rows. *39 (39: 40: 41: 41) sts*
Break yarn and leave sts on a holder.

SLEEVE FRONT

Cast on 38 (38: 39: 40: 40) sts using 4mm (US 6) needles.
ROW 1 (RS): K to last 4 sts, (P1, K1) twice.
ROW 2: K1, (P1, K1) twice, P to end.
Rep last 2 rows 9 times more, inc 1 st at beg of
9th (**11th**) of these rows. *15 (15: 16: 17: 17) sts*

JOIN SECTIONS

Handknit DK Cotton version

NEXT ROW (RS): Inc in first st of sleeve front, K to last
5 sts of this section, then with WS of sleeve front
against RS of sleeve back, K tog next st of sleeve
front with first st of sleeve back, K tog rem 4 sts of
sleeve front with next 4 sts of sleeve back, K to last st
of sleeve back, inc in last st. *51 (51: 53: 55: 55) sts*

Denim version

NEXT ROW (RS): K to last 5 sts of sleeve front, then with
RS of sleeve back against WS of sleeve front, K tog
next st of sleeve front with first st of sleeve back, K tog
rem 4 sts of sleeve front with next 4 sts of sleeve back,
K to end of sleeve back. *49 (49: 51: 53: 53) sts*

Both versions

Complete as given for left sleeve.

finishing

Handknit DK Cotton version

Press all pieces as described on the information page.

Denim version

DO NOT PRESS.

Both versions

Join both shoulder seams using back stitch or mattress
stitch if preferred.

BUTTON BAND

Slip 7 sts left on holder for button band onto 3¼mm
(US 3) needles and rejoin yarn with RS facing.
Cont in moss (seed) st as set until band, when slightly
stretched, fits up left front to neck shaping, ending
with a WS row.
Cast (bind) off.
Slipstich band in place.
Mark positions for 5 buttons on this band, the lowest
button to come in 3rd row of band, the top button
1.5cm (¾in) below neck shaping and the rem 3
buttons evenly spaced between.

BUTTONHOLE BAND

Work as given for button band, rejoining yarn with
WS facing and with the addition of 5 buttonholes to
correspond with positions marked for buttons, as folls:
BUTTONHOLE ROW (RS): Moss (seed) st 2, cast (bind) off
2 sts, moss (seed) st to end and back, casting on 2 sts
over those cast (bound) off on previous row.
Slipstich band in place.

COLLAR

Cast on 83 (87: 87: 95: 95) sts using 3¼mm (US 3)
needles.
ROW 1 (RS): K3, (P1, K1) to last 4 sts, P1, K3.

ROW 2: K1, P2, K2, (P1, K1) to last 4 sts, K1, P2, K1.
These 2 rows set the sts.
Keeping sts correct as set, cont as folls:
ROW 3 (RS): K3, P1, M1, moss (seed) st to last 4 sts,
M1, P1, K3. *85 (89: 89: 97: 97) sts*
ROW 4: K1, P2, K1, moss (seed) st to last 4 sts, K1, P2,
K1.
ROW 5: K3, P1, moss (seed) st to last 4 sts, P1, K3.
ROW 6: K1, P2, K1, M1, moss (seed) st to last 4 sts,
M1, K1, P2, K1. *87 (91: 91: 99: 99) sts*
ROW 7: As row 5.
ROW 8: As row 4.
Rep rows 3 to 8, 2 (**3**) times more, and then rows
3 to 6 (**4**) again. *99 (103: 103: 111: 111) sts* for
Handknit DK Cotton or *101 (105: 105: 113: 113) sts*
for Denim.
Cast (bind) off in patt.

LEFT CUFF

Cast on 47 (47: 49: 51: 51) sts using 3¼mm (US 3)
needles.
Work in moss (seed) st as given for back for 6 rows.
ROW 7 (BUTTONHOLE ROW) (RS): Moss (seed) st 2, cast
(bind) off 2 sts, moss (seed) st to end.
ROW 8: Moss (seed) st to end, casting on 2 sts over
those cast (bound) off on previous row.
Work another 8 rows in moss (seed) st.
Cast (bind) off in moss (seed) st.

RIGHT CUFF

Work as given for left cuff, rev position of buttonhole
as folls:
ROW 7 (BUTTONHOLE ROW) (RS): Moss (seed) st to last 4
sts, cast (bind) off 2 sts, moss (seed) st to end.

POCKET FLAPS (MAKE 2)

Cast on 25 sts using 3¼mm (US 3) needles.
ROW 1 (RS): K3, P1, moss (seed) st to last 4 sts, P1, K3.
ROW 2: K1, P2, K1, moss (seed) st to last 4 sts, K1, P2,
K1.
These 2 rows set the sts.
Keeping sts correct as set, cont as folls:
Rep last 2 rows 5 (**6**) times more.
NEXT ROW (RS): K3, P1, P2tog, moss (seed) st to last 6
sts, P2tog, P1, K3.
NEXT ROW: K1, P2, K1, K2tog, moss (seed) st to last 6
sts, K2tog, K1, P2, K1. *21 sts*
Rep last 2 rows twice more and then first of these
2 rows again. *11 sts*
NEXT ROW (WS): K1, P2, K1, sl1, K2tog, psso, K1, P2,
K1.
NEXT ROW: K3, sl1, P2tog, psso, K3.
NEXT ROW: K1, P1, sl1, P2tog, psso, P1, K1.
NEXT ROW: K1, sl1, K2tog, psso, K1.
NEXT ROW: Sl1, K2tog, psso.
Fasten off.
After all knitting is complete, machine wash all
Denim pieces as described on ball band before sewing
together.
Sew cast-on edge of collar to neck edge, positioning
ends of collar halfway across top of front bands. Join
sleeve seams, then with RS facing, sew cast- (bound-)
off edge of cuff to lower edge of sleeve using back
stitch. Fold cuff down. Sew pocket flaps in place at
top of front moss (seed) st panels as in photograph.
See information page for finishing instructions,
setting in sleeves using the set-in method. Sew
buttons to front bands and cuffs to correspond with
buttonholes, and through all layers to secure pocket
flaps in place.

palm by Kim Hargreaves

SIZE	XS	S	M	L	XL	
To fit bust	81	86	91	97	102	cm
	32	34	36	38	40	in
Actual width	45.5	48.5	51	53.5	56	cm
	18	19	20	21	22	cm
Length	47	48	49	50	51	cm
	18½	19	19½	19½	20	in
Sleeve length	40	41	41	42	42	cm
	15½	16	16	16½	16½	in

YARN
Rowan Cotton Glacé 50gm (1¾oz) balls:

Pixie 723	11	11	12	12	13

NEEDLES
1 pair 2¾mm (US 2) needles
1 pair 3¼mm (US 3) needles

FASTENINGS
1 button
3 snaps

TENSION (GAUGE)
23 sts and 39 rows to 10cm (4in) measured over moss (seed) stitch using 3¼mm (US 3) needles

back
Cast on 93 (99: 105: 111: 117) sts using 2¾mm (US 2) needles.
Work 5 rows in garter st (knit every row), ending with a RS row.
Change to 3¼mm (US 3) needles and work in moss (seed) st as folls:
ROW 1 (WS): P1, *K1, P1, rep from * to end.
ROW 2: As row 1.
Cont in moss (seed) st, shaping side seams by inc 1 st at each end of 6th and every foll 12th row until there are 105 (111: 117: 123: 129) sts.
Cont straight until back measures 28 (28: 29: 29: 30)cm (11¼ [11¼: 11½: 11½: 12]in) from cast-on edge, ending with a WS row.
SHAPE ARMHOLES
Keeping patt correct, cast (bind) off 3 (4: 4: 5: 5) sts at beg of next 2 rows. *99 (103: 109: 113: 119) sts*
Dec 1 st at each end of next 7 (7: 9: 9: 11) rows, then on every foll alt row until 73 (75: 77: 79: 81) sts rem.
Cont straight until armhole measures 19 (20: 20: 21: 21)cm (7½ [7¾: 7¾: 8¼: 8¼]in), ending with a WS row.
SHAPE SHOULDERS AND BACK NECK
Keeping patt correct, cast (bind) off 5 (6: 6: 6: 6) sts at

beg of next 2 rows. *63 (63: 65: 67: 69) sts*
NEXT ROW (RS): Cast (bind) off 5 (6: 6: 6: 6) sts, patt until there are 10 (9: 9: 10: 11) sts on right needle and turn, leaving rem sts on a holder.
Work each side of neck separately.
Cast (bind) off 4 sts at beg of next row.
Cast (bind) off rem 6 (5: 5: 6: 7) sts.
With RS facing, rejoin yarn to rem sts, cast (bind) off center 33 (33: 35: 35: 35) sts, patt to end.
Work to match first side, rev shaping.

left front
Cast on 51 (54: 57: 60: 63) sts using 2¾mm (US 2) needles.
Work 5 rows in garter st, ending with a RS row.
Change to 3¼mm (US 3) needles and work in moss (seed) st as folls:
ROW 1 (WS): P1 (0: 1: 0: 1), *K1, P1, rep from * to end.
ROW 2: *P1, K1, rep from * to last 1 (0: 1: 0: 1) st, P1 (0: 1: 0: 1).
Cont in moss (seed) st, shaping side seam by inc 1 st at beg of 6th and every foll 12th row until there are 57 (60: 63: 66: 69) sts.
Cont straight until left front matches back to beg of armhole shaping, ending with a WS row.
SHAPE ARMHOLE
Keeping patt correct, cast (bind) off 3 (4: 4: 5: 5) sts at beg of next row. *54 (56: 59: 61: 64) sts*
Work 1 row. Dec 1 st at armhole edge of next 7 (7: 9: 9: 11) rows, then on every foll alt row until 41 (42: 43: 44: 45) sts rem.
Cont straight until there are 25 (25: 27: 27: 27) rows fewer than on back to start of shoulder shaping, ending with a RS row.
SHAPE NECK
Keeping patt correct, cast (bind) off 13 sts at beg of next row. *28 (29: 30: 31: 32) sts*
Dec 1 st at neck edge of next 7 rows, then on every foll alt row until 16 (17: 17: 18: 19) sts rem.
Work 7 rows, ending with a WS row.
SHAPE SHOULDER
Keeping patt correct, cast (bind) off 5 (6: 6: 6: 6) sts at beg of next and foll alt row.
Work 1 row.
Cast (bind) off rem 6 (5: 5: 6: 7) sts.

right front
Cast on 51 (54: 57: 60: 63) sts using 2¾mm (US 2) needles.

Work 5 rows in garter st, ending with a RS row.
Change to 3¼mm (US 3) needles and work in moss
(seed) st as folls:
ROW 1 (WS): *P1, K1, rep from * to last 1 (0: 1: 0: 1)
st, P1 (0: 1: 0: 1).
ROW 2: P1 (0: 1: 0: 1), *K1, P1, rep from * to end.
Cont as for left front, rev shaping, until there are
30 (30: 32: 32: 32) rows fewer than on back to start of
shoulder shaping, ending with a WS row.
NEXT ROW (RS) (BUTTONHOLE ROW): Moss (seed) st 3,
cast (bind) off 2 sts, moss (seed) st to end.
NEXT ROW: Moss (seed) st to end, casting on 2 sts over
those cast (bound) off on previous row.
Complete to match left front, rev shaping.

sleeves (both alike)
Cast on 47 (47: 49: 49: 51) sts using 2¾mm (US 2)
needles.
Work 5 rows in garter st, ending with a RS row.
Change to 3¼mm (US 3) needles and work in moss
(seed) st as for back, inc 1 st at each end of 8th and
every foll 12th row to 63 (63: 65: 53: 55) sts, then on
every foll 10th row until there are 71 (73: 75: 77: 79)
sts, taking inc sts into patt.
Cont straight until sleeve measures 40 (41: 41: 42:
42)cm (15¾ [16¼: 16¼: 16½: 16½]in) from cast-on
edge, ending with a WS row.
SHAPE TOP
Keeping patt correct, cast (bind) off 3 (4: 4: 5: 5) sts at
beg of next 2 rows. *65 (65: 67: 67: 69) sts*
Dec 1 st at each end of next 3 rows, then on foll
3 alt rows. *53 (53: 55: 55: 57) sts*
Work 3 rows, ending with a WS row.
Dec 1 st at each end of next and every foll 4th row
until 43 (41: 45: 43: 47) sts rem, then on every foll alt
row until 39 sts rem.
Dec 1 st at each end on next 5 rows, ending with a
WS row. *29 sts*
Cast (bind) off 4 sts at beg of next 2 rows.
Cast (bind) off rem 21 sts.

finishing
Press all pieces as described on the information page.
Join shoulder seams using back stitch.
NECKBAND
With RS facing and 2¾mm (US 2) needles, pick up
and knit 42 (42: 44: 44: 44) sts up right side of neck,
41 (41: 43: 43: 43) sts from back and 42 (42: 44: 44:
44) sts down left side of neck.
125 (125: 131: 131: 131) sts
Work 4 rows in garter st.
Cast (bind) off knitwise (on WS).

See information page for finishing instructions.
Sew on button to correspond with buttonhole in
right front. Sew press fastenings in line with
buttonhole at regular intervals along front opening
edge to avoid gaping.

opal by Kim Hargreaves

TENSION (GAUGE)
23 sts and 32 rows to 10cm (4in) measured over stocking (stockinette) stitch using 3¼mm (US 3) needles

left front

Cast on 115 (121: 127: 133: 139) sts using 3¼mm (US 3) needles.
Beg with a K row, work in st st throughout as folls:
Work 97 (101: 101: 105: 105) rows, ending with a RS row.

SHAPE FRONT SLOPE

**Dec 1 st at beg of next row and at same edge on every foll row until 64 (70: 76: 82: 88) sts rem, ending with a WS row.

SHAPE ARMHOLE

Cast (bind) off 7 (8: 8: 9: 9) sts at beg and dec 1 st at end of next row. *56 (61: 67: 72: 78) sts*
Dec 1 st at beg of next row.
Dec 1 st at both ends of next 7 (7: 9: 9: 11) rows, then on foll 8 (9: 9: 10: 10) alt rows. *25 (28: 30: 33: 35) sts*
Work 1 row.
Dec 1 st at front slope edge only on next and foll 0 (5: 9: 14: 15) alt rows. *24 (22: 20: 18: 19) sts*

For XS, S and M sizes

Work 3 rows.
Dec 1 st at front slope edge only on next and every foll 4th row until 16 (17: 17) sts rem.

For all sizes

Cont straight until armhole measures 21 (21: 22: 22: 23)cm (8¼ [8¼: 8½: 8½: 9]in), ending with a WS row.

SHAPE SHOULDER

Cast (bind) off 5 (6: 6: 6: 6) sts at beg of next and foll alt row.
Work 1 row. Cast (bind) off rem 6 (5: 5: 6: 7) sts.

right front

Cast on 91 (96: 102: 107: 113) sts using 3¼mm (US 3) needles.
Beg with a K row, work in st st throughout as folls:
Work 4 rows.
Inc 1 st at beg of next and every foll 4th row until there are 115 (121: 127: 133: 139) sts.
Work 3 rows.

SHAPE FRONT SLOPE

Cast (bind) off 3 sts at beg of next and foll alt row. *109 (115: 121: 127: 133) sts*
Complete to match left front from **, rev shaping.

SIZE	XS	S	M	L	XL	
To fit bust	81	86	91	97	102	cm
	32	34	36	38	40	in
Actual width	50	52.5	55	58	60.5	cm
	19½	20½	21½	23	24	cm
Length	68	69	70	71	72	cm
	27	27	27½	28	28½	in

YARN

Rowan Cotton Glacé 50gm (1¾oz) balls:

Fizz 722	10	11	12	12	13

NEEDLES

1 pair 2¾mm (US 2) needles
1 pair 3¼mm (US 3) needles
1 2¾mm (US 2) circular needle

back

Cast on 115 (121: 127: 133: 139) sts using 3¼mm (US 3) needles.

Beg with a K row, work in st st throughout as folls:
Cont straight until back measures same as fronts to start of armhole shaping, ending with a WS row.

SHAPE ARMHOLES

Cast (bind) off 7 (8: 8: 9: 9) sts at beg of next 2 rows.
101 (105: 111: 115: 121) sts

Dec 1 st at each end of next 7 (7: 9: 9: 11) rows, then on every foll alt row until 71 (73: 75: 77: 79) sts rem.
Cont straight until back matches fronts to start of shoulder shaping, ending with a WS row.

SHAPE SHOULDERS AND BACK NECK

Cast (bind) off 5 (6: 6: 6: 6) sts at beg of next 2 rows.
61 (61: 63: 65: 67) sts

NEXT ROW (RS): Cast (bind) off 5 (6: 6: 6: 6) sts, K until there are 10 (9: 9: 10: 11) sts on right needle and turn, leaving rem sts on a holder.
Work each side of neck separately.
Cast (bind) off 4 sts at beg of next row.
Work 1 row. Cast (bind) off rem 6 (5: 5: 6: 7) sts.
With RS facing, rejoin yarn to rem sts, cast (bind) off center 31 (31: 33: 33: 33) sts, K to end.
Work to match first side, rev shaping.

finishing

Press all pieces as described on the information page.
Join shoulder seams using back stitch.

FRONT OPENING AND NECK EDGING

With RS facing and 2¾mm (US 2) circular needle, starting at right front cast-on edge, pick up and knit 77 (80: 80: 83: 83) sts up right front opening edge to start of front slope shaping, 103 (103: 106: 106: 109) sts up right front slope, 39 (39: 41: 41: 41) sts from back, 103 (103: 106: 106: 109) sts down left front slope and 74 (77: 77: 80: 80) sts down left front opening edge to lower edge.
396 (402: 410: 416: 422) sts
Cast (bind) off knitwise (on WS).

ARMHOLE BORDERS

With RS facing and 2¾mm (US 2) needles, pick up and knit 110 (112: 118: 120: 124) sts evenly around armhole edge.
Cast (bind) off knitwise (on WS).
Join side and armhole border seams using back stitch, leaving seams open for first 40 rows.

SIDE-SEAM-OPENING BORDERS

With RS facing and 2¾mm (US 2) needles, pick up and knit 30 sts up first side of side-seam opening, and 30 sts down other side of opening. *60 sts*
Cast (bind) off knitwise (on WS).

Make 4 twisted cords, each about 40cm (16in) long, and knot one end. Attach 2 of these cords to inside corner of front slope and remaining 2 cords to corresponding side seam.
See information page for finishing instructions.

butterfly cardigan by Kim Hargreaves

SIZE	XS	S	M	L	XL	
To fit bust	81	86	91	97	102	cm
	32	34	36	38	40	in
Actual width	43	45.5	48	50.5	53	cm
	17	18	19	20	21	in
Length	44	45	46	47	48	cm
	17½	17½	18	18½	19	in
Sleeve length	41	41	42	42	43	cm
	16	16	16½	16½	17	in

YARN

Rowan Cotton Glacé 50gm (1¾oz) balls:

Orchid 120	10	11	12	12	13

Leftover yarn in contrast color for embroidery (optional); trimmed with Bonny 104 in photograph.

NEEDLES

1 pair 2¼mm (US 1) needles
1 pair 3mm (US 2/3) needles

BUTTONS

9

TENSION (GAUGE)

28 sts and 36 rows to 10cm (4in) measured over stocking (stockinette) stitch using 3mm (US 3) needles

back

Cast on 113 (119: 128: 134: 143) sts using 2¼mm (US 1) needles.
Work border as folls:
Knit 3 rows.
ROW 4 (WS): P2, *yrn, P2tog, P1, rep from * to end.
ROWS 5 TO 7: Knit.
ROW 8: Knit, inc 2 (2: 1: 1: 0) sts at end(s) of this row.
115 (121: 129: 135: 143) sts
These 8 rows complete border.
Change to 3mm (US 3) needles and, beg with a K row, cont in st st as folls:
Inc 1 st at each end of 9th and every foll 16th row until there are 121 (127: 135: 141: 149) sts.
Cont straight until back measures 24 (25: 25: 26: 26)cm (9½ [9¾: 9¾: 10¼: 10¼]in) from cast-on edge, ending with a WS row.

SHAPE ARMHOLES

Cast (bind) off 3 (4: 4: 5: 5) sts at beg of next 2 rows.
115 (119: 127: 131: 139) sts
Dec 1 st at each end of next 7 (7: 9: 9: 11) rows, then on every foll alt row until 85 (87: 91: 93: 97) sts rem.
Cont straight until armhole measures 20 (20: 21: 21: 22)cm (7¾ [7¾:8¼: 8¼: 8½]in), ending with a WS row.

SHAPE SHOULDERS AND BACK NECK

Cast (bind) off 6 (6: 7: 7: 8) sts at beg of next 2 rows.
73 (75: 77: 79: 81) sts
NEXT ROW (RS): Cast (bind) off 6 (6: 7: 7: 8) sts, K until there are 11 sts on right needle and turn, leaving rem sts on a holder.
Work each side of neck separately.
Cast (bind) off 4 sts at beg of next row.
Cast (bind) off rem 7 sts.
With RS facing, rejoin yarn to rem sts, cast (bind) off center 39 (41: 41: 43: 43) sts, K to end.
Work to match first side, rev shaping.

left front

Cast on 56 (59: 65: 68: 71) sts using 2¼mm (US 1) needles.
Work border-patt rows 1 to 7 as for back.
ROW 8: Knit, inc 2 (2: 0: 0: 1) sts at end(s) of this row.
58 (61: 65: 68: 72) sts
Change to 3mm (US 3) needles and, beg with a K row, cont in st st as folls:
Inc 1 st at beg of 9th and every foll 16th row until there are 61 (64: 68: 71: 75) sts.
Cont straight until left front matches back to beg of armhole shaping, ending with a WS row.

SHAPE ARMHOLE

Cast (bind) off 3 (4: 4: 5: 5) sts at beg of next row.
58 (60: 64: 66: 70) sts
Work 1 row.
Dec 1 st at armhole edge of next 7 (7: 9: 9: 11) rows, then on every foll alt row until 43 (44: 46: 47: 49) sts rem. Cont straight until left front is 23 (23: 25: 25: 25) rows shorter than back to start of shoulder shaping, ending with a RS row.

SHAPE NECK

Cast (bind) off 11 (12: 11: 12: 12) sts at beg of next row and 4 sts at beg of foll alt row.
28 (28: 31: 31: 33) sts
Dec 1 st at neck edge on next 5 rows, then on every foll alt row until 19 (19: 21: 21: 23) sts rem.
Work 7 rows, ending with a WS row.

SHAPE SHOULDER

Cast (bind) off 6 (6: 7: 7: 8) sts at beg of next and foll alt row.
Work 1 row. Cast (bind) off rem 7 sts.

right front

Cast on 56 (59: 65: 68: 71) sts using 2¼mm (US 1) needles.

Work border-patt rows 1 to 7 as for back.

ROW 8: Knit, inc 2 (2: 0: 0: 1) sts at end(s) of this row. *58 (61: 65: 68: 72) sts*

Change to 3mm (US 3) needles and, beg with a K row, cont in st st as folls:

Inc 1 st at end of 9th and every foll 16th row until there are 61 (64: 68: 71: 75) sts.

Complete to match left front, rev all shaping.

sleeves (both alike)

Cast on 56 (56: 59: 59: 62) sts using 2¼mm (US 1) needles.

Work border-patt rows 1 to 7 as for back.

ROW 8: Knit. *56 (56: 59: 59: 62) sts*

Change to 3mm (US 3) needles and, beg with a K row, cont in st st as folls:

Inc 1 st at each end of 5th and every foll 8th row to 70 (64: 71: 65: 70) sts, then on every foll 6th row until there are 92 (94: 97: 99: 102) sts.

Cont straight until sleeve measures 41 (41: 42: 42: 43)cm (16¼ [16¼: 16½: 16½: 17]in) from cast-on edge, ending with a WS row.

SHAPE TOP

Cast (bind) off 3 (4: 4: 5: 5) sts at beg of next 2 rows. *86 (86: 89: 89: 92) sts*

Dec 1 st at each end of next 7 rows, then on foll 6 (6: 7: 6: 7) alt rows. *60 (60: 61: 63: 64) sts*

Work 3 rows.

Dec 1 st at each end of next and every foll 4th row until 52 (52: 53: 53: 54) sts rem, then on every foll alt row until 46 (46: 47: 47: 48) sts rem.

Dec 1 st at each end of next 3 rows, ending with a WS row. *40 (40: 41: 41: 42) sts*

Cast (bind) off 5 sts at beg of next 2 rows, then 4 sts at beg of foll 2 rows.

Cast (bind) off rem 22 (22: 23: 23: 24) sts.

finishing

Press all pieces as described on the information page. Join both shoulder seams using back stitch.

NECKBAND

With RS facing and 2¼mm (US 1) needles, pick up and knit 36 (37: 38: 39: 39) sts up right side of neck, 47 (48: 49: 50: 50) sts from back and 36 (37: 38: 39: 39) sts down left side of neck. *119 (122: 125: 128: 128) sts*

Knit 4 rows.

ROW 5 (WS): P2, *yrn, P2tog, P1, rep from * to end.

ROWS 6 TO 8: Knit.

Cast (bind) off knitwise (on WS).

FRONT BORDERS (BOTH ALIKE)

With RS facing and 2¼mm (US 1) needles, pick up and knit 110 (113: 113: 116: 119) sts along one front opening edge between cast-on edge and top of neck border. Work rows 1 to 8 as for neck border.

Cast (bind) off knitwise (on WS).

Work border along other front opening edge in same way. See information page for finishing instructions.

Using eyelet holes of right front border as buttonholes, sew on buttons, the lowest button level with eyelets worked in left front border, the top button level with eyelets on neck border and the rem 7 buttons evenly spaced between.

embroidery (optional)

Using contrasting yarn, embroider a bullion stitch on eyelet row of all borders midway between eyelet holes.

butterfly vest by Kim Hargreaves

SIZE	XS	S	M	L	XL	
To fit bust	81	86	91	97	102	cm
	32	34	36	38	40	in
Actual width	33	33.5	38	40.5	43	cm
	13	14	15	16	17	cm
Length	21	22	22	23	23	cm
	8½	8½	8½	9	9	in

YARN

Rowan Cotton Glacé 50gm (1¾oz) balls:
Orchid 120   2   3   3   3   4
Leftover yarn in contrast color for embroidery
(optional); trimmed with Bonny 104 in photograph.

NEEDLES

1 pair 2mm (US 0) needles
1 pair 2¼mm (US 1) needles
1 pair 3mm (US 3) needles

TENSION (GAUGE)

28 sts and 36 rows to 10cm (4in) measured over
stocking (stockinette) stitch using 3mm (US 3)
needles

back and front (both alike)

Cast on 83 (89: 95: 101: 110) sts using 2¼mm
(US 1) needles.
Work border as folls:
Knit 3 rows.
ROW 4 (WS): P2, *yrn, P2tog, P1, rep from * to end.
ROWS 5 TO 7: Knit.
ROW 8: Knit, inc 0 (0: 2: 2: 1) sts at end(s) of this row.
83 (89: 97: 103: 111) sts
These 8 rows complete border.
Change to 3mm (US 3) needles and, beg with a
K row, cont in st st as folls:
Inc 1 st at each end of 3rd and every foll 10th row
until there are 93 (99: 107: 113: 121) sts.
Cont straight until work measures 21 (22: 22: 23:
23)cm (8¼ [8½: 8½: 9: 9]in) from cast-on edge,
ending with a WS row.
SHAPE ARMHOLES
Cast (bind) off 4 (5: 5: 6: 6) sts at beg of next 2 rows.
85 (89: 97: 101: 109) sts
Dec 1 st at each end of next 7 (7: 9: 9: 11) rows, then
on every foll alt row until 61 (63: 67: 69: 73) sts rem.
Work 1 row.

SHAPE NECK

NEXT ROW (RS): K2tog, K17 and turn, leaving rem sts
on a holder.
Work each side of neck separately.
Cast (bind) off 6 sts at beg of next row. Dec 1 st at
beg of next row. Cast (bind) off 4 sts at beg of next
and foll alt row. Cast (bind) off rem 3 sts.
With RS facing, rejoin yarn to rem sts, cast (bind) off
center 23 (25: 29: 31: 35) sts, K to end.
Work to match first side, rev shaping.

finishing

Press all pieces as described on the information page.
FRONT AND BACK NECK EDGING (BOTH ALIKE)
With RS facing and using 2¼mm (US 1) needles,
pick up and K 58 (61: 64: 67: 70) sts evenly along
upper shaped edge.
ROW 1 (WS): Knit.
ROW 2 AND EVERY RS ROW: Inc in first st, K to last st,
inc in last st.
ROW 3: Knit.
ROW 5: P2, *yrn, P2tog, P1, rep from * to end.
ROW 7: Knit.
ROW 8: As row 2.
Cast (bind) off knitwise (on WS).
SHOULDER STRAPS AND ARMHOLE EDGINGS (BOTH ALIKE)
Using 2mm (US 0) needles and thumb method, cast
on 81 (82: 84: 84: 86) sts for shoulder strap.
Break yarn and put to one side.
With RS facing and using 2¼mm (US 1) needles,
starting at top of left front side seam, pick up and
K 32 (33: 35: 38: 40) sts along left front armhole edge
to top of front edging, K across 81 (82: 84: 84: 86) sts
of shoulder strap, then pick up and K 32 (33: 35: 38:
40) sts along left back armhole edge, starting at top of
back edging and ending at top of left back side seam.
145 (148: 154: 160: 166) sts
ROW 1 (WS): Knit.
ROW 2 AND EVERY RS ROW: K2tog, K to last 2 sts, K2tog.
ROW 3: P2, *yrn, P2tog, P1, rep from * to end.
ROW 5: Knit.
ROW 6: As row 2.
Change to 2mm (US 0) needles and cast (bind) off
knitwise (on WS).
Embroidery (optional; see page 108)
See information page for finishing instructions.

tune by Kim Hargreaves

SIZE	XS	S	M	L	XL	
To fit bust	81	86	91	97	102	cm
	32	34	36	38	40	in
Actual width	40.5	43	45.5	48	50.5	cm
	16	17	18	19	20	cm
Length	45	46	47	48	49	cm
	17½	18	18½	19	19½	in

YARN
Rowan 4 ply Cotton 50gm (1¾oz) balls:
Wider-stripe vest

A Pool 124	3	4	4	5	5
B Ripple 121	2	2	2	2	2

Narrower-stripe vest

A Marine 102	3	3	3	3	3
B Bleached 113	2	2	3	3	3

NEEDLES
1 pair 2¼mm (US 1) needles
1 pair 3mm (US 3) needles

TENSION (GAUGE)
28 sts and 38 rows to 10cm (4in) measured over stocking (stockinette) stitch using 3mm (US 3) needles

wider-stripe vest
back
Cast on 100 (107: 114: 121: 128) sts using 2¼mm (US 1) needles and yarn A. Knit 4 rows.
Change to 3mm (US 3) needles and, beg with a K row, work in striped st st as folls:
ROWS 1 AND 2: Use yarn B.
ROWS 3 TO 6: Use yarn A.
These 6 rows form stripe patt.
**Keeping patt correct, inc 1 st at each end of 13th row from beg of stripes and every foll 12th row until there are 114 (121: 128: 135: 142) sts.
Cont straight until back measures 25 (26: 26: 27: 27)cm (9¾ [10¼: 10¼: 10¾: 10¾]in), ending with a WS row.
SHAPE ARMHOLES
Cast (bind) off 4 (5: 5: 6: 6) sts at beg of next 2 rows.
106 (111: 118: 123: 130) sts
Dec 1 st at each end of next 9 (9: 11: 11: 13) rows, then on foll 3 (4: 4: 5: 5) alt rows.
82 (85: 88: 91: 94) sts
Cont straight until armhole measures about 11cm (4¼in), ending after row 2.

Break off yarn B and cont in st st using yarn A only.
Cont straight until armhole measures 19 (19: 20: 20: 21)cm (7½ [7½: 7¾: 7¾: 8¼]in), ending with a WS row.
SHAPE BACK NECK
NEXT ROW (RS): K17 (18: 19: 20: 21) sts and turn, leaving rem sts on a holder.
Work each side of neck separately.
Cast (bind) off 5 sts at beg of next row.
12 (13: 14: 15: 16) sts
Dec 1 st at neck edge of next 2 rows.
10 (11: 12: 13: 14) sts
SHAPE SHOULDER
Cast (bind) off 3 (3: 3: 4: 4) sts at beg and dec 1 st at end of next row.
Work 1 row. Rep last 2 rows once more.
Cast (bind) off rem 2 (3: 4: 3: 4) sts.
With RS facing, rejoin yarn to rem sts, cast (bind) off center 48 (49: 50: 51: 52) sts, K to end.
Work to match first side, rev shaping.

front
Work as given for back until there are 6 rows fewer than on back to start of back neck shaping (this is 10 rows down from shoulder shaping), ending with a WS row.
SHAPE BACK NECK
NEXT ROW (RS): K20 (21: 22: 23: 24) sts and turn, leaving rem sts on a holder.
Work each side of neck separately.
Cast (bind) off 5 sts at beg of next row.
15 (16: 17: 18: 19) sts
Dec 1 st at neck edge of next 5 rows, then on foll alt row. *9 (10: 11: 12: 13) sts*
Work 1 row, ending with a WS row.
SHAPE SHOULDER
Cast (bind) off 3 (3: 3: 4: 4) sts at beg and dec 1 st at end of next row.
Work 1 row.
Cast (bind) off 3 (3: 3: 4: 4) sts at beg of next row.
Work 1 row.
Cast (bind) off rem 2 (3: 4: 3: 4) sts.
With RS facing, rejoin yarn to rem sts, cast (bind) off center 42 (43: 44: 45: 46) sts, K to end.
Work to match first side, rev shaping.

narrower-stripe vest
back
Cast on 100 (107: 114: 121: 128) sts using 2¼mm (US 1) needles and yarn A.
Knit 4 rows.
Change to 3mm (US 3) needles and, beg with a K row, work in striped st st as folls:
ROWS 1 AND 2: Use yarn B.
ROWS 3 AND 4: Use yarn A.
These 4 rows form stripe patt.
Working in stripes throughout, complete as given for back of wider-stripe vest from **.

front
Work as given for front of wider-stripe vest, working in narrower stripes throughout.

finishing
Press all pieces as described on the information page. Join right shoulder seam using back stitch or mattress stitch if preferred.
NECKBAND
With RS facing, using 2¼mm (US 1) needles and yarn A, pick up and knit 18 sts down left side of front neck, 42 (43: 44: 45: 46) sts from front, 18 sts up right side of front neck, 12 sts down right side of back neck, 48 (49: 50: 51: 52) sts from back and 12 sts up left side of back neck. *150 (152: 154: 156: 158) sts*
*ROW 1 (WS)**: Knit.
ROW 2: Purl.
ROWS 3 AND 4: As rows 1 and 2.
Cast (bind) off knitwise (on WS).
Join left shoulder and neckband seam using back stitch or mattress stitch if preferred.
ARMHOLE BORDERS (BOTH ALIKE)
With RS facing, using 2¼mm (US 1) needles and yarn A, pick up and knit 138 (140: 146: 148: 154) sts evenly around armhole edge.
Work from * to * as given for neckband.
See information page for finishing instructions.

raewyn by Debbie Bliss

SIZES

	CHILDREN'S (YRS)				LADIES'			MEN'S		
	4–6	6–8	8–10	S	M	L	S	M	L	
To fit chest	64	69	76	84	91	99	99	107	114	cm
	25	27	30	33	36	39	39	42	45	in
Actual width	46	50	54	58	62	66	66	70	74	cm
	18	19½	21½	23	24½	26	26	27½	29	in
Length	45	51	57	73	74	75	66	67	68	cm
	17½	20	22½	28½	29	29½	26	26½	27	in
Sleeve length	33	38	43	49	49	49	55	55	55	cm
	13	15	17	19½	19½	19½	21½	21½	21½	in

YARNS

Rowan Handknit DK Cotton 50gm (1¾oz) balls:

10	12	15	20	21	22	22	23	24

Rowan Denim 50gm (1¾oz) balls:

12	14	17	22	24	25	24	25	27

(Children's photographed in Handknit DK in Chime 204, ladies' photographed in Denim in Memphis 229, men's in Handknit DK in Zing 300)

NEEDLES

1 pair 3¼mm (US 3) needles
1 pair 4mm (US 6) needles
Cable needle

TENSION (GAUGE)

Handknit DK Cotton
20 sts and 28 rows to 10cm (4in) measured over stocking (stockinette) stitch using 4mm (US 6) needles

Denim (before washing)
20 sts and 28 rows to 10cm (4in) measured over stocking (stockinette) stitch using 4mm (US 6) needles

PATTERN NOTE

Denim will shrink in length when washed for the first time. Allowances have been made in this pattern for shrinkage.
The pattern is written for the 3 children's sizes, followed by the 3 ladies' sizes in **bold**, followed by the 3 men's sizes.

SHAPING NOTE

To keep cast- (bound-) off edges neat and to avoid them stretching too much, it is advisable to work 2 sts tog over tops of cables when casting binding off. Stitch counts given do NOT take into account these decreases.

SPECIAL ABBREVIATIONS

TW3R = Twist 3 right: Slip next st onto cable needle and leave at back of work, K2, then P1 from cable needle

TW3L = Twist 3 left: Slip next 2 sts onto cable needle and leave at front of work, P1, then K2 from cable needle

TW3RB = Slip next st onto cable needle and leave at back of work, (K1 tbl) twice, then P1 from cable needle

TW3LB = Slip next 2 sts onto cable needle and leave at front of work, P1, then (K1 tbl) twice from cable needle

C4F = Cable 4 front: Slip next 2 sts onto cable needle and leave at front of work, K2, then K2 from cable needle

C4B = Cable 4 back: Slip next 2 sts onto cable needle and leave at back of work, K2, then K2 from cable needle

C4FB = Slip next 2 sts onto cable needle and leave at front of work, (K1 tbl) twice, then (K1 tbl) twice from cable needle

TW5R = Slip next 2 sts onto cable needle and leave at front of work, K2, P1, then K2 from cable needle

MB = Make bobble as folls: P1, pick up loop lying between needles and (K1, P1) twice into this loop, turn and P4, turn and K4tog, P1, then pass bobble st over this P st

back

Children's and men's sizes only

Cast on 92 (100: 108) (132: 140: 148) sts using 3¼mm (US 3) needles.

ROW 1 (RS): *K1, P1, rep from * to end.

ROW 2: *P1, K1, rep from * to end. Rep last 2 rows 2 (3) times more.

Change to 4mm (US 6) needles.

Ladies' sizes only

Cast on 118 (124: 132:) sts using 4mm (US 6) needles.

All sizes

Handknit DK Cotton version

Beg with a K row, cont in st st until back measures 21 (24: 27: **35: 36: 37:** 31: 32: 33)cm (8¼ [9½: 10¾: **13¾: 14¼: 14½:** 12¼: 12½: 13]in) from cast-on edge, ending with a WS row.

Denim version

Beg with a K row, cont in st st until back measures 24.5 (28: 31.5: **41: 42: 43:** 36: 37.5: 38.5)cm (9¾ [11¼: 12½: **16¼: 16½: 17:** 14¼: 14¾: 15¼]in) from cast-on edge, ending with a WS row.

Both versions

NEXT ROW (RS): *K1, P1, rep from * to end.

NEXT ROW: *P1, K1, rep from * to end.

These 2 rows form moss (seed) st.

Work another 1 row in moss (seed) st.

Children's sizes only

NEXT ROW (WS): Moss (seed) st 8 (12: 16), inc once in each of next 2 sts, moss (seed) st 9, inc in next st, moss (seed) st 4, inc once in each of next 2 sts, moss (seed) st 7, inc once in each of next 2 sts, (moss (seed) st 10, inc once in each of next 2 sts) twice, moss (seed) st 7, inc once in each of next 2 sts, moss (seed) st 4, inc in next st, moss (seed) st 9, inc once in each of next 2 sts, moss (seed) st 8 (12: 16). *108 (116: 124) sts*

Ladies' and men's sizes only

NEXT ROW (WS): Moss (seed) st **2 (5: 9:** 9: 13: 17), inc once in each of next 2 sts, moss (seed) st 7, inc in next st, moss (seed) st 1, inc in next st, moss (seed) st 7, inc once in each of next 2 sts, moss (seed) st 9, inc in next st, moss (seed) st 4, inc once in each of next 2 sts, moss (seed) st 7, (inc once in each of next 2 sts, moss (seed) st 10) twice, inc once in each of next 2 sts, moss (seed) st 7, inc once in each of next 2 sts, moss (seed) st 4, inc in next st, moss (seed) st 9, inc once in each of next 2 sts, moss (seed) st 7, inc in next st, moss (seed) st 1, inc in next st, moss (seed) st 7, inc once in each of next 2 sts, moss (seed) st **2 (5: 9:** 9: 13: 17) *142 (**148: 156:** 156: 164: 172) sts*

All sizes

Starting and ending rows as indicated and repeating the patt rows throughout, cont in patt from chart as folls:

NEXT ROW (RS): Moss (seed) st 6 (10: 14: **0: 3: 7:** 7: 11: 15), work next 96 (**142:** 142) sts as row 1 of chart, moss (seed) st 6 (10: 14: **0: 3: 7:** 7: 11: 15).

This row sets position of chart with edge sts worked in moss (seed) st.

Handknit DK Cotton version

Cont straight until back measures 45 (51: 57: **70: 71: 72:** 66: 67: 68)cm (17¾ [20: 22½: **27½: 28: 28¼:** 26: 26¼: 26¾]in) from cast-on edge, ending with a WS row.

Denim version

Cont straight until back measures 52.5 (59.5: 66.5: **81.5: 83: 84:** 77: 78: 79.5)cm (20¾ [23½: 26¼: **32: 32½: 33:** 30: 30¾: 31¼]in) from cast-on edge, ending with a WS row.

Both versions

SHAPE SHOULDERS AND BACK NECK

Keeping chart correct, cast (bind) off 13 (14: 15: **16: 17: 18:** 18: 20: 21) sts at beg of next 2 rows.

82 (88: 94: 110: 114: 120: 120: 124: 130) sts

NEXT ROW (RS): Cast (bind) off 13 (14: 15: **16: 17: 18:** 18: 20: 21) sts, patt until there are 16 (17: 18: **20: 21: 23:** 23: 23: 25) sts on right needle and turn, leaving rem sts on a holder.

Work each side of neck separately.

Cast (bind) off 4 sts at beg of next row.

Cast (bind) off rem 12 (13: 14: **16: 17: 19:** 19: 19: 21) sts.

With RS facing, rejoin yarn to rem sts, cast (bind) off center 24 (26: 28: **38: 38)** sts, patt to end.

Work to match first side, rev shaping.

front

Handknit DK Cotton version

Work as given for back until there are 14 (**16: 18)** rows fewer than on back to start of shoulder shaping, ending with a WS row.

Denim version

Work as given for back until there are 16 (**20: 22)** rows fewer than on back to start of shoulder shaping, ending with a WS row.

Both versions

SHAPE NECK

NEXT ROW (RS): Patt 46 (49: 52: **61: 64: 68:** 68: 72: 76) sts and turn, leaving rem sts on a holder.

Work each side of neck separately.

Ladies' and men's sizes only

Cast (bind) off **4 (4)** sts at beg of next row.

*57 (60: 64: **64: 68: 72)** sts*

All sizes

Dec 1 st at neck edge of next 5 (**7: 7)** rows, then on foll 3 (**2: 2)** alt rows.

*38 (41: 44: **48: 51: 55:** 55: 59: 63) sts*

Cont straight until front matches back to start of shoulder shaping, ending at side edge.

SHAPE SHOULDER

Keeping chart correct, cast (bind) off 13 (14: 15: **16: 17: 18:** 18: 20: 21) sts at beg of next and foll alt row.

KEY

□	K on RS, P on WS
⊡	P on RS, K on WS
TW3R	TW3R
TW3L	TW3L
TW3RB	TW3RB
TW3LB	TW3LB
C4F	C4F
C4B	C4B
C4FB	C4FB
TW5R	TW5R
MB	MB

YOKE

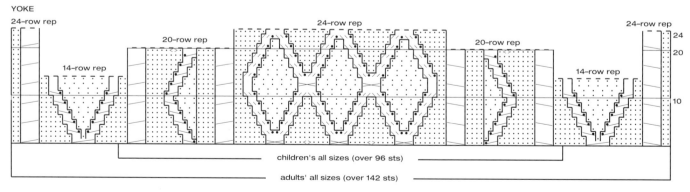

24-row rep   20-row rep   14-row rep   24-row rep   20-row rep   14-row rep   24-row rep

children's all sizes (over 96 sts)

adults' all sizes (over 142 sts)

Work 1 row.

Cast (bind) off rem 12 (13: 14: **16: 17: 19:** 19: 19: 21) sts.
With RS facing, rejoin yarn to rem sts, cast (bind) off
center 16 (18: 20: **20: 20)** sts, patt to end.
Work to match first side, rev shaping.

sleeves (both alike)

Cast on 42 (44: 46: **50: 54)** sts using 3¼mm (US 3)
needles.
Work in moss (seed) st as given for back for 8 (**2: 8)**
rows, ending with a WS row.

Ladies' sizes only

ROW 3 (RS): Moss (seed) st 4, *MB, moss (seed) st 8,
rep from * to last 6 sts, MB, moss (seed) st 4.
Work another 3 rows in moss (seed) st, ending with a
WS row.

All sizes

Change to 4mm (US 6) needles.
Beg with a K row, cont in st st as folls:

Handknit DK Cotton version

Inc 1 st at each end of 5th (**next:** 7th) and every foll
4th (**6th:** 6th) row until there are 64 (72: 78: **76:** 82) sts.
Work 1 (**5:** 3) rows, ending with a WS row.
Work in moss (seed) st for 3 rows, inc 1 st at each end
of 3rd (**1st:** 3rd) of these rows. 66 (74: 80: **78:** 84) sts
NEXT ROW (WS): Moss (seed) st 0 (0: 2: **1:** 4), (inc once in
each of next 2 sts) 0 (0: 1: **1:** 1) times, moss (seed) st 6
(10: 9: **9:** 9), inc in next st, moss (seed) st 4, inc once in
each of next 2 sts, moss (seed) st 7, (inc once in each of
next 2 sts, moss (seed) st 10) twice, inc once in each of
next 2 sts, moss (seed) st 7, inc once in each of next 2
sts, moss (seed) st 4, inc in next st, moss (seed) st 6 (10: 9:
9: 9), (inc once in each of next 2 sts) 0 (0: 1: **1:** 1) times,
moss (seed) st 0 (0: 2: **1:** 4). 78 (86: 96: **94:** 100) sts
Starting and ending rows as indicated and rep the patt
throughout, cont in patt, foll chart for sleeve as folls:
Inc 1 st at each end of 3rd (**3rd:** 5th) and every foll
6th (**4th:** 4th) row until there are 88 (96: 108: **114:**
118) sts, taking inc sts into patt.
Cont straight until sleeve measures 33 (38: 43: **49:** 55)cm
(13 [15: 17: **19¼:** 21½]in), ending with a WS row.

Denim version

Inc 1 st at each end of 5th (**next:** 7th) and every foll
6th (**6th:** 6th) row until there are 60 (66: 72: **80:** 86) sts.
Work 5 (3: 1: **5:** 5) rows, ending with a WS row.
Work in moss (seed) st for 3 rows, inc 1 st at each end
of 1st (3rd: 3rd: **1st:** 1st) of these rows.
*62 (68: 74: **82:** 88) sts*
NEXT ROW (WS): Moss (seed) st 0 (**3:** 6), (inc once in
each of next 2 sts) 0 (0: 1: **1:** 1) times, moss (seed) st 4
(7: 8: **9:** 9), inc in next st, moss (seed) st 4, inc once in
each of next 2 sts, moss (seed) st 7, (inc once in each of
next 2 sts, moss (seed) st 10) twice, inc once in each of
next 2 sts, moss (seed) st 7, inc once in each of next 2
sts, moss (seed) st 4, inc in next st, moss (seed) st 4 (7:
8: **9:** 9), (inc once in each of next 2 sts) 0 (0: 1: **1:** 1)
time, moss (seed) st 0 (**3:** 6). 74 (80: 90: **98:** 104) sts
Starting and ending rows as indicated and repeating
the patt rows throughout, cont in patt, foll chart for
sleeve as folls:
Inc 1 st at each end of 3rd and every foll 4th (**6th:**
8th) row until there are 88 (96: 108: **114:** 118) sts,
taking inc sts into patt.
Cont straight until sleeve measures 38.5 (44.5: 50: **57:**
64)cm (15¼ [18: 19¾: **22½:** 25¼]in) ending with a
WS row.

Both versions

Cast (bind) off in patt.

These 2 rows form rib.

Work in rib for another 3 (5) rows, ending with a WS row.

Beg with a K row, work in st st for 6 rows.

Ladies' sizes only

Work in moss (seed) st as given for back for 1 row.

ROW 2 (RS): Moss (seed) st 6, *MB, moss (seed) st 8, rep from * to last 8 sts, MB, moss (seed) st 6.

Work another 3 rows in moss (seed) st.

All sizes

Cast (bind) off.

Ladies' sizes only

HEM EDGING

With RS facing and using 3¼mm (US 3) needles, pick up and knit **121 (121: 132)** sts across cast-on edge of back.

ROW 1 (WS): K1, *P1, K1, rep from * to end.

This row sets position of moss (seed) st.

Work another 2 rows in moss (seed) st, ending with a WS row.

**Keeping moss (seed) st correct, cont as folls:

NEXT ROW (RS): Moss (seed) st 11 and turn.

Work on this set of 11 sts only for first point.

Work 5 rows, dec 1 st at each end of 2nd and foll alt row. *7 sts*

NEXT ROW: Work 2 tog, moss (seed) st 1, (K1, P1) twice into next st, turn and P4, turn and K4, turn and (P2tog) twice, turn and K2tog, moss (seed) st 1, work 2 tog. *5 sts*

Work 3 rows, dec 1 st at each end of 2nd of these rows. *3 sts*

NEXT ROW: Sl1, work 2 tog, psso.

Fasten off.

Return to rem sts and rejoin yarn with RS facing.***

Rep from ** to *** until all sts have been worked.

Work edging across cast-on edge of front in same way.

All sizes

After all knitting is complete, machine wash all Denim pieces as described on ball band before sewing together.

See information page for finishing instructions, setting in sleeves using the straight cast-off method.

finishing

Handknit DK Cotton version

Press all pieces as described on the information page.

Denim version

DO NOT PRESS.

Both versions

Join right shoulder seam using back stitch or mattress stitch if preferred.

NECKBAND

With RS facing and using 3¼mm (US 3) needles, pick up and knit 17 (**24**: 24) sts down left side of neck, 16 (18: 20: **20**: 20) sts from front, 17 (**24**: 24) sts up right side of neck and 32 (34: 36: **46**: 46) sts from back. *82 (86: 90: **114**: 114) sts*

Children's and men's sizes only

ROW 1 (WS): P2, *K2, P2, rep from * to end.

ROW 2: K2, *P2, K2, rep from * to end.

KEY

☐	K on RS, P on WS
⊡	P on RS, K on WS
⊡⟋	TW3R
⟍⊡	TW3L
⊡⟋⟋	TW3RB
⟍⟍⊡	TW3LB
⟋	C4F
⟋	C4B
⧓	C4FB
⟋⟋	TW5R
⧓	MB

SLEEVE

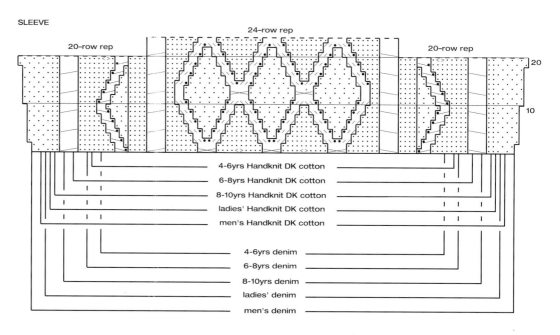

hope by Kim Hargreaves

KEY

☐ K on RS,
P on WS

▣ P on RS,
K on WS

⬜ C3B

⬜ C3F

⬜ CR3R

⬜ CR3L

⬜ C6B

⬜ C6F

SIZE

SIZE	XS	S	M	L	XL	
To fit bust	81	86	91	97	102	cm
	32	34	36	38	40	in
Actual width	47	50.5	53	56.5	59	cm
	18½	20	21	22	23	in
Length	47	48	49	50	51	cm
	18½	19	19½	19½	20	in
Sleeve length	41	41	42	42	42	cm
	16	16	16½	16½	16½	in

YARN

Rowan All Seasons Cotton 50gm (1¾oz) balls:

Bleached 182	10	11	12	12	13

NEEDLES

1 pair 4½mm (US 7) needles
1 pair 5mm (US 8) needles
Cable needle

TENSION (GAUGE)

17 sts and 24 rows to 10cm (4in) measured over stocking (stockinette) stitch using 5mm (US 8) needles

SPECIAL ABBREVIATIONS

CR3R = Cross 3 right: Slip next st onto cable needle and leave at back of work, K2, then P1 from cable needle

CR3L = Cross 3 left: Slip next 2 sts onto cable needle and leave at front of work, P1, then K2 from cable needle

C3B = Cable 3 back: Slip next st onto cable needle and leave at back of work, K2, then K1 from cable needle

C3F = Cable 3 front: Slip next 2 sts onto cable needle and leave at front of work, K1, then K2 from cable needle

C6B = Cable 6 back: Slip next 3 sts onto cable needle and leave at back of work, K3, then K3 from cable needle

C6F = Cable 6 front: Slip next 3 sts onto cable needle and leave at front of work, K3, then K3 from cable needle

back

Cast on 86 (92: 98: 104: 110) sts using 4½mm (US 7) needles.

ROW 1 (RS): P3 (0: 3: 0: 3), K2, (P4, K2) 5 (6: 6: 7: 7) times, P2, K12, P2, (K2, P4) 5 (6: 6: 7: 7) times, K2, P3 (0: 3: 0: 3).

ROW 2: K3 (0: 3: 0: 3), P2, (K4, P2) 5 (6: 6: 7: 7) times, K2, P12, K2, (P2, K4) 5 (6: 6: 7: 7) times, P2, K3 (0: 3: 0: 3).

Rep these 2 rows 6 times more.

Change to 5mm (US 8) needles.

Starting and ending rows as indicated and repeating the patt rows as detailed throughout, cont in patt from chart as folls:

Inc 1 st at each end of next and every foll 8th row until there are 98 (104: 110: 116: 122) sts, taking inc sts into patt.

Cont straight until back measures 27 (28: 28: 29: 29)cm (10¾ [11¼: 11¼: 11½: 11½]in), ending with a WS row.

SHAPE ARMHOLES

Keeping patt correct, cast (bind) off 3 (4: 4: 5: 5) sts at beg of next 2 rows. *92 (96: 102: 106: 112) sts*

Dec 1 st at each end of next 5 (5: 7: 7: 9) rows, then

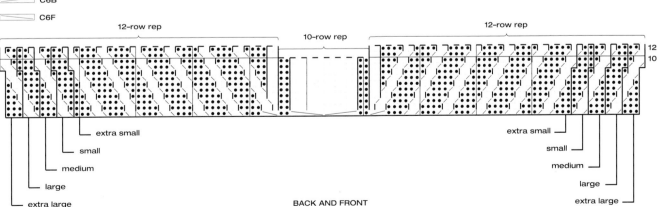

12-row rep 10-row rep 12-row rep

extra small
small
medium
large
extra large

extra small
small
medium
large
extra large

BACK AND FRONT

on foll 4 (5: 5: 6: 6) alt rows. *74 (76: 78: 80: 82) sts*
Cont straight until armhole measures 20 (20: 21: 21: 22)cm (7¾ [7¾: 8¼: 8¼: 8½]in), ending with a WS row.

SHAPE SHOULDERS AND BACK NECK
Cast (bind) off 6 (7: 7: 7: 8) sts at beg of next 2 rows. *62 (62: 64: 66: 66) sts*
NEXT ROW (RS): Cast (bind) off 6 (7: 7: 7: 8) sts, patt until there are 11 (10: 11: 12: 11) sts on right needle and turn, leaving rem sts on a holder.
Work each side of neck separately.
Cast (bind) off 4 sts at beg of next row.
Cast (bind) off rem 7 (6: 7: 8: 7) sts.
With RS facing, slip center 28 sts onto a holder, rejoin yarn to rem sts, patt to end.
Work to match first side, rev shaping.

front

Work as given for back until there are 14 rows fewer than on back to start of shoulder shaping, ending with a WS row.

SHAPE NECK
NEXT ROW (RS): Patt 26 (27: 28: 29: 30) sts and turn, leaving rem sts on a holder.
Work each side of neck separately.
Dec 1 st at neck edge of next 4 rows, then on foll 3 alt rows. *19 (20: 21: 22: 23) sts*
Work 3 rows, ending with a WS row.

SHAPE SHOULDER
Cast (bind) off 6 (7: 7: 7: 8) sts at beg of next and foll alt row.
Work 1 row. Cast (bind) off rem 7 (6: 7: 8: 7) sts.
With RS facing, slip center 22 sts onto a holder, rejoin yarn to rem sts, patt to end.
Work to match first side, rev shaping.

left sleeve

Cast on 54 (54: 56: 58: 58) sts using 4½mm (US 7) needles.
ROW 1 (RS): P2 (2: 3: 4: 4), *K2, P4, rep from * to last 4 (4: 5: 6: 6) sts, K2, P2 (2: 3: 4: 4).
ROW 2: K2 (2: 3: 4: 4), *P2, K4, rep from * to last 4 (4: 5: 6: 6) sts, P2, K2 (2: 3: 4: 4).
Rep these 2 rows 6 times more.

Change to 5mm (US 8) needles.
Starting and ending rows as indicated and rep the 12 patt rows throughout, cont in patt from chart as folls:
Inc 1 st at each end of 3rd and every foll 10th row to 70 (64: 68: 70: 62) sts, then on every foll 0 (8th: 8th: 8th: 8th) row until there are 70 (72: 74: 76: 78) sts, taking inc sts into patt.
Cont straight until left sleeve measures 41 (41: 42: 42: 42)cm (16¼ [16¼: 16½: 16½: 16½]in), ending with a WS row.

SHAPE TOP
Keeping patt correct, cast (bind) off 3 (4: 4: 5: 5) sts at beg of next 2 rows. *64 (64: 66: 66: 68) sts*
Dec 1 st at each end of next 5 rows, then on foll 2 alt rows, then on every foll 4th row until 44 (44: 46: 46: 48) sts rem. Work 1 row.
Dec 1 st at each end of next and foll 1 (1: 2: 2: 3) alt rows, then on foll 5 rows, ending with a WS row. *30 sts*
Cast (bind) off 4 sts at beg of next 2 rows.
Cast (bind) off rem 22 sts.

right sleeve

Work as given for left sleeve, foll chart for right sleeve.

finishing

Press all pieces as described on the information page.
Join right shoulder seam using back stitch or mattress stitch if preferred.

NECKBAND
With RS facing and using 4½mm (US 7) needles, pick up and knit 20 sts down left side of neck, patt across 22 sts from front holder, pick up and knit 19 sts up right side of front neck and 6 sts from right side of back neck, patt across 28 sts from back holder, then pick up and knit 7 sts from left side of back neck. *102 sts*
ROW 1 (WS): P1, (K2, P2) 3 times, K2, P12, K2, (P2, K2) 9 times, P12, (K2, P2) 6 times, P1.
This row sets position of rib with center front and back sts still worked as cable.
Keeping cable correct, work 16 rows.
Cast (bind) off, dec 6 sts across top of each cable.
See information page for finishing instructions, setting in sleeves using the set-in method.

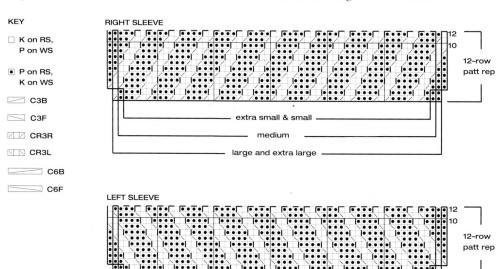

KEY

☐ K on RS, P on WS

▣ P on RS, K on WS

◿ C3B

◹ C3F

CR3R

CR3L

C6B

C6F

RIGHT SLEEVE

12
10
12-row patt rep

extra small & small
medium
large and extra large

LEFT SLEEVE

12
10
12-row patt rep

extra small & small
medium
large and extra large

bark pullover and tunic by Louisa Harding

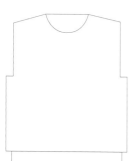

SIZE
Tunic

One size to fit up to	97	cm
	38	in
Actual width	58.5	cm
	23	in
Length	69.5	cm
	27½	in
Sleeve length	49	cm
	19¼	in

Pullover

One size to fit up to	107	cm
	42	in
Actual width	62.5	cm
	24½	in
Length	66	cm
	26	in
Sleeve length	49	cm
	19¼	in

YARN
Rowan Wool Cotton 50gm (1¾oz) balls:
Tunic
Dream 929   17
Pullover
Camel 945   17

NEEDLES
1 pair 3mm (US 3) needles
1 pair 3¾mm (US 5) needles

TENSION (GAUGE)
24 sts and 32 rows to 10cm (4in) measured over
textured pattern 3¾mm (US 5) needles

PATTERN NOTE
The pattern is written for the tunic followed by the
pullover in **bold**; where only 1 figure is given, this
refers to both versions.

back
Cast on 130 (**140**) sts using 3mm (US 3) needles.
Tunic only
Work 32 rows in patt from chart.
Change to 3¾mm (US 5) needles and cont in patt from
chart until chart row 140 has been completed and AT
THE SAME TIME inc 1 st at each end of next row and
4 foll 22nd rows to 140 sts, ending with a WS row.
Pullover only
Work 6cm (2½in) in K2, P2 rib, ending with a RS row.
NEXT ROW (WS) (INC): Rib 12, (M1, rib 13) 9 times,
M1, rib 11. *150 sts*
Change to 3¾mm (US 5) needles and, beg at chart
row 30, cont in patt from chart until chart row 140
completed, ending with a WS row.
Tunic and pullover
SHAPE ARMHOLE
Cast (bind) off 6 sts at beg of next 2 rows.
Cont without further shaping until chart row 222 has
been completed, ending with a WS row.
Tunic only
SHAPE SHOULDERS AND TURTLE NECK
Change to 3mm (US 3) needles.
Cast (bind) off 8 sts at beg of next 2 rows and 6 sts at
beg of foll 6 rows. *76 sts*
Dec 1 st at each end of next 4 rows and 4 foll alt
rows. *60 sts*
Cont without further shaping until chart row 260 has
been completed.
Cast (bind) off loosely and evenly.

Pullover only

SHAPE SHOULDERS AND BACK NECK

Cast (bind) off 15 sts, patt 37 sts, turn, leaving rem sts on a holder.

Work each side separately.

Cast (bind) off 3 sts at beg of next row, patt to end.

Cast (bind) off 16 sts, patt to last 2 sts, k2tog.

NEXT ROW: K2tog, patt to end.

Cast (bind) off rem 16 sts.

With RS facing, rejoin yarn to rem sts, cast (bind) off center 34 sts, patt to end.

Complete to match first side.

front

Tunic

Work as for back.

Pullover

Work as for back until chart row 204 has been completed.

SHAPE FRONT NECK

Patt 61 sts, turn, leaving rem sts on a holder.

Work each side separately.

Cast (bind) off 3 sts at beg of next row and foll alt row.

Dec 1 st at neck edge on the next 4 rows and 4 foll alt rows. *47 sts*

Cont without further shapiing until chart row 222 has been completed, ending with a WS row.

SHAPE SHOULDER

Cast (bind) off 15 sts at beg of next row and 16 at beg of foll alt row.

Work 1 row.

Cast (bind) off rem 16 sts.

With RS facing, rejoin yarn to rem sts, cast (bind) off center 16 sts, patt to end.

Complete to match first side.

sleeves (both alike)

Cast on 50 sts using 3mm (US 3) needles.

ROW 1 (WS): K2, (P2, K2) to end.

ROW 2: P2, (K2, P2) to end.

Rep these 2 rows until work measures 8 (**6**)cm (3¼ [**2½**]in) from cast-on edge, ending with a RS row.

NEXT ROW (WS) (INC): Rib 8, (M1, rib 7) 5 times, M1 rib 7. *56 sts*

Change to 3¾mm (US 5) needles and work 130 (**138**) rows in patt from chart and AT THE SAME TIME shape sides by inc 1 st at each end of 3rd row, 4 foll 3rd rows and then every foll 4th row to 120 sts.

Cast (bind) off loosely and evenly.

finishing

Press pieces as described on the information page, taking care not to flatten textured pattern.

Tunic

To keep the shoulder seam from stretching during wearing, join shoulder and neck seams using a very firm back stitch.

Pullover

Join right shoulder seam.

With RS facing and 3mm (US 3) needles, pick up and K 22 sts down left front neck, 16 sts across center front, 22 sts up right front neck and 44 sts across back neck. *104 sts*

Work 3cm (1¼in) in K2, P2 rib.

Cast (bind) off loosely and evenly.

See information page for finishing instructions.

KEY

☐ K on RS,
    P on WS

⊡ P on RS,
    K on WS

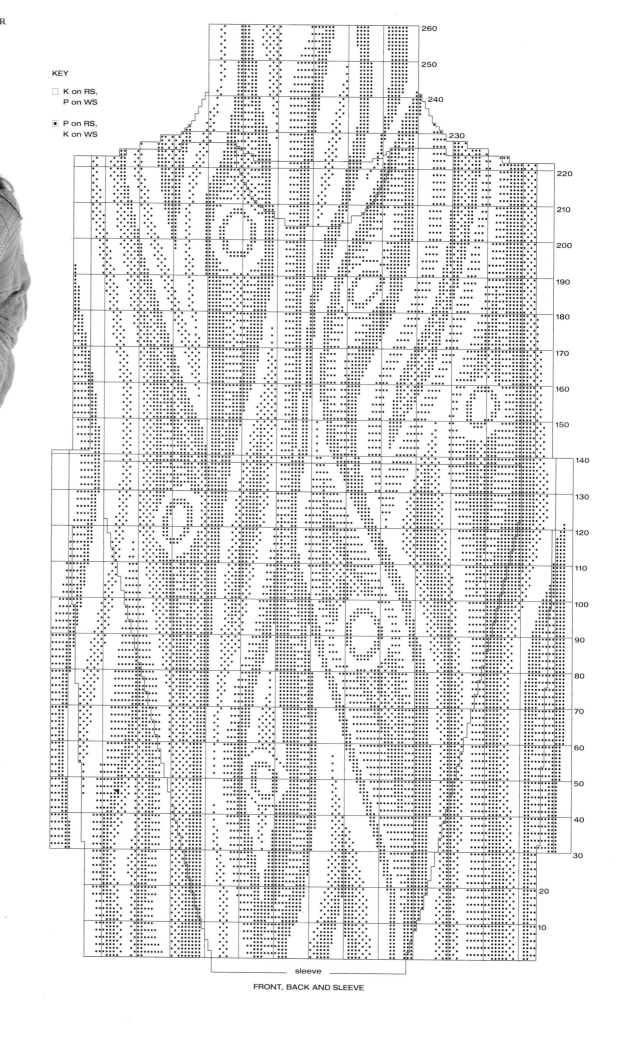

260
250
240
230
220
210
200
190
180
170
160
150
140
130
120
110
100
90
80
70
60
50
40
30
20
10

sleeve

FRONT, BACK AND SLEEVE

faye by Kim Hargreaves

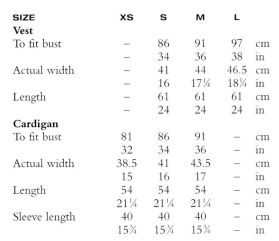

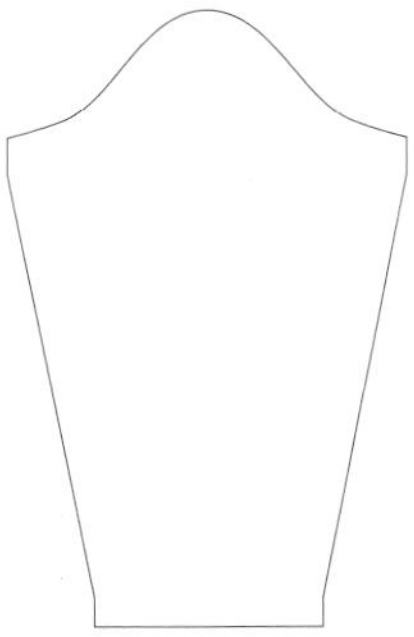

SIZE	XS	S	M	L	
Vest					
To fit bust	–	86	91	97	cm
	–	34	36	38	in
Actual width	–	41	44	46.5	cm
	–	16	17¼	18¼	in
Length	–	61	61	61	cm
	–	24	24	24	in
Cardigan					
To fit bust	81	86	91	–	cm
	32	34	36	–	in
Actual width	38.5	41	43.5	–	cm
	15	16	17	–	in
Length	54	54	54	–	cm
	21¼	21¼	21¼	–	in
Sleeve length	40	40	40	–	cm
	15¾	15¾	15¾	–	in

YARNS
Rowan 4-ply Cotton 50gm (1¾oz) balls:
Vest

Cobalt 108	–	5	6	6

Cardigan

Opaque 112	7	8	8	–

NEEDLES
1 pair 2¼mm (US 1) needles
1 pair 3mm (US 3) needles

BUTTONS
7

BEADS (CARDIGAN ONLY)
About 5,000 tiny glass beads. Thread beads onto yarn before beginning to knit. Beads are then slipped along yarn and into position as required.

TENSION (GAUGE)
31 sts and 43 rows to 10cm (4in) measured over cardigan beaded pattern using 3mm (US 3) needles; 29 sts and 38 rows to 10cm measured over vest textured pattern using 3mm (US 3) needles

PATTERN NOTE
The cardigan and vest are both given in three sizes but, as tension varies between designs, these three sizes also vary. Only the cardigan is available in extra small (following first set of figures), and only the vest in large (following third set of figures). For the small-size cardigan, follow the second set of figures, but for the small vest, follow the first set of figures. For the medium-size cardigan, follow the third set of figures, but for the medium vest, follow the second set of figures.

SPECIAL ABBREVIATIONS
M2 = Make 2 sts as folls: pick up horizontal loop lying between needles onto left needle and K then P into back of it.
BEAD 1 = Bring yarn to front of work and slip next st, slide bead along yarn so that it sits in front of slipped st, take yarn to back of work. K next st tightly, ensuring bead sits neatly over previous st.

cardigan and vest
back
LEFT BACK PANEL
Cast on 25 (29: 33) sts using 2¼mm (US 1) needles.
ROW 1 (RS): K1, *P1, K1, rep from * to end.
This row forms moss (seed) st.
Work another 5 rows in moss (seed) st.
ROW 7 (RS) (INC): K1, P1, M2, patt to end. *27 (31: 35) sts*
Patt 5 rows.
ROW 13: As row 7. *29 (33: 37) sts*
Patt 3 rows, thus ending with a WS row.
Break yarn and leave sts on a holder.

CENTER BACK PANEL
Cast on 55 sts using 2¼mm (US 1) needles.
Work 6 rows in moss (seed) st as for left back panel.
ROW 7 (RS) (INC): K1, P1, M2, patt to last 2 sts, M2, P1, K1. *59 sts*
Patt 5 rows.
ROW 13: As row 7. *63 sts*
Patt 3 rows, thus ending with a WS row.
Break yarn and leave sts on another holder.

RIGHT BACK PANEL
Cast on 25 (29: 33) sts using 2¼mm (US 1) needles.
Work 6 rows in moss (seed) st as for left back panel.
ROW 7 (RS) (INC): Patt to last 2 sts, M2, P1, K1.
27 (31: 35) sts
Patt 5 rows.
ROW 13: As row 7. *29 (33: 37) sts*
Patt 3 rows, thus ending with a WS row.

JOIN PANELS
NEXT ROW (RS): Patt to last st of right back panel, holding center panel in front of right back panel, K last st of right back panel together with first st of center panel, patt to last st of center panel, holding center panel in front of left back panel, K last st of center panel together with first st of left back panel,

patt to end. *119 (127: 135) sts*
P 1 row.
Change to 3mm (US 3) needles and work in patt
as folls:

Cardigan only
ROW 1 (RS): K3 (7: 11), *bead 1, K7, rep from * to last
4 (8: 12) sts, bead 1, K3 (7: 11).
ROW 2: Purl.

Vest only
ROW 1 (RS): K3 (7: 11), *P1, K7, rep from * to last
4 (8: 12) sts, P1, K3 (7: 11).
ROW 2: Purl.

Cardigan and vest
These 2 rows form patt.

SHAPE SIDE SEAMS AND DARTS
Place markers on 28th (32nd: 36th) st from each end
of last row.
ROW 3 (RS) (DEC): K2tog, (patt to within 2 sts of
marked st, sl1, K1, psso, patt marked st, K2tog) twice,
patt to last 2 sts, K2tog. *113 (121: 129) sts*
Patt 15 rows.
Rep last 16 rows twice more, then row 3 again.
95 (103: 111) sts
Patt 19 rows, thus ending with a WS row.
ROW 71 (RS) (INC): Inc in first st, (patt to marked st,
M1, patt marked st, M1) twice, patt to last st, inc in
last st. *101 (109: 117) sts*
Patt 13 rows.
Rep last 14 rows twice more, then row 71 again.
119 (127: 135) sts
Patt 25 rows, thus ending with a WS row.

SHAPE ARMHOLES
Keeping patt correct, cast (bind) off 4 (6: 8) sts at beg
of next 2 rows. *111 (115: 119) sts*
Dec 1 st at each end of next 9 rows, then on every
foll alt row until 79 (83: 87) sts rem.

Cardigan only
Patt 51 rows, thus ending with a WS row.

SHAPE BACK NECK AND SHOULDERS
Cast (bind) off 6 (7: 7) sts at beg of next 2 rows.
67 (69: 73) sts
NEXT ROW (RS): Cast (bind) off 6 (7: 7) sts, patt until
there are 10 (10: 12) sts on right needle and turn,
leaving rem sts on a holder.
Work each side of neck separately.
Cast (bind) off 4 sts at beg of next row.
Cast (bind) off rem 6 (6: 8) sts.

Vest only
Work 1 row, thus ending with a WS row.
Dec 1 st at each end of next and every foll 4th row
until 71 (75: 79) sts rem.
Patt 37 rows, thus ending with a WS row.

SHAPE BACK NECK AND SHOULDERS
Cast (bind) off 5 (5: 6) sts at beg of next 2 rows.
61 (65: 67) sts
NEXT ROW (RS): Cast (bind) off 5 (5: 6) sts, patt until
there are 8 (10: 10) sts on right needle and turn,
leaving rem sts on a holder.
Work each side of neck separately.
Cast (bind) off 4 sts at beg of next row.
Cast (bind) off rem 4 (6: 6) sts.

Cardigan and vest
With RS facing, rejoin yarn to rem sts, cast (bind) off
center 35 sts, patt to end.
Work to match first side, rev shaping.

cardigan and vest
left front
LEFT CENTER PANEL
Cast on 31 sts using 2¼mm (US 1) needles.
Work 6 rows in moss (seed) st as for left back panel.
ROW 7 (RS) (INC): K1, P1, M2, patt to end. *33 sts*
Patt 5 rows.
ROW 13: As row 7. *35 sts*
Patt 2 rows, thus ending with a RS row.
ROW 16 (WS): Patt 5 sts and slip these sts onto a safety
for button band, M1, patt to end. *31 sts*
Break yarn and leave sts on a holder.

LEFT SIDE PANEL
Work as for right back panel. *29 (33: 37) sts*

JOIN PANELS
NEXT ROW (RS): Patt to last st of left side panel, holding
left center panel in front of left side panel, K last st of
side panel together with first st of center panel, patt to
end. *59 (63: 67) sts*
P 1 row.
Change to 3mm (US 3) needles and work in patt as folls:

Cardigan only
ROW 1 (RS): K3 (7: 11), *bead 1, K7, rep from * to end.
ROW 2: Purl.

Vest only
ROW 1 (RS): K3 (7: 11), *P1, K7, rep from * to end.
Row 2: Purl.

Cardigan and vest
These 2 rows form patt.

SHAPE SIDE SEAM AND DART
Place marker on 28th (32nd: 36th) st from end
of last row.
ROW 3 (RS) (DEC): K2tog, patt to within 2 sts of marked
st, sl1, K1, psso, patt marked st, K2tog, patt to end. *56
(60: 64) sts*
Patt 15 rows.
Rep last 16 rows twice more, then row 3 again.
47 (51: 55) sts
Patt 19 rows, thus ending with a WS row.
ROW 71 (RS) (INC): Inc in first st, patt to marked st, M1,
patt marked st, M1, patt to end. *50 (54: 58) sts*
Patt 13 rows.
Rep last 14 rows twice more, then row 71 again.
59 (63: 67) sts
Cont in patt until left front matches back to start of
armhole shaping, ending with a WS row.

SHAPE ARMHOLE
Keeping patt correct, cast (bind) off 4 (6: 8) sts at beg
of next row. *55 (57: 59) sts*
Work 1 row.
Dec 1 st at armhole edge on next 9 rows, then on
every foll alt row until 43 (45: 47) sts rem, thus ending
with a RS row.

SHAPE NECK
Keeping patt correct, cast (bind) off 6 sts at beg of next
row. *37 (39: 41) sts*
Dec 1 st at armhole edge on next row. *36 (38: 40) sts*
Cast (bind) off 4 sts at beg of next row. *32 (34: 36) sts*
Dec 1 st at each end of next row.
Dec 1 st at neck edge only on next row.
Rep last 2 rows once more and then first of these
2 rows again. *24 (26: 28) sts*
Work 1 row, thus ending with a WS row.

Cardigan only
Dec 1 st at neck edge only on next and foll 2 alt rows,
then on every foll 4th row until 18 (20: 22) sts rem.
Cont without further shaping until left front matches
back to start of shoulder shaping, ending with a WS row.

SHAPE SHOULDER

Cast (bind) off 6 (7: 7) sts at beg of next and foll alt row.

Work 1 row.

Cast (bind) off rem 6 (6: 8) sts.

Vest only

Dec 1 st at armhole edge on next and foll 4th row and AT THE SAME TIME dec 1 st at neck edge on next and every foll alt row. *19 (21: 23) sts*

Work 3 rows, thus ending with a WS row.

Dec 1 st at each end of next and foll 4th row. *15 (17: 19) sts*

Work 3 rows.

Dec 1 st at neck edge only on next row. *14 (16: 18) sts*

Cont without further shaping until left front matches back to start of shoulder shaping, ending with a WS row.

SHAPE SHOULDER

Cast (bind) off 5 (5: 6) sts at beg of next and foll alt row.

Work 1 row.

Cast (bind) off rem 4 (6: 6) sts.

cardigan and vest
right front

RIGHT SIDE PANEL

Work as for left back panel. *29 (33: 37) sts*

Break yarn and leave sts on a holder.

RIGHT CENTER PANEL

Cast on 31 sts using 2¼mm (US 1) needles.

Work 4 rows in moss (seed) st as for left back panel.

ROW 5 (RS) (BUTTONHOLE ROW): K1, P1, (yrn) twice (to make a st-drop extra loop on next row), P2tog, patt to end.

Work 1 row.

ROW 7 (RS) (INC): Patt to last 2 sts, M2, P1, K1. *33 sts*

Patt 5 rows.

ROW 13: As row 7. *35 sts*

Patt 2 rows, thus ending with a RS row.

ROW 16 (WS): Patt to last 5 sts, M1 and turn, leaving last 5 sts on a safety pin for buttonhole band. *31 sts*

JOIN PANELS

NEXT ROW (RS): Patt to last st of right center panel, holding center panel in front of right side panel, K last st of center panel together with first st of side panel, patt to end. *59 (63: 67) sts*

P 1 row.

Change to 3mm (US 3) needles and work in patt as folls:

Cardigan only

ROW 1 (RS): *K7, bead 1, rep from * to last 3 (7: 11) sts, K3 (7: 11).

ROW 2: Purl.

Vest only

ROW 1 (RS): *K7, P1, rep from * to last 3 (7: 11) sts, K3 (7: 11).

ROW 2: Purl.

Cardigan and vest

These 2 rows form patt.

SHAPE SIDE SEAM AND DART

Place markers on 28th (32nd: 36th) st from beg of last row.

ROW 3 (RS) (DEC): Patt to within 2 sts of marked st, sl 1, K1, psso, patt marked st, K2tog, patt to last 2 sts, K2tog. *56 (60: 64) sts*

Patt 15 rows.

Rep last 16 rows twice more, then row 3 again. *47 (51: 55) sts*

Patt 19 rows, thus ending with a WS row.
ROW 71 (RS) (INC): Patt to marked st, M1, patt marked st, M1, patt to last st, inc in last st. *50 (54: 58) sts*
Patt 13 rows.
Rep last 14 rows twice more, then row 71 again. *59 (63: 67) sts*
Complete to match left front, rev shaping.

cardigan
sleeves (both alike)
Cast on 57 sts using 2¼mm (US 1) needles.
Work 17 rows in moss (seed) st as for left back panel, inc 1 st at each end of 11th row, ending with a RS row. *59 sts*
P 1 row.
Change to 3mm (US 3) needles and patt as folls:
ROW 1 (RS): Inc in first st, K4, *bead 1, K7, rep from * to last 6 sts, bead 1, K4, inc in last st. *61 sts*
ROW 2: Purl.
These 2 rows set patt.
Cont in patt as now set, shaping sides by inc 1 st at each end of every foll 8th (8th: 6th) row (from previous inc) until there are 67 (87: 71) sts, then on every foll 10th (10th: 8th) row until there are 89 (93: 97) sts, taking inc sts into patt.
Cont without further shaping until sleeve measures 40cm (15¾in), ending with a WS row.
SHAPE TOP
Keeping patt correct, cast (bind) off 4 (6: 8) sts at beg of next 2 rows. *81 sts*
Dec 1 st at each end of next 7 rows, then on every foll alt row until 59 sts rem.
Work 3 rows, thus ending with a WS row.
Dec 1 st at each end of next and every foll 4th row until 49 sts rem.
Work 1 row, thus ending with a WS row.
Dec 1 st at each end of next and foll 3 alt rows. *41 sts*
Dec 1 st at each end of next 5 rows, thus ending with a WS row. *31 sts*
Cast (bind) off 5 sts at beg of next 4 rows.
Cast (bind) off rem 11 sts.

finishing
Press all pieces as described on the information page.
Join both shoulder seams using back stitch.
BUTTON BAND
Slip rem 5 sts on left front safety pin on 2¼mm (US 1) needles and rejoin yarn with RS facing.
Cont in moss (seed) st as set until band, when slightly stretched, fits up left front opening edge to neck shaping, ending with a WS row.
Break yarn and leave sts on a safety pin.
Slipstich band in place.
Mark positions for 7 buttons on this band, the first level with buttonhole in right front, the last 0.5cm (¼in) above neck shaping, and the rem spaced evenly between.
BUTTONHOLE BAND
Slip rem 5 sts on right front safety pin on 2¼mm (US 1) needles and rejoin yarn with WS facing.
Work to match button band, with the addition of another 6 buttonholes worked to correspond with positions marked for buttons as folls:
BUTTONHOLE ROW (RS): K1, P1, (yrn) twice (to make a st-drop extra loop on next row), P2tog, K1.
When completed, do NOT break yarn.
Slipstitch band in place.

NECKBAND
With RS facing and using 2¼mm (US 1) needles, patt across 5 sts of buttonhole band, pick up and knit 54 sts up right front neck, 43 sts across back neck, and 54 sts down left front neck, then patt across 5 sts of button band left on safety pin. *161 sts*
Keeping moss (seed) st correct as set by bands, proceed as folls:
Work 1 row, thus ending with a WS row.
NEXT ROW (RS) (BUTTONHOLE ROW): K1, P1, (yrn) twice (to make a st-drop extra loop on next row), P2tog, patt to end.
Work 3 rows, thus ending with a WS row.
Cast (bind) off loosely and evenly in patt.
See information page for finishing instructions.

seville by Louisa Harding

SIZE	S	M	L	
To fit bust	81–86	86–91	91–97	cm
	32–34	34–36	36–38	in
Actual width	43	47	51	cm
	17	18½	20	in
Length	36	36	36	cm
	14	14	14	in
Sleeve length	6	6	6	cm
	2½	2½	2½	in

YARNS
Rowan Fine Cotton Chenille 50gm (1¾oz) balls:

Cornflower 412	5	5	6

See information page for special notes on knitting with Chenille.

NEEDLES
1 pair 3¼mm (US 3) needles
Cable needle

TENSION (GAUGE)
25 sts and 36 rows to 10cm (4in) measured over reversed stocking (stockinette) stitch using 3¼mm (US 3) needles.

SPECIAL ABBREVIEATIONS
DL = Drop loop: Drop yo of previous row off needle.
INC = Increase: Knit into front and back of yo on previous row.
MP = Make picot: Working into first st on needle and using cable method, cast on 2 sts, K2, slip first st knitted over 2nd st, knit next st, slip 2nd st over 3rd (first st on needle); this creates the picot edge.

back
Cast on 108 (118: 128) sts using 3¼mm (US 3) needles.
Work 4 rows in garter st (knit every row).
Beg with a P row, cont in reversed st st until work measures 16cm (6¼in) from cast-on edge, ending with a WS row.
SHAPE ARMHOLES
Cast (bind) off 4 sts at beg of next 2 rows and 3 sts at beg of foll 2 rows. Dec 1 st at each end on next 4 rows and 4 foll alt rows.
Work 3 rows.
Dec 1 st at each end of next row and foll 4th row. *74 (84: 94)sts*
Cont without further shaping until work measures 20cm (7¾in) from start of armhole shaping, ending with a WS row.

SHAPE SHOULDERS AND BACK NECK
Cast (bind) off 4 (6: 7) sts at beg of next 2 rows.
Cast (bind) off 4 (6: 7) sts, patt 8 (9: 12), turn and leave rem sts on a holder.
Work each side of neck separately.
Cast (bind) off 4 sts, patt to end.
Cast (bind) off rem 4 (5: 8) sts.
With RS facing, rejoin yarns to rem sts, cast (bind) off 42 sts very loosely, patt to end.
Complete to match first side, rev all shaping.

front
Work as for back until front is 16 rows shorter than back to shoulder shaping, ending with a WS row.
SHAPE FRONT NECK
Patt 22 (27: 32)sts, turn and leave rem sts on a holder.
Work each side of neck separately.
Cast (bind) off 4 sts at beg of next row.
Dec 1 st at neck edge on next 4 rows and 2 foll alt rows. *12 (17: 22) sts*
Cont without further shaping until front matches back to shoulder shaping, ending with a WS row.
SHAPE SHOULDER
Cast (bind) off 4 (6: 7) sts at beg of next row and foll alt row. Work 1 row.
Cast (bind) off rem 4 (5: 8) sts.
With RS facing, rejoin yarn to rem sts, cast (bind) off 30 sts very loosely, patt to end.
Complete to match first side, rev all shaping.

sleeves (both alike)
Cast on 72 sts using 3¼mm (US 3) needles.
Work 4 rows in garter st.
Cont in reversed st st, starting with a P row, and AT THE SAME TIME shape sides by inc 1 st at each end of 3rd row and every foll 3rd row to 82 sts. Cont without further shaping until sleeve measures 6cm (2½in) from cast-on edge.
SHAPE SLEEVE HEAD
Cast (bind) off 4 sts at beg of next 2 rows and 3 sts at beg of foll 2 rows.
Dec 1 st at each end on next 5 rows and 4 foll alt rows. *50 sts*
Work 3 rows.
Dec 1 st at each end on next row, 2 foll 4th rows and 5 foll alt rows. *34 sts*
Work 1 row.
Dec 1 st at each end of next 4 rows. *26 sts*
Cast (bind) off 4 sts at beg of next 2 rows.
Cast (bind) off rem 18 sts loosely and evenly.

finishing

Press all pieces as described on the information page.
Join both shoulder seams using back stitch.
Join side and sleeve seams.
Set sleeve head into armhole.

WORK LACE EDGING

Cast on 18 sts using 3¼mm (US 3) needles and knit 1 row.

PREPARATION ROW: K5, K2tog, K2, yo, K1, K2tog, yo, K2tog, K1, yo, K3.

ROW 1 (RS): K3, yo, slip yo of previous row, K2, inc, K3, slip next 2 sts onto cable needle, hold at front, K3, then K2 from cable needle, yo, K2tog, K1. *20 sts*

ROW 2: MP, K6, K2tog, yo, K2tog, K4, (K1, P1) into both yo loops tog, as if they were a single loop, K3. *19 sts*

ROW 3: K2, K2tog, yo, K2tog, K10, yo, K2tog, K1. *18 sts*

ROW 4: K5, (yo, K1) twice, K2tog, yo, K2tog, K3, yo, DL, K3. *19 sts*

ROW 5: K3, (K1, P1) into yo of previous row, K7, inc, K1, inc, K2, yo, K2tog, K1. *22 sts*

ROW 6: MP, K4, yo, K2, yo, K2tog, K1, yo, (K1, K2tog, yo, K2tog) twice, K2. *22 sts*

ROW 7: K3, yo, DL, K6, (yo, K2tog, K1) 4 times. *22 sts*

Row 8: K5, (yo, K2tog, K1) 3 times, yo, K2tog, K2, (K1, P1) into yo of previous row, K3. *23 sts*

ROW 9: K2, K2tog, yo, K2tog, K5, (yo, K2tog, K1) 4 times. *22 sts*

ROW 10: MP, K4, (yo, K2tog, K1) 3 times, yo, K2tog, K2, yo, DL, K3. *22 sts*

ROW 11: K3, (K1, P1) into yo of previous row, K6, (yo, K2tog, K1) 4 times. *23 sts*

ROW 12: K5, (yo, K2tog, K1) 4 times, K2tog, yo, K2tog, K2. *22 sts*

ROW 13: As row 7.

ROW 14: MP, K4, (yo, K2tog, K1) 3 times, yo, K2tog, K2, (K1, P1) into yo of the previous row, K3. *23 sts*

ROW 15: As row 9.

ROW 16: K5, (yo, K2tog, K1) 3 times, yo, K2tog, K2, yo, DL, K3. *22 sts*

ROW 17: K3, (K1, P1) into yo of previous row, K6, yo, (K2tog, K1) twice, (yo, K2tog, K1) twice. *22 sts*

ROW 18: MP, K4, yo, K2tog, K1, K2tog, yo, K2tog, K1, yo, K3, K2tog, yo, K2tog, K2. *21 sts*

ROW 19: K3, yo, DL, K7, yo, K2tog, K2, (yo, K2tog, K1) twice. *21 sts*

ROW 20: K5, yo, (K2tog) twice, yo, K2tog, K1, yo, K5, (K1, P1) into yo of previous row, K3. *22 sts*

ROW 21: K2, K2tog, yo, K2tog, K7, (K2tog, K1) twice, yo, K2tog, K1. *19 sts*

ROW 22: K5, K2tog, K2, yo, K1, K2tog, yo, K2tog, K1, yo, DL, K3. *18 sts*

Rep rows 1-22 until edging is long enough to fit around lower edge of back and front, leave sts on a holder.
Slipstitch into place, adjust length if necessary.
Cast (bind) off.

LACE EDGING FOR NECK AND SLEEVES (WORK 3 LENGTHS)

Cast on 5 sts using 3¼mm (US 3) needles and K 1 row.

ROWS 1, 2 AND 3: K2, yo, K2tog, K1.

ROW 4: MP, K1, yo, K2tog, K1.

Rep these 4 rows until each edging is long enough to fit around neck edge and edge of each sleeve, leave sts on a holder. Slip st into place, adjust length if necessary.
Cast (bind) off.
See information page for finishing instructions.

peace by Kim Hargreaves

SIZE	1ST	2ND	3RD	4TH	5TH	
To fit bust	81	86	91	97	102	cm
	32	34	36	38	40	in
Actual width	43	44.5	48	51	53.5	cm
	17	18	19	20	21	cm
Length	55.5	56.5	57.5	58.5	59.5	cm
	22	22¼	22½	23	23½	in
Sleeve length	25	25	25.5	25.5	26	cm
	9½	9½	10	10	10½	in

YARN
Rowan Cotton Glacé 50gm (1¾oz) balls:

Vest						
Steel 798	6	6	6	7	7	

Cardigan						
Butter 795	7	8	8	9	9	

NEEDLES
1 pair 2¾mm (US 2) needles
1 pair 3¼mm (US 3) needles

TENSION (GAUGE)
23 sts and 32 rows to 10cm (4in) measured over stocking (stockinette) stitch using 3¼ mm (US 3) needles

BUTTONS
5 buttons or 9 large hooks and eyes

vest and cardigan
back
Cast on 99 (105: 111: 117: 123) sts using 2¾mm (US 2) needles.
Knit 4 rows.
Change to 3¼mm (US 3) needles and, beg with a K row, work 10 rows in st st, ending with a WS row.
Mark the 25th (27th: 29th: 31st: 33rd) st in from each side with a colored thread.
SHAPE SIDES
NEXT ROW (RS) (DEC): K2, K2tog, K to 1 st before marker, K3tog, K to 1 st before 2nd marker, K3tog tbl, K to last 4 sts, K2tog tbl, K2.
93 (99: 105: 111: 117) sts
Work 9 rows in st st.
Rep the last 10 rows twice more and then rep dec row once more. *75 (81: 87: 93: 99) sts*
Work without shaping until work measures 19cm (7½in) from cast-on edge, ending with a WS row.

NEXT ROW (RS) (INC): K2, M1, K to marked st, M1, K1, M1, K to marked st, M1, K1, M1, K to last 2 sts, M1, K2. *81 (87: 93: 99: 105) sts*
Work 11 rows.
Rep the last 12 rows twice more and then rep inc row once more. *99 (105: 111: 117: 123) sts*
Cont without shaping until work measures 36.5cm (14¼in) from cast-on edge, ending with a WS row.
SHAPE ARMHOLES
Vest only
Cast (bind) off 6 sts at beg of next 2 rows.
Dec 1 st at each end of next 7 rows and 8 (9: 10: 11: 12) foll alt rows. *57 (61: 65: 69: 73) sts*
Cont without further shaping until work measures 19 (20: 21: 22: 23)cm (7½ [7¾: 8¼: 8½: 9]in) from beg of armhole shaping, ending with a WS row.
SHAPE SHOULDERS AND BACK NECK
Cast (bind) off 3 (3: 3: 4: 4) sts at beg of next 2 rows.
Cast (bind) off 3 (3: 4: 4: 4) sts, K7 (8: 8: 8: 9) sts, turn and leave rem sts on a holder.
Work each side of neck separately.
Cast (bind) off 4 sts, P to end.
Cast (bind) off rem 3 (4: 4: 4: 5) sts.
Cardigan only
Cast (bind) off 4 sts at beg of next 2 rows.
Dec 1 st at each end of next 7 rows and 6 (7: 8: 9: 10) foll alt rows. *65 (69: 73: 77: 81) sts*
Cont without further shaping until work measures 19 (20: 21: 22: 23)cm (7½ [7¾: 8¼: 8½: 9]in) from beg of armhole shaping, ending with a WS row.
SHAPE SHOULDERS AND BACK NECK
Cast (bind) off 4 (4: 5: 5: 5) sts at beg of next 2 rows.
Cast (bind) off 4 (5: 5: 5: 6) sts, K9 (9: 9: 10: 10), turn and leave rem sts on a holder.
Work each side of neck separately.
Cast (bind) off 4 sts, P to end.
Cast (bind) off rem 5 (5: 5: 6: 6) sts.
Vest and cardigan
With RS facing, rejoin yarn to rem sts, cast (bind) off center 31 (33: 35: 37: 39) sts, K to end.
Complete to match first side, rev shaping.

left front
Cast on 50 (53: 56: 59: 62) sts, using 2¾mm (US 2) needles and work as folls:
ROW 1 (RS): K to last 8 sts, (P1, K1) to end.
ROW 2: (K1, P1) 4 times, K to end.
Rep these 2 rows once more.
Change to 3¼mm (US 3) needles.
Now keeping 8 sts at center front in moss (seed) st

and rem sts in st st, cont as folls:

NEXT ROW (RS): K to last 8 sts, (P1, K1) to end.

NEXT ROW: (K1, P1) 4 times, P to end.

Rep these 2 rows 4 times more, ending with a WS row. Mark 25th (27th: 29th: 31st: 33rd) st in from side edge with a colored thread.

SHAPE SIDES

NEXT ROW (RS) (DEC): K2, K2tog, K to 1 st before marker, K3tog, work to end. *47 (50: 53: 56: 59) sts*

Work 9 rows.

Rep the last 10 rows twice more and then rep dec row once more. *38 (41: 44: 47: 50) sts*

Cont until work measures 19cm (7½in) from cast-on edge, ending with a WS row.

NEXT ROW (RS) (INC): K2, M1, K to marked st, M1, K1, M1, work to end.

Work 11 rows.

Rep the last 12 rows twice more and then rep the inc row once more. *50 (53: 56: 59: 62) sts*

Cont until front is 16 rows shorter than back to beg of armhole shaping.

SHAPE FRONT SLOPE

NEXT ROW (RS) (DEC): K until 13 sts rem on LH needle, K2tog tbl, K3, moss (seed) st to end. *49 (52: 55: 58: 61) sts*

Work 7 rows.

Rep last 8 rows once more (when front should match armhole shaping). *48 (51: 54: 57: 60) sts*

Cont shaping front as before on next row and 3 foll 8th rows and AT THE SAME TIME shape armholes as folls:

SHAPE ARMHOLE

Vest only

Cast (bind) off 6 sts, K until 13 sts rem on, LH needle, K2tog tbl, K3, moss (seed) st to end. *41 (44: 47: 50: 53) sts*

Work 1 row.

Dec 1 st at armhole edge on next 7 rows and 8 (9: 10: 11: 12) foll alt rows. *23 (25: 27: 29: 31) sts*

Cont until front is 25 (29: 29: 31: 31) rows shorter than back to beg of shoulder shaping, ending with a RS row.

SHAPE FRONT NECK

NEXT ROW (WS): Moss (seed) st 8 and leave these 8 sts on a holder for neckband, K to end.

Dec 1 st at neck edge on next row, 3 (3: 5: 5: 7) foll alt rows and 2 (3: 2: 3: 2) foll 4th rows. *9 (10: 11: 12: 13) sts*

Cont without shaping until front matches back to shoulder shaping, ending with a WS row.

SHAPE SHOULDER

Cast (bind) off 3 (3: 3: 4: 4) sts at beg of next row and 3 (3: 4: 4: 4) sts at beg of foll alt row.

Work 1 row. Cast (bind) off rem 3 (4: 4: 4: 5) sts.

Cardigan only

Cast (bind) off 4 sts, K until 13 sts rem on LH needle, K2tog tbl, K3, moss (seed) st to end. *43 (46: 49: 52: 55) sts*

Dec 1 st at armhole edge on next 7 rows and 6 (7: 8: 9: 10) foll alt rows. *27 (29: 31: 33: 35) sts*

Cont until front is 25 (29: 29: 31: 31) rows shorter than back to beg of shoulder shaping, ending with a RS row.

SHAPE FRONT NECK

NEXT ROW (WS): Moss (seed) st 8 and leave these 8 sts on a holder for neckband, K to end.

Dec 1 st at neck edge on next row, 3 (3: 5: 5: 7) foll alt rows and 2 (3: 2: 3: 2) foll 4th rows. *13 (14: 15: 16: 17) sts*

Cont without shaping until front matches back to shoulder shaping, ending with a WS row.

SHAPE SHOULDER

Cast (bind) off 4 (4: 5: 5: 5) sts at beg of next row and 4 (5: 5: 5: 6) sts at beg of foll alt row.

Work 1 row.

Cast (bind) off rem 5 (5: 5: 6: 6) sts.

BUTTON VERSION

Mark position of 5 buttons, 1cm (½in) in from center front edge, the 1st to come 9cm (3½in) from cast-on edge, the 5th 3 rows below the start of front slope shaping and the rem spaced evenly between.

right front

Cast on 50 (53: 56: 59: 62) sts, using 2¾mm (US 2) needles and work as folls:

ROW 1 (RS): (K1, P1) 4 times, K to end.

ROW 2: K to last 8 sts, (P1, K1) to end.

Rep these 2 rows once more.

Change to 3¼mm (US 3) needles

Work as for left front, rev shaping.

cardigan
sleeves (both alike)

Cast on 55 (57: 57: 59: 59) sts using 2¾mm (US 2) needles and work in moss (seed) st, setting sts as folls:

ROW 1 (RS): (K1, P1), to last st, K1.

Rep this row until 8 rows in all have been completed.

Change to 3¼mm (US 3) needles.

Work 2 rows in st st, beg with a K row.

NEXT ROW (RS) (INC): K2, M1, K to last 2 sts, M1, K2. *57 (59: 59: 61: 61) sts*

Work 5 rows.

Inc as before on next row and every foll 6th row to 73 (75: 73: 73: 75) sts and then for 3rd, 4th and 5th sizes only every foll 4th row to 79 (81: 83) sts. *73 (75: 79: 81: 83) sts*

Cont without shaping until sleeve measures 25 (25: 25.5: 25.5: 26)cm (9¾ [9¾: 10: 10: 10¼]in) from cast-on edge, ending with a WS row.

SHAPE SLEEVEHEAD

Cast (bind) off 4 sts at beg of next 2 rows.

Dec 1 st at each end of next 5 rows, 3 (4: 5: 6: 7) foll alt rows and 4 foll 4th rows. *41 (41: 43: 43: 43) sts*

Work 1 row.

Dec 1 st at each end of next row, 2 foll alt rows and 5 foll rows. *25 (25: 27: 27: 27) sts*

Cast (bind) off 5 sts at beg of next 2 rows.

Cast (bind) off rem 15 (15: 17: 17: 17) sts.

finishing

Press all pieces as described on the information page. Join both shoulder seams.

NECK EDGING

With RS of right front facing and using 2¾mm (US 2) needles, slip 8 sts from holder onto RH needle, join yarn and pick up and knit 29 (33: 37: 39: 43) sts up right front neck, 39 (41: 43: 45: 47) sts across back neck and 29 (33: 37: 39: 43) sts down left front neck, patt across 8 sts on holder. *113 (123: 133: 139: 149) sts*

Keeping patt correct, work 7 rows in moss (seed) st.

Cast (bind) off in pattern.

See information page for finishing instructions.

Vest only

ARMHOLE EDGINGS (BOTH ALIKE)

With RS facing and using 2¾mm (US 2) needles,

pick up and knit 101 (107: 113: 115: 121) sts evenly around armhole edge.

Work 5 rows in moss (seed) st.

Cast (bind) off in moss (seed) st.

See information page for finishing instructions.

Button version only

BUTTON LOOPS (MAKE 5)

Cast on 16 sts using 2¾mm (US 2) needles.

Cast (bind) off.

Fold strip in half to make a loop, pin in place on inside of right front to correspond with button markers on left front. Adjust loop to match size of button and sew securely in place.

Sew on buttons.

Hook-and-eye version

Sew hooks and eyes into position on WS, the 1st pair to come 1cm (½in) from cast-on edge, the 9th pair to come just below start of front slope shaping and the rem spaced evenly between.

sumba by Martin Storey

	CHILD'S		MEN'S		
SIZES	4-6 YRS	M	L	XL	
To fit chest	64	97	102	107	cm
	25	38	40	42	in
Actual width	40.5	58.5	61.5	63	cm
	16	23	24	24	in
Length	53	65	68	70.5	cm
	20¾	25½	27	28	in
Sleeve length	33	51	51	51	cm
	13	20	20	20	in

YARNS

Rowan Handknit DK Cotton 50gm (1¾oz) balls:

A	Turkish plum 277	11	18	18	19
B	Rosso 215	1	1	1	2
C	Linen 205	2	2	3	3

NEEDLES

1 pair 3¼mm (US 3) needles
1 pair 4mm (US 6) needles

TENSION (GAUGE)

22 sts and 25 rows to 10cm (4in) measured over patterned stocking (stockinette) stitch using 4mm (US 6) needles;
23 sts and 28 rows to 10cm (4in) measured over rib patt using 4mm (US 6) needles

PATTERN NOTE

The pattern is written for the child's size, followed by the men's sizes.

front

Cast on 93 (135: 141: 147) sts using 3¼mm (US 3) needles and yarn A.
Beg with a K row, work 8 rows in st st.
NEXT ROW (RS): K3, *P3, K3, rep from * to end.
NEXT ROW: P3, *K3, P3, rep from * to end.
These 2 rows form rib patt.**
Work another 11 (27: 27: 27) rows in rib patt, thus ending with a RS row.
NEXT ROW (WS) (DEC): P11 (19: 20: 17), *P2tog, P21 (17: 18: 14), rep from * to last 13 (21: 21: 18) sts, P2tog, P11 (19: 19: 16). *89 (129: 135: 139) sts*
Change to 4mm (US 6) needles.
Using the Fair Isle technique described on the information page and beg with chart row 11 (1: 1: 1), work 66 (58: 66: 72) rows in patt from chart, which is worked entirely in st st, beg with a K row and thus ending with a WS row.

SHAPE ARMHOLES

Keeping patt correct, cast (bind) off 4 (7: 7: 7) sts at beg of next 2 rows. *81 (115: 121: 125) sts*

Men's sizes only

Dec 1 st at each end of next and foll 6 alt rows. *101 (107: 111) sts*

All sizes

Cont without further shaping until chart row 120 (122: 130: 136) is completed, thus ending with a WS row.

SHAPE NECK

NEXT ROW (RS): Patt 34 (41: 44: 46) sts and turn, leaving rem sts on a holder.
Work each side of neck separately.
Cast (bind) off 3 (4: 4: 4) sts at beg of next row. *31 (37: 40: 42) sts*
Dec 1 st at neck edge on next 4 (5: 5: 5) rows. *27 (32: 35: 37) sts*

Child's size only

Work 1 row, thus ending with a RS row.
Dec 1 st at neck edge on next and foll alt row, thus ending with a WS row. *25 sts*

SHAPE SHOULDER

Cast (bind) off 8 sts at beg of next and foll alt row.
Work 1 row.
Cast (bind) off rem 9 sts.

Men's sizes only

Work 1 row, then dec 1 st at neck edge on next row. *31 (34: 36) sts*
Work 1 row, thus ending with a WS row.

SHAPE SHOULDER

Cast (bind) off 5 (6: 6) sts at beg and dec 1 st at end of next row.
Work 1 row.
Cast (bind) off 6 (6: 7) sts at beg and dec 1 st at end of next row.
Work 1 row.
Cast (bind) off 6 (6: 7) sts at beg of next row, and 6 (7: 7) sts at beg of foll alt row.
Work 1 row.
Cast (bind) off rem 6 (7: 7) sts.

All sizes

With RS facing, slip center 13 (19: 19: 19) sts on a holder, rejoin yarn to rem sts, patt to end.
Work to match first side, rev shaping.

KEY
☐ A
⊡ B
▣ C

146
140
130
120
110
100
90
80

child

medium
large
extra large

medium
large
extra large

FRONT FOR ADULT AND CHILD

back

Work as for front to **.

Work another 12 (28: 28: 28) rows in rib patt, thus ending with a WS row.

Change to 4mm (US 6) needles and cont in rib patt until back matches front to start of armhole shaping, ending with a WS row.

SHAPE ARMHOLES

Keeping rib patt correct, cast (bind) off 4 (7: 7: 7) sts at beg of next 2 rows. *85 (121: 127: 133) sts*

Men's sizes only

Dec 1 st at each end of next and foll 6 alt rows. *107 (113: 119) sts*

All sizes

Cont without further shaping until back matches front to start of shoulder shaping, ending with a WS row.

SHAPE SHOULDERS

Cast (bind) off 9 (6: 6: 7) sts at beg of next 4 (8: 2: 6) rows, then 8 (7: 7: 8) sts at beg of foll 2 (2: 8: 4) rows.

Leave rem 33 (45: 45: 45) sts on a holder.

sleeves (both alike)

Cast on 45 sts using 3¼mm (US 3) needles and yarn A.

Beg with a K row, work 8 rows in st st.

Work 20 rows in rib patt as for front, thus ending with a WS row.

Change to 4mm (US 6) needles and cont in rib patt, shaping sides by inc 1 st at each end of next 3rd and every foll alt 3rd row until there are 97 (117: 117: 117) sts, taking inc sts into rib patt.

Cont without further shaping until sleeve measures 33 (51: 51: 51)cm (13 [20: 20: 20]in), ending with a WS row.

SHAPE TOP

Child's size only

Cast (bind) off loosely and evenly.

Men's sizes only

Cast (bind) off 7 sts at beg of next 2 rows. *103 sts*

Cast (bind) off 5 sts at beg of next 6 rows, 3 sts at beg of foll 10 rows, then 6 sts at beg of next 4 rows.

Cast (bind) off rem 19 sts.

finishing

Press all pieces as described on the information page.

Join right shoulder seam using back stitch.

NECKBAND

With RS facing, using 3¼mm (US 3) needles and yarn A, pick up and knit 15 (20: 20: 20) sts down left front neck, K13 (19: 19: 19) sts from holder at center front, pick up and K14 (21: 21: 21) sts up right front neck and K33 (45: 45: 45) sts from holder at back neck. *75 (105: 105: 105) sts*

Work 7 (21: 21: 21) rows in rib patt as for front, thus ending with a WS row.

Beg with a K row, work 8 rows in st st.

Cast (bind) off.

See information page for finishing instructions.

laurel leaf by Kim Hargreaves

SIZE	XS	S	M	L	XL	
To fit bust	81	86	91	97	102	cm
	32	34	36	38	40	in
Actual width	48.5	51	53.5	56	58.5	cm
	19	20	21	22	23	cm
Length	48	49	50	52	52	cm
	19	19½	19½	20½	20½	in
Sleeve length	40	40	42	42	43	cm
	15½	15½	16½	16½	17	in

YARN

Rowan Cotton Glacé 50gm (1¾oz) balls:

A Fizz 722	8	8	9	9	9
B Pepper 796	2	2	2	2	2
C Mint 748	1	1	1	2	2
D Pear 780	1	1	1	1	1

NEEDLES

1 pair 2¾mm (US 2) needles
1 pair 3¼mm (US 3) needles

BUTTONS

10

TENSION (GAUGE)

23 sts and 32 rows to 10cm (4in) measured over patterned stocking (stockinette) stitch using 3¼mm (US 3) needles

back

Cast on 99 (105: 111: 117: 123) sts using 2¾mm (US 2) needles and yarn B.
**Join yarn A.
Using yarn A, knit 3 rows.
ROW 4 (WS): Using yarn B, *P2tog, yrn, rep from * to last st, P1.
Using yarn A, knit 2 rows.**
Change to 3¼mm (US 3) needles.
Using the intarsia technique described on the information page, joining and breaking colors as required and beg with a K row, work in patt from chart, which is worked entirely in st st, as folls:
Work 2 (2: 2: 4: 4) rows.
Inc 1 st at each end of next and every foll 14th row until there are 111 (117: 123: 129: 135) sts, taking inc sts into patt.
Work 11 (15: 15: 17: 17) rows, ending with chart row 84 (88: 88: 92: 92).

SHAPE ARMHOLES

Keeping chart correct, cast (bind) off 3 (4: 4: 5: 5) sts

at beg of next 2 rows. *105 (109: 115: 119: 125) sts*
Dec 1 st at each end of next 7 (7: 9: 9: 11) rows, then on every foll alt row until 79 (81: 83: 85: 87) sts rem.
Cont straight until chart row 148 (152: 156: 160: 162) has been completed, ending with a WS row.

SHAPE SHOULDERS AND BACK NECK

Keeping chart correct, cast (bind) off 7 (8: 8: 8: 8) sts at beg of next 2 rows. *65 (65: 67: 69: 71) sts*
NEXT ROW (RS): Cast (bind) off 7 (8: 8: 8: 8) sts, patt until there are 12 (11: 11: 12: 12) sts on right needle and turn, leaving rem sts on a holder.
Work each side of neck separately.
Cast (bind) off 4 sts at beg of next row.
Cast (bind) off rem 8 (7: 7: 8: 8) sts.
With RS facing, rejoin yarn to rem sts, cast (bind) off center 27 (27: 29: 29: 31) sts, patt to end.
Work to match first side, rev shaping.

left front

Cast on 49 (53: 55: 59: 61) sts using 2¾mm (US 2) needles and yarn B.
Work as for back from ** to **, inc 1 (0: 1: 0: 1) st at end of last row. *50 (53: 56: 59: 62) sts*
Change to 3¼mm (US 3) needles and work in patt from body chart as folls:
Work 2 (2: 2: 4: 4) rows.
Inc 1 st at beg of next and every foll 14th row until there are 56 (59: 62: 65: 68) sts, taking inc sts into patt.
Work 11 (15: 15: 17: 17) rows, ending with chart row 84 (88: 88: 92: 92).

SHAPE ARMHOLE

Keeping chart correct, cast (bind) off 3 (4: 4: 5: 5) sts at beg of next row. *53 (55: 58: 60: 63) sts*
Work 1 row.
Dec 1 st at armhole edge of next 7 (7: 9: 9: 11) rows, then on every foll alt row until 40 (41: 42: 43: 44) sts rem.
Work 11 (9: 9: 7: 5) rows, ending with chart row 116 (120: 122: 126: 126).

SHAPE NECK

Keeping chart correct, dec 1 st at neck edge of next 9 rows, then on every foll alt row until 22 (23: 23: 24: 24) sts rem.
Work 5 rows, ending with chart row 148 (152: 156: 160: 162).

SHAPE SHOULDER

Keeping chart correct, cast (bind) off 7 (8: 8: 8: 8) sts at beg of next and foll alt row.
Work 1 row.
Cast (bind) off rem 8 (7: 7: 8: 8) sts.

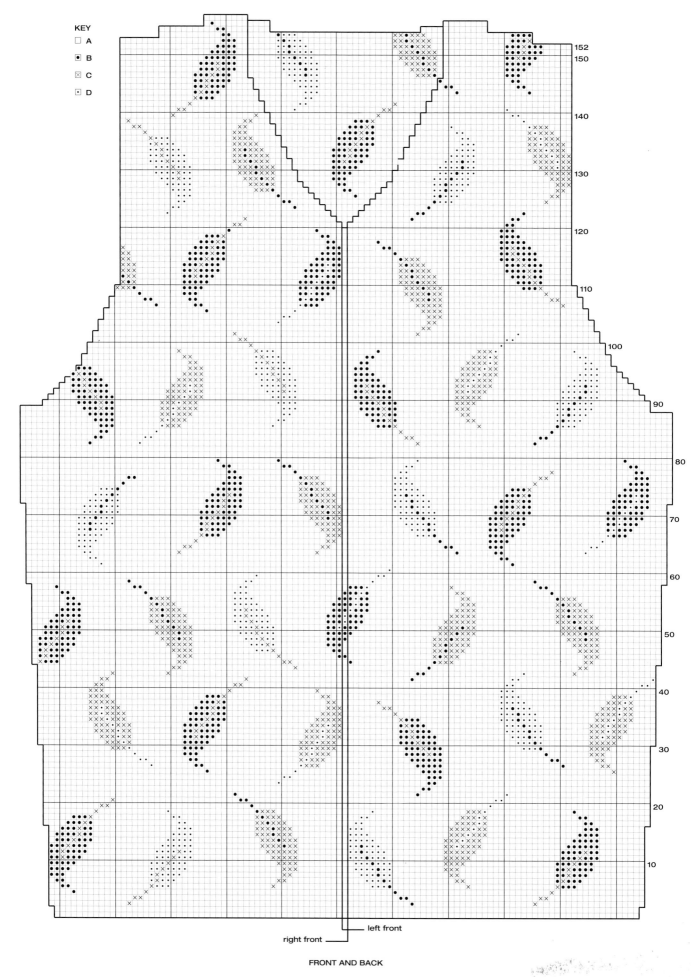

KEY
□ A
▣ B
☒ C
⊡ D

152
150
140
130
120
110
100
90
80
70
60
50
40
30
20
10

left front
right front

FRONT AND BACK

right front

Cast on 49 (53: 55: 59: 61) sts using 2¾mm (US 2) needles and yarn B.

Work as for back from ** to **, inc 1 (0: 1: 0: 1) st at beg of last row. *50 (53: 56: 59: 62) sts*

Change to 3¼mm (US 3) needles and work in patt from body chart as folls:

Work 2 (2: 2: 4: 4) rows.

Inc 1 st at end of next and every foll 14th row until there are 56 (59: 62: 65: 68) sts, taking inc sts into patt.

Complete to match left front, rev shaping.

sleeves (both alike)

Cast on 47 (47: 47: 51: 51) sts using 2¾mm (US 2) needles and yarn B.

Work as for back from ** to **.

Change to 3¼mm (US 3) needles and work in patt from sleeve chart as folls:

Work 2 rows.

Inc 1 st at each end of next and every foll 10th row until there are 63 (55: 51: 63: 59) sts, then on every foll 8th row until there are 73 (75: 77: 79: 81) sts, taking inc sts into patt.

Work 11 rows, ending with chart row 124 (124: 128: 128: 132).

SHAPE TOP

Keeping chart correct, cast (bind) off 3 (4: 4: 5: 5) sts at beg of next 2 rows. *67 (67: 69: 69: 71) sts*

Dec 1 st at each end of next 3 rows, then on foll 3 alt rows. *55 (55: 57: 57: 59) sts*

Work 3 rows, ending with a WS row.

Dec 1 st at each end of next and every foll 4th row until 47 (47: 49: 49: 51) sts rem, then on every foll alt row until 35 sts rem.

Dec 1 st at each end on next 3 rows. *29 sts*

Cast (bind) off 4 sts at beg of next 2 rows.

Cast (bind) off rem 21 sts.

finishing

Press all pieces as described on the information page. Join both shoulder seams using back stitch.

NECK BORDER

With RS facing, 2¾mm (US 2) needles and yarn A, pick up and knit 31 (31: 34: 34: 36) sts up right side of neck, 35 (35: 37: 37: 39) sts from back, and 31 (31: 34: 34: 36) sts down left side of neck. *97 (97: 105: 105: 111) sts*

ROWS 1 AND 2: Using yarn A, knit.

ROW 3 (WS): Using yarn B, *P2tog, yrn, rep from * to last st, P1.

ROWS 4 AND 5: Using yarn A, knit.

ROW 6: Using yarn B, knit.

Cast (bind) off knitwise (on WS) using yarn B.

FRONT BORDERS (BOTH ALIKE)

With RS facing, 2¾mm (US 2) needles and yarn A, pick up and knit 91 (93: 95: 97: 97) sts along one front opening edge between cast-on edge and top of neck border.

Work rows 1–6 as for neck border.

Cast (bind) off knitwise (on WS) using yarn B.

See information page for finishing instructions, using eyelet holes of right front border as buttonholes.

KEY

☐ A
⊡ B
☒ C
⊡ D

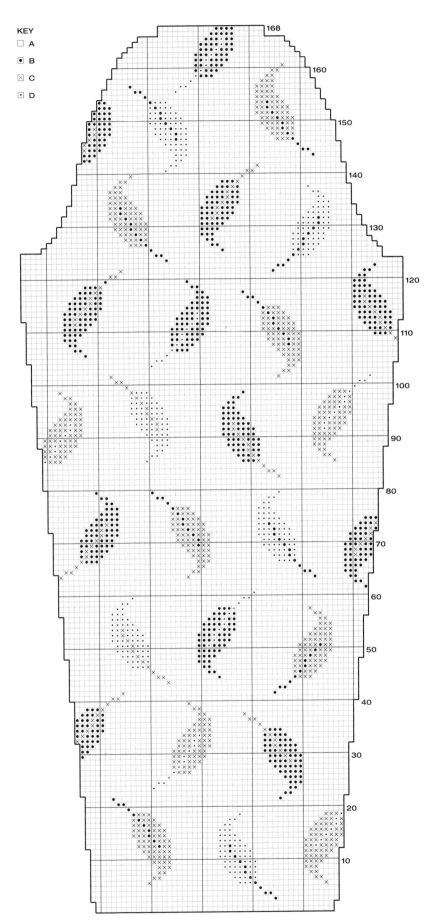

SLEEVE

iris cardigan by Sharon Peake

SIZE

	S	M	
To fit bust	81–86	91–97	cm
	32–34	36–38	in
Actual width	49.5	52	cm
	19½	20½	in
Length	49	51	cm
	19	20	in
Sleeve length	39	40	cm
	15½	16	in

YARN

Rowan 4ply Cotton 50gm (1¾oz) balls:

A Violet 114		7	7
B Bonny 104		2	2
C Olive 118		2	2

NEEDLES

One pair 2¼ mm (US 1) needles
One pair 3mm (US 2/3) needles

BUTTONS

8

TENSION

28 sts and 38 rows to 10cm (4in) measured over stocking (stockinette) stitch pattern using 3mm (US 3) needles

SPECIAL ABBREVIATIONS

P2SSO = Pass 2 slipped stitches over.
PULL UP LOOP = Insert point of right-hand needle upward under the 2 strands in front of sl sts, knit the next st, then lift the 2 strands off over the point of the right hand needle.

back

Cast on 171 sts using 3mm (US 3) needles.

WORK SCALLOP EDGE

ROW 1 (RS): K3, *sl1, K1, psso, sl2, K3tog, p2sso, K2tog, K4, rep from * to last 12 sts, sl1, K1, psso, sl2, K3tog, p2sso, K2tog, K3.
ROW 2: P4, *yrn, P1, yrn, P6, rep from * to last 5 sts, yrn, P1, yrn, P4.
ROW 3: K1, yf, *K2, sl1, K1, psso, K1, K2tog, K2, yf, rep from * to last st, K1.
ROW 4: P2, *yrn, P2, yrn, P3, yrn, p2, yrn, P1, rep from * to last st, P1.
ROW 5: K2, yf, K1,*yf, sl1, K1, psso, K1, sl1, K2tog, psso, K1, K2tog, (yf, K1) 3 times, rep from * to last 12 sts, yf, sl1, K1, psso, K1, sl1, K2tog, psso, K1, K2tog, yf,

K1, yf, K2.
ROW 6: Purl.
ROW 7: K5, *yf, sl2, K3tog, p2sso, yf, K7, rep from * to last 10 sts, yf, sl2, K3tog, p2sso, yf, K5. *133 sts*
ROW 8: Knit across row, dec 1 st at each end of row. *131 sts*
ROWS 9, 10 AND 11: Knit.

WORK TRELLIS PATTERN

Change to yarn B.
ROW 12 (WS): K1, P3, *with yarn at front, sl3 purlwise, P3, rep from * to last st, K1.
ROW 13: P1, K3, *with yarn at back, sl3 purlwise, K3, rep from * to last st, P1.
Change to yarn A.
ROW 14: K1, P3, *K3, P3, rep from * to last st, K1.
ROW 15: P1, K3, *P3, K3, rep from * to last st, K1.
ROW 16: K5, *pull up loop, K5, rep from * to end.
ROW 17: Work as row 15.
Change to yarn B.
ROW 18: P1, *with yarn at front, sl3 purlwise, P3, rep from * to last 4 sts, sl3 purlwise, P1.
ROW 19: K1, *with yarn at back, sl3 purlwise, K3, rep from * to last 4 sts, sl3 purlwise, K1.
Change to yarn A.
ROW 20: Work as row 15.
ROW 21: Work as row 14.
Row 22: K2, *pull up loop, K5, rep from * to last 3 sts, pull up loop, K2.
ROW 23: K4, *P3, K3, rep from * to last 7 sts, P3, K4.
ROWS 24-35: Work as rows 12-23.
ROW 36 (WS) (DEC): K1, *K2tog, K12 (40), rep from * to last 4 sts, K2tog, K2. *121 (127) sts*
Cont in patt from chart for back, joining and breaking colors as required and using the intarsia method described on the information page. Work until chart row 40 is complete, shaping sides by inc 1 st at each end of chart row 3 and every foll 8th row. *131 (137) sts*
Cont in patt, rep the 40-row rep throughout and inc every 8th row as before to 139 (145) sts, ending with a RS row.
Work 3 (9) rows.

SHAPE ARMHOLE

Cast (bind) off 6 sts at beg of next 2 rows.
Dec 1 st at each end of next 5 rows and 9 (10) foll alt rows. *99 (103) sts*
Cont without shaping until work measures 20cm (8in) from beg of armhole shaping, ending with a WS row.

SHAPE SHOULDER AND BACK NECK

Cast (bind) off 8 (9) sts at beg of next 2 rows.

Cast (bind) off 8 (9) sts, patt 13 sts, turn and leave rem sts on a holder.
Work each side of neck separately.
Cast (bind) off 4 sts, patt to end.
Cast (bind) off rem 9 sts.
With RS facing, rejoin yarn to rem sts, cast (bind) off center 41 sts, patt to end.
Complete to match first side, rev shaping.

left front

Cast on 93 sts using 3mm (US 3) needles and yarn A.
Work 7 rows of scallop patt as given for back. *73 sts*
ROW 8 (WS) (DEC): K2tog, *K8, K2tog, rep from * to last st, K1. *65 sts*
ROWS 9, 10 AND 11: Knit.

WORK TRELLIS PATTERN
Change to yarn B.
ROW 12 (WS): K1, P3, *with yarn at front, sl3 purlwise, P3, rep from * to last st, K1.
ROW 13: P1, K3, *with yarn at back, sl3 purlwise, K3, rep from * to last st, K1.
Change to yarn A.
ROW 14: K1, P3, *K3, P3, rep from * to last st, K1.
ROW 15: P1, K3, *P3, K3, rep from * to last st, P1.
ROW 16: K5, *pull up loop, K5, rep from * to end.
ROW 17: Work as row 15.
Change to yarn B.
ROW 18: P1, *with yarn at front, sl3 purlwise, P3, rep from * to last 4 sts, sl3 purlwise, P1.
ROW 19: K1, *with yarn at back, sl3 purlwise, K3, rep from * to last 4 sts, sl3 purlwise, K1.
Change to yarn A.
ROW 20: Work as row 15.
ROW 21: Work as row 14.
ROW 22: K2, *pull up loop, K5, rep from * to last 3 sts, pull up loop, K2.
ROW 23: K4, *P3, K3, rep from * to last 7 sts, P3, K4.
ROWS 24-35: Work as rows 12-23.
Smaller size only
Row 36 (WS) (DEC): K9, K2tog, K12 to end. *61 sts ***
Larger size only
Dec 1 st at end of last row. *64 sts ***
Both sizes
Cont in patt from chart for left front until chart row 40 is complete, shaping side by inc 1 st at beg of chart row 3 and every foll 8th row. *66 (69) sts*
Cont in patt, rep the 40-row rep throughout and inc every 8th row as before to 70 (73) sts, ending with a RS row.
Work 3 (9) rows.
SHAPE ARMHOLE AND FRONT NECK
Cast (bind) off 6 sts at beg of next row.
Work 1 row.
Dec 1 st at armhole edge on next 5 rows.
Work 1 row.
Dec 1 st at each end of next row and 8 (9) foll alt rows. *41 (42) sts*
Work 1 row.
Cont dec at neck edge on next row and every alt row until 31 (30) sts rem and then every foll 4th row to 25 (27) sts.
Cont until front matches back to shoulder, ending with a WS row.
SHAPE SHOULDER
Cast (bind) off 8 (9) sts at beg of next row and foll alt row.
Work 1 row.
Cast (bind) off rem 9 sts.

right front

Work as given for left front to **.
Complete as given for left front, following chart for right front and rev shaping.

sleeves (both alike)

Cast on 62 sts using 2¼mm (US 1) needles and yarn A.

ROW 1 (RS): K2, *P2, K2, rep from * to end.

ROW 2: P2, *K2, P2, rep from * to end.

Rep the last 2 rows until work measures 7.5cm (3in) from cast-on edge, ending with a WS row and inc 1 st at end of last row. *63 sts*

Change to 3mm (US 3) needles. Work 40 rows in patt from chart, working between markers for sleeves and inc each end of 3rd row and every foll 6th row. *77 sts*

Cont in patt, rep the 40-row patt throughout and inc every 6th row as before to 99 sts, taking extra-stitches into pattern. Cont until work measures 39 (40)cm (15½ [15¾]in) from cast-on edge, ending with a WS row.

SHAPE SLEEVE HEAD

Cast (bind) off 6 sts at beg of next 2 rows.

Dec 1 st at each end of next 7 rows and 6 foll alt rows. *61 sts*

Work 3 rows.

Dec 1 st at each end of next row, 4 foll 4th rows and 4 foll alt rows. *43 sts*

Work 1 row.

Dec 1 st at each end of next 7 rows.

Cast (bind) off 4 sts at beg of next 2 rows. Cast (bind) off rem 21 sts.

finishing

Press all pieces as described on the information page. Join both shoulders seams using back stitch.

FRONT BAND

With RS facing, using 2¼mm (US 1) needles and yarn A, pick up and knit 21 sts from cast-on edge to top of trellis pattern, 58 (64) sts to start of front neck shaping, 52 sts to shoulder, 49 sts across back neck, 52 sts down to start of front neck shaping, 58 (64) sts down to top of trellis pattern and 21 sts to cast-on edge. *311 (323) sts*

Knit 1 row.

NEXT ROW (BUTTONHOLE ROW) (RS): K3 (2), [K2tog, (yon, drop one of these loop on next row) twice, K8 (9)] 7 times, K2tog, (yon) twice, knit to end.

Knit 2 rows. Cast (bind) off knitwise. See information page for finishing instructions. Sew on buttons.

KEY □ A ▪ B ⋈ Using B, K1, P1, K1, into next st, P3tog ╱ C

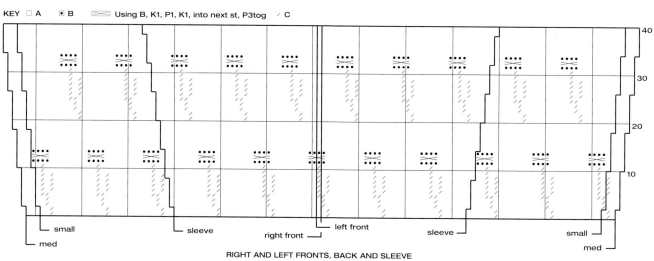

RIGHT AND LEFT FRONTS, BACK AND SLEEVE

courthouse steps by Kaffe Fassett

SIZE	XS	S	M	L	XL	
To fit bust	81	86	91	97	102	cm
	32	34	36	38	40	in
Actual width	52	54.5	57	59	61.5	cm
	20½	21½	22½	23	24	cm
Length	51	53	53	54	55	cm
	20	21	21	21½	21½	in
Sleeve length	39	39	40	40	41	cm
	15½	15½	15½	15½	16	in

YARN
Rowan 4 ply Cotton and Cotton Glacé
50gm (1¾oz) balls:

			XS	S	M	L	XL
A	4 ply	Bonny 104	1	1	1	1	1
B	4 ply	Vine 103	2	2	2	2	2
C	4 ply	Nightsky 115	2	2	2	2	2
D	4 ply	Vamp 117	1	1	2	2	2
E	Glacé	Nightshade 746	2	2	2	3	3
F	4 ply	Magenta 106	1	1	1	1	1
G	Glacé	Poppy 741	2	2	2	2	2
H	Glacé	Cr. Rose 793	2	2	2	2	2
J	Glacé	Pepper 796	2	2	2	2	2
M	Glacé	Bubbles 724	2	2	2	2	2
N	Glacé	Dijon 739	2	2	2	2	2
P	Glacé	Pear 780	1	1	1	1	1
R	Glacé	Terracotta 786	2	2	2	2	2
S	Glacé	Hyacinth 787	1	1	2	2	2
T	Glacé	Bl.Orange 445	2	2	2	2	2

NEEDLES
1 pair 3mm (US 3) needles
1 pair 3¼mm (US 3) needles

TENSION (GAUGE)
25 sts and 35 rows to 10cm (4in) measured over
patterned stocking (stockinette) stitch using 3¼mm
(US 3) needles

back and front (both alike)
Cast on 130 (136: 142: 148: 154) sts using 3mm
(US 3) needles and yarn E.
ROW 1 (RS): Using yarn E, P3 (2: 1: 4: 3), *K4, P4, rep
from * to last 7 (6: 5: 8: 7) sts, K4, P3 (2: 1: 4: 3).
ROW 2: Using yarn B, K3 (2: 1: 4: 3), *P4, K4, rep
from * to last 7 (6: 5: 8: 7) sts, P4, K3 (2: 1: 4: 3).
These 2 rows form rib.
Work another 18 rows in rib using colors as folls:
ROW 3: Use yarn B.
ROWS 4 TO 6: Use yarn T.
ROWS 7 AND 8: Use yarn D.

ROW 9: Use yarn R.
ROWS 10 AND 11: Use yarn J.
ROWS 12 AND 13: Use yarn S.
ROWS 14 TO 16: Use yarn N.
ROWS 17 AND 18: Use yarn H.
ROWS 19 AND 20: Use yarn B.
Change to 3¼mm (US 3) needles.
Using the intarsia technique described on the
information page and starting and ending rows as
indicated, cont in patt, foll chart, which is worked
entirely in st st, as folls:
Work 86 (90: 90: 92: 92) rows, ending with a WS row.

SHAPE ARMHOLES
Keeping chart correct, cast (bind) off 5 sts at beg of
next 2 rows. *120 (126: 132: 138: 144) sts*
Dec 1 st at each end of next 9 rows.
102 (108: 114: 120: 126) sts
Cont straight until chart row 144 (148: 150: 152: 156)
has been completed, ending with a WS row.
Change to 3mm (US 3) needles.
ROW 1 (RS): Using yarn E, K1 (4: 3: 2: 1), *P4, K4, rep
from * to last 5 (8: 7: 6: 5) sts, P4, K1 (4: 3: 2: 1).
ROW 2: Using yarn B, P1 (4: 3: 2: 1), *K4, P4, rep

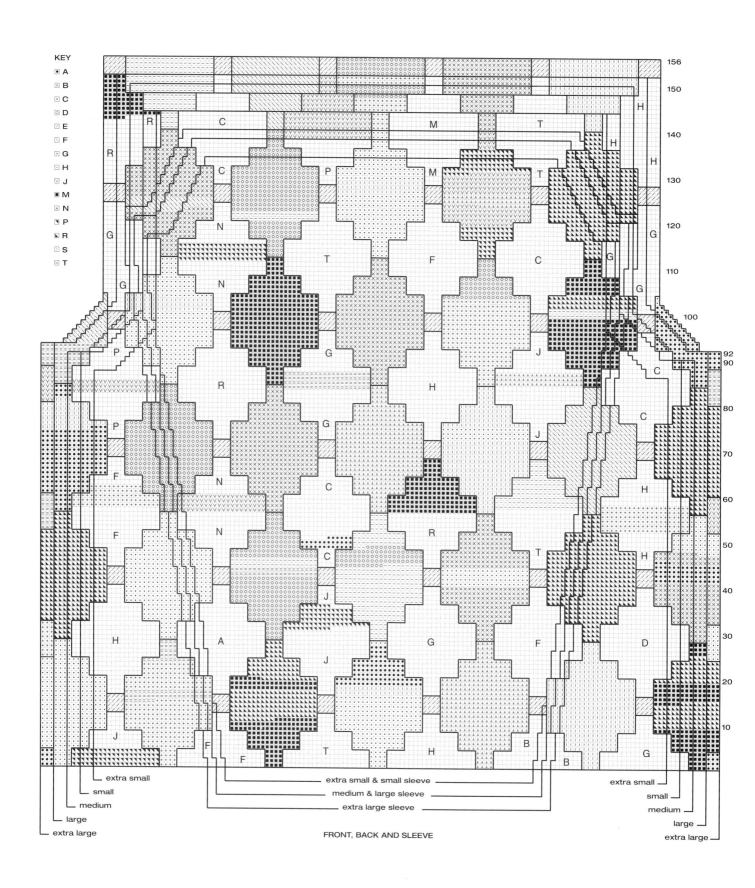

FRONT, BACK AND SLEEVE

from * to last 5 (8: 7: 6: 5) sts, K4, P1 (4: 3: 2: 1).
These 2 rows set position of rib.
Work another 14 rows in rib using colors as folls:
ROW 3: Use yarn B.
ROWS 4 TO 6: Use yarn T.
ROWS 7 AND 8: Use yarn D.
ROW 9: Use yarn R.
ROWS 10 AND 11: Use yarn J.
ROWS 12 AND 13: Use yarn S.
ROWS 14 TO 16: Use yarn N.
SHAPE SHOULDERS
Keeping rib correct, cont as folls:
Using yarn H, cast (bind) off 6 (7: 8: 9: 10) sts at beg
of next 2 rows. *90 (94: 98: 102: 106) sts.*
Using yarn B, cast (bind) off 6 (7: 8: 9: 10) sts at beg
of next 2 rows.
Cast (bind) off rem 78 (80: 82: 84: 86) sts.

sleeves (both alike)

Cast on 70 (70: 74: 74: 78) sts using 3mm (US 3)
needles and yarn E.
ROW 1 (RS): Using yarn E, K1 (1: 3: 3: 1), *P4, K4, rep
from * to last 5 (5: 7: 7: 5) sts, P4, K1 (1: 3: 3: 1).
ROW 2: Using yarn B, P1 (1: 3: 3: 1), *K4, P4, rep
from * to last 5 (5: 7: 7: 5) sts, K4, P1 (1: 3: 3: 1).
These 2 rows form rib.
Work another 18 rows in rib using colors as given for
back and front.
Change to 3¼mm (US 3) needles.
Using the intarsia technique described on the
information page and starting and ending rows as
indicated, cont in patt foll chart as folls:
Inc 1 st at each end of 3rd and every foll 6th row
until there are 106 (106: 112: 112: 116) sts, taking inc
sts into patt.
Cont straight until chart row 116 (116: 120: 120: 122)
has been completed, ending with a WS row.
SHAPE TOP
Keeping chart correct, cast (bind) off 5 sts at beg of
next 2 rows. *96 (96: 102: 102: 106) sts*
Dec 1 st at each end of next and foll 7 alt rows.
Work 1 row, ending with chart row 134 (134: 138:
138: 140).
Cast (bind) off rem 80 (80: 86: 86: 90) sts.

finishing

Press all pieces as described on the information page.
Join both shoulder seams using back stitch or mattress
stitch if preferred, and leaving 31 (32: 33: 34: 34.5)cm
(12¼ [12½: 13: 13½: 13¾]in) open at center for neck.
See information page for finishing instructions, setting
in sleeves using the shallow set-in method.

autumn

Easy-to-wear designs in rich earth colors—versatile enough to take you from the end of summer and through autumn to the first days of winter.

tulip cardigan by Kim Hargreaves

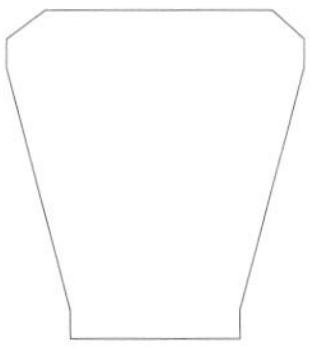

SIZES	6 MTHS	9 MTHS	1-2 YRS	2-3 YRS	3-4 YRS	4-6 YRS	6-8 YRS	
Actual width	27	29.5	32.5	35.5	38	41	44	cm
	10½	11½	13	14	15	16	17½	in
Length	26	28	31	32	35.5	38.5	42	cm
	10	11	12	12½	14	15	16½	in
Sleeve length	22	23.5	26.5	30	32	34	39	cm
	8½	9½	10½	12	12½	13½	15½	in

YARN
Rowan Hand Knit Cotton 50gm (1¾oz) balls:

3	3	3	4	4	5	6

(Photographed in Frost 552 and Viola 581)

NEEDLES
1 pair 2¾mm (US 2) needles
1 pair 3¼mm (US 3) needles

BUTTONS
5

TENSION (GAUGE)
28 sts and 36 rows to 10cm (4in) measured over stocking (stockinette) stitch using 3¼mm (US 3) needles

SHAPING NOTE
All decreases are worked 3 sts in from ends of rows. To dec 2 sts at beg of rows, work: K3, K3tog, K to end.
To dec 2 sts at end of rows, work: K to last 6 sts, K3tog tbl, K3.
All increases are worked 2 sts in from ends of rows.
To inc 1 st at beg of rows, work: K2, M1, K to end.
To inc 1 st at end of rows, work: K to last 2 sts, M1, K2.

back
Cast on 75 (83: 91: 99: 107: 115: 123) sts using 3¼mm (US 3) needles.
Knit 2 rows.
Beg with a K row, now work in st st throughout as folls:
Work straight until back measures 10 (12: 14: 14: 17: 17.5: 21)cm (4 [4¾: 5½: 5½: 6½: 6¾: 8¼]in), ending with a WS row.
SHAPE ARMHOLES
Cast (bind) off 2 sts at beg of next 2 rows.
71 (79: 87: 95: 103: 111: 119) sts
Dec 2 sts at each end of next and foll alt row.
63 (71: 79: 87: 95: 103: 111) sts
Cont straight until armholes measure 13 (13: 14: 15:

15.5: 18: 18)cm (5 [5: 5½: 6: 6¼: 7: 7] in), ending with a WS row.
SHAPE SHOULDERS AND BACK NECK
Cast (bind) off 6 (7: 8: 9: 11: 12: 13) sts at beg of next 2 rows. *51 (57: 63: 69: 73: 79: 85) sts*
NEXT ROW (RS): Cast (bind) off 6 (7: 8: 9: 11: 12: 13) sts, K until there are 11 (12: 13: 14: 14: 15: 17) sts on right needle and turn, leaving rem sts on a holder.
Work each side of neck separately.
Cast (bind) off 4 sts at beg of next row.
Cast (bind) off rem 7 (8: 9: 10: 10: 11: 13) sts.
With RS facing, rejoin yarn to rem sts, cast (bind) off center 17 (19: 21: 23: 23: 25: 25) sts, K to end.
Work to match first side, rev shaping.

pocket linings (make two)
Cast on 19 (21: 21: 23: 23: 25: 25) sts using 3¼mm (US 3) needles.
Beg with a K row, now work 28 rows in st st, thus ending with a WS row.
Break yarn and leave sts on a holder.

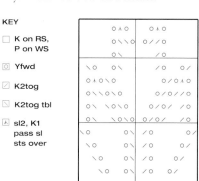

KEY

☐ K on RS, P on WS

Ⓞ Yfwd

▱ K2tog

◺ K2tog tbl

⬧ sl2, K1 pass sl sts over

MOTIF CHART

left front

Cast on 42 (47: 50: 55: 59: 62: 66) sts using 3¼mm (US 3) needles.
Knit 2 rows.
NEXT ROW (RS): K to last 6 sts, M1 and turn, leaving last 6 sts on a safety pin for button border.
37 (42: 45: 50: 54: 57: 61) sts
Purl 1 row.

PLACE MOTIF
NEXT ROW (RS): K9 (12: 13: 16: 18: 19: 21), work next 19 sts as row 1 of motif chart, K9 (11: 13: 15: 17: 19: 21).
This row sets position of motif chart worked on a st st background.
Cont as now set until all 26 rows of motif chart are complete, thus ending with a WS row.

PLACE POCKET
NEXT ROW (RS): K9 (11: 12: 14: 16: 16: 18), slip next 19 (21: 21: 23: 23: 25: 25) sts onto a holder and, in their place, K across 19 (21: 21: 23: 23: 25: 25) sts of first pocket lining, K9 (10: 12: 13: 15: 16: 18).
Beg with a P row, cont in st st until left front matches back to start of armhole shaping, ending with a WS row.

SHAPE ARMHOLE
Cast (bind) off 2 sts at beg of next row.
35 (40: 43: 48: 52: 55: 59) sts
Work 1 row.

1st, 3rd, 6th and 7th sizes
Dec 2 sts at armhole edge on next and foll alt row.
31 (39: 51: 55) sts
Work 3 rows, thus ending with a WS row.

SHAPE FRONT SLOPE
Dec 2 sts at end of next and every foll 6th row until 19 (25: 35: 39) sts rem.

2nd, 4th and 5th sizes
Dec 2 sts at armhole edge on next row. *38 (46: 50) sts*
Work 1 row, thus ending with a WS row.

SHAPE FRONT SLOPE
Dec 2 sts at both ends of next row. *34 (42: 46) sts*
Work 3 (5: 5) rows, thus ending with a WS row.
Dec 2 sts at front slope edge only on next and every foll 6th row until 22 (28: 32) sts rem.

All sizes
Work straight until left front matches back to start of shoulder shaping, ending with a WS row.

SHAPE SHOULDER
Cast (bind) off 6 (7: 8: 9: 11: 12: 13) sts at beg of next and foll alt row.
Work 1 row.
Cast (bind) off rem 7 (8: 9: 10: 10: 11: 13) sts.

right front

Cast on 42 (47: 50: 55: 59: 62: 66) sts using 3¼mm (US 3) needles. Knit 2 rows.
NEXT ROW (RS): K6 and slip these sts on a safety pin for buttonhole border, M1, K to end.
37 (42: 45: 50: 54: 57: 61) sts
Purl 1 row.

PLACE MOTIF
NEXT ROW (RS): K9 (11: 13: 15: 17: 19: 21), work next 19 sts as row 1 of motif chart, K9 (12: 13: 16: 18: 19: 21).
This row sets position of motif chart worked on a st st background.
Cont as now set until all 26 rows of motif chart are complete, thus ending with a WS row.

PLACE POCKET
NEXT ROW (RS): K9 (10: 12: 13: 15: 16: 18), slip next 19 (21: 21: 23: 23: 25: 25) sts onto a holder and, in their place, K across 19 (21: 21: 23: 23: 25: 25) sts of second pocket lining, K9 (11: 12: 14: 16: 16: 18).
Beg with a P row, cont in st st and complete to match left front, rev shaping.

sleeves (both alike)

Cast on 39 (39: 41: 47: 47: 51: 51) sts using 2¾mm (US 2) needles. Knit 4 (4: 6: 6: 6: 6: 6) rows.
Change to 3¼mm (US 3) needles.
Beg with a K row, now work in st st, shaping sides by inc 1 st at each end of 3rd and every foll 4th row until there are 73 (69: 73: 67: 65: 93: 75) sts.

2nd, 3rd, 4th, 5th, 6th and 7th sizes
Inc 1 st at each end of every foll 6th row (from previous inc) until there are 73 (79: 85: 87: 101: 101) sts.

All sizes
Cont without further shaping until sleeve measures 22 (23.5: 26.5: 30: 32: 34: 39)cm (8½ [9¼: 10½: 12: 12½: 13½: 15½] in), ending with a WS row.

SHAPE TOP
Cast (bind) off 2 sts at beg of next 2 rows.
69 (69: 75: 81: 83: 97: 97) sts
Dec 2 sts at each end of next and foll alt row.
Work 1 row, thus ending with a WS row.
Cast (bind) off rem 61 (61: 67: 73: 75: 89: 89) sts.

finishing

Press all pieces as described on the information page.
Join both shoulder seams using back stitch.

BUTTON BORDER
Slip 6 sts on left front safety pin onto 2¾mm (US 2) needles and rejoin yarn with RS facing.
Cont in garter st (knit every row) until border, when slightly stretched, fits up left front opening edge to shoulder and across to center back neck, ending with a WS row.
Cast (bind) off.
Slip st border in place.
Mark positions for 5 buttons on this border, the 1st to come in first row of border, the last to come 1cm(½in) below start of front slope shaping and the rem 3 buttons evenly spaced between.

BUTTONHOLE BORDER
Work to match button border, rejoining yarn with WS facing and with the addition of 5 buttonholes worked to correspond with positions marked for buttons as folls:
BUTTONHOLE ROW (RS): K2, yfwd, K2tog, K2.
Slipstitch border in place, joining ends at center back.
Join side seams using back stitch.

LOWER EDGING
Cast on 7 sts using 3¼mm (US 3) needles.
ROW 1 (RS): K2, yfwd, K2tog, yfwd, K3. *8 sts*
ROW 2, AND ALL WS ROWS: Knit.
ROW 3: K2, yfwd, K2tog, yfwd, K4. *9 sts*
ROW 5: K2, yfwd, K2tog, yfwd, K5. *10 sts*
ROW 7: K2, yfwd, K2tog, yfwd, K6. *11 sts*
ROW 9: K2, yfwd, K2tog, yfwd, K7. *12 sts*
ROW 11: K2, yfwd, K2tog, yfwd, K8. *13 sts*
ROW 12: Cast (bind) off 6 sts, K to end. *7 sts*
Rep these 12 rows until edging fits along lower edge of body, ending with row 12. Cast (bind) off.
Slipstitch edging in place.

POCKET TOPS
Slip 19 (21: 21: 23: 23: 25: 25) sts left on pocket holder onto 2¾mm (US 2) needles and rejoin yarn with RS facing. Knit 3 rows.
Cast (bind) off knitways (on WS).
See information page for finishing instructions.

scamp by Kim Hargreaves

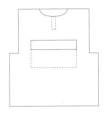

SIZES	1ST	2ND	3RD	4TH	5TH	6TH	7TH	
To fit chest	1–2	2–3	3–4	4–5	6–7	8–9	9–10	yrs
	51	56	58	61	66	71	76	cm
	20	22	23	24	26	28	30	in
Actual width	33.5	37.5	40.5	43.5	46.5	50.5	55.5	cm
	13	15	16	17	18½	20	22	in
Length	33	37	42	45	48.5	54	58	cm
	13	14½	16½	17½	19	21	23	in
Sleeve length	18	21.5	23	26	30.5	33	35.5	cm
	7	8½	9	10	12	13	14	in

(All measurements after washing)

YARNS

Crewneck pullover
Rowan Handknit Cotton DK 50gm (1¾oz) balls:

Raindrop 206	5	7	8	9	10	12	14

Rowan Denim 50gm (1¾oz) balls:

	6	7	8	10	11	13	15

Collared pullover
Rowan Handknit Cotton DK 50gm (1¾oz) balls:

	6	8	9	10	12	14	16

Rowan Denim 50gm (1¾oz) balls:

Nashville 225	7	8	9	11	13	15	17

NEEDLES
1 pair 3¼mm (US 3) needles
1 pair 4mm (US 6) needles

BUTTONS
2 for collared pullover
7.5cm (3in) of Velcro for collared pullover

TENSION (GAUGE)
Handknit DK Cotton
20 sts and 28 rows to 10cm (4in) measured over stocking (stockinette) stitch using 4mm (US 6) needles
Denim (before washing)
20 sts and 28 rows to 10cm (4in) measured over stocking (stockinette) stitch using 4mm (US 6) needles

PATTERN NOTE
Denim will shrink in length when washed for the first time. Allowances have been made in this pattern for shrinkage.

back

Cast on 67 (75: 81: 87: 93: 101: 111) sts using 3¼mm (US 3) needles.
Beg with a K row, work 6 rows in st st.
Starting and ending rows as indicated and rep rows 1 to 8 only, cont in patt from chart as folls:
Work 6 (6: 6: 6: 8: 8: 8) rows.
Change to 4mm (US 6) needles.

Handknit DK Cotton version
Cont straight until back measures about 16 (18.5: 22.5: 24: 26.5: 30.5: 33)cm (6¼ [7¼: 8¾: 9½: 10½: 12: 13]in) from lower edge, allowing first 6 rows to roll to RS and ending with chart row 8.

Denim version
Cont straight until back measures about 19.5 (22.5: 27.5: 29: 32: 37: 40)cm (7¾ [8¾: 11: 11½: 12½: 14½: 15¾]in) from lower edge, allowing first 6 rows to roll to RS and ending with chart row 8.

Both versions
Work chart rows 9–4, ending with a WS row.

SHAPE ARMHOLES
Keeping chart correct, cast (bind) off 4 (5: 5: 5: 6: 6: 6) sts at beg of next 2 rows.
*59 (65: 71: 77: 81: 89: 99) sts***
Work chart rows 17–36 and then rep chart rows 15–36 only, cont as folls:

Handknit DK Cotton version

Cont straight until armhole measures 14 (15.5: 16.5: 18: 19: 20.5: 22)cm (5½ [6: 6½: 7: 7½: 8: 8½]in), ending with a WS row.

Denim version

Cont straight until armhole measures 17 (19: 20: 22: 23: 25: 26.5)cm (6½ [7½: 7¾: 8½: 9: 9¾: 10½]in), ending with a WS row.

Both versions

SHAPE SHOULDERS AND BACK NECK

NEXT ROW (RS): Patt until there are 21 (23: 26: 28: 29: 32: 36) sts on right needle and turn, leaving rem sts on a holder.

Work each side of neck separately.

Cast (bind) off 4 sts at beg of next row.

Cast (bind) off rem 17 (19: 22: 24: 25: 28: 32) sts.

With RS facing, rejoin yarn to rem sts, cast (bind) off center 17 (19: 19: 21: 23: 25: 27) sts, patt to end.

Work to match first side, rev shapings.

crewneck pullover
front

Work as for back until there are 12 (12: 14: 14: 16: 16: 18) rows fewer than on back to shoulder cast (bind) off, ending with a WS row.

SHAPE NECK

NEXT ROW (RS): Patt 24 (26: 30: 32: 34: 37: 42) sts and turn, leaving rem sts on a holder.

Work each side of neck separately.

Cast (bind) off 4 sts at beg of next row.

Dec 1 st at neck edge of next 3 rows, then on foll 0 (0: 1: 1: 2: 2: 3) alt rows. *17 (19: 22: 24: 25: 28: 32) sts*

Work 7 rows.

SHAPE SHOULDER

Cast (bind) off rem 17 (19: 22: 24: 25: 28: 32) sts.

With RS facing, rejoin yarn to rem sts, cast (bind) off center 11 (13: 11: 13: 13: 15: 15) sts, patt to end.

Work to match first side, rev shapings.

collared pullover
pocket lining

Cast on 49 (51: 53: 55: 57: 59: 61) sts using 4mm (US 6) needles.

Handknit DK Cotton version

Beg with a K row, work 12 (12.5: 12.5: 14: 14: 16: 16)cm (4¾ [5: 5: 5½: 5½: 6¼: 6¼]in) in st st, ending with a RS row.

Denim version

Beg with a K row, work 14 (15: 15: 17: 17: 19: 19)cm (5½ [6: 6: 6½: 6½: 7½: 7½]in) in st st, ending with a RS row.

Both versions

Break yarn and leave sts on a holder.

front

Work as for back to **.

Keeping patt correct as for back, cont as folls:

Work 2 rows.

PLACE POCKET

NEXT ROW (RS): Patt 5 (7: 9: 11: 12: 15: 19) sts, cast (bind) off next 49 (51: 53: 55: 57: 59: 61) sts in patt, patt to end.

NEXT ROW: Patt 5 (7: 9: 11: 12: 15: 19) sts, with WS facing now patt across 49 (51: 53: 55: 57: 59: 61) sts of pocket lining, patt to end.

Handknit DK Cotton version

Cont in patt until armhole measures 7.5 (8: 8: 9: 10: 11: 11)cm (3 [3¼: 3¼: 9½: 4: 4¼: 4¼]in), ending with a WS row.

Denim version

Cont in patt until armhole measures 9 (10: 10: 11: 12: 13: 13)cm (3½ [4: 4: 4¼: 4¾: 5: 5]in), ending with a WS row.

Both versions

DIVIDE FOR FRONT OPENING

NEXT ROW (RS): Patt 27 (30: 33: 36: 38: 42: 47) sts, [K1, P1] twice, K1 and turn, leaving rem sts on a holder. *32 (35: 38: 41: 43: 47: 52) sts.*

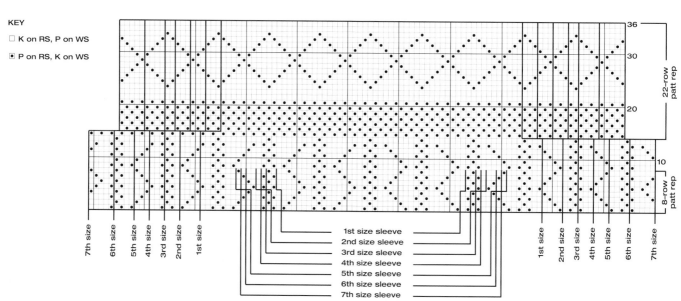

KEY

□ K on RS, P on WS

▪ P on RS, K on WS

36
30
22-row patt rep
20
10
8-row patt rep

7th size
6th size
5th size
4th size
3rd size
2nd size
1st size

1st size sleeve
2nd size sleeve
3rd size sleeve
4th size sleeve
5th size sleeve
6th size sleeve
7th size sleeve

1st size
2nd size
3rd size
4th size
5th size
6th size
7th size

FRONT, BACK AND SLEEVE

Work each side of neck separately.
NEXT ROW: K1, [P1, K1] twice, patt to end.
Last 2 rows set position of 5-st front-opening border worked in moss (seed) st.
Keeping border and patt correct, cont as folls:
Cont straight until there are 10 (10: 12: 12: 14: 14: 16) rows fewer than on back to shoulder cast (bind) off, ending with a WS row.

SHAPE NECK
NEXT ROW (RS): Patt 24 (26: 30: 32: 34: 37: 42) sts and turn, leaving rem 8 (9: 8: 9: 9: 10: 10) sts on a holder.
Cast (bind) off 4 sts at beg of next row.
Dec 1 st at neck edge of next 3 rows, then on foll 0 (0: 1: 1: 2: 2: 3) alt rows. *17 (19: 22: 24: 25: 28: 32) sts*
Work 5 rows.

SHAPE SHOULDER
Cast (bind) off rem 17 (19: 22: 24: 25: 28: 32) sts.
With RS facing, rejoin yarn to rem sts and cont as folls:
NEXT ROW (RS): Cast on 5 sts, work across these 5 sts as folls: [K1, P1] twice, K1, patt to end.
NEXT ROW: Patt to last 5 sts, K1, [P1, K1] twice.
Last 2 rows set position of 5-st front-opening border worked in moss (seed) st.
Keeping border and patt correct, cont as folls:
Cont straight until 10 (10: 12: 12: 14: 14: 16) rows fewer than on back to shoulder cast (bind) off, ending with a WS row.

SHAPE NECK
NEXT ROW (RS): Patt 8 (9: 8: 9: 9: 10: 10) sts and slip these sts onto a holder, patt to end.
24 (26: 30: 32: 34: 37: 42) sts
Work 1 row. Cast (bind) off 4 sts at beg of next row.
Dec 1 st at neck edge of next 3 rows, then on foll 0 (0: 1: 1: 2: 2: 3) alt rows. *17 (19: 22: 24: 25: 28: 32) sts*
Work 5 rows.

SHAPE SHOULDER
Cast (bind) off rem 17 (19: 22: 24: 25: 28: 32) sts.

sleeves (both alike)
Cast on 35 (39: 41: 43: 47: 49: 51) sts using 3¼mm (US 3) needles.
Beg with a K row, work 6 rows in st st.
Starting and ending rows as indicated and rep rows 1–8 only throughout, cont in patt from chart as folls:
Work 4 rows.
Change to 4mm (US 6) needles.

Handknit DK Cotton version
Inc 1 st at each end of next and every foll 4th (4th: 4th: 4th: 6th: 6th: 6th) row to 51 (65: 69: 75: 59: 59: 61) sts, then on every foll alt (alt: alt: alt: 4th: 4th: 4th) row until there are 61 (67: 71: 77: 81: 87: 93) sts, taking inc sts into patt.
Cont straight until sleeve measures 20 (24: 25.5: 28.5: 33.5: 36: 38.5)cm (7¾ [9½: 10: 11¼: 13: 14¼: 15¼]in) from lower edge, allowing first 6 rows to roll to RS and ending with a WS row.

Denim version
Inc 1 st at each end of next and every foll 4th (6th: 6th: 6th: 6th: 6th: 6th) row to 57 (47: 53: 57: 75: 77: 79) sts, then on every foll alt 4th row until there are 61 (67: 71: 77: 81: 87: 93) sts, taking inc sts into patt.
Cont straight until sleeve measures 24 (29: 30.5: 34: 40: 43: 46)cm (9½ [11½: 12: 13½: 15¾: 17: 18]in) from lower edge, allowing first 6 rows to roll to RS and ending with a WS row.

Both versions
Cast (bind) off loosely.

finishing
Press all pieces as described on the information page.

Crewneck pullover only
Join right shoulder seam using back stitch.

NECK BORDER
With RS facing and 3¼mm (US 3) needles, pick up and knit 15 (15: 17: 17: 19: 19: 21) sts down left front neck, 11 (13: 11: 13: 13: 15: 15) sts across front neck, 15 (15: 17: 17: 19: 19: 21) sts up right front neck, and 25 (27: 27: 29: 31: 33: 35) sts across back neck.
66 (70: 72: 76: 82: 86: 92) sts

Handknit DK Cotton version
Beg with a P row, work 11 rows in st st.

Denim version
Beg with a P row, work 13 rows in st st.

Both versions
Cast (bind) off loosely knitwise.
Join left shoulder and neck-border seam using back stitch, rev seam for st st roll.

Collared pullover only
Join shoulder seams using back stitch.

COLLAR
With RS facing and 3¼mm (US 3) needles, sl 8 (9: 8: 9: 9: 10: 10) sts from right front holder onto right needle, rejoin yarn and pick up and knit 15 (15: 17: 17: 19: 19: 21) sts up right front neck, 25 (27: 27: 29: 31: 33: 35) sts across back neck and 15 (15: 17: 17: 19: 19: 21) sts down left front neck, then patt across 8 (9: 8: 9: 9: 10: 10) sts from left front holder.
71 (75: 77: 81: 87: 91: 97) sts

Handknit DK Cotton version
Work 7 (7: 7.5: 7.5: 8.5: 8.5: 8.5)cm (2¾ [2¾: 3: 3: 3½: 3½: 3½]in) in moss (seed) st as set by front borders.

Denim version
Work 8 (8: 9: 9: 10: 10: 10)cm (3¼ [3¼: 3½: 3½: 3½: 4: 4]in) in moss (seed) st as set by front borders.
Cast (bind) off loosely and evenly in moss (seed) st.

POCKET FLAP
Cast on 51 (53: 55: 57: 59: 61: 63) sts using 4mm (US 6) needles.
ROW 1 (RS): K1, *P1, K1, rep from * to end.
Keeping moss (seed) st correct as set by last row, cont as folls:
Work 5 rows.
BUTTONHOLE ROW (RS): Moss (seed) st 4, cast (bind) off 2 sts, moss (seed) st to last 6 sts, cast (bind) off 2 sts, moss (seed) st to end.
NEXT ROW: Moss (seed) st to end, casting on 2 sts over those cast (bind) off on previous row.
Work 8 (8: 8: 10: 10: 10: 10) rows.
Cast (bind) off in patt.
Sew pocket flap to front above pocket opening as in photograph. Sew on buttons. Attach Velcro to pocket flap and pocket front halfway between buttons to prevent sagging.

See information page for finishing instructions, setting in sleeves using the square set-in method.

basic stripe by Kim Hargreaves

	CHILDREN'S (YRS)						ADULTS'				
SIZES	1	3	5	7	9	11	S	M	L	XL	
To fit chest	–	–	–	–	–	–	86–91	97–102	97–102	102–107	cm
	–	–	–	–	–	–	34–36	38–40	38–40	40–42	in
Actual width	30.5	34	38	43.5	47	51.5	58.5	63.5	63.5	69	cm
	12	13½	15	17	18½	20¼	23	25	25	27¼	in
Length	32	34.5	40.5	46	51	54	61.5	66.5	66.5	68.5	cm
	12½	13½	16	18	20	21¼	24¼	26¼	26¼	27	in
Sleeve length	22.5	25	29	31.5	33.5	36	39.5	39.5	44.5	44.5	cm
	8¾	9¾	11½	12¼	13¼	14¼	15½	15½	17½	17½	in

YARNS

Rowan Cotton Glacé 50gm (1¾oz) balls:

Two-color version

A	2	3	4	5	5	5	6	6	7	9	
B without hood	3	4	5	6	7	7	8	8	9	10	
B with hood	4	5	6								

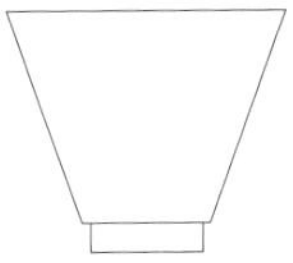

Three-color version

A	1	2	3	3	4	4	5	6	6	7	
B without hood	3	4	5	6	7	7	8	8	9	10	
B with hood	4	5	6								
C	1	1	1	1	1	1	1	1	2	2	

Note: For the three-color design, all the ribs and edgings remain the same as for the two-color design; only the narrow stripes on the sleeves are changed from yarn A to yarn C.

PHOTOGRAPHED IN	A	B	C
Large	736	725	737
Medium	743	745	
11 years	727	725	742
5 years	742	727	745
5 years	741	740	
5 years	736	725	
1 year	743	725	741

NEEDLES

1 pair 2¾mm (US 2) needles
1 pair 3¼mm (US 3) needles

BUTTONS

Pullover with hood (1, 3 and 5 years only): 3 buttons
Pullover with neckband (all sizes): 4 buttons

TENSION (GAUGE)

23 sts and 32 rows to 10cm (4in) measured over stocking (stockinette) stitch using 3¼mm (US 3) needles

back

Cast on 68 (76: 84: 92: 100: 108: 120: 128: 128: 136) sts using 2¾mm (US 2) needles and yarn A.
Work 1 row in K2, P2 rib.
Change to yarn B and cont in rib as set until work measures 4 (4: 5: 5: 6.5: 6.5: 6.5: 6.5: 6.5: 6.5)cm (1½ [1½: 2: 2: 2¾: 2¾: 2¾: 2¾: 2¾: 2¾]in) from beg, ending with a RS row.

NEXT ROW (INC) 1 AND 3 YEARS ONLY: Rib 22 (25), M1, rib 24 (26), M1, rib 22 (25). *70 (78) sts*

5, 7 AND 9 YEARS ONLY: Rib 12 (4: 8), [M1, rib 20 (12: 12)] 3 (7: 7) times, M1, rib 12 (4: 8). *88 (100: 108) sts*

11 YEARS AND SMALL ADULT: Rib 8, [M1, rib 10 (8)] 10 (14) times. *118 (134) sts*

MEDIUM, LARGE AND EXTRA LARGE ADULT: Rib 5, [M1, rib 7 (7: 6)] 17 (17: 21) times, M1, rib 4 (4: 5). *146 (146: 158) sts ***

Change to 3¼mm (US 3) needles and work 88 (96: 112: 130: 140: 150: 176: 192: 192: 200) rows in st st, beg with a K row in stripes of 6 rows A, 6 rows B.

SHAPE BACK NECK AND SHOULDERS

1, 3, 5, 7, 9 & 11 years only

With RS facing, K24 (28: 33: 37: 41: 46) sts, turn and leave rem sts on a holder.

Work each side of neck separately.
Cast (bind) off 4 sts, P to end.
Cast (bind) off rem 20 (24: 29: 33: 37: 42) sts.
With RS facing, rejoin yarn to rem sts, cast (bind) off center 22 (22: 22: 26: 26: 26) sts, K to end.
Complete to match first side, rev all shaping.

Small, medium, large and extra large adults' only

Cast (bind) off 16 (18: 18: 20) sts at beg of next 2 rows.
Cast (bind) off 16 (18: 18: 20) sts, K22 (23: 23: 24) sts, turn and leave rem sts on a holder.
Work each side of neck separately.
Cast (bind) off 6 sts, P to end.
Cast (bind) off rem 16 (17: 17: 18) sts.
With RS facing, rejoin yarn to rem sts, cast (bind) off center 26 (28: 28: 30) sts, K to end. Complete to match first side, rev all shaping.

front

Work as given for back to **.

1, 3 and 5 years only (pockets)

Change to 3¼mm (US 3) needles and cont in st st, beg with a K row, in stripes as for back as folls:
K18 (21: 24) sts, leave these sts on a holder, K34 (36: 40) sts, leave rem 18 (21: 24) sts on a holder. Keeping stripe sequence correct, cont on center 34 (36: 40) sts until front pocket measures 9.5 (11: 12.5)cm (3¾ [4¼: 5]in), ending with a WS row.
Leave sts on a holder.
Using a separate length of the yarn used for first stripe and 3¼mm (US 3) needles, cast on 34 (36: 40) sts for pocket lining. Then with RS facing, slip first 18 (21: 24) sts (already knitted) onto RH 3¼mm (US 3) needle and knit across sts of pocket lining. Complete row by working across rem 18 (21: 24) sts.

70 (78: 88) sts
Cont in stripe sequence until work measures same as front pocket.
Complete pocket as folls:
K18 (21: 24) sts, then holding pocket flap sts at front, take 1 st from pocket flap and 1 st from main knitting and K both sts tog. Cont in this manner until all pocket sts have been worked, then K across rem 18 (21: 24) sts. Cont in st st until 56 (60: 72) rows have been completed.

7, 9 & 11 years, small, medium, large and extra large adults'

Change to 3¼mm (US 3) needles and cont in stripe sequence until 86 (88: 98: 118: 128: 128: 132) rows have been completed.

All sizes

DIVIDE FOR NECK

K33 (37: 42: 48: 52: 57: 64: 70: 70: 76) sts, turn and leave rem sts on a holder.
Work each side of neck separately.
Cont in st st until a total of 77 (81: 97: 113: 123: 133: 157: 169: 169: 173) rows have been completed in stripe sequence.

SHAPE FRONT NECK

Keeping stripe sequence correct, cast (bind) off 3 (3: 3: 3: 3: 3: 4: 4: 4: 4) sts at beg of next row, P to end.
Work 1 row.
Cast (bind) off 3 sts at beg of next row.
Dec 1 st at neck edge on next 6 (4: 4: 6: 6: 6: 2: 2: 2: 2) rows, then on foll 1 (3: 3: 3: 3: 3: 6: 7: 7: 6) alt rows and then every 4th row 0 (0: 0: 0: 0: 0: 1: 1: 1: 3) times. *20 (24: 29: 33: 37: 42: 48: 53: 53: 58) sts*
Cont without further shaping until front matches back to shoulder, ending with a WS row.

SHAPE SHOULDER

1, 3, 5, 7, 9 & 11 years only

Cast (bind) off rem sts.

Small, medium, large and extra large adults' only

Cast (bind) off 16 (18: 18: 20) sts at beg of next row and foll alt row. Work 1 row.
Cast (bind) off rem 16 (17: 17: 18) sts.
With RS facing, rejoin yarn to rem sts, cast (bind) off center 4 (4: 4: 4: 4: 6: 6: 6: 6) sts, K to end.
Complete to match first side, rev all shaping.

sleeves (both alike)

Cast on 32 (32: 36: 36: 40: 44: 48: 48: 48: 48) sts using 2¾mm (US 2) needles and yarn A.
Work 1 row in K2, P2 rib.
Change to yarn B and cont in rib as set until work measures 5 (5: 6.5: 6.5: 6.5: 6.5: 6.5: 6.5: 6.5: 6.5)cm (2 [2: 2¾.2¾: 2¾: 2¾: 2¾: 2¾: 2¾: 2¾]in) from beg, ending with a RS row.
NEXT ROW (INC) Rib 4 (4: 3: 3: 6: 6: 6: 6: 2: 2), (M1, rib 8 (8: 6: 6: 4: 11: 12: 12: 4: 4) to last 4 (4: 3: 3: 6: 5: 6: 6: 2: 2) sts, M1, rib 4 (4: 3: 3: 6: 5: 6: 6: 2: 2).
36 (36: 42: 42: 48: 48: 52: 52: 60: 60) sts
Change to 3¼mm (US 3) needles and work 56 (64: 72: 80: 86: 94: 106: 106: 122: 122) rows in stripe sequence of 2 rows A, 6 rows B (or 2 rows C, 6 rows B) and AT THE SAME TIME, shape sides by inc 1 st at each end of every 3rd row until there are 70 (70: 86: 86: 92: 92: 116: 116: 128: 128) sts.
Cast (bind) off.

hoods

1, 3 & 5 years only

Cont on 80 (82: 84) sts using 3¼mm (US 3) needles

and yarn B.
Work 70 (76: 80) rows in st st, beg with a K row, in stripe sequence for sleeves. Cast (bind) off.
Fold hood in half with wrong sides tog, then sew cast (bound) off edge of hood together.

HOOD EDGING

With RS of hood facing and 2¾mm (US 2) needles, pick up and K112 (118: 122) sts evenly around front edge of hood.
Work 5 rows in K2, P2 rib using yarn B.
Change to yarn A and work 1 row in rib as set.
Cast (bind) off evenly in rib using yarn A.

pocket edgings

1, 3 & 5 years only
With RS facing, 2¾mm (US 2) needles and yarn B, pick up and K30 (34: 36) sts evenly up left side of pocket. Work 5 rows in K2, P2 rib using yarn B.
Change to yarn A and work 1 row in rib as set.
Cast (bind) off evenly in rib using yarn A.
Work right side of pocket to match.
Sew pocket tops in place on RS.

finishing

Press all pieces (except ribbing) on WS using a warm iron over a damp cloth.
Join both shoulder seams using back stitch.
Place markers 15 (15: 18.5: 18.5: 20: 20: 25: 25: 27.5: 27.5)cm (6 [6: 7¼: 7¼: 7¾: 7¾: 9¾: 9¾: 11: 11]in) below shoulder seams on back and front.
Sew sleeve top between markers using back stitch.
Join side and sleeve seams using back stitch on main knitting and an edge-to-edge st on ribs.

BUTTON BAND (LEFT SIDE FOR LADIES', RIGHT SIDE FOR MEN'S)

With RS facing, 2¾mm (US 2) needles and yarn B, pick up and K18 (18: 22: 24: 30: 30: 34: 36: 36: 36) sts evenly along appropriate front edge. Work 5 rows in K2, P2 rib using yarn B.
Change to yarn A and work 1 row in rib as set.
Cast (bind) off evenly in rib using yarn A.

BUTTONHOLE BAND

With RS facing, 2¾mm (US 2) needles and yarn B, pick up and K sts along rem edge as for button band.
Work 2 rows in K2, P2 rib.
NEXT ROW (BUTTONHOLE): Rib 3, cast (bind) off 2, rib 3 (3: 5: 6: 9: 9: 11: 12: 12: 12) sts twice, cast (bind) off 2, rib 3.
NEXT ROW: Work across row in rib, casting on 2 sts in place of those cast (bound) off on previous row.
Work 1 more row in rib using yarn B, then change to yarn A and work 1 more row.
Cast (bind) off evenly in rib using yarn A.
Slipstitch front bands into place.

1, 3 & 5 years only (pullover with hood)

Slipstitch hood evenly into place around neck.

All sizes (pullover with neckband)

With RS facing, 2¾mm (US 2) needles and yarn B, pick up and K84 (88: 88: 96: 96: 104: 108: 110: 110: 114) sts evenly around neck edge, including front bands.
Work 5 rows in K2, P2 rib using yarn B and making a buttonhole in line with those previously worked on rows 2 and 3.
Change to yarn A and work 1 row in rib as set.
Cast (bind) off evenly in rib using yarn A.
Press seams.
Sew on buttons to correspond with buttonholes.

zoe by Rowan Design Studio

SIZES	1ST	2ND	3RD	4TH	5TH	6TH	7TH	8TH	9TH	
To fit	6 mths	9 mths	1–2 yrs	2–3 yrs	3–4 yrs	4–6 yrs	6–8 yrs	8–9 yrs	9–10 yrs	
Actual width	30	32.5	34.5	37.5	41	44	47	51	55	cm
	11¾	12¾	13½	14¾	16	17¼	18½	20	21½	in
Length	30.5	33	38	42	45	49.5	53.5	57	61	cm
	12	13	15	16½	18	19½	21	22½	24	in
Sleeve length	20	21.5	22.5	24.5	28	30.5	35.5	38	40.5	cm
	8	8½	9	9½	11	12	14	15	16	in

YARN
Rowan Wool Cotton 50gm (1¾oz) balls:

Gypsy 910	14	3	4	4	5	6	7	8	10	12

NEEDLES
1 pair 3¼mm (US 3) needles
1 pair 4mm (US 6) needles

BUTTONS
1st, 2nd, 3rd and 4th sizes only
4

TENSION (GAUGE)
22 sts and 30 rows to 10cm (4in) measured over
stocking (stockinette) stitch using 4mm (US 6) needles

back
Cast on 66 (72: 76: 82: 90: 96: 104: 112: 122) sts using
3¼mm (US 3) needles and work 6 (6: 8: 8: 8: 8: 10:
10: 10) rows in garter stitch (knit every row).
Change to 4mm (US 6) needles.
NEXT ROW (RS): K4 (5: 5: 6: 6: 5: 5: 5: 6) sts, K2, *P2, K2,
rep from * to last 4 (5: 5: 6: 6: 5: 5: 5: 6) sts, K4 (5: 5: 6: 6:
5: 5: 5: 6) sts.
NEXT ROW: K4 (5: 5: 6: 6: 5: 5: 5: 6) sts, P2, *K2, P2, rep
from * to last 4 (5: 5: 6: 6: 5: 5: 5: 6) sts, K4 (5: 5: 6: 6:
5: 5: 5: 6) sts.
Rep these 2 rows 1 (1: 2: 2: 2: 2: 3: 3: 3) times more. **
Cont in st st, beg with a K row, until work measures
30.5 (33: 38: 42: 45: 49.5: 53.5: 57: 61)cm (12 [13: 15:
16½: 17¾: 19½: 21: 22½: 24]in), or length required
from cast-on edge, ending with a WS row.
SHAPE SHOULDERS AND BACK NECK
Cast (bind) off 20 (22: 23: 26: 28: 31: 34: 37: 42) sts,
K26 (28: 30: 30: 34: 34: 36: 38: 38) sts and leave these
on a holder, K to end.
1st, 2nd, 3rd & 4th sizes only
Work 2 rows in st st to form band for shoulder buttons.
All sizes
Cast (bind) off.

pocket lining (make 2)
Cast on 14 (16: 16: 18: 22: 24: 26: 26: 26) sts using
4mm (US 6) needles and work 18 (20: 22: 24: 26: 28:
30: 30: 30) rows in st st, beg with a K row.
Leave sts on a holder.

front
Work as for back to **.
Work 18 (20: 22: 24: 26: 28: 30: 30: 30) rows in st st,
beg with a K row.
PLACE POCKET LININGS
NEXT ROW (RS): K10 (10: 11: 12: 12: 12: 14: 16: 20) sts,
slip next 14 (16: 16: 18: 22: 24: 26: 26: 26) sts onto a
holder and replace these with first pocket lining, K18
(20: 22: 22: 22: 24: 24: 28: 30) sts, slip next 14 (16: 16:
18: 22: 24: 26: 26: 26) sts onto holder and replace
these with second pocket lining and knit to end.
Cont in st st until front is 12 (12: 14: 14: 16: 16: 18:
18: 18) rows shorter than back to shoulder shaping,
ending with a WS row.
SHAPE FRONT NECK
NEXT ROW: K28 (30: 32: 35: 38: 41: 44: 48: 53, turn,
leaving rem sts on a holder, work each side separately.
Dec 1 st at neck edge on next 8 (8: 9: 9: 10: 10: 10:
11: 11) rows.
20 (22: 23: 26: 28: 31: 34: 37: 42) sts
Cont without further shaping until front matches
back to shoulder, ending with a WS row. ***
5th, 6th, 7th, 8th & 9th sizes only
Cast (bind) off rem sts.
1st, 2nd, 3rd & 4th sizes only
Work buttonhole band for shoulder fastening as folls:
Knit 2 rows.
BUTTONHOLE ROW (RS): K2, (yon, K2tog, K4 (5: 5: 6)
twice, yon, K2tog, K4 (4: 5: 6)
Knit 1 row. Cast (bind) off.

All sizes

Return to stitches on holder and with RS facing slip center 10 (12: 12: 12: 14: 14: 16: 16: 16) sts onto a holder, rejoin yarn and K to end.

Work as for first side to *** rev shaping. Cast (bind) off.

sleeves (both alike)

Cast on 32 (32: 36: 40: 42: 44: 48: 48: 48) sts using 3¼mm (US 3) needles and work 6 (6: 8: 8: 8: 8: 8: 8: 8) rows in st st, beg with a K row.

Work 6 (6: 8: 8: 8: 8: 8: 8: 8) rows in K2, P2 rib.

Change to 4mm (US 6) needles and cont in st st, shaping sides by inc as folls:

NEXT ROW (INC): K2, M1, K to last 2 sts, M1, K2.

Work 3 rows.

Rep these 4 rows until there are 56 (58: 64: 70: 76: 82: 90: 94: 100) sts on needle.

Cont without further shaping until work measures 18 (19.5: 20.5: 22.5: 26: 28.5: 33.5: 36: 38.5)cm (7 [7¾: 8: 8¾: 10¼:11¼: 13: 14¼: 15¼]in) from beg of rib, ending with a WS row.

Work 6 rows in K2, P2 rib.

Cast (bind) off loosely and evenly in rib.

finishing

Press all pieces except ribbing on wrong side, using a warm iron over a damp cloth.

Join right shoulder seam using back stitch.

NECKBAND

With RS facing, using 3¼mm (US 3) needles and beg at left shoulder, on first 4 sizes only pick up and K2 sts across buttonhole band, 12 (12: 14: 14: 16: 16: 18: 18: 18) sts down left front neck, 10 (12: 12: 12: 14: 14: 16: 16: 16) sts from holder across center front, 12 (12: 14: 14: 16: 16: 18: 18: 18) sts up right front neck and 26 (28: 30: 30: 34: 34: 36: 38: 38) sts from holder across back neck. On first 4 sizes only, pick up and K2 sts from button band.

64 (68: 74: 74: 80: 80: 88: 90: 90) sts

1st, 2nd, 3rd & 4th sizes only

Work 2 rows in K2, P2 rib.

NEXT ROW (BUTTONHOLE) (WS): Rib to last 4 sts, rib 2tog, yon, rib 2.

Work 1 more row in rib.

Work 6 rows in st st, beg with a P row.

Cast (bind) off loosely and evenly.

Join back and front at left shoulder edge, overlapping front onto back. Sew on buttons.

5th, 6th, 7th, 8th & 9th sizes only

Work 6 rows in K2, P2 rib.

Work 8 rows in st st, beg with a P row.

Cast (bind) off loosely and evenly.

Join left shoulder seam using a back stitch and join neckband seam using a flat stitch.

All sizes

POCKET TOPS

With RS facing, slip sts from holder onto a 3¼mm (US 3) needle and work 6 (6: 6: 8: 8: 8: 8: 8: 8) rows in garter st. Cast (bind) off.

Place markers about 12.5 (13: 14.5: 16: 17: 18.5: 20.5: 21.5: 22.5)cm (5 [5: 5¾: 6¼: 6½: 7¼: 8: 8½: 8¾:]in), down from shoulder seam on back and front.

Sew in sleeves between markers, matching center of sleeve to shoulder seam and slightly stretching rib at top of sleeve.

See information page for finishing instructions, leaving garter-st rows at bottom of garment open to form vent.

carpenter by Kim Hargreaves

SIZES	XS	S	M	L	XL	
To fit bust	81	86.5	91.5	96.5	102	cm
	32	34	36	38	40	in
Actual width	46	48.5	50.5	54	56	cm
	18	19	20	21½	22	in
Length	50	60	61	62	63	cm
	23	23½	24	24½	25	in
Sleeve length	42	42	43	43	43	cm
	16½	16½	17	17	17	in

YARNS

Rowan Magpie Aran 100gm (3½oz) balls:
Natural 002   6   6   6   7   7

NEEDLES

1 pair 4½mm (US 7) needles
1 pair 5mm (US 8) needles

TENSION (GAUGE)

18 sts and 23 rows to 10cm (4in) measured over stocking (stockinette) stitch using 5mm (US 8) needles

back

Cast on 83 (87: 91: 97: 101) sts using 4½mm (US 7) needles.
ROW 1 (RS): K1, *P1, K1, rep from * to end.
ROW 2: P1, *K1, P1, rep from * to end.
Rep last 2 rows 6 times more.
Change to 5mm (US 8) needles.
ROW 1 (RS): Knit.
ROW 2: Purl.
ROW 3: K2 (4: 3: 3: 2), *yfwd, K2tog, K4, rep from * to last 3 (5: 4: 4: 3) sts, yfwd, K2tog, K1 (3: 2: 2: 1).
Beg with a purl row, now work in st st throughout as follows:
Work 3 (3: 3: 5: 5) rows, thus ending with a WS row.
SHAPE SIDE SEAMS AND DARTS
Place markers on 21st (22nd: 23rd: 24th: 25th) st from each end of last row.
NEXT ROW (RS) (DEC): K2, K2tog, K to within 1 st of marked st, K3tog, K to within 1 st of 2nd marked st, K3tog tbl, K to last 4 sts, K2tog tbl, K2.
Work 11 rows.
Rep last 12 rows once more and then first (dec) row again. 65 (69: 73: 79: 83) sts
Work 11 (13: 13: 13: 13) rows, ending with a WS row.
NEXT ROW (RS) (INC): K3, M1, *K to marked st, M1, K marked st, M1, rep from * once more, K to last 3 sts, M1, K3.
Work 13 rows.

Rep last 14 rows once more and then first (inc) row again. 83 (87: 91: 97: 101) sts
Cont straight until back measures 39 (40: 40: 41: 41)cm (15½ [15¾: 15¾: 16¼: 16¼]in), ending with a WS row.
SHAPE ARMHOLES
Cast (bind) off 3 (4: 5: 5: 6) sts at beg of next 2 rows.
77 (79: 81: 87: 89) sts
NEXT ROW (RS) (DEC): K3, K3tog, K to last 6 sts, K3tog tbl, K3.
Work 1 row.
Rep last 2 rows 2 (2: 2: 3: 3) times more.
65 (67: 69: 71: 73) sts
NEXT ROW (RS) (DEC): K3, K3tog, K to last 6 sts, K3tog tbl, K3.
Work 3 rows.
Rep last 4 rows once more. 57 (59: 61: 63: 65) sts
Cont without further shaping until armhole measures 20 (20: 21: 21: 22)cm (7¾ [7¾: 8¼: 8¼: 8½]in), ending with a WS row.
SHAPE SHOULDERS AND BACK NECK
Cast (bind) off 4 sts at beg of next 2 rows.
49 (51: 53: 55: 57) sts
NEXT ROW (RS): Cast (bind) off 4 sts, K until there are 7 (7: 8: 8: 9) sts on right needle and turn, leaving rem sts on a holder.
Work each side of neck separately.
Cast (bind) off 4 sts at beg of next row.
Cast (bind) off rem 3 (3: 4: 4: 5) sts.
With RS facing, rejoin yarn to rem sts, cast (bind) off center 27 (29: 29: 31: 31) sts, K to end.
Work to match first side, rev shaping.

front

Work as given for back until there are 8 rows fewer than on back to start of shoulder and back neck shaping.
SHAPE NECK
NEXT ROW (RS): K17 (17: 18: 18: 19) and turn, leaving rem sts on a holder.
Work each side of neck separately.
Work 1 row.
NEXT ROW (RS) (DEC): K to last 5 sts, K3tog tbl, K2.
Rep last 2 rows twice more. 11 (11: 12: 12: 13) sts
Work 1 row, thus ending with a WS row.
SHAPE SHOULDER
Cast (bind) off 4 sts at beg of next and foll alt row.
Work 1 row.
Cast (bind) off rem 3 (3: 4: 4: 5) sts.
With RS facing, rejoin yarn to rem sts, cast (bind) off

center 23 (25: 25: 27: 27) sts, K to end.
Work 1 row.
NEXT ROW (RS) (DEC): K2, K3tog, K to end.
Rep last 2 rows twice more. *11 (11: 12: 12: 13) sts*
Work 2 rows, thus ending with a RS row.
SHAPE SHOULDER
Cast (bind) off 4 sts at beg of next and foll alt row.
Work 1 row.
Cast (bind) off rem 3 (3: 4: 4: 5) sts.

sleeves (both alike)

Cast on 39 (41: 43: 45: 47) sts using 4½mm (US 7)
needles.
Work 22 rows in rib as given for back, inc 1 st at
each end of 15th row and thus ending with a WS
row. *41 (43: 45: 47: 49) sts*
Change to 5mm (US 8) needles.
Beg with a K row, work in st st, shaping sleeve seam
by inc 1 st at each end of next and every foll 8th row
until there are 59 (61: 63: 65: 67) sts.
Cont without further shaping until sleeve measures
42 (42: 43: 43: 43)cm (16½ [16½: 17: 17: 17]in),
ending with a WS row.
SHAPE TOP
Cast (bind) off 3 (4: 5: 5: 6) sts at beg of next 2 rows.
53 (53: 53: 55: 55) sts
NEXT ROW (RS) (DEC): K3, K3tog, K to last 6 sts,
K3tog tbl, K3.
Work 1 row.
NEXT ROW (RS) (DEC): K3, K3tog, K to last 6 sts,
K3tog tbl, K3.
Work 3 rows. *45 (45: 45: 47: 47) sts*
NEXT ROW (RS) (DEC): K3, K3tog, K to last 6 sts,
K3tog tbl, K3.
Work 5 rows.
Rep last 6 rows 1 (1: 1: 1: 2) times more.
37 (37: 37: 39: 35) sts
NEXT ROW (RS) (DEC): K3, K3tog, K to last 6 sts,
K3tog tbl, K3.
Work 3 rows.
Rep last 4 rows 0 (0: 1: 1: 0) times more.
33 (33: 29: 31: 31) sts
NEXT ROW (RS) (DEC): K3, K3tog, K to last 6 sts,
K3tog tbl, K3.
Work 1 row.
Rep last 2 rows 2 (2: 1: 1: 1) times more.
21 (21: 21: 23: 23) sts
Cast (bind) off 4 sts at beg of next 2 rows.
Cast (bind) off rem 13 (13: 13: 15: 15) sts.

finishing

Press all pieces as described on the information page.
Join right shoulder seam using back stitch.
NECK BORDER
With RS facing and using 5mm (US 8) needles, pick
up and knit 12 sts down left front neck, 23 (25: 25:
27: 27) sts across front neck, 12 sts up right front
neck and 34 (36: 36: 38: 38) sts across back neck.
81 (85: 85: 89: 89) sts
Beg with a WS row, work 8cm (3¼in) in rib as given
for back.
Cast (bind) off loosely in rib.
Make twisted cord approx 150cm (60in) long and
knot ends. Thread in and out of eyelet holes above
body rib.
See information page for finishing instructions.

betsy by Kim Hargreaves

SIZES

	S	M	L	
To fit bust	81–86	86–91	91–97	cm
	32–34	34–36	36–38	in
Actual width	50.5	53	56	cm
	20	21	22	in
Length	51.5	54	56.5	cm
	20½	21½	22	in
Sleeve length	43	43	43	cm
	17	17	17	in

YARNS

Rowan Wool Cotton 50gm (1¾oz) balls:

Amazon 905	9	10	10	

NEEDLES

1 pair 3¼mm (US 3) needles
1 pair 3¾mm (US 5) needles
1 pair 4mm (US 6) needles

BUTTONS

7

TENSION (GAUGE)

22 sts and 30 rows to 10cm (4in) measured over stocking (stockinette) stitch using 4mm (US 6) needles.

back

Cast on 111 (117: 123) sts using 3¾mm (US 5) needles.
ROW 1 (RS): K1, *P1, K1, rep from * to end.
This row forms moss (seed) st.
Work another 43 rows in moss (seed) st, thus ending with a WS row.
Change to 4mm (US 6) needles.
Beg with a K row, work in st st throughout as folls:
Cont straight until back measures 28 (30.5: 33)cm (11¼ [12: 13]in), ending with a WS row.
SHAPE RAGLAN ARMHOLES
Cast (bind) off 3 (4: 5) sts at beg of next 2 rows.
105 (109: 113) sts
NEXT ROW (DEC) (RS): K3, K3tog, K to last 6 sts, K3tog tbl, K3.
Work 1 row.
Rep last 2 rows 1 (3: 5) times more. *97 (93: 89) sts*
NEXT ROW (DEC) (RS): K3, K3tog, K to last 6 sts, K3tog tbl, K3.
Work 3 rows.
Rep last 4 rows 14 (13: 12) times more, and then first 2 of these rows again, ending with a WS row. *33 sts*
SHAPE BACK NECK
NEXT ROW (RS): K6 and turn, leaving rem sts on a holder.

Work each side of neck separately. Cast (bind) off 4 sts at beg of next row. K2tog and fasten off.
With RS facing, rejoin yarn to rem sts, cast (bind) off center 21 sts, K to end. Work to match first side, rev shapings.

pocket linings (make two)

Cast on 27 sts using 4mm (US 6) needles.
Beg with a K row, work 26 rows in st st.
Break yarn and leave sts on a holder.

left front

Cast on 62 (65: 68) sts using 3¾mm (US 5) needles.
ROW 1 (RS): *K1, P1, rep from * to last 0 (1: 0) st, K0 (1: 0).
ROW 2: K0 (1: 0), *P1, K1, rep from * to end.
These 2 rows form moss (seed) st.
Work another 41 rows in moss (seed) st, ending with a RS row.
PLACE POCKET
NEXT ROW (WS): Patt 7 sts and slip these sts on a safety pin for button border, M1, patt 14 (16: 18), cast (bind) off next 27 sts in patt, patt to end.
Change to 4mm (US 6) needles.
NEXT ROW (RS): K14 (15: 16), K across 27 sts of first pocket lining, K15 (17: 19). *56 (59: 62) sts*
Beg with a P row, work in st st throughout as folls:
Cont straight until left front matches back to start of armhole shaping, ending with a WS row.
SHAPE RAGLAN ARMHOLE
Cast (bind) off 3 (4: 5) sts at beg of next row.
53 (55: 57) sts
Work 1 row.
NEXT ROW (DEC) (RS): K3, K3tog, K to end.
Work 1 row.
Rep last 2 rows 1 (3: 5) times more. *49 (47: 45) sts*
NEXT ROW (DEC) (RS): K3, K3tog, K to end.
Work 3 rows.
Rep last 4 rows 9 (8: 7) times more, and then first 3 of these rows again, thus ending with a RS row. *27 sts*
SHAPE NECK
Cast (bind) off 5 sts at beg of next row. *22 sts*
NEXT ROW (RS): K3, K3tog, K16. *20 sts*
Cast (bind) off 5 sts at beg of next row. *15 sts*
Dec 1 st at neck edge on next 2 rows. *13 sts*
NEXT ROW (RS): K3, K3tog, K5, K2tog. *10 sts*
Work 3 rows, dec 1 st at neck edge on 2nd of these rows. *9 sts*
NEXT ROW (RS): K3, K3tog, K1, K2tog. *6 sts*

Work 3 rows, dec 1 st at neck edge on 2nd of these rows. *5 sts*
NEXT ROW (RS): K1, K4tog.
Work 3 rows on rem 2 sts.
NEXT ROW: K2tog and fasten off.

right front

Cast on 62 (65: 68) sts using 3¾mm (US 5) needles.
ROW 1 (RS): K0 (1: 0), *P1, K1, rep from * to end.
ROW 2: *K1, P1, rep from * to last 0 (1: 0) st, K0 (1: 0).
These 2 rows form moss (seed) st. Work another 34 rows in moss (seed) st, thus ending with a WS row.
NEXT ROW (BUTTONHOLE ROW) (RS): Patt 3 sts, yrn (to make a buttonhole), work 2 tog, patt to end.
Work another 6 rows in moss (seed) st, end with a RS row.

PLACE POCKET

NEXT ROW (WS): Patt 14 (15: 16) sts, cast (bind) off next 27 sts in patt, patt to last 7 sts, M1 and turn, leaving rem 7 sts on a safety pin for buttonhole border.
Change to 4mm (US 6) needles.
NEXT ROW (RS): K15 (17: 19), K across 27 sts of 2nd pocket lining, K14 (15: 16). *56 (59: 62) sts*
Beg with a P row, work in st st throughout as folls:
Cont straight until left front matches back to start of armhole shaping, ending with a RS row.

SHAPE RAGLAN ARMHOLE

Cast (bind) off 3 (4: 5) sts at beg of next row.
53 (55: 57) sts
NEXT ROW (DEC) (RS): K to last 6 sts, K3tog tbl, K3.
Work 1 row.
Rep last 2 rows 1 (3: 5) times more. *49 (47: 45) sts*
NEXT ROW (DEC) (RS): K to last 6 sts, K3tog tbl, K3.
Work 3 rows. Rep last 4 rows 10 (9: 8) times more, thus ending with a WS row. *27 sts*

SHAPE NECK

NEXT ROW (RS): Cast (bind) off 5 sts, K to last 6 sts, K3tog tbl, K3. *20 sts*
Work 1 row. Cast (bind) off 5 sts at beg of next row.
15 sts
Dec 1 st at neck edge on next row. *14 sts*
NEXT ROW (RS): K2tog, K6, K3tog tbl, K3. *11 sts*
Dec 1 st at neck edge on next and foll alt row. *9 sts*
NEXT ROW (RS): K3, K3tog tbl, K3. *7 sts*
Dec 1 st at neck edge on next and foll alt row. *5 sts*
NEXT ROW (RS): K3tog, K2. *3 sts*
Dec 1 st at neck edge on next row.
Work 2 rows on rem 2 sts.
NEXT ROW: K2tog and fasten off.

left sleeve

Cast on 47 sts using 3¾mm (US 3) needles.
Work 10 rows in moss (seed) st as given for back, thus ending with a WS row.
Change to 4mm (US 6) needles.
Beg with a K row, work in st st throughout as folls:
Work 6 rows.
NEXT ROW (RS) (INC): K2, M1, K to last 2 sts, M1, K2.
Working increases 2 sts in from ends of rows as set by last row, shape sides by inc 1 st at each end of every foll 6th row until there are 67 (75: 83) sts.

Small and medium sizes only

Inc 1 st at each end of every foll 8th row until there are 79 (81) sts.

All sizes

Cont without further shaping until sleeve measures 43cm (17in), ending with a WS row.

SHAPE RAGLAN

Cast (bind) off 3 (4: 5) sts at beg of next 2 rows. *73 sts*
NEXT ROW (DEC) (RS): K3, K3tog, K to last 6 sts, K3tog tbl, K3.
Work 3 rows.
Rep last 4 rows 14 times more, thus ending with a WS row. *13 sts*
Work 2 rows.
NEXT ROW (RS): K3, K3tog, K1, K3tog tbl, K3. *9 sts**
Work 2 rows, thus ending with a RS row.

SHAPE NECK

Cast (bind) off 4 sts at beg of next row, then 3 sts at beg of foll alt row.
NEXT ROW: K2tog and fasten off.

right sleeve

Work as given for left sleeve to **.
Work 1 row, thus ending with a WS row.

SHAPE NECK

Cast (bind) off 4 sts at beg of next row, then 3 sts at beg of foll alt row. Work 1 row.
NEXT ROW: K2tog and fasten off.

finishing

Press all pieces as described on the information page.
Join raglan seams using back stitch.

BUTTON BORDER

Slip the 7 sts on left front safety pin onto 3¾mm (US 5) needles and rejoin yarn with RS facing.
Cont in moss (seed) st as set until border, when slightly stretched, fits up left front opening edge, ending with a WS row. Cast (bind) off. Slipstitch border in place.
Mark positions for 7 buttons on this border, the first to come level with buttonhole in right front, the last to come 1cm (½in) below neck shaping and the rem 5 buttons evenly spaced between.

BUTTONHOLE BORDER

Work to match button border, rejoining yarn with WS facing and with the addition of another 6 buttonholes worked to correspond with positions marked for buttons as folls:
BUTTONHOLE ROW (RS): Patt 3 sts, yrn (to make a buttonhole), work 2 tog, patt 2 sts.

COLLAR

Cast on 127 sts using 3¼mm (US 3) needles.
Knit 2 rows.
ROW 3 (DEC): K13, sl1, K2tog, psso, K to last 16 sts, sl1, K2tog, psso, K13. *123 sts*
Knit 1 row.
ROW 5: K12, sl1, K2tog, psso, K to last 15 sts, sl1, K2tog, psso, K12. *119 sts*
Cont in this way, dec on every foll alt row and working 1 fewer st before and after decreases, until the following row has been worked:
NEXT ROW: Sl1, K2tog, psso, K to last 3 sts, sl1, K2tog, psso.
Knit 1 row. Cast (bind) off.
Sew cast- (bound-) off edge of collar to neck edge, positioning ends of collar midway across top of borders.
See information page for finishing instructions.

cheesecake by Kim Hargreaves

SIZES	1ST	2ND	3RD	4TH	5TH	
To fit	3–4	4–5	6–7	8–9	9–10	yrs
Chest size	58	61	66	71	76	cm
	23	24	26	28	30	in
Actual width	33	35.5	39	43.5	46	cm
	13	14	15½	17	18	in
Length	34	36.5	39	42	44	cm
	13½	14½	15½	16½	17½	in
Sleeve length	26.5	29.5	33.5	37	40.5	cm
	10½	11½	13	14½	16	in

YARN

Rowan Cotton Glacé 50gm (1¾oz) balls:

A	Bl Orange 445	2	2	2	2	2
B	Mint 748	1	2	2	2	2
C	Butter 795	2	2	2	2	2
D	Candy Fl 747	1	1	1	1	1
E	Hyacinth 787	1	1	2	2	2
F	Terracotta 786	1	1	1	1	1
G	Pear 780	1	1	1	1	2
H	Bubbles 724	2	2	2	3	3

NEEDLES

1 pair 2¾mm (US 2) needles
1 pair 3¼mm (US 3) needles
2¾mm (US 2) circular needle

BUTTONS

7

TENSION (GAUGE)

23 sts and 32 rows to 10cm (4in) measured over stocking (stockinette) stitch using 3¼mm (US 3) needles

back

Cast on 76 (82: 90: 100: 106) sts using 2¾mm (US 2) needles and yarn H.
Beg with a K row, work in striped st st from chart A as folls:
Work 8 rows.
Change to 3¼mm (US 3) needles and cont from chart A until row 28 has been completed, ending with a WS row.
Using the Fair Isle technique described on the information page, starting and ending rows as indicated and beg with a K row, work 10 rows in patt from chart B, which is worked entirely in st st.
Beg with a K row, cont in striped st st from chart C as folls:

Cont straight until back measures 19 (20.5: 22: 24: 25)cm (7½ [8: 8½: 9½: 9¾]in) from cast-on edge, ending with a WS row.

SHAPE ARMHOLES

Cast (bind) off 3 (3: 4: 4: 4) sts at beg of next 2 rows.
70 (76: 82: 92: 98) sts
Dec 1 st at each end of next 3 rows.
64 (70: 76: 86: 92) sts
Cont straight until armhole measures 16 (17: 18: 19: 20)cm (6¼ [6½: 7: 7½: 7¾]in), ending with a WS row.

SHAPE SHOULDERS AND BACK NECK

Cast (bind) off 6 (7: 7: 9: 9) sts at beg of next 2 rows.
52 (56: 62: 68: 74) sts
NEXT ROW (RS): Cast (bind) off 6 (7: 7: 9: 9) sts, patt until there are 9 (10: 12: 12: 14) sts on right needle and turn, leaving rem sts on a holder.
Work each side of neck separately.
Cast (bind) off 4 sts at beg of next row.
Cast (bind) off rem 5 (6: 8: 8: 10) sts.
With RS facing, rejoin yarn to rem sts, cast (bind) off center 22 (22: 24: 26: 28) sts, patt to end.
Work to match first side, rev shaping.

left front

Cast on 39 (42: 46: 51: 54) sts using 2¾mm (US 2) needles and yarn H.
Beg with a K row, work in striped st st from chart A as folls:
Work 8 rows.
Change to 3¼mm (US 3) needles and cont from chart A until row 28 is complete, ending with a WS row.
Now work 10 rows in patt from chart B.
Beg with a K row, cont in striped st st from chart C as folls:
Cont straight until left front matches back to beg of armhole shaping, ending with a WS row.

SHAPE ARMHOLES

Cast (bind) off 3 (3: 4: 4: 4) sts at beg of next row.
36 (39: 42: 47: 50) sts
Work 1 row.
Dec 1 st at armhole edge of next 3 rows.
33 (36: 39: 44: 47) sts
Cont straight until there are 22 (22: 24: 24: 26) rows fewer than on back to start of shoulder shaping, ending with a WS row.

SHAPE NECK

Dec 1 st at neck edge of every row until 17 (20: 22: 26: 28) sts rem.
Work 6 (6: 7: 6: 7) rows.

SHAPE SHOULDERS AND BACK NECK

Cast (bind) off 6 (7: 7: 9: 9) sts at beg of next and foll alt row.

Work 1 row.

Cast (bind) off rem 5 (6: 8: 8: 10) sts.

right front

Work to match left front, rev shaping.

sleeves (both alike)

Cast on 38 (40: 42: 44: 46) sts using 2¾mm (US 2) needles and yarn H.

Beg with a K row, work in striped st st from chart A as folls:

Work 8 (8: 10: 10: 10) rows.

Change to 3¼mm (US 3) needles and cont from chart A, inc 1 st at each end of next and every foll 4th (6th: 6th: 6th: 6th) row until row 28 is complete, ending with a WS row.

48 (48: 48: 50: 52) sts

Now work 10 rows in patt from chart B, inc 1 st at each end of row 1 (5: 1: 1: 1) and every foll 4th (4th: 6th: 6th: 6th) row.

54 (52: 52: 54: 56) sts

Beg with a K row, cont in striped st st from chart C as folls:

Inc 1 st at each end of row 3 and every foll 4th (4th: 6th: 6th: 6th) row until there are 74 (78: 58: 64: 72) sts.

7th, 8th and 9th sizes only

Inc 1 st at each end of every foll 4th row until there are 82 (88: 92) sts.

All sizes

Cont straight until sleeve measures 27.5 (30.5: 34.5: 38: 41.5)cm (11 [12: 13½: 15: 16¼]in) from cast-on edge, ending with a WS row.

SHAPE TOP

Cast (bind) off 3 (3: 4: 4: 4) sts at beg of next 2 rows.

68 (72: 74: 80: 84) sts

Dec 1 st at each end of next and foll 2 alt rows.

Work 1 row.

Cast (bind) off rem 62 (66: 68: 74: 78) sts.

finishing

Press all pieces as described on the information page. Join shoulder seams using back stitch.

FRONT BORDER

With RS facing, yarn C and 2¾mm (US 2) circular needle, starting and ending 2 rows up from lower cast-on edge, pick up and knit 66 (72: 78: 84: 90) sts up right front opening edge to start of neck shaping, 22 (22: 24: 24: 28) sts up right front neck, 28 (28: 30: 32: 34) sts across back neck, 22 (22: 24: 24: 28) sts down left front neck to start of neck shaping and 66 (72: 78: 84: 90) sts down left front opening edge.

204 (216: 234: 248: 270) sts

Beg with a K row, work in st st as folls:

Work 1 row.

NEXT ROW (RS) (BUTTONHOLE ROW): P2, *yrn, P2tog, P8 (9: 10: 11: 12), rep from * 5 times more, yrn, P2tog, P to end.

Work 2 rows.

Cast (bind) off knitwise (on WS).

See information page for finishing instructions, setting in sleeves using the shallow set-in method and allowing 1cm (½in) at cast-on edges of sleeves and body to roll out to RS.

KEY

- ▪ A
- ☒ B
- ⊙ C
- ☑ D
- ⊞ E
- ⊟ F
- ☑ G
- ▫ H

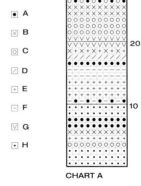

CHART A

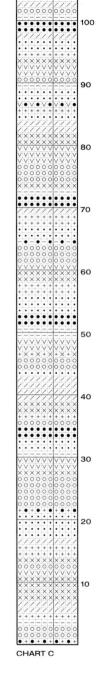

CHART C

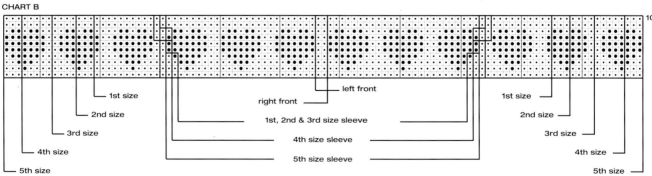

CHART B

1st size
2nd size
3rd size
4th size
5th size

right front
left front
1st, 2nd & 3rd size sleeve
4th size sleeve
5th size sleeve

1st size
2nd size
3rd size
4th size
5th size

fish pullover by Louisa Harding

SIZES

	1ST	2ND	3RD	4TH	5TH	6TH	
	2–3	3–4	4–6	6–8	8–9	9–10	yrs
Actual width	38	41	44	47	51	55	cm
	15	16	17	18½	20	21½	in
Length	42	45	49.5	53.5	57	61	cm
	16½	18	19½	21	22½	24	in
Sleeve length	25	28	30.5	35.5	38	40.5	cm
	10	11	12	14	15	16	in

YARNS

Rowan Handknit DK Cotton 50gm (1¾oz) balls:

A Ecru 251	6	7	8	9	10	12
B Turkish Pl 277	3	3	4	4	5	5

NEEDLES

1 pair 3¼mm (US 3) needles
1 pair 4mm (US 6) needles

TENSION GAUGE)

20 sts and 28 rows to 10cm (4in) measured over patt stocking (stockinette) stitch using 4mm (US 6) needles

back

Cast on 76 (82: 88: 94: 102: 110) sts using 3¼mm (US 3) needles and yarn B.
ROW 1 (RS): (K2, P2) to last 0 (2: 0: 2: 2: 2) sts, K0 (2: 0: 2: 2: 2).
ROW 2: P0 (2: 0: 2: 2: 2) sts, (K2, P2) to end.
Rep these 2 rows twice more.
Change to 4mm (US 6) needles, joining in yarn A and, using a mixture of Fair Isle and intarsia techniques as described on the information page, cont in patt from chart for back until row 106 (114: 128: 138: 148: 160) is complete, ending with a WS row.

SHAPE BACK NECK
Patt 26 (28: 31: 33: 36: 40) sts and turn, leaving rem sts on a holder.
Work each side of neck separately.
Dec 1 st at neck edge on next 3 rows.
23 (25: 28: 30: 33: 37) sts

SHAPE SHOULDER
Cast (bind) off rem sts.
With RS facing, slip center 24 (26: 26: 28: 30: 30) sts onto a holder, rejoin yarns to rem sts, work to end.
Complete to match first side, rev shaping.

front

Work as for back until chart row 92 (100: 112: 122: 130: 142) is complete, ending with a WS row.

SHAPE FRONT NECK
Patt 30 (32: 35: 38: 41: 45) sts and turn, leaving rem sts on a holder.
Work each side of neck separately.
Dec 1 st at neck edge on next 4 (4: 4: 5: 5: 5) rows and 3 foll alt rows. *23 (25: 28: 30: 33: 37) sts*
Cont without further shaping until front matches back to shoulder shaping, ending with a WS row.

SHAPE SHOULDER
Cast (bind) off rem sts.
With RS facing, slip center 16 (18: 18: 18: 20: 20) sts onto a holder, rejoin appropriate yarns to rem sts, patt to end.
Complete as for first side, rev shaping.

sleeves (both alike)

Cast on 36 (40: 40: 46: 46: 46) sts using 3¼mm (US 3) needles and yarn B.
Work 6 rows in K2, P2 rib, ending with a WS row.
Change to 4mm (US 6) needles and working between appropriate markers, cont in patt from chart until row 64 (72: 80: 94: 100: 108) is complete and AT THE SAME TIME shape sides by inc 1 st at each end of 3rd row and every foll 4th row to 64 (70: 74: 80: 80: 80) sts and then for 3 larger sizes only every foll 6th row to 82 (86: 92) sts, ending with a WS row.
64 (70: 74: 82: 86: 92) sts
Cast (bind) off loosely and evenly.

finishing

Press all pieces except ribbing on wrong side using a warm iron over a damp cloth.
Join right shoulder seam using back stitch.

NECK BAND
With RS facing, using 3¼mm (US 3) needles and yarn A, beg at left shoulder, pick up and knit 18 (18: 20: 20: 22: 22) sts down left front neck, 16 (18: 18: 18: 20: 20) sts from holder at center front, 18 (18: 20: 20: 22: 22) sts up right front neck and 3 sts down back neck. K24 (26: 26: 28: 30: 30) sts from holder at center back, pick up and knit 3 sts up back neck to shoulder. *82 (86: 90: 92: 100: 100) sts*
Work 5 rows in K2, P2 rib. Cast (bind) off in rib.
Join left shoulder seam using back stitch and join neck band using edge-to-edge stitch. See information page for finishing instructions.

KEY
□ A
⊡ B

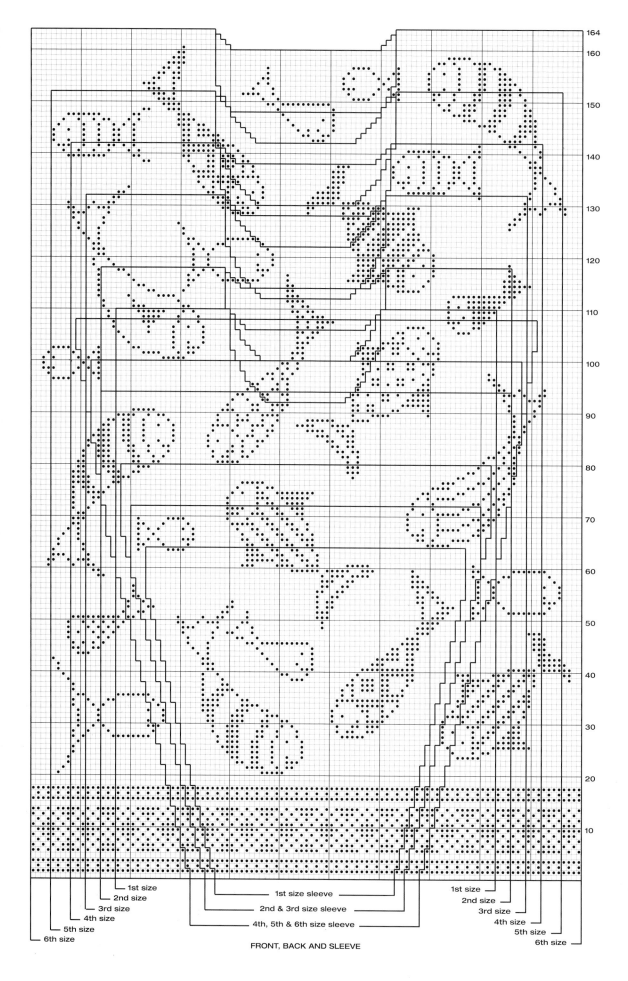

1st size
2nd size
3rd size
4th size
5th size
6th size

1st size sleeve
2nd & 3rd size sleeve
4th, 5th & 6th size sleeve

1st size
2nd size
3rd size
4th size
5th size
6th size

FRONT, BACK AND SLEEVE

maddy by Kim Hargreaves

SIZES	CHILDREN'S			ADULTS'					
	1ST	2ND	3RD	1ST	2ND	3RD	4TH	5TH	
To fit	6–7 yrs	8–9 yrs	9–10 yrs	32	34	36	38	40	
To fit chest	66	71	76	81	86.5	91.5	96.5	102	cm
	26	28	30	32	34	36	38	40	in
Actual width	37	39.5	42.5	45	47.5	50.5	53	56	cm
	14	15½	16½	17½	18½	20	21	22	in
Length	30	36	45						cm
	12	14	17½						in
Longer length				60	61	61	62	62	cm
				23½	24	24	24½	24½	in
Shorter length				54	55	55	56	56	cm
				21½	21½	21½	22	22	in
Sleeve length	30	34	38	42	42	43	43	43	cm
	12	13½	15	16½	16½	17	17	17	in

YARNS

Rowan Wool Cotton or Designer DK 50gm (1¾oz) balls:

Children's version

| Pinky 902 | 5 | 7 | 8 |

About 1 skein of embroidery silk in each of 3 different colors

Adults' longer version

| Wool Cotton DK, Misty 903 | 10 | 10 | 11 | 11 | 12 |

1 meter (1yd) of very narrow satin ribbon and approx 6 skeins of embroidery silk

Adults' shorter version

| Designer DK, Black 62 | 8 | 8 | 9 | 9 | 10 |

NEEDLES

1 pair 3¼mm (US 3) needles
1 pair 4mm (US 6) needles

BUTTONS

7 for adults' version, or 5 for children's version.

TENSION (GAUGE)

22 sts and 30 rows to 10cm (4in) measured over stocking (stockinette) stitch using 4mm (US 6) needles

adults' longer version
back

Cast on 105 (111: 117: 123: 129) sts using 3¼mm (US 3) needles. Knit 5 rows.
ROW 6 (WS): P1, *K1, P1, rep from * to end.
Last row forms moss (seed) st. Work another 6 rows in moss (seed) st, ending with a WS row.
Change to 4mm (US 6) needles.

Beg with a K row, work 8 rows in st st.
Now work in eyelet patt as follows:
PATT ROW 1 (RS): K4 (7: 10: 13: 16), * yfwd, K2tog, K14, rep from * to last 5 (8: 11: 14: 17) sts, yfwd, K2tog, K3 (6: 9: 12: 15).
Purl 1 row.
Beg with a K row, work 18 rows in st st, shaping side seams by dec 1 st at each end of next and every foll 4th row. *95 (101: 107: 113: 119) sts*
PATT ROW 21 (RS): K7 (10: 13: 16: 3), * yfwd, K2tog, K14, rep from * to last 8 (11: 14: 17: 4) sts, yfwd, K2tog, K6 (9: 12: 15: 2).
Purl 1 row.
Work another 18 rows in st st, cont to dec 1 st at each end of every foll 4th row from previous dec. *85 (91: 97: 103: 109) sts*
Last 40 rows set position of eyelet patt (see chart).
Keeping patt correct, dec 1 st at each end of foll 3rd row. *83 (89: 95: 101: 107) sts*
Work 9 rows, thus ending with a WS row.

Inc 1 st at each end of next and every foll 4th row until there are 99 (105: 111: 117: 123) sts, taking inc sts into patt. Cont straight until back measures 38cm (15in), ending with a WS row.

SHAPE ARMHOLES
Keeping patt correct, cast (bind) off 4 (4: 5: 5: 6) sts at beg of next 2 rows. *91 (97: 101: 107: 111) sts*
Dec 1 st at each end on next 5 (7: 7: 9: 9) rows, then on foll 5 (5: 6: 6: 7) alt rows. *71 (73: 75: 77: 79) sts*
Cont without further shaping until armhole measures 22 (23: 23: 24: 24)cm (8½ [9: 9: 9½: 9½]in), ending with a WS row.

SHAPE SHOULDERS AND BACK NECK
Keeping patt correct, cast (bind) off 4 sts at beg of next 2 rows.
63 (65: 67: 69: 71) sts
NEXT ROW (RS): Cast (bind) off 4 sts, patt until there are 7 (7: 8: 8: 9) sts on right needle and turn, leaving rem sts on a holder.
Work each side of neck separately.
Cast (bind) off 4 sts at beg of next row.
Cast (bind) off rem 3 (3: 4: 4: 5) sts.
With RS facing, rejoin yarn to rem sts, cast (bind) off center 41 (43: 43: 45: 45) sts, patt to end.
Work to match first side, rev shaping.

left front

Cast on 58 (61: 64: 67: 70) sts using 3¼mm (US 3) needles. Knit 5 rows.
ROW 6 (WS): P0 (1: 0: 1: 0), *K1, P1, rep from * to end.
Last row sets position of moss (seed) st as given for back.
Work another 5 rows in moss (seed) st, ending with a RS row.
Row 12 (WS): Patt 6 sts and slip these sts onto a safety pin, M1, patt to end. *53 (56: 59: 62: 65) sts*
**Change to 4mm (US 6) needles.
Beg with a K row, work 8 rows in st st.
Now work in eyelet patt as follows:
PATT ROW 1 (RS): K4 (7: 10: 13: 16), * yfwd, K2tog, K14, rep from * to last st, K1.
Purl 1 row.
Beg with a K row, work 18 rows in st st, shaping side seam by dec 1 st at beg of next and every foll 4th row. *48 (51: 54: 57: 60) sts*
PATT ROW 21 (RS): K7 (10: 13: 16: 3), * yfwd, K2tog, K14, rep from * to last 9 sts, yfwd, K2tog, K7.
Purl 1 row.
Work another 18 rows in st st, continuing to dec 1 st at beg of every foll 4th row from previous dec.
43 (46: 49: 52: 55) sts
Last 40 rows set position of eyelet patt.
Keeping patt correct, dec 1 st at beg of foll 3rd row. *42 (45: 48: 51: 54) sts*
Work 9 rows, thus ending with a WS row.
Inc 1 st at beg of next and every foll 4th row until there are 50 (53: 56: 59: 62) sts, taking inc sts into patt.
Cont straight until left front matches back to start of armhole shaping, ending with a WS row.

SHAPE ARMHOLE
Keeping patt correct, cast (bind) off 4 (4: 5: 5: 6) sts at beg of next row. *46 (49: 51: 54: 56) sts*
Work 1 row.
Dec 1 st at armhole edge on next 5 (7: 7: 9: 9) rows, then on foll 5 (5: 6: 6: 7) alt rows.
36 (37: 38: 39: 40) sts
Cont without further shaping until there are 13 rows fewer than on back to start of shoulder shaping, thus ending with a RS row.

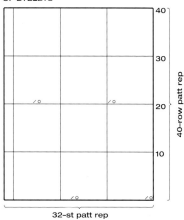

yfwd,
K2tog

40-row patt rep
40
30
20
10

32-st patt rep

SHAPE NECK
Keeping patt correct, cast (bind) off 13 (14: 14: 15: 15) sts at beg of next row, and 6 sts at beg of foll alt row. *17 (17: 18: 18: 19) sts*
Dec 1 st at neck edge on next 3 rows, then on foll 3 alt rows. *11 (11: 12: 12: 13) sts*
Work 1 row, thus ending at armhole edge.

SHAPE SHOULDER
Keeping patt correct, cast (bind) off 4 sts at beg of next and foll alt row.
Work 1 row. Cast (bind) off rem 3 (3: 4: 4: 5) sts.

right front

Cast on 58 (61: 64: 67: 70) sts using 3¼mm (US 3) needles. Knit 5 rows.
ROW 6 (WS): *P1, K1, rep from * to last 0 (1: 0: 1: 0) st, P0 (1: 0: 1: 0).
Last row sets position of moss (seed) st as given for back.
Work another 2 rows in moss (seed) st, ending with a WS row.
ROW 9 (BUTTONHOLE ROW) (RS): Patt 2 sts, yrn twice to make a buttonhole (drop extra loop on next row), work 2 tog, patt to end.
Work another 2 rows in moss (seed) st, ending with a RS row.
ROW 12 (WS): Patt to last 6 sts, M1 and turn, leaving last 6 sts on a safety pin. *53 (56: 59: 62: 65) sts*
Change to 4mm (US 6) needles.
Complete to match left front from **, rev all shapings and setting position of eyelets as folls:
PATT ROW 1 (RS): K16, *yfwd, K2tog, K14, rep from * to last 5 (8: 11: 14: 17) sts, yfwd, K2tog, K3 (6: 9: 12: 15).
PATT ROW 21 (RS): K8, * yfwd, K2tog, K14, rep from * to last 8 (11: 14: 17: 4) sts, yfwd, K2tog, K6 (9: 12: 15: 2).

sleeves (both alike)

Cast on 43 (43: 45: 45: 47) sts using 3¼mm (US 3) needles. Knit 5 rows.
Work 7 rows in moss (seed) st as given for back, thus ending with a WS row. Change to 4mm (US 6) needles.
Beg with a K row, work 8 rows in st st, shaping sleeve seam by inc 1 st at each end of 3rd row.
45 (45: 47: 47: 49) sts
Now work in eyelet patt as follows:
PATT ROW 1 (RS): Inc in first st, K5 (5: 6: 6: 7), *yfwd, K2tog, K14, rep from * to last 7 (7: 8: 8: 9) sts, yfwd, K2tog, K4 (4: 5: 5: 6), inc in last st. *47 (47: 49: 49: 51) sts.*
Purl 1 row. Work 18 rows in st st, shaping sleeve seam by inc 1 st at end of every foll 6th row from previous inc. *53 (53: 55: 55: 57) sts*

PATT ROW 21 (RS): K2 (2: 3: 3: 4), *yfwd, K2tog, K14, rep from * to last 3 (3: 4: 4: 5) sts, yfwd, K2tog, K1 (1: 2: 2: 3).
Purl 1 row. Work 18 rows in st st, inc 1 st at end of 6th row from previous inc and every foll 8th (6th: 6th: 6th: 6th) row. *57 (59: 61: 61: 63) sts*
Last 40 rows form eyelet patt.
Keeping patt correct, inc 1 st at each end of every foll 8th (6th: 6th: 6th: 6th) row from previous inc until there are 71 (63: 63: 71: 71) sts, taking inc sts into patt.

2nd, 3rd, 4th & 5th sizes only
Inc 1 st at each end of every foll 8th row until there are (73: 75: 77: 79) sts.

All sizes
Cont without further shaping until sleeve measures 42 (42: 43: 43: 43)cm (16½ [16½: 17: 17: 17]in), ending with a WS row.

SHAPE TOP
Keeping patt correct, cast (bind) off 4 (4: 5: 5: 6) sts at beg of next 2 rows. *63 (65: 65: 67: 67) sts*
Dec 1 st at each end of next 3 rows, then on foll 3 alt rows. *51 (53: 53: 55: 55) sts*
Work 3 rows, thus ending with a WS row.
Dec 1 st at each end of next and every foll 4th row until 41 (43: 43: 45: 45) sts rem, then on every foll alt row until 37 sts rem.
Dec 1 st at each end on next 5 rows, thus ending with a WS row. *27 sts*
Cast (bind) off 4 sts at beg of next 2 rows.
Cast (bind) off rem 19 sts.

adults' shorter version
back
Cast on 99 (105: 111: 117: 123) sts using 3¼mm (US 3) needles. Knit 5 rows.
ROW 6 (WS): P1, *K1, P1, rep from * to end.
Last row forms moss (seed) st. Work another 6 rows in moss (seed) st, ending with a WS row.
Change to 4mm (US 6) needles.
Beg with a K row, work in st st, shaping side seams by dec 1 st at each end of 5th row (from beg of st st) and every foll 4th row until 83 (89: 95: 101: 107) sts rem.
Work 9 rows, thus ending with a WS row.
Inc 1 st at each end of next and every foll 4th row until there are 99 (105: 111: 117: 123) sts.
Cont straight until back measures 32cm (12½in), ending with a WS row.

SHAPE ARMHOLES
Cast (bind) off 4 (4: 5: 5: 6) sts at beg of next 2 rows. *91 (97: 101: 107: 111) sts*
Dec 1 st at each end on next 5 (7: 7: 9: 9) rows, then on foll 5 (5: 6: 6: 7) alt rows. *71 (73: 75: 77: 79) sts*
Cont without further shaping until armhole measures 22 (23: 23: 24: 24)cm (8½ [9: 9: 9½: 9½]in), ending with a WS row.

SHAPE SHOULDERS AND BACK NECK
Cast (bind) off 7 sts at beg of next 2 rows. *57 (59: 61: 63: 65) sts*
NEXT ROW (RS): Cast (bind) off 7 sts, K until there are 10 (10: 11: 11: 12) sts on right needle and turn, leaving rem sts on a holder.
Work each side of neck separately.
Cast (bind) off 4 sts at beg of next row.
Cast (bind) off rem 6 (6: 7: 7: 8) sts.
With RS facing, rejoin yarn to rem sts, cast (bind) off center 23 (25: 25: 27: 27) sts, K to end.
Work to match first side, rev shaping.

left front
Cast on 55 (58: 61: 64: 67) sts using 3¼mm (US 3) needles. Knit 5 rows.
ROW 6 (WS): P1 (0: 1: 0: 1), *K1, P1, rep from * to end.
Last row sets position of moss (seed) st as given for back. Work another 5 rows in moss (seed) st, ending with a RS row.
ROW 12 (WS): Patt 6 sts and slip these sts onto a safety pin, M1, patt to end. *50 (53: 56: 59: 62) sts*
**Change to 4mm (US 6) needles.
Beg with a K row, work in st st, shaping side seam by dec 1 st at beg of 5th row (from beg of st st) and every foll 4th row until 42 (45: 48: 51: 54) sts rem.
Work 9 rows, thus ending with a WS row.
Inc 1 st at beg of next and every foll 4th row until there are 50 (53: 56: 59: 62) sts.
Cont straight until left front matches back to start of armhole shaping, ending with a WS row.

SHAPE ARMHOLE
Cast (bind) off 4 (4: 5: 5: 6) sts at beg of next row. *46 (49: 51: 54: 56) sts*
Work 1 row.
Dec 1 st at armhole edge on next 5 (7: 7: 9: 9) rows, then on foll 5 (5: 6: 6: 7) alt rows. *36 (37: 38: 39: 40) sts*
Cont without further shaping until there are 23 rows fewer than on back to start of shoulder shaping, thus ending with a RS row.

SHAPE NECK
Cast (bind) off 4 (5: 5: 6: 6) sts at beg of next row and 4 sts at beg of foll alt row. *28 (28: 29: 29: 30) sts*
Dec 1 st at neck edge on next 3 rows, then on foll 3 alt rows. *22 (22: 23: 23: 24) sts*
Work 3 rows.
Dec 1 st at neck edge on next and foll 4th row. *20 (20: 21: 21: 22) sts*
Work 3 rows, thus ending at armhole edge.

SHAPE SHOULDER
Cast (bind) off 7 sts at beg of next and foll alt row. Work 1 row. Cast (bind) off rem 6 (6: 7: 7: 8) sts.

right front
Cast on 55 (58: 61: 64: 67) sts using 3¼mm (US 3) needles. Knit 5 rows.
ROW 6 (WS): *P1, K1, rep from * to last 1 (0: 1: 0: 1) st, P1 (0: 1: 0: 1).
Last row sets position of moss (seed) st as given for back. Work another 2 rows in moss (seed) st, ending with a WS row.
ROW 9 (BUTTONHOLE ROW) (RS): Patt 2 sts, yrn twice to make a buttonhole (drop extra loop on next row), work 2 tog, patt to end.
Work another 2 rows in moss (seed) st, ending with a RS row.
ROW 12 (WS): Patt to last 6 sts, M1 and turn, leaving last 6 sts on a safety pin. *50 (53: 56: 59: 62) sts*
Complete to match left front from **, rev shaping.

sleeves (both alike)
Cast on 43 (43: 45: 45: 47) sts using 3¼mm (US 3) needles. Knit 5 rows.
Work 7 rows in moss (seed) st as given for back, thus ending with a WS row.
Change to 4mm (US 6) needles.
Beg with a K row, work in st st, shaping sleeve seam by inc 1 st at each end of 3rd row and every foll 6th row to 55 (59: 63: 71: 71) sts, then on every foll 8th row until there are 71 (73: 75: 77: 79) sts.
Cont without further shaping until sleeve measures

2 (42: 43: 43: 43)cm (16½ [16½: 17: 17: 17]in), ending
with a WS row.

SHAPE TOP

Cast (bind) off 4 (4: 5: 5: 6) sts at beg of next 2 rows.
63 (65: 65: 67: 67) sts

Dec 1 st at each end of next 3 rows, then on foll
3 alt rows. *51 (53: 53: 55: 55) sts*

Work 3 rows, thus ending with a WS row.

Dec 1 st at each end of next and every foll 4th row
until 41 (43: 43: 45: 45) sts rem, then on every foll alt
row until 37 sts rem.

Dec 1 st at each end of next 5 rows, thus ending with
a WS row. *27 sts*

Cast (bind) off 4 sts at beg of next 2 rows. Cast (bind)
off rem 19 sts.

finishing

Press all pieces as described on the information page.
Join shoulder seams using back stitch.

BUTTON BORDER

Slip the 6 sts on left front safety pin onto 3¼mm
(US 3) needles and rejoin yarn with RS facing.
Cont in moss (seed) st as set until border, when
slightly stretched, fits up left front opening edge to
neck, ending with a WS row.
Cast (bind) off. slipstitch border in place.
Mark positions for 7 buttons on this border, the lowest
button level with buttonhole already worked in right
front, the top button 1cm (½in) below neck shaping
and the rem 5 buttons evenly spaced between.

BUTTONHOLE BORDER

Work as given for button border, rejoining yarn
with WS facing and with the addition of another 6
buttonholes to correspond with positions marked for
buttons worked as follows:

BUTTONHOLE ROW (RS): Patt 2 sts, yrn twice to make a
buttonhole (drop extra loop on next row), work 2tog,
patt 2 sts.
Slipstitch border in place.

Longer version only

NECK BORDER

With RS facing and using 3¼mm (US 3) needles,
starting and ending midway across top of borders,
pick up and knit 35 sts up right front neck, 49 (51:
51: 53: 53) sts across back neck, and 35 sts down left
front neck. *119 (121: 121: 123: 123) sts*

Work 1 row in moss (seed) st as given for back.
Keeping moss (seed) st correct, proceed as follows:

NEXT ROW (RS): Patt 1 (2: 2: 3: 3) sts, *yrn (to make a
hole), work 2 tog, patt 2 sts, rep from * to last 2 (3: 3:
4: 4) sts, yrn, work 2 tog, patt 0 (1: 1: 2: 2) sts.

Work another 3 rows in moss (seed) st. Knit 3 rows.
Cast (bind) off knitwise (on WS).
Thread ribbon through eyelet holes.
Using embroidery silk, oversew around each eyelet
hole on body and sleeves, using chart on page 172 as
a guide.

Shorter version only

NECK BORDER

With RS facing and using 3¼mm (US 3) needles,
starting and ending midway across top of borders,
pick up and knit 35 sts up right front neck, 31 (33:
33: 35: 35) sts across back neck and 35 sts down left
front neck. *101 (103: 103: 105: 105) sts*

Work 5 rows in moss (seed) st as given for back.
Knit 3 rows. Cast (bind) off knitwise (on WS).

Both versions

See information page for finishing instructions.

children's version
back

Cast on 81 (87: 93) sts using 3¼mm (US 3) needles.
Knit 5 rows.

ROW 6 (WS): P1, *K1, P1, rep from * to end.
Last row forms moss (seed) st.
Work another 6 rows in moss (seed) st, ending with a
WS row. Change to 4mm (US 6) needles.
Beg with a K row, work 8 rows in st st.
Now work in eyelet patt as follows:

PATT ROW 1 (RS): K8 (11: 14), *yfwd, K2tog, K14, rep
from * to last 9 (12: 15) sts, yfwd, K2tog, K7 (10: 13).
Purl 1 row. Work 18 rows in st st.

PATT ROW 21 (RS): K16 (3: 6), *yfwd, K2tog, K14, rep
from * to last 17 (4: 7) sts, yfwd, K2tog, 15 (2: 5).
Purl 1 row. Work 18 rows in st st.

Last 40 rows form eyelet patt (see chart on page 172).
Cont in patt until back measures 15 (19: 26)cm (6
[7½: 10¼]in), ending with a WS row.

SHAPE ARMHOLES

Keeping patt correct, cast (bind) off 5 sts at beg of next
2 rows. *71 (77: 83) sts*

Cont without further shaping until armhole measures 15 (17: 19)cm (6 [6½: 7½]in), ending with a WS row.

SHAPE SHOULDERS AND BACK NECK
Keeping patt correct, cast (bind) off 7 (8: 9) sts at beg of next 2 rows. *57 (61: 65) sts*

NEXT ROW (RS): Cast (bind) off 7 (8: 9) sts, patt until there are 12 (12: 13) sts on right needle and turn, leaving rem sts on a holder.
Work each side of neck separately.
Cast (bind) off 4 sts at beg of next row.
Cast (bind) off rem 8 (8: 9) sts.
With RS facing, rejoin yarn to rem sts, cast (bind) off center 19 (21: 21) sts, patt to end.
Work to match first side, rev shaping.

left front

Cast on 46 (49: 52) sts using 3¼mm (US 3) needles.
Knit 5 rows.

ROW 6 (WS): P0 (1: 0), *K1, P1, rep from * to end.
Last row sets position of moss (seed) st as given for back.
Work another 5 rows in moss (seed) st, ending with a RS row.

ROW 12 (WS): Patt 6 sts and slip these sts onto a safety pin, M1, patt to end. *41 (44: 47) sts*
**Change to 4mm (US 6) needles.
Beg with a K row, work 8 rows in st st.
Now work in eyelet patt as follows:

ROW 1 (RS): K8 (11: 14), (yfwd, K2tog, K14) twice, K1.
Purl 1 row. Work 18 rows in st st.

ROW 21 (RS): K16 (3: 6), *yfwd, K2tog, K14, rep from * to last 9 sts, yfwd, K2tog, K7.
Purl 1 row. Work 18 rows in st st.
Last 40 rows form eyelet patt.
Cont in patt until left front matches back to start of armhole shaping, ending with a WS row.

SHAPE ARMHOLE
Keeping patt correct, cast (bind) off 5 sts at beg of next row. *36 (39: 42) sts*
Cont straight until there are 11 rows fewer than on back to start of shoulder shaping, thus ending with a RS row.

SHAPE NECK
Keeping patt correct, cast (bind) off 4 (5: 5) sts at beg of next row, and 4 sts at beg of foll alt row. *28 (30: 33) sts*
Dec 1 st at neck edge on next 4 rows, then on foll 2 alt rows. *22 (24: 27) sts*

SHAPE SHOULDER
Keeping patt correct, cast (bind) off 7 (8: 9) sts at beg of next and foll alt row.
Work 1 row. Cast (bind) off rem 8 (8: 9) sts.

right front

Cast on 46 (49: 52) sts using 3¼mm (US 3) needles.
Knit 5 rows.

ROW 6 (WS): *P1, K1, rep from * to last 0 (1: 0) st, P0 (1: 0).
Last row sets position of moss (seed) st as given for back.
Work another 2 rows in moss (seed) st, ending with a WS row.

ROW 9 (BUTTONHOLE ROW) (RS): Patt 2 sts, yrn twice to make a buttonhole (drop extra loop on next row), work 2 tog, patt to end. Work another 2 rows in moss (seed) st, ending with a RS row.

ROW 12 (WS): Patt to last 6 sts, M1 and turn, leaving last 6 sts on a safety pin. *41 (44: 47) sts*
Complete to match left front from **, rev all shaping and setting eyelet patt as follows:

ROW 1 (RS): K16, yfwd, K2tog, K14, yfwd, K2tog, K7 (10: 13).
Beg with a P row, work 19 rows in st st.

ROW 21 (RS): K8, (yfwd, K2tog, K14) twice, (yfwd, K2tog) 0 (1: 1) time, K1 (2: 5).
Beg with a P row, work 19 rows in st st.

sleeves (both alike)

Cast on 37 (39: 41) sts using 3¼mm (US 3) needles.
Knit 5 rows.
Work 7 rows in moss (seed) st as given for back, thus ending with a WS row.
Change to 4mm (US 6) needles.
Beg with a K row, work 8 rows in st st, shaping sleeve seam by inc 1 st at each end of 3rd and foll 4th row. *41 (43: 45) sts*
Now work in eyelet patt as follows:

PATT ROW 1 (RS): K4 (5: 6), (yfwd, K2tog, K14) twice, yfwd, K2tog, K3 (4: 5).
Purl 1 row. Work 18 rows in st st, shaping sleeve seam by inc 1 st at each end of every foll 4th row from previous inc. *51 (53: 55) sts*

PATT ROW 21 (RS): K1 (2: 3), (yfwd, K2tog, K14) 3 times, yfwd, K2tog, K0 (1: 2).
Purl 1 row. Work 18 rows in st st, inc 1 st at each end of the next and every foll 4th row. *61 (63: 65) sts*
Last 40 rows form eyelet patt.
Keeping patt correct, inc 1 st at each end of every 4th row until there are 65 (73: 81) sts, taking inc sts into patt.
Cont without further shaping until sleeve measures 30 (34: 38)cm (12 [13½: 15]in), ending with a WS row. Cast (bind) off loosely.

finishing

Press all pieces as described on the information page. Join shoulder seams using back stitch.

BUTTON BORDER
Slip the 6 sts on left front safety pin onto 3¼mm (US 3) needles and rejoin yarn with RS facing.
Cont in moss (seed) st as set until border, when slightly stretched, fits up left front opening edge to neck, ending with a WS row.
Cast (bind) off. slipstitch border in place.
Mark positions for 5 buttons on this border, the lowest button level with buttonhole already worked in right front, the top button 1cm (½in) below neck shaping and the rem 3 buttons evenly spaced between.

BUTTONHOLE BORDER
Work as given for button border, rejoining yarn with WS facing and with the addition of another 4 buttonholes to correspond with positions marked for buttons worked as follows:

BUTTONHOLE ROW (RS): Patt 2 sts, yrn twice to make a buttonhole (drop extra loop on next row), work 2 tog, patt 2 sts. Slipstitch border in place.

COLLAR
Cast on 75 (79: 81) sts using 3¼mm (US 3) needles.
Knit 5 rows.
Now work in moss (seed) st as given for back until collar measures 7cm (2¾in). Cast (bind) off in patt.
Sew cast- (bound-) off edge of collar to neck edge, positioning ends of collar midway across top of borders.
Using embroidery silk and colors at random, oversew around each eyelet hole on body and sleeves, using the photographs as a guide.
See information page for finishing instructions.

fleet by Kim Hargreaves

SIZES	CHILDREN'S (YRS)						LADIES'			MEN'S			
	3-4	4-6	6-8	8-9	9-11	12-14	**S**	**M**	**L**	M	L	XL	
To fit chest	–	–	–	–	–	–	**86**	**91**	**97**	97	102	107	cm
	–	–	–	–	–	–	**34**	**36**	**38**	38	40	42	in
Actual width	41.5	44.5	47.5	51.5	53.5	56.5	**58.5**	**61.5**	**63.5**	63.5	66.5	68.8	cm
	16½	17½	18½	20½	21	22	**23**	**24**	**25**	25	26	27	in
Length	41	44	47	51	53	56	**58.5**	**58.5**	**58.5**	61.5	61.5	61.5	cm
	16	17½	18½	20	21	22	**23**	**23**	**23**	24	24	24	in
Sleeve length	30.5	33	38	40.5	43	45	**47.7**	**47.5**	**47.5**	50.5	50.5	50.5	cm
	12	13	15	16	17	17½	**18½**	**18½**	**18½**	20	20	20	in

(All measurements after washing)

YARNS

Rowan Denim 50gm (1¾oz) balls:

10	11	12	14	16	17	**18**	**19**	**20**	20	21	22

(Children's photographed in Ecru 324, men's in Nashville 225)

NEEDLES

1 pair 3¼mm (US 3) needles
1 pair 4mm (US 6) needles

TENSION (GAUGE) BEFORE WASHING

20 sts and 28 rows to 10cm (4in) measured over stocking (stockinette) stitch using 4mm (US 6) needles.

PATTERN NOTE

Denim will shrink in length when washed for the first time. Allowances have been made in this pattern for shrinkage.
The pattern is written for the six children's sizes, followed by the ladies' sizes in **bold**, followed by the men's sizes.

back

Cast on 83 (89: 95: 103: 107: 113: **117: 123: 127:** 127: 133: 137) sts using 3¼mm (US 3) needles.
Beg and ending rows as indicated, work 10 (10: 10: 10: 10: 10: **12: 12: 12:** 12: 12: 12) rows foll relevant chart.
Change to 4mm (US 6) needles.
Cont, foll chart, until row 78 (84: 90: 104: 108: 118: **120: 120: 120:** 130: 130: 130) is complete, ending with a WS row.

SHAPE ARMHOLES

Children's sizes only

Cast (bind) off 5 sts at beg of next 2 rows.
73 (79: 85: 93: 97: 103) sts

Adults' sizes only

Cast (bind) off 4 sts at beg of next 2 rows.
Dec 1 st at each end on next 6 rows.
*97 (**103: 107:** 107: 113: 117) sts*

All sizes

Cont without further shaping until chart row 136 (146: 156: 170: 176: 186: **194: 194: 194:** 204: 204: 204) is complete, ending with a WS row.

SHAPE SHOULDERS AND BACK NECK

NEXT ROW (RS): Patt 25 (28: 30: 34: 35: 38: **35: 38: 40:** 39: 42: 44) and turn, leaving rem sts on a holder.
Work each side of neck separately.
Cast (bind) off 4 sts at beg of next row.
Break yarn and leave 21 (24: 26: 30: 31: 34: **31: 34: 36:** 35: 38: 40) sts on a holder.
With RS facing, rejoin yarn to rem sts, cast (bind) off center 23 (23: 25: 25: 27: 27: **27: 27: 27:** 29: 29: 29) sts, patt to end.
Complete to match first side, rev shaping.

front

Work as given for back until chart row 122 (132: 142: 154: 160: 170: **174: 174: 174:** 180: 180: 180) is complete, thus ending with a WS row.

SHAPE NECK

NEXT ROW (RS): Patt 31 (34: 36: 40: 42: 45: **43: 46: 48:** 47: 50: 52) and turn, leaving rem sts on a holder.
Work each side of neck separately.
Cast (bind) off 4 sts at beg of next row.
Dec 1 st at neck edge on next 3 rows, then on every foll alt row until 21 (24: 26: 30: 31: 34: **33: 36: 38:** 37: 40: 42) sts rem.

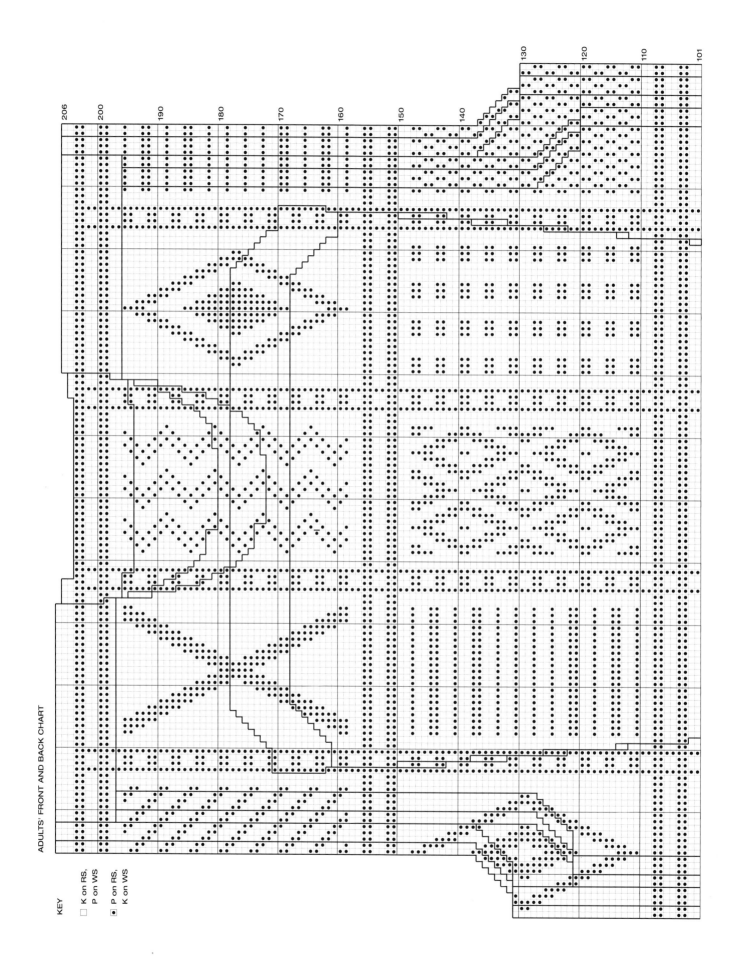

ADULTS' FRONT AND BACK CHART

KEY

K on RS,
P on WS

☐

P on RS,
K on WS

⊡

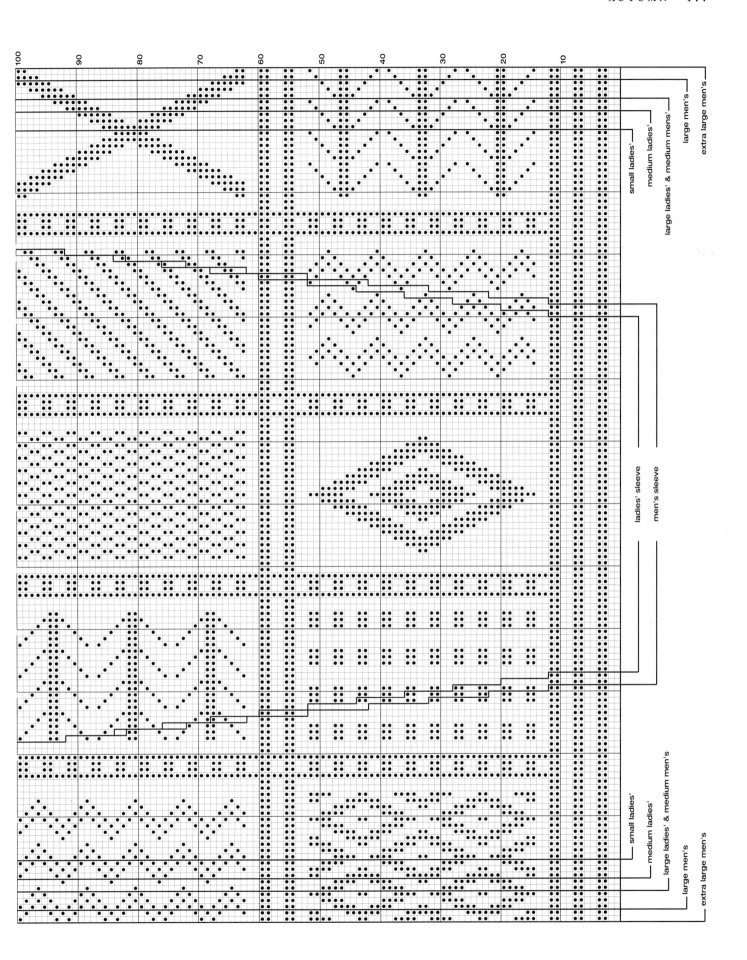

CHILDREN'S
FRONT AND
BACK CHART

KEY

☐ K on RS,
P on WS

▣ P on RS,
K on WS

Adults' sizes only

Dec 1 st at neck edge on every foll 4th row (from previous dec) until **31** (**34: 36**: 35: 38: 40) sts rem.

All sizes

Cont without further shaping until chart row 138 (148: 158: 172: 178: 188: **196: 196: 196**: 206: 206: 206) is complete, ending with a WS row.

SHAPE SHOULDER

Break yarn and leave rem 21 (24: 26: 30: 31: 34: **31: 34: 36**: 35: 38: 40) sts on a holder.

With RS facing, rejoin yarn to rem sts, cast (bind) off center 11 (11: 13: 13: 13: 13: **11: 11: 11**: 13: 13: 13) sts, patt to end.

Complete to match first side, rev shaping.

sleeves (both alike)

Cast on 39 (41: 43: 47: 49: 51: **57: 57: 57**: 61: 61: 61) sts using 3¼mm (US 3) needles.

Beg and ending rows as indicated, work 10 (10: 10: 10: 10: 10: **12: 12: 12**: 12: 12: 12) rows foll relevant chart.

Change to 4mm (US 6) needles.

Cont foll chart, shaping sides by inc 1 st at each end on next and every foll 4th (4th: 4th: 6th: 6th: 6th: **8th: 8th: 8th**: 10th: 10th: 10th) row until there are 59 (59: 49: 67: 69: 55: **81: 81: 81**: 85: 85: 85) sts.

Inc 1 st at each end on every foll 6th (6th: 6th: 8th: 8th: 8th: **10th: 10th: 10th**: 12th: 12th: 12th) row (from previous inc) until there are 73 (77: 81: 81: 85: 85: **91: 91: 91**: 91: 91: 91) sts.

Cont without further shaping until chart row 102 (110: 128: 136: 144: 152: **160: 160: 160**: 170: 170: 170) is complete, ending with a WS row.

Children's sizes only

Cast (bind) off loosely and evenly.

Adults' sizes only

Cast (bind) off 4 sts at beg of next 2 rows.

Dec 1 st at each end on next 6 rows.

Cast (bind) off rem 71 sts loosely and evenly.

finishing

DO NOT PRESS.

Join right shoulder seam by casting (binding) off sts tog on RS.

NECK BAND

With RS facing and 3¼mm (US 3) needles, pick up and knit 14 (14: 14: 16: 17: 17: **20: 20: 20**: 24: 24: 24) sts down left front neck, 11 (11: 13: 13: 13: 13: **11: 11: 11**: 13: 13: 13) sts across center front, 14 (14: 14: 16: 17: 17: **20: 20: 20**: 24: 24: 24) sts up right front neck, 4 sts down right back neck, 23 (23: 25: 25: 27: 27: **27: 27: 27**: 29: 29: 29) sts across center back, and 4 sts up left back neck.

70 (70: 74: 78: 82: 82: 86: 86: 86: 98: 98: 98) sts

ROW 1 (WS): P2, *K2, P2, rep from * to end.

ROW 2: K2, *P2, K2, rep from * to end.

Rep last 2 rows 2 (2: 2: 2: 2: 2: **4: 4: 4**: 4: 4: 4) times more, and then first of these 2 rows again.

Beg with a K row, work 6 (6: 6: 6: 6: 6: **8: 8: 8**: 8: 8: 8) rows in st st.

Cast (bind) off loosely and evenly.

Join left shoulder seam by casting off sts tog on RS.

Machine wash all pieces tog before sewing tog (see ball band for washing instructions).

See information pages for finishing instructions.

lottie by Kim Hargreaves

SIZES	S	M	L	
To fit bust	81–86.5	86.5–91.5	91.5–96.5	cm
	32–34	34–36	36–38	in
Actual width	47	51	55	cm
	18½	20	21½	in
Length	64	65	66	cm
	25	25½	26	in
Sleeve length	43	43	43	cm
	17	17	17	in

YARNS
Rowan Fine Cotton Chenille 50gm (1¾oz) balls:

Ruby 407	8	9	9

NEEDLES
1 pair 2¾mm (US 2) needles
1 pair 3¼mm (US 3) needles

BUTTONS
11

TENSION (GAUGE)
28 sts and 28 rows to 10cm (4in) measured over pattern using 3¼mm (US 3) needles

back
Cast on 132 (143: 154) sts using 2¾mm (US 2) needles.
Knit 8 rows.
Change to 3¼mm (US 3) needles.
ROW 9 (RS): *K2tog, K2, inc in next st by knitting into front and back of next 2 sts, K3, sl1, K1, psso, rep from * to end.
ROW 10: Purl.
ROWS 11 AND 12: As rows 9 and 10.
ROW 13: As row 9.
Knit 5 rows, dec 1 st at each end of first of these rows, ending with a WS row. *130 (141: 152) sts*
Row 19: K4, inc in next st, K3, sl1, K1, psso, *K2tog, K2, inc once in each of next 2 sts, K3, sl1, K1, psso, rep from *to last 10 sts, K2tog, K2, inc in next st, K5.
Row 20: P2tog, P to last 2 sts, P2tog.
128 (139: 150) sts
ROW 21: K3, inc in next st, K3, sl1, K1, psso, *K2tog, K2, inc once in each of next 2 sts, K3, sl1, K1, psso, rep from * to last 9 sts, K2tog, K2, inc in next st, K4.
ROW 22: Purl.
ROW 23: As row 21.
Knit 5 rows, dec 1 st at each end of 3rd of these rows, ending with a WS row. *126 (137: 148) sts*
ROW 29: K2, inc in next st, K3, sl1, K1, psso, *K2tog,

K2, inc once in each of next 2 sts, K3, sl1, K1, psso, rep from * to last 8 sts, K2tog, K2, inc in next st, K3.
ROW 30: Purl.
ROW 31: As row 29.
ROW 32: P2tog, P to last 2 sts, P2tog. *124 (135: 146) sts*
ROW 33: K1, inc in next st, K3, sl1, K1, psso, *K2tog, K2, inc once in each of next 2 sts, K3, sl1, K1, psso, rep from * to last 7 sts, K2tog, K2, inc in next st, K2.
Knit 5 rows, dec 1 st at each end of 5th of these rows, ending with a WS row. *122 (133: 144) sts*
ROW 39 (RS): Inc in first st, K3, sl1, K1, psso, *K2tog, K2, inc once in each of next 2 sts, K3, sl1, K1, psso, rep from * to last 6 sts, K2tog, K2, inc in next st, K1.
ROW 40: Purl.
Last 2 rows form patt.
Patt another 3 rows, thus ending with a RS row.
Keeping patt correct, dec 1 st at each end of next and every foll 6th row until there are 110 (121: 132) sts.
Work 7 rows, ending with a RS row.
Inc 1 st at each end of next and every foll 4th row until there are 132 (143: 154) sts, taking inc sts into patt.
Work 14 rows, ending with a WS row.
Work measures about 45cm [17¾in].
SHAPE ARMHOLES
Keeping patt correct, cast (bind) off 6 sts at beg of next 2 rows. *120 (131: 142) sts*
Dec 1 st at each end of next 10 rows, then on foll 6 alt rows. *88 (99: 110) sts*
Cont without further shaping until armhole measures 19 (20: 21)cm (7½ [7¾: 8¼]in), ending with a WS row.
SHAPE SHOULDERS AND BACK NECK
Keeping patt correct, cast (bind) off 4 (5: 6) sts at beg of next 2 rows. *80 (89: 98) sts*
NEXT ROW (RS): Cast (bind) off 4 (5: 6) sts, patt until there are 7 (8: 11) sts on right needle and turn, leaving rem sts on a holder.
Work each side of neck separately.
Cast (bind) off 4 sts at beg of next row.
Cast (bind) off rem 3 (4: 7) sts.
With RS facing, rejoin yarn to rem sts, cast (bind) off center 58 (63: 64) sts, patt to end.
Work to match first side, rev shaping.

left front
Cast on 61 (66: 72) sts using 2¾mm (US 2) needles.
Knit 8 rows.
Change to 3¼mm (US 3) needles.
ROW 9 (RS): *K2tog, K2, inc once in each of next 2 sts, K3, sl1, K1, psso, rep from * to last 6 (0: 6) sts, (K2tog, K2, inc once in next st, K1) 1 (0: 1) time.

ROW 10: Purl.

ROWS 11 AND 12: As rows 9 and 10.

ROW 13: As row 9.

Knit 5 rows, dec 1 st at end of first of these rows, ending with a WS row. *60 (65: 71) sts*

ROW 19: K4, inc in next st, K3, sl1, K1, psso, *K2tog, K2, inc once in each of next 2 sts, K3, sl1, K1, psso, rep from * to last 6 (0: 6) sts, (K2tog, K2, inc once in next st, K1) 1 (0: 1) time.

ROW 20: P to last 2 sts, P2tog. *59 (64: 70) sts*

ROW 21: K3, inc in next st, K3, sl1, K1, psso, *K2tog, K2, inc once in each of next 2 sts, K3, sl1, K1, psso, rep from * to last 6 (0: 6) sts, (K2tog, K2, inc once in next st, K1) 1 (0: 1) time.

ROW 22: Purl.

ROW 23: As row 21.

Knit 5 rows, dec 1 st at end of 3rd of these rows and ending with a WS row. *58 (63: 69) sts*

ROW 29: K2, inc in next st, K3, sl1, K1, psso, *K2tog, K2, inc once in each of next 2 sts, K3, sl1, K1, psso, rep from * to last 6 (0: 6) sts, (K2tog, K2, inc once in next st, K1) 1 (0: 1) time.

ROW 30: Purl.

ROW 31: As row 29.

ROW 32: P to last 2 sts, P2tog. *57 (62: 68) sts*

ROW 33: K1, inc in next st, K3, sl1, K1, psso, *K2tog, K2, inc once in each of next 2 sts, K3, sl1, K1, psso, rep from * to last 6 (0: 6) sts, (K2tog, K2, inc once in next st, K1) 1 (0: 1) time.

Knit 5 rows, dec 1 st at end of 5th of these rows, ending with a WS row. *56 (61: 67) sts*

ROW 39 (RS): Inc in first st, K3, sl1, K1, psso, *K2tog, K2, inc once in each of next 2 sts, K3, sl1, K1, psso, rep from * to last 6 (0: 6) sts, (K2tog, K2, inc once in next st, K1) 1 (0: 1) time.

ROW 40: Purl.

Last 2 rows form patt.

**Patt another 3 rows, thus ending with a RS row.

Keeping patt correct, dec 1 st at end of next and every foll 6th row until there are 50 (55: 61) sts.

Work 7 rows, ending with a RS row.

Inc 1 st at end of next and every foll 4th row until there are 61 (66: 72) sts, taking inc sts into patt.

Work 14 rows, ending with a WS row.

SHAPE ARMHOLES

Keeping patt correct, cast (bind) off 6 sts at beg of next row. *55 (60: 66) sts*

Work 1 row.

Dec 1 st at armhole edge of next 10 rows, then on foll 6 alt rows. *39 (44: 50) sts*

Cont straight until there are 13 rows fewer than on back to start of shoulder and back neck shaping, ending with a RS row.

SHAPE NECK

Keeping patt correct, cast (bind) off 13 (15: 16) sts at beg of next row, and 6 sts at beg of foll alt row. *20 (23: 28) sts*

Dec 1 st at neck edge on next 9 rows. *11 (14: 19) sts*

Work 1 row, ending at armhole edge.

SHAPE SHOULDER

Keeping patt correct, cast (bind) off 4 (5: 6) sts at beg of next and foll alt row.

Work 1 row.

Cast (bind) off rem 3 (4: 7) sts.

right front

Cast on 61 (66: 72) sts using 2¾mm (US 2) needles.
Knit 8 rows.
Change to 3¼mm (US 3) needles.
ROW 9 (RS): (Inc in first st, K3, sl1, K1, psso) 1 (0: 1)
time, *K2tog, K2, inc once in each of next 2 sts, K3,
sl1, K1, psso, rep from * to end.
ROW 10: Purl.
ROWS 11 AND 12: As rows 9 and 10.
ROW 13: As row 9.
Knit 5 rows, dec 1 st at beg of first of these rows,
ending with a WS row. *60 (65: 71) sts*
ROW 19: (Inc in first st, K3, sl1, K1, psso) 1 (0: 1) time,
*K2tog, K2, inc once in each of next 2 sts, K3, sl1,
K1, psso, rep from * to last 10 sts, K2tog, K2, inc in
next st, K5.
ROW 20: P2tog, P to end. *59 (64: 70) sts*
ROW 21: (Inc in first st, K3, sl1, K1, psso) 1 (0: 1) time,
*K2tog, K2, inc once in each of next 2 sts, K3, sl1,
K1, psso, rep from * to last 9 sts, K2tog, K2, inc in
next st, K4.
ROW 22: Purl.
ROW 23: As row 21.
Knit 5 rows, dec 1 st at beg of 3rd of these rows,
ending with a WS row. *58 (63: 69) sts*
ROW 29: (Inc in first st, K3, sl1, K1, psso) 1 (0: 1) time,
*K2tog, K2, inc once in each of next 2 sts, K3, sl1,
K1, psso, rep from * to last 8 sts, K2tog, K2, inc in
next st, K3.
ROW 30: Purl.
ROW 31: As row 29.
ROW 32: P2tog, P to end. *57 (62: 68) sts*
ROW 33: (Inc in first st, K3, sl1, K1, psso) 1 (0: 1) time,
*K2tog, K2, inc once in each of next 2 sts, K3, sl1,
K1, psso, rep from * to last 7 sts, K2tog, K2, inc in
next st, K2.
Knit 5 rows, dec 1 st at beg of 5th of these rows,
ending with a WS row. *56 (61: 67) sts*
ROW 39 (RS): (Inc in first st, K3, sl1, K1, psso) 1 (0: 1)
time, *K2tog, K2, inc once in each of next 2 sts, K3,
sl1, K1, psso, rep from * to last 6 sts, K2tog, K2, inc in
next st, K1.
ROW 40: Purl.
Last 2 rows form patt.
Complete to match left front from **, rev shaping.

sleeves (both alike)

Cast on 55 sts using 2¾mm (US 2) needles. Knit 8
rows, inc 1 st at each end of 6th of these rows. *57 sts*
Change to 3¼mm (US 3) needles.
ROW 9 (RS): K1, *K2tog, K2, inc once in each of next
2 sts, K3, sl1, K1, psso, rep from * to last st, K1.
ROW 10: Purl.
ROW 11: As row 9.
ROW 12: Inc in first st, P to last st, inc in last st. *59 sts*
ROW 13: K2, *K2tog, K2, inc once in each of next 2
sts, K3, sl1, K1, psso, rep from * to last 2 sts, K2.
Knit 5 rows, inc 1 st at each end of 5th of these rows,
ending with a WS row. *61 sts*
ROW 19: K3, *K2tog, K2, inc once in each of next 2
sts, K3, sl1, K1, psso, rep from * to last 3 sts, K3.
ROW 20: Purl.
ROWS 21 AND 22: As rows 19 and 20.
ROW 23: As row 19.
Knit 5 rows, inc 1 st at each end of first of these rows,
ending with a WS row. *63 sts*
ROW 29: K4, *K2tog, K2, inc once in each of next
2 sts, K3, sl1, K1, psso, rep from * to last 4 sts, K4.

ROW 30: Inc in first st, P to last st, inc in last st. *65 sts*
ROW 31: K5, *K2tog, K2, inc once in each of next 2
sts, K3, sl1, K1, psso, rep from * to last 5 sts, K5.
ROW 32: Purl.
ROW 33: As row 31.
Knit 5 rows, inc 1 st at each end of 3rd of these rows,
ending with a WS row. *67 sts*
ROW 39 (RS): Inc in first st, K3, sl1, K1, psso, *K2tog,
K2, inc once in each of next 2 sts, K3, sl1, K1, psso,
rep from * to last 6 sts, K2tog, K2, inc in next st, K1.
ROW 40: Purl.
Last 2 rows form patt.
Cont in patt as now set, shaping sleeve seam by inc
1 st at each end of every foll 6th row from previous
inc to 77 (85: 93) sts, then on every foll 8th row until
there are 91 (93: 95) sts, taking inc sts into st st until
there are sufficient sts to take into patt.
Work 8 rows, ending with a WS row.
Work measures approx 43cm [17in].
SHAPE TOP
Keeping patt correct, cast (bind) off 6 sts at beg of
next 2 rows. *79 (81: 83) sts*
Dec 1 st at each end of next 5 rows, then on foll
3 alt rows. *63 (65: 67) sts*
Work 3 rows, ending with a WS row.
Dec 1 st at each end of next and every foll 4th row
until 55 (57: 59) sts rem, then on every foll alt row
until 51 sts rem.
Dec 1 st at each end on next 5 rows, ending with a
WS row. *41 sts*
Cast (bind) off 4 sts at beg of next 4 rows.
Cast (bind) off rem 25 sts.

finishing

Press all pieces as described on the information page.
Join shoulder seams using back stitch.
NECK BORDER
With RS facing and using 2¾mm (US 2) needles,
pick up and knit 32 (35: 36) sts up right front neck,
66 (71: 72) sts across back neck and 32 (35: 36) sts
down left front neck. *130 (141: 144) sts*
ROW 1 (WS): Knit.
ROW 2: (Inc in next st, K3, sl1, K1, psso, K2tog, K2,
inc in next st) 2 (0: 2) times, (K2tog, K2, inc once in
each of next 2 sts, K3, sl1, K1, psso) 0 (2: 0) times, K
to last 23 (22: 23) sts, (inc in next st, K3, sl1, K1, psso,
K2tog, K2, inc in next st) 2 (0: 2) times, K1 (0: 1),
(K2tog, K2, inc once in each of next 2 sts, K3, sl1,
K1, psso) 0 (2: 0) times.
Rep last 2 rows once more.
Cast (bind) off knitwise (on WS).
BUTTON BORDER
With RS facing and using 2¾mm (US 2) needles,
pick up and knit 135 sts down left front opening edge
from top of neck border to cast-on edge.
Knit 2 rows. Cast (bind) off knitwise (on WS).
BUTTONHOLE BORDER
With RS facing and using 2¾mm (US 2) needles,
pick up and knit 135 sts up right front opening edge
from cast-on edge to top of neck border.
ROW 1 (WS) (BUTTONHOLE ROW): K2, *yfwd twice to
make a buttonhole (drop extra loop on next row),
K2tog, K11, rep from * 9 times more, yfwd twice,
K2tog, K1.
Knit 1 row.
Cast (bind) off knitwise (on WS).
See information page for finishing instructions.

cool cagoule by Martin Storey

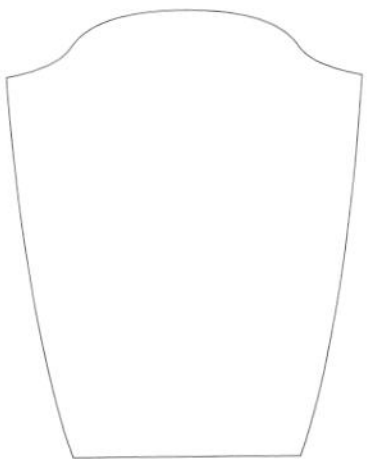

SIZES

	LADIES'		MENS'				
	S	M	L	M	L	XL	
To fit bust (chest)	76–81	86–91	97–102	97–102	107–112	117–122	cm
	30–32	34–36	38–40	38–40	42–44	46–48	in
Actual width	55	60.5	65.5	65.5	71	76	cm
	21½	23½	26	26	28	30	in
Length	60	62	64	64	66	68.5	cm
	23½	24½	25	25	26	27	in
Sleeve length	44	46	48	48	50	52	cm
	17½	18	19	19	19½	20½	in

YARN

Rowan Cotton Glacé 50gm (1¾oz) balls:

Dijon 739	15	17	19			
Pepper 796				19	21	22

NEEDLES

1 pair 2¾mm (US 2) needles
1 pair 3¼mm (US 3) needles
2 double-pointed 3¼mm (US 3) needles
Cable needle

BUTTONS

2

TENSION (GAUGE)

23 sts and 32 rows to 10cm (4in) measured over stocking (stockinette) stitch using 3¼mm (US 3) needles.

SPECIAL ABBREVIATIONS

C4B = Cable 4 back: Slip next 2 sts onto cable needle and leave at back of work, K2, then K2 from cable needle.
C4F = Cable 4 front: Slip next 2 sts onto cable needle and leave at front of work, K2, then K2 from cable needle

back

Cast on 127 (139: 151: 151: 163: 175) sts using 3¼mm (US 3) needles.
Beg with a K row, work 7 rows in st st.
NEXT ROW (WS): Knit (to form fold line).**
Beg with a K row, work another 8 rows in st st.
Place markers at both ends of last row.
ROW 1 (RS): Knit.
ROW 2: P31 (35: 39: 39: 43: 47), K3, P59 (63: 67: 71: 71: 75), K3, P31 (35: 39: 39: 43: 47).
Rows 1 and 2 form patt.
Cont in patt until back measures 33 (34: 35: 35: 36:

37)cm (13 [13½: 13¾: 13¾: 14¼: 14½]in) from markers, ending with a WS row.
Work 4 rows in garter st (knit every row).
Beg with a K row, complete back in st st as folls:
Work 2 rows, thus ending with a WS row.

SHAPE ARMHOLES

Cast (bind) off 5 sts at beg of next 2 rows.
117 (129: 141: 141: 153: 165) sts
Dec 1 st at each end of next 3 rows, then on every foll 3rd row until 103 (115: 127: 127: 139: 151) sts rem.
Cont straight until armhole measures
23 (24: 25: 25: 26: 27)cm (9 [9½: 9¾: 9¾: 10¼: 10¾]in), ending with a WS row.

SHAPE SHOULDERS

Cast (bind) off 7 (8: 9: 9: 10: 11) sts at beg of next 8 rows, then 6 (7: 8: 8: 9: 10) sts at beg of foll 2 rows.
Leave rem 35 (37: 39: 39: 41: 43) sts on a holder.

POCKET FLAP

Cast on 65 (69: 73: 73: 77: 81) sts using 2¾mm (US 2) needles, beg with a RS row, work 4 rows in garter st.
Change to 3¼mm (US 3) needles and patt as folls:
ROW 1 (RS): Knit.
ROW 2: K3, P to last 3 sts, K3.
Patt another 2 rows.
NEXT ROW (RS) (BUTTONHOLE ROW): K14 (15: 16: 16: 18), cast (bind) off 2 sts, K to last 16 (17: 18: 18: 19: 20) sts, cast (bind) off 2 sts, K to end.
NEXT ROW: Patt to end, casting on 2 sts over those cast (bound) off on previous row.
Work in patt for another 14 rows, ending with a WS row.
Break yarn and leave sts on a spare needle.

front

Work as for back to **.

Beg with a K row, work another 4 rows in st st.

NEXT ROW (EYELET ROW) (RS): K58 (64: 70: 70: 76: 82), K2tog, yfwd, K7, yfwd, K2tog tbl, K to end.

Beg with a P row, work 3 rows in st st.

Place markers at both ends of last row.

ROW 1 (RS): Knit.

ROW 2: P31 (35: 39: 39: 43: 47), K3, P59 (63: 67: 67: 71: 75), K3, P31 (35: 39: 39: 43: 47).

Rows 1 and 2 form patt.

Cont in patt until front measures 10 (11: 12: 12: 13: 14)cm (4 [4¼: 4¾: 4¾: 5: 5½]in) from markers, ending with a WS row.

DIVIDE FOR POCKET

NEXT ROW: K31 (35: 39: 39: 43: 47) and slip these sts onto a holder for left front, K65 (69: 73: 73: 77: 81) and turn, leaving rem 31 (35: 39: 39: 43: 47) sts on another holder for right front.

Work on this center set of 65 (69: 73: 73: 77: 81) sts only for pocket front as folls: Knit 2 rows.

NEXT ROW (WS) (INC): K13 (14: 15: 15: 16: 17), M1, K2, M1, K35 (37: 39: 39: 41: 43), M1, K2, M1, K13 (14: 15: 15: 16: 17). *69 (73: 77: 77: 81: 85) sts*

Cont in cable patt as folls:

ROW 1 (RS): K12 (13: 14: 14: 15: 16), P1, K4, P1, K33 (35: 37: 37: 39: 41), P1, K4, P1, K12 (13: 14: 14: 15: 16).

ROW 2: K3, P9 (10: 11: 11: 12: 13), K1, P4, K1, P33 (35: 37: 37: 39: 41), K1, P4, K1, P9 (10: 11: 11:12: 13), K3.

ROW 3: K12 (13: 14: 14: 15: 16), P1, C4B, P1, K33 (35: 37: 37: 39: 41), P1, C4F, P1, K12 (13: 14: 14: 15: 16).

ROW 4: As row 2.

Rows 1–4 form patt.

Cont in patt until pocket front measures about 20cm (8in) from dividing row, ending with patt row 4.

Change to 2¾mm (US 2) needles.

NEXT ROW (RS) (DEC): K13 (14: 15: 15: 16: 17), K2tog twice, K35 (37: 39: 39: 41: 43), (K2tog) twice, K13 (14: 15: 15: 16: 17). *65 (69: 73: 73: 77: 81) sts*

Beg with a WS row, work 3 rows in garter st.

Cast (bind) off evenly knitwise.

Return to sts left on holders and, using 3¼mm (US 3) needles, cont as folls:

NEXT ROW (RS): Sl 31 (35: 39: 39: 43: 47) sts from left front holder onto right needle, rejoin yarn and cast on 65 (69: 73: 73: 77: 81) sts for pocket back, then K across 31 (35: 39: 39: 43: 47) sts from right front holder. *127 (139: 151: 151: 163: 175) sts*

Beg with a P row, cont in st st until front measures 33 (34: 35: 35: 36: 37)cm (13 [13½: 13¾: 13¾: 14¼: 14½]in) from markers, ending with a WS row.

PLACE POCKET FLAP

NEXT ROW (RS): K31 (35: 39: 43: 47), holding WS of pocket flap against RS of front, K tog first st of flap with next st of front, K tog rem 64 (68: 72: 72: 76: 80) sts of flap with sts from front in the same way, K rem 31 (35: 39: 39: 43: 47) sts of front. *127 (139: 151: 151: 163: 175) sts*

Work 3 rows in garter st.

Beg with a K row, complete front in st st as folls: Work 2 rows, thus ending with a WS row.

SHAPE ARMHOLES

Cast (bind) off 5 sts at beg of next 2 rows. *117 (129: 141: 141: 153: 165) sts*

Dec 1 st at each end of next 3 rows, then on every foll 3rd row until 103 (115: 127: 127: 139: 151) sts rem.

Cont straight until armhole measures 6 (7: 8: 8: 9: 10)cm (2½ [2¾: 3¼: 3¼: 3½: 4]in), ending with a WS row.

DIVIDE FOR FRONT OPENING

NEXT ROW (RS): K46 (52: 58: 58: 64: 70) and turn, leaving rem sts on a holder.

Work each side of neck separately.

Cont straight until front is 14 (14: 16: 16: 16: 18) rows shorter than back to start of shoulder shaping.

SHAPE NECK

NEXT ROW (RS): K to last 4 (5: 5: 5: 6: 6) sts and turn, leaving last 4 sts on a holder. *42 (47: 53: 53: 58: 64) sts*

Dec 1 st at neck edge on next 4 rows, then on every foll alt row until 34 (39: 44: 44: 49: 54) sts rem.

Work 1 row.

SHAPE SHOULDERS

Cast (bind) off 7 (8: 9: 9: 10: 11) sts at beg of next and foll 3 alt rows. Work 1 row. Cast (bind) off rem 6 (7: 8: 8: 9: 10) sts.

With RS facing, rejoin yarn to rem 57 (63: 69: 69: 75: 81) sts, cast (bind) off 11 sts, K to end. *46 (52: 58: 58: 64: 70) sts*

Work to match first side, rev shaping.

sleeves (both alike)

Cast on 59 (61: 59: 59: 61: 63) sts using 3¼mm (US 3) needles.

ROW 1 (RS) (INC): K3 (4: 0: 0: 0: 0), P0 (0: 1: 1: 2: 3), inc in next st 0 (0: 2: 2: 2: 2) times, *P3, K3, P3, inc in next st twice, rep from * to last 12 (13: 1: 1: 2: 3) sts, P3 (3: 1: 1: 2: 3), [K3, P3] 1 (1: 0: 0: 0: 0) time, K3 (4: 0: 0: 0: 0). *67 (69: 71: 71: 73: 75) sts*

ROW 2: P3 (4: 0: 0: 0: 0), K0 (0: 1: 1: 2: 3), P0 (0: 4: 4: 4: 4), *K3, P3, K3, P4, rep from * to last 12 (13: 1: 1: 2: 3) sts, K3 (3: 1: 1: 2: 3), [P3, K3] 1 (1: 0: 0: 0: 0) time, P3 (4: 0: 0: 0: 0).

ROW 3: K3 (4: 0: 0: 0: 0), P0 (0: 1: 1: 2: 3), C4B 0 (0: 1: 1: 1: 1) times, *P3, K3, P3, C4B, rep from * to last 12 (13: 1: 1: 2: 3) sts, P3 (3: 1: 1: 2: 3), [K3, P3] 1 (1: 0: 0: 0: 0) time, P3 (4: 0: 0: 0: 0).

ROW 4: As row 2.

ROW 5: K3 (4: 0: 0: 0: 0), P0 (0: 1: 1: 2: 3), K0 (0: 4: 4: 4: 4), *P3, K3, P3, K4, rep from * to last 12 (13: 1: 1: 2: 3) sts, P3 (3: 1: 1: 2: 3), [K3, P3] 1 (1: 0: 0: 0: 0) time, P3 (4: 0: 0: 0: 0).

Rows 2–5 form patt.

Cont in patt as set, inc 1 st at each end of 2nd and every foll 6th row to 101 (105: 105: 105: 109: 109) sts, then on every foll 4th row until there are 113 (117: 123: 123: 127: 133) sts, taking inc sts into patt.

Cont straight until sleeve measures 44 (46: 48: 48: 50: 52)cm (17¼ [18: 18¾: 18¾: 19¾: 20½]in) from cast-on edge, ending with a WS row.

SHAPE TOP

Keeping patt correct, cast (bind) off 5 sts at beg of next 4 rows, 3 sts at beg of foll 14 rows and 5 sts at beg of foll 6 rows.

Cast (bind) off rem 21 (25: 31: 31: 35: 41) sts.

finishing

Press all pieces as described on the information page.

FRONT OPENING BORDERS (BOTH ALIKE)

With RS facing and 3¼mm (US 3) needles, pick up and K 37 sts evenly along one side of front opening, between center front cast- (bound-) off sts and neck shaping.

ROW 1 (WS): P2, *K3, P2, rep from * to end.

ROW 2: K2, *P3, K2, rep from * to end.

Rows 1 and 2 form rib. Work another 2 rows in rib.

ROW 5 (WS) (EYELET ROW): P2, *K2tog, yfwd, K1, P2, rep from * to end.

Work another 2 rows in rib. Cast (bind) off in rib.

Sew ends of borders to center front cast- (bound-) off sts at base of opening so that cast- (bound-) off edges meet at center. Join shoulder seams using back stitch.

COLLAR

With RS facing and 3¼mm (US 3) needles, pick up and K6 sts across top of right front border, 4 (5: 5: 5: 6: 6) sts from right front holder, 33 (34: 38: 38: 38: 40) sts up right side of neck, 35 (37: 39: 39: 41: 43) sts from back neck holder, inc 1 (0: 0: 0: 1: 0) st at center, 33 (34: 38: 38: 38: 40) sts down left side of neck, 4 (5: 5: 5: 6: 6) sts from left front holder, and 6 sts across top of left front border.

122 (127: 137: 137: 142: 147) sts

Beg with row 2, work in rib as for front borders for 10 (10: 12: 12: 12: 12)cm (4 [4: 4¾: 4¾: 4¾: 4¾]in).

Cast (bind) off loosely in rib.

Sew cast-on edge of pocket back in place behind pocket front. Topstitch edges of pocket front in position, matching the 3 border sts with garter st ridge on body. Sew on buttons.

Set sleeves into armhole using back stitch. Join side and sleeve seams using back stitch.

Fold lower edge of body to WS along knit-row ridge and catch into place.

HEM DRAWSTRING

Cast on 3 sts using 3¼mm (US 3) double-pointed needles.

ROW 1 (RS): K3 (all 3 sts now on right needle), *slip sts to opposite end of this needle and transfer this needle to left hand, without turning work (and taking yarn snugly across back of work) K same 3 sts again (all 3 sts on right needle again), rep from * until cord measures 146cm (57½in).

NEXT ROW: K3tog and fasten off.

Thread hem drawstring through hem casing using eyelet holes at front.

NECK TIE

Work as for hem drawstring, making cord 81cm (32in) long.

Thread neck tie in and out of eyelet holes of front borders as in photograph.

laurel by Louisa Harding

SIZE

To fit bust	81–86	cm
	32–34	in
Actual width	43	cm
	17	in
Shirt length	66.5	cm
	26½	in
Waistcoat length	76.5	cm
	30	in
Sleeve length	42	cm
	16½	in

YARNS

Rowan Designer DK 50gm (1¾oz) balls or
Lurex 25gm (⅞oz) balls:

Shirt

| DDK 639 | 11 |
| Lurex | 26 |

Waistcoat

| DDK 660 | 8 |
| Lurex Gold 842 | 21 |

NEEDLES

1 pair 3¼mm (US 3) needles
1 pair 4mm (US 6) needles

Lurex: Please replace 3¼mm (US 3) with 4mm (US 6), and 4mm (US 6) with 5mm (US 8) throughout or with needles that give correct tension.

BUTTONS

16 for shirt
8 for waistcoat

TENSION (GAUGE)

20 sts and 30 rows to 10cm (4in) measured over lace pattern using 4mm (US 6) needles

STITCH NOTE

When working lace pattern, the first and last stitch is knitted on every row to give a neat edge for stitching together.

LACE PATTERN

ROW 1 (RS): K5, *yf, sl1, K1, psso, K1 (K2tog,yf) twice, K3, rep from * to last st, K1.
ROW 2 AND ALL WS ROWS: K1, purl to last st, K1.
ROW 3: K1, *K3, (yf, sl1, K1, psso) twice, K1, K2tog, yf, rep from * to last 5 sts, K5.

ROW 5: K3, *(yf, sl1, K1, psso) 3 times, K4, rep from * to last 3 sts, yf, sl1, K1, psso, K1.
ROW 7: K2, *(yf, sl1, K1, psso) 4 times, K2, rep from * to last 4 sts, yf, sl1, K1, psso, K2.
ROW 9: As row 5.
ROW 11: As row 3.
ROW 13: As row 1.
ROW 15: K1, K2tog, yf, *K4, (K2tog, yf) 3 times, rep from * to last 3 sts, K3.
ROW 17: K2, K2tog, yf, *K2, (K2tog, yf) 4 times, rep from * to last 2 sts, K2.
ROW 19: As row 15.
ROW 20: K1, purl to last st, K1.
These 20 rows form the patt and are repeated throughout.

shirt and waistcoat
back

Cast on 106 sts using 4mm (US 6) needles and work 4 rows in garter stitch (knit every row).

Waistcoat only

Work 30 rows in patt without shaping (this is for extra length), then cont to work as for:

Shirt and waistcoat

Work 106 rows in lace patt, shaping sides by dec 1 st at each end of 9th and every foll 8th row. *80 sts*
Keeping patt correct, work 10 rows without shaping.
Work 18 rows in patt, inc 1 st at each end of next and every foll 6th row. *86 sts*

SHAPE ARMHOLES

Cast (bind) off 4 sts at beg of next 2 rows.
Dec 1 st at each end of next 5 rows and foll 2 alt rows. *64 sts*
Keeping patt correct, work 55 rows without further shaping or until work measures 22cm (8½in)from beg of armhole shaping, ending with a WS row.

SHAPE SHOULDER AND BACK NECK

Dec 1 st at each end of next 10 rows. *44 sts*
NEXT ROW: Cast (bind) off 1 st, patt 11, turn and leave rem sts on a holder.
Work each side of neck separately.
Dec 1 st at each end of next 4 rows.
NEXT ROW: K1, K2tog, psso, fasten off.
With RS facing, rejoin yarn to rem sts, cast (bind) off center 20 sts, patt to end.
Complete to match first side, rev shaping.

left front

Cast on 56 sts using 4mm (US 6) needles and work 4 rows in garter st.

Waistcoat only

Work 30 rows in patt without shaping (this is for extra length), then cont to work as for:

Shirt and waistcoat

Work 106 rows in lace patt, shaping side by dec 1 st at side edge on 9th and every 8th row. *43 sts*
Keeping lace patt correct, work 10 rows without shaping.
Work 18 rows, inc 1 st at side edge on next and every foll 6th row. *46 sts*

SHAPE ARMHOLE

NEXT ROW (RS): Cast (bind) off 4 sts, patt to end.
Patt 1 row.
Dec 1 st at armhole edge on next 5 rows and foll 2 alt rows. *35 sts*
Keeping patt correct, work 40 rows without shaping or until work measures 17cm (6½in) from beg of armhole shaping, ending with a RS row.

SHAPE FRONT NECK

NEXT ROW (WS): Cast (bind) off 7 sts, patt to end.
Dec 1 st at neck edge on next 9 rows and foll 2 alt rows. *17 sts*
Patt 1 row.

SHAPE SHOULDER

Dec 1 st at armhole edge on next 15 rows.
NEXT ROW: K2tog, fasten off.

right front

Work as given for left front, rev all shaping.

sleeve cuffs (both alike)

Shirt only

Cast on 46 sts using 4mm (US 6) needles and work 4 rows in garter st.
Work 30 rows in lace patt.
Cast (bind) off evenly.

sleeves (both alike)

Cast on 46 sts using 4mm (US 6) needles.
Working in lace patt throughout, shape sides by inc 1 st at each end of 5th and every foll 4th row to 86 sts, working extra sts into patt as they occur.
Cont without further shaping until work measures 32cm (12½in) from beg, ending with a WS row.

SHAPE TOP

Cast (bind) off 4 sts at beg of next 2 rows.
Dec 1 st at each end of next 5 rows, then every alt row to 40 sts, ending with a WS row.
Cast (bind) off 3 sts at beg of next 8 rows. *16 sts*
Cast (bind) off rem sts.

finishing

Shirt and waistcoat

Press all pieces as described on the information page.
Join shoulder seams.

BUTTON BAND

Instructions are given for shirt followed by waistcoat in **bold**.
With RS facing, using 3¼mm (US 3) needles, rejoin yarn and pick up and knit 136 (**150**) sts evenly along left front edge.
NEXT ROW (WS): Knit to end.
Knit 4 more rows.
Cast (bind) off evenly.

BUTTONHOLE BAND

With RS facing, using 3¼mm (US 3) needles, rejoin yarn and pick up and knit 136 (**150**) sts evenly along right front edge.
ROW 1 (WS): Knit.
BUTTONHOLE ROW (RS): K4, cast (bind) off 2 sts, [K16 (**18**), cast (bind) off 2 sts] 7 times, K4.
ROW 3: Knit, casting on 2 sts over those cast (bound) off on previous row.
Knit 2 rows.
Cast (bind) off evenly.

COLLAR AND NECKBAND

With RS facing and using 3¼mm (US 3) needles, rejoin yarn and pick up and knit 34 sts evenly up right front neck, 28 sts along back neck and 34 sts evenly down left front neck. *96 sts*

Shirt only

COLLAR

Work 30 rows in lace patt, and AT THE SAME TIME inc 1 st at each end of the 3rd row and every foll 4th row as folls:
INC ROW (RS): K1, M1, patt to last st, M1, K1, working extra sts into patt as they occur.
Work 3 rows in garter st.
Cast (bind) off knitwise.
Join side and sleeve seams.
Beg halfway along center back of sleeve, join cast-(bound-) off edge of cuff to cast-on edge of sleeve, overlapping cuff by 4cm (1½in). (The overlap should face toward the back of sleeve.)
Sew 4 buttons down overlap on each cuff.
Set in sleeves.

Waistcoat only

NECKBAND

Work 3 rows in garter st.
Cast (bind) off evenly knitwise.

ARMHOLE EDGINGS (BOTH ALIKE)

With RS facing and using 3¼mm (US 3) needles, pick up and K 94 sts evenly around armhole edge.
Work 3 rows in garter st.
Cast (bind) off evenly knitwise.
Join side seams.
See information page for finishing instructions.

cardigan with chenille collar
by Louisa Harding

SIZES

To fit bust	86–91	cm
	34–36	in
Actual width	51	cm
	20	in
Length	48	cm
	19	in
Sleeve length	52.5	cm
	20¾	in

YARN

Rowan Wool Cotton and Rowan Fine Cotton Chenille 50gm (1¾oz) balls:

A	Wool Cotton, Camel 943	10
B	Wool Cotton, Violet 933	1
C	Chenille, Cornflower 412	1
D	Wool Cotton, Russet 910	1

NEEDLES

1 pair 3¼mm (US 3) needles
1 pair 4mm (US 6) needles
Cable needle

BUTTONS

6

TENSION (GAUGE)

22 sts and 30 rows to 10cm (4in) measured over stocking (stockinette) stitch using 4mm (US 6) needles

back

Cast on 126 sts using 3¼mm (US 3) needles and yarn D.

ROW 1: Using yarn D, *P2, K2, rep from * to last 2 sts. P2.

ROW 2: Using yarn D, *K2, P2, rep from * to last sts, K2.

Then, joining and breaking off colors as required, work next 40 rows in patt from chart, rep 32-st patt 3 times across row and working last 30 sts on RS rows and first 30 sts on WS rows as indicated.

Change to 4mm (US 6) needles and work 38 rows in patt from chart, repeating stitch patt as before and rows 41-50 throughout.

SHAPE ARMHOLES

Keeping patt correct, cast (bind) off 5 sts at beg of next 2 rows. *116 sts*

Work another 62 rows in patt.

SHAPE SHOULDERS

Cast (bind) off 37 sts at beg of next 2 rows.
Cast (bind) off rem 42 sts.

left front

Cast on 62 sts using 3¼ mm (US 3) needles and yarn D. Work first 2 rows in rib as given for back. Then, joining and breaking colors as required, work next 40 rows in patt from chart for left front.

Change to 4mm (US 6) needles and work 38 rows in patt from chart, working between markers for left front as before and rep chart rows 41-50 throughout.

SHAPE ARMHOLE

Cast (bind) off 5 sts at beg of next row, patt to end. *57 sts*

Work another 42 rows in patt, ending with a RS row.

SHAPE FRONT NECK

Cast (bind) off 7 sts at beg of next row, patt to end.
Dec 1 st at neck edge on next 8 rows.
Work 1 row, then dec 1 st at neck edge on next row and foll 4 alt rows.
Work 2 rows in patt. Cast (bind) off rem 37 sts.

right front

Work as given for left front, rev all shaping.

sleeves (both alike)

Cast on 54 sts using 3¼ mm (US 3) needles and yarn D. Work first 2 rows in rib as given for back. Then, joining and breaking colors as required, work in patt from chart, setting patt sts as folls:

NEXT ROW: Using yarn A (P2, K2) 3 times, work next 30 sts from chart row 1 between sleeve markers, using yarn A (K2, P2) 3 times.

NEXT ROW: Using yarn A (K2, P2) 3 times, work next 30 sts from chart row 2 between sleeve markers, using yarn A (P2, K2) 3 times.

Keeping 12 sts at either side in rib patt as set, cont to work through chart rows to row 40. AT THE SAME TIME, begin shaping sides by inc 1 st at each end of 25th row and every foll 6th row until there are 60 sts.

Change to 4mm (US 6) needles and using yarn A only, work 118 rows in st st, beg with a K row. AT THE SAME TIME, shape sides by inc 1 st at each end of 3rd row and every foll 6th row until there are 98 sts. Cast (bind) off.

finishing

Press all pieces (except ribbing) very gently on WS using a warm iron over a damp cloth.

Join both shoulder seams using back stitch.

Sew sleeve top into armhole, the straight sides at top of sleeve to form a neat right angle to cast- (bound) off sts at armhole on back and fronts.

Join side and sleeve seams.

BUTTON BAND

Cast on 9 sts using 3¼mm (US 3) needles and yarn D.

ROW 1: K3, P3, K3.

ROW 2: P3, K3, P3.

Change to yarn A and cont in rib as set until band, when slightly stretched, fits up front to start of neck shaping.

Sew band into position as you go along.

Cast (bind) off evenly in rib.

BUTTONHOLE BAND

Work to correspond with button band with the addition of 6 buttonholes, the first to come 2cm (¾in) up from bottom edge, the 3rd to come at top of patterned rib, the 2nd to come halfway between 1st and 3rd, the last to come 1.5cm (½in) down from cast- (bound-) off edge of band and the remaining 2 buttons spaced evenly between the 3rd and 6th buttonholes.

First mark position of buttons with pins to ensure even spacing, then work buttonholes to correspond.

TO MAKE A BUTTONHOLE:

ROW 1: K3, cast (bind) off 2, P1, K3.

ROW 2: Work across row in rib, casting on 2 sts in place of those cast (bound) off on previous row.

COLLAR

Cast on 105 sts using 3¼ mm (US 3) needles and yarn C.

Cont in moss (seed) stitch as folls:

NEXT ROW: *K1, P1, rep from * to last st, K1.

Rep this row 19 more times and AT THE SAME TIME shape sides by inc 1 st (make inc st 1 st in from each side edge) at each end of 2nd row and 4 foll 4th rows. *115 sts*

Cast (bind) off loosely and evenly in moss (seed) stitch. slipstitch collar into place, matching center of collar with center back neck and finishing halfway across front bands.

Sew on buttons to correspond with buttonholes.

Press seams.

See information page for finishing instructions.

KEY

- ▨▨▨▨ Slip next 2 sts onto cable needle and hold at back of work, K2, then P2 from cable needle.
- ▨▨▨▨ Slip next 2 sts onto cable needle and hold at front of work, P2, then K2 from cable needle.
- ▨▨▨ Slip next st onto cable needle and hold at back of work, K2, then P1 from cable needle.
- ▨▨▨ Slip next 2 sts onto cable needle and hold at front of work, P1, then K2 from cable needle.
- ☐ Using yarn A, K on RS, P on WS.
- ● Using yarn A, P on RS, K on WS.
- ◉ Using yarn B, K on RS, P on WS.
- ▣ Using yarn C, K on RS, P on WS.
- ✕ Using yarn C, K on RS, P on WS.

PATTERN CHART

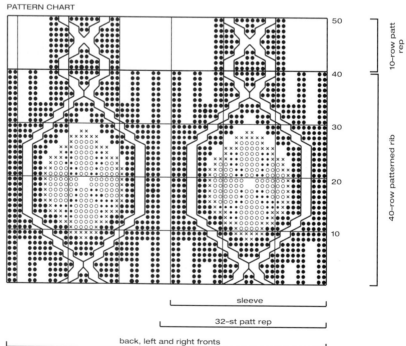

10-row patt rep

40-row patterned rib

sleeve

32-st patt rep

back, left and right fronts

paris by Sharon Peake

SIZES	S	M	L	
To fit bust	86	91	97	cm
	34	36	38	in
Actual width	43	45.5	48	cm
	17	18	19	in
Length	62	62	62	cm
	24½	24½	24½	in
Sleeve length	43	43	43	cm
	17	17	17	in

YARNS

Rowan True 4-ply Botany 50gm (1¾oz) balls:
Poodle cardigan

A Redwood 549	8	9	9
B Jet 546	1	1	1
C Camel 582	1	1	1
D Grape 585	1	1	1
E Lavender 571	1	1	1

One-color cardigan

Burnt 566???	8	8	9

BUTTONS

9

NEEDLES

1 pair 3mm (US 2) needles
1 pair 3¼mm (US 3) needles

TENSION (GAUGE)

27 sts and 34 rows to 10cm (4in) over stocking (stockinette) stitch using 3¼mm (US 3) needles

PATTERN NOTE

For one-color garments, follow pattern for patterned cardigan, ignoring all color changes.

back

Cast on 122 (126: 134) sts using 3mm (US 2) needles and yarn A.
Knit 2 rows using yarn B.
Knit 2 rows using yarn A.
Change to 3¼mm (US 3) needles and work 32 rows in textured stitch as folls:
ROW 1 (RS): Using yarn A, K1, purl to last st, K1.
ROW 2: K1, *(K1, P1, K1) into next st, P3tog, rep from * to last st, K1.
ROW 3: K1, purl to last st, K1.
ROW 4: K1, *P3tog, (K1, P1, K1) into next st, rep from * to last st, K1.

Rep these 4 rows 7 times more, inc 1 st at each end of last row on medium size only. *122 (128: 134) sts*
Joining and breaking colors as required and using the intarsia technique, work 12 rows in patt from chart for back, ending with a WS row.
SHAPE SIDES AS FOLLS:
Dec 1 st at each end of next row and 1 foll 12th row. Work 5 rows.
Dec 1 st at each end of next row and every foll 3rd row to 100 (106: 112) sts.
Cont without shaping until chart row 60 is complete, ending with a WS row.
Inc 1 st at each end of next row and 8 foll 6th rows, then cont without further shaping until chart row 114 is complete, ending with a WS row. *118 (124: 130) sts*
SHAPE ARMHOLES
Cast (bind) off 6 sts at beg of next 2 rows.
Dec 1 st at each end of next 9 (10: 11) rows.
88 (92: 96) sts
Work until chart row 170 is complete, ending with a WS row.
SHAPE BACK NECK
Patt 36 (38: 40) sts, turn and leave rem sts on a holder. Work each side of neck separately.
Dec 1 st at neck edge on next 6 rows. *30 (32: 34) sts*
Work 1 row. Cast (bind) off loosely and evenly.
With RS facing, rejoin yarn to rem sts, cast (bind) off center 16 sts, patt to end.
Complete to match first side, rev shaping.

left front

Note: The button band is worked at the same time as the front.
Cast on 78 (78: 82) sts using 3mm (US 2) needles and yarn A.
**Knit 2 rows using yarn B.
Knit 2 rows using yarn A.
Change to 3¼mm (US 3) needles and work 32 rows in textured st as given for back, ending with a WS row. **
Cont working front edging and patt from chart for left front as folls:
Small size only
CHART ROW 1 (RS): K2tog, K to last 18 sts, K1, P16, K1. *77 sts*
Med size only
CHART ROW 1 (RS): K1, M1, K to last 18 sts, M1, K1, P16, K1. *80 sts*
Large size only
CHART ROW 1 (RS): K1, M1, K to last 18 sts, K1, P16, K1. *83 sts*

All sizes
CHART ROW 2: K1, *(K1, P1, K1) into next st, P3tog, rep from * 3 times more, K1, work 59 (62: 65) sts in patt from chart.
Keeping patt on 18 sts of button band correct, cont until 12 rows in patt from chart are complete, ending with a WS row.

SHAPE SIDE AS FOLLS:
Dec 1 st at beg of next row and 1 on foll 12th row. Work 5 rows.
Dec 1 st at beg of next row and every foll 3rd row to 66 (69: 72) sts.
Work without shaping until chart row 60 is complete, ending with a WS row.
Inc 1 st at beg of next row and every foll 6th row to 75 (78: 81) sts then cont without further shaping until chart row 114 is complete, ending with a WS row.

SHAPE ARMHOLE
Cast (bind) off 6 sts at beg of next row.
Work 1 row. Dec 1 st at armhole edge on every foll row to 60 (62: 64) sts.
Cont from chart until row 145 is complete, ending with a RS row.

SHAPE FRONT NECK
Cast (bind) off 21 sts at neck edge on next row.
Work 1 row. Dec 1 st at neck edge on next 4 rows and 5 foll alt rows. 30 (32: 34) sts
Work without shaping until front matches back to shoulder shaping, ending with a WS row.
Cast (bind) off loosely and evenly.

right front

Note: The buttonhole band is worked at the same time as the front.
Cast on 78 (78: 82) sts using 3mm (US 3) needles and yarn A.
Work as given for left front from ** to ** with the addition of buttonholes worked on rows 9 and 29 as folls:
ROWS 9 AND 29 (RS) (BUTTONHOLE): K1, P6, cast (bind) off 3 sts, patt to end.
NEXT ROW: Keeping sts correct, work in patt, inc 3 sts over those cast (bound) off on previous row.
Cont working front edging and patt from chart as folls:

Small size only
CHART ROW 1 (RS): K1, P16, K1, K to last 2 sts, K2tog. *77 sts*

Med size only
CHART ROW 1 (RS): K1, P16, K1, M1, K to last st, M1, K1. *80 sts*

Large size only
CHART ROW 1 (RS): K1, P16, K1, K to last st, M1, K1. *83 sts*

All sizes
CHART ROW 2: Work 59 (62: 65) sts in patt from chart, K1, *(K1, P1, K1) into next st, P3tog, rep from * 3 more times, K1.
Keeping patt on 18 sts of button band correct, complete as given for left front, rev shaping and with the addition of buttonholes worked as before on chart rows 13, 33, 53, 73, 93, 113 and 133.

sleeves (both alike)

Cast on 62 sts using 3mm (US 3) needles and yarn A and work turnback cuff as folls:
Knit 2 rows using yarn B.
Knit 2 rows using yarn A.
Change to 3¼mm (US 3) needles and work 8 rows in textured patt as given for back.
Keeping patt correct, dec 1 st at each end of next row and 3 foll 6th rows, ending with a RS row. *54 sts*

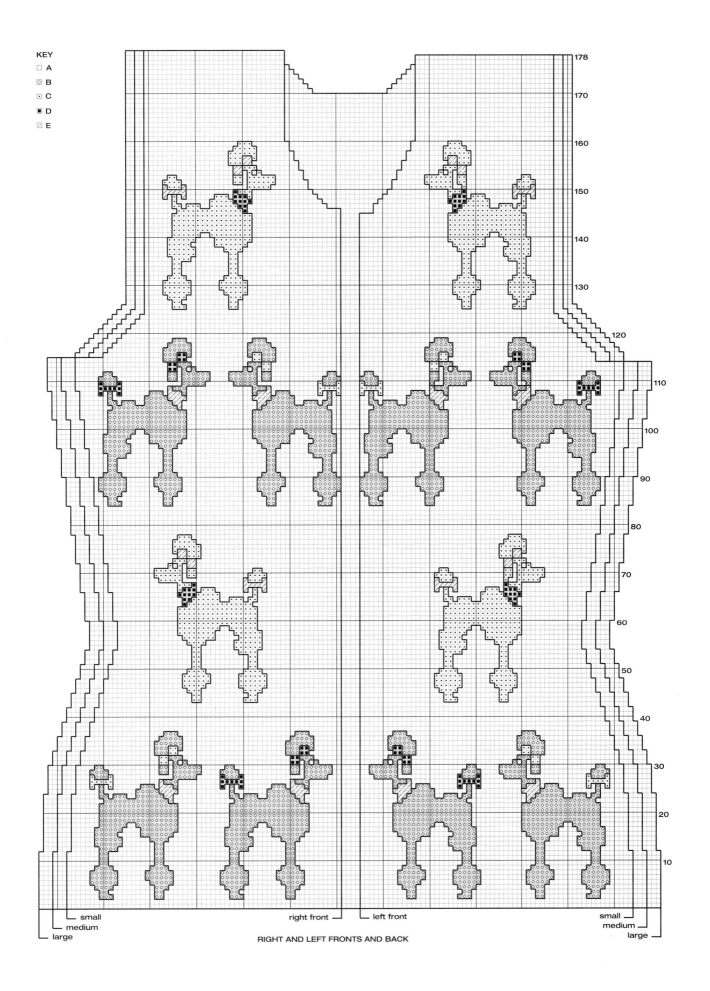

KEY
□ A
⊡ B
⊡ C
■ D
◪ E

RIGHT AND LEFT FRONTS AND BACK

Work 5 more rows in pattern, ending with a WS row. From this point, the WS of cuff becomes the RS of sleeve:

NEXT ROW (WS): Purl 1 row.

Work in patt from chart for sleeve shaping by inc 1 st at each end of row 7, 10 foll 6th rows and then every foll 8th row to 90 sts.

Work until chart row 146 is complete, ending with a WS row.

SHAPE SLEEVE HEAD

Cast (bind) off 6 sts at beg of next 2 rows and 4 sts at beg of foll 2 rows. *70 sts*

Dec 1 st at each end of next 7 rows and 3 foll alt rows. *50 sts*

Work 3 rows. Dec 1 st at each end of next row, 3 foll 4th rows, 4 foll alt rows and 5 foll rows. *24 sts*

Cast (bind) off 5 sts at beg of next 2 rows.

Cast (bind) off rem 14 sts.

finishing

Press all pieces, including all textured edgings, as described on the information page.

Join both shoulder seams using back stitch.

COLLAR

Cast on 126 sts using 3¼mm (US 3) needles and yarn A and work collarband and underside of collar as folls:

Knit 2 rows.

Work 4 rows in texture stitch as given for back.

NEXT ROW (BUTTONHOLE ROW) (RS): K1, P6, cast (bind) off 3 sts, patt to end.

NEXT ROW: Keeping sts correct, work in patt, inc 3 sts over those cast (bound) off on previous row.

Work 2 more rows in patt.

Change to 3mm (US 3) needles and working in st st, beg with a knit row, cast (bind) off 12 sts at beg of next 2 rows. *102 sts*

Cont until 9cm (3½in) of st st is complete, ending with a WS row.

Place a marker at each end of the last row; this is the fold line.

Work upper side of collar and collar band as follows:

Knit 2 rows using yarn A.

Knit 2 rows using yarn B.

Knit 2 rows using yarn A.

Change to 3¼mm (US 3) needles and cont in textured patt as given for back until work measures 9cm (3½in) from marker, ending with a WS row.

Keeping patt correct, cast on 12 sts at beg of next 2 rows. *126 sts*

Work 8 more rows in textured st, working a buttonhole as before on 3rd and 4th rows.

Knit 2 rows. Cast (bind) off loosely and evenly.

Join upper side to lower side of collar along edges as folls:

With WS together, fold collar along fold line.

With upper side facing, using 3mm (US 2) needles and yarn A and working through both layers, pick up and knit 28 sts along collar edge from fold line to where 12 sts are cast (bound) off.

Knit 1 row using yarn A.

Knit 2 rows using yarn B.

Knit 1 row using yarn A.

Cast (bind) off in yarn A.

Work other side to match.

Slipstitch edges of band together.

Starting and ending at front edges and matching center of collar with center back neck, slipstitch cast-on and cast- (bound-) off edges of collar neatly into place.

See information page for finishing instructions.

KEY

☐ A
◉ B
⊡ C
◼ D
☑ E

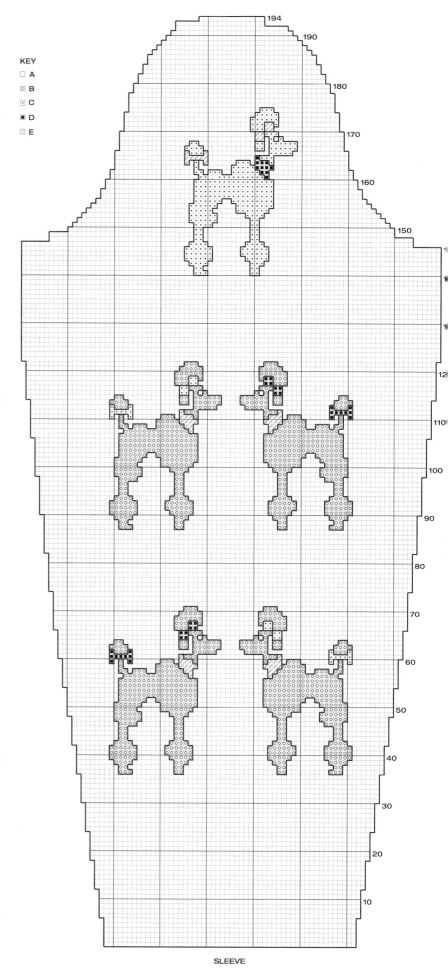

SLEEVE

knight by Kim Hargreaves

SIZES

	XS	S	M	L	
To fit bust	81	86.5	91.5	102	cm
	32	34	36	40	in
Actual width	60.5	64	66	68.5	cm
	24	25	26	27	in
Length	68	72	75	79	cm
	27	28½	29½	31	in
Sleeve length	43	46	48	49	cm
	17	18	19	19½	in

YARNS

Rowan Magpie Aran and Magpie Tweed 100gm (3½oz) balls:

		XS	S	M	L
A	M Tweed Indigo 776	5	6	6	6
B	M Tweed Leafy 774	4	4	4	4
C	M Tweed Jewel 775	1	1	1	1
D	M Admiral 504	1	1	1	1
E	M Tweed Ivy 765	1	2	2	2

NEEDLES

1 pair 4mm (US 6) needles
1 pair 5mm (US 8) needles

BUTTONS

5

TENSION (GAUGE)

18 sts and 23 rows to 10cm (4in) measured over patterned stocking (stockinette) stitch using 5mm (US 8) needles

back

Cast on 109 (115: 119: 123) sts using 4mm (US 6) needles and yarn A.
ROW 1 (RS): K1, *P1, K1, rep from * to end.
This row forms moss (seed) st.
Work another 6 rows in moss (seed) st, ending with a RS row.
Purl 1 row.
Change to 5mm (US 8) needles.
Using the intarsia technique described on the information page and beg with a RS row, work in patt from chart until back measures 44 (47: 50: 53)cm, (17¼ [18½: 19¾: 21]in), ending with a WS row.
SHAPE ARMHOLES
Keeping chart correct, cast (bind) off 4 sts at beg of next 2 rows. *101 (107: 111: 115) sts*
Dec 1 st at each end of next 5 rows.
91 (97: 101: 105) sts

Cont without further shaping until armhole measures 24 (25: 25: 26)cm (9½ [9¾: 9¾: 10¼]in), ending with a WS row.
SHAPE SHOULDERS AND BACK NECK
Keeping chart correct, cast (bind) off 10 (11: 12: 12) sts at beg of next 2 rows. *71 (75: 77: 81) sts*
NEXT ROW (RS): Cast (bind) off 10 (11: 12: 12) sts, patt until there are 15 (15: 15: 16) sts on right needle and turn, leaving rem sts on a holder.
Work each side of neck separately.
Cast (bind) off 4 sts at beg of next row.
Cast (bind) off rem 11 (11: 11: 12) sts.
With RS facing, rejoin yarn to rem sts, cast (bind) off center 21 (23: 23: 25) sts, patt to end.
Work to match first side, rev shapings.

pocket linings (make 2)

Cast on 25 sts using 5mm (US 8) needles and yarn A.
Beg with a K row, work 36 rows in st st.
Break yarn and leave sts on a holder.

left front

Cast on 58 (61: 63: 65) sts using 4mm (US 6) needles and yarn A.
ROW 1 (RS): *K1, P1, rep from * to last 0 (1: 1: 1) st, K0 (1: 1: 1).
This row sets position of moss (seed) st as for back.
Work another 6 rows in moss (seed) st, end with a RS row.
ROW 8 (WS): Patt 8 sts and leave these on a safety pin, M1, purl to end. *51 (54: 56: 58) sts*
Change to 5mm (US 8) needles and work in patt from chart as follows:
Work 36 (38: 38: 40) rows, ending with a WS row.
PLACE POCKET
NEXT ROW (RS): Patt 13 (15: 16: 17) sts, slip next 25 sts onto a holder and, in their place, patt across 25 sts from first pocket lining, patt rem 13 (14: 15: 16) sts.
**Cont in patt until left front matches back to start of armhole shaping, ending with a WS row.
SHAPE ARMHOLE
Keeping chart correct, cast (bind) off 4 sts at beg of next row.
47 (50: 52: 54) sts
Work 1 row.
Dec 1 st at armhole edge of next 5 rows.
42 (45: 47: 49) sts
Cont straight until there are 15 rows fewer than on back to start of shoulder and back neck shaping, thus ending with a RS row.

SHAPE NECK

Keeping chart correct, cast (bind) off 4 (5: 5: 6) sts at beg of next row. *38 (40: 42: 43) sts*
Dec 1 st at neck edge on next 5 rows, then on foll 2 alt rows. *31 (33: 35: 36) sts*
Work 5 rows, thus ending with a WS row.

SHAPE SHOULDER

Keeping chart correct, cast (bind) off 10 (11: 12: 12) sts at beg of next and foll alt row.
Work 1 row. Cast (bind) off rem 11 (11: 11: 12) sts.

right front

Cast on 58 (61: 63: 65) sts using 4mm (US 6) needles and yarn A.
ROW 1 (RS): K0 (1: 1: 1), *P1, K1, rep from * to end.
This row sets position of moss (seed) st as for back.
Work another 6 rows in moss (seed) st, ending with a RS row.
ROW 8 (WS): Purl to last 8 sts, M1 and turn, leaving these last 8 sts on a safety pin. *51 (54: 56: 58) sts*
Change to 5mm (US 8) needles and work in patt from chart as follows:
Work 36 (38: 38: 40) rows, ending with a WS row.

PLACE POCKET

NEXT ROW (RS): Patt 13 (14: 15: 16) sts, slip next 25 sts onto a holder and, in their place, patt across 25 sts from second pocket lining, patt rem 13 (15: 16: 17) sts.
Complete to match left front from **, rev all shapings.

sleeves (both alike)

Cast on 51 (53: 55: 57) sts using 4mm (US 6) needles and yarn A.
Work 7 rows in moss (seed) st as given for back, thus ending with a RS row.
Purl 1 row.
Change to 5mm (US 8) needles and work in patt from chart as follows:
Inc 1 st at each end of 3rd and every foll 4th row to 77 (77: 69: 69) sts, then on every foll 6th row until there are 87 (91: 91: 93) sts, taking inc sts into patt.
Cont without further shaping until sleeve measures 43 (46: 48: 49) cm (17 [18: 18¾: 19¼]in), ending with a WS row.

SHAPE SLEEVE HEAD

Keeping chart correct, cast (bind) off 4 sts at beg of next 2 rows. *79 (83: 83: 85) sts*
Dec 1 st at each end on next 8 rows.
Cast (bind) off rem 63 (67: 67: 69) sts.

finishing

Press all pieces as described on the information page. Join shoulder seams using back stitch.

BUTTON BORDER

Slip the 8 sts on left front safety pin onto 4mm (US 6) needles and rejoin yarn A with RS facing.
Cont in moss (seed) st as set until border, when slightly stretched, fits up left front opening edge to neck, ending with a WS row. Cast (bind) off in patt.
Slipstitch border in place.
Mark positions for 5 buttons on this border, the lowest button level with the pocket opening, the top button 2cm (¾in) below neck shaping and the rem 3 buttons evenly spaced between.

BUTTONHOLE BORDER

Work as given for button border, rejoining yarn with WS facing and with the addition of 5 buttonholes to correspond with positions marked for buttons worked as follows:
BUTTONHOLE ROW (RS): Patt 2 sts, work 2 tog, yrn twice to make a buttonhole (drop extra loop on next row), patt 4 sts.
Slipstitch border in place.

COLLAR

Cast on 79 (83: 83: 87) sts using 4mm (US 6) needles and yarn A. Knit 5 rows.
Now work in moss (seed) st as given for back until collar measures 9cm (3½in). Cast (bind) off in patt.
Sew cast-off edge of collar to neck edge, positioning ends of collar midway across top of borders.

POCKET TOPS (BOTH ALIKE)

Slip the 25 sts from pocket holder onto 4mm (US 6) needles and rejoin yarn A with RS facing.
Knit 1 row.
Work 3 rows in moss (seed) st as given for back.
Cast (bind) off in patt.

POCKET FLAPS (make 2)

Cast on 29 sts using 4mm (US 6) needles and yarn A.
Work 8 rows in moss (seed) st as given for back.
Dec 1 st at each end of next and foll 3 alt rows. *21 sts*
Work 1 row. Cast (bind) off in patt.
Sew cast-on edge of pocket flaps to fronts 1cm (½in) above pocket opening.
See information page for finishing instructions.

KEY

- □ A
- ⊡ B
- ■ C
- ⊙ D
- ⊠ E

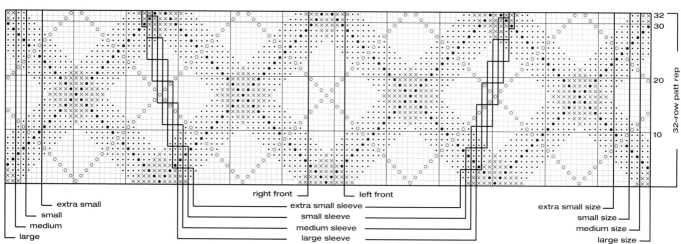

RIGHT AND LEFT FRONTS, BACK AND SLEEVE

bunny by Kim Hargreaves

SIZES	3–4YRS	4–6YRS	6–8YRS	
Actual width	41	44	47	cm
	16	17½	18½	in
Length	42	44.5	47.5	cm
	16½	17½	18½	in
Sleeve length	26	28.5	33.5	cm
	10	11	13	in

YARNS

Rowan True 4-ply Botany 50gm (1¾oz) balls:

A Redwood 549	8	9	9
B Strawberry 560	1	1	1

NEEDLES

1 pair 2¾mm (US 2) needles
1 pair 3¼mm (US 3) needles

BUTTONS

9

TENSION (GAUGE)

28 sts and 36 rows to 10cm (4in) measured over patt using 3¼mm (US 3) needles

SPECIAL ABBREVIATIONS

MB = Make bobble: (K1, P1) 3 times into next st, then slip 2nd, 3rd, 4th, 5th and 6th sts over first.

back

Cast on 115 (123: 131) sts using 2¾mm (US 2) needles and yarn A.
Knit 14 rows, thus ending with a WS row.
Change to 3¼mm (US 3) needles and using the intarsia technique described on the information page, work 76 (82: 88) rows in patt from chart, which is worked mainly in st st, beg with a knit row and thus ending with a WS row.

SHAPE ARMHOLES

Keeping chart correct, cast (bind) off 4 sts at beg of next 2 rows. *107 (115: 123) sts*
Dec 1 st at each end of next 3 rows. *101 (109: 117) sts*
Cont without further shaping until chart row 140 (150: 160) is complete, thus ending with a WS row.

SHAPE SHOULDERS AND BACK NECK

Keeping chart correct, cast (bind) off 7 (7: 8) sts at beg of next 6 (2: 4) rows, then 0 (8: 9) sts at beg of foll 0 (4: 2) rows. *59 (63: 67) sts*
NEXT ROW (RS): Cast (bind) off 7 (8: 9) sts, patt until there are 11 (12: 13) sts on right needle and turn, leaving rem sts on a holder.

Work each side of neck separately. Cast (bind) off 4 sts at beg of next row. Cast (bind) off rem 7 (8: 9) sts.
With RS facing, rejoin yarn to rem sts, cast off center 23 sts, patt to end.
Work to match first side, rev shapings.

left front

Cast on 66 (70: 74) sts using 2¾mm (US 2) needles and yarn A.
Knit 13 rows, thus ending with a RS row.
NEXT ROW (WS): K9 and slip these sts onto a safety pin for button border, M1, K to end. *58 (62: 66) sts*
Change to 3¼mm (US 3) needles and work 76 (82: 88) rows in patt from chart, ending with a WS row.

SHAPE ARMHOLES

Keeping chart correct, cast (bind) off 4 sts at beg of next row. *54 (58: 62) sts*
Patt 1 row.
Dec 1 st at armhole edge on next 3 rows.
51 (55: 59) sts
Cont without further shaping until chart row 125 (135: 145) is complete, thus ending with a RS row.

SHAPE NECK

Keeping chart correct, cast (bind) off 9 sts at beg of next row. *42 (46: 50) sts*
Dec 1 st at neck edge on next 3 rows, then on foll 2 alt rows.
37 (41: 45) sts
Patt 3 rows.
Dec 1 st at neck edge on next row. *36 (40: 44) sts*
Patt 3 rows.

SHAPE SHOULDER

Cast (bind) off 7 (7: 8) sts at beg and dec 1 st at end of next row. *28 (32: 35) sts*
Patt 1 row.
Cast (bind) off 7 (8: 8) sts at beg of next row, then 7 (8: 9) sts at beg of foll 2 alt rows.
Patt 1 row.
Cast (bind) off rem 7 (8: 9) sts.

right front

Cast on 66 (70: 74) sts using 2¾mm (US 2) needles and yarn A.
Knit 13 rows, thus ending with a RS row.
NEXT ROW (WS): K to last 9 sts, M1 and turn, leaving rem 9 sts on a safety pin for buttonhole border.
58 (62: 66) sts
Complete to match left front, rev shaping.

sleeves (both alike)

Cast on 57 sts using 2¾mm (US 2) needles and yarn A.
Knit 14 rows, thus ending with a WS row.
Change to 3¼mm (US 3) needles and work in patt
from chart, shaping sides by inc 1 st at each end of
3rd row and every foll 4th row to 89 (93: 105) sts,
then on every foll alt row until there are 99 (105:
111) sts, taking inc sts into patt.
Patt 9 rows, thus ending with chart row 82 (92: 110)
and a WS row.

SHAPE TOP

Keeping chart correct, cast (bind) off 4 sts at beg of
next 2 rows. *91 (97: 103) sts*
Dec 1 st at each end of next 2 rows.
Cast (bind) off rem 87 (93: 99) sts loosely and evenly.

finishing

Press all pieces as described on the information page.
Join shoulder seams using back stitch.

BUTTON BORDER

Slip the 9 sts from left front safety pin onto 2¾mm
(US 2) needles and rejoin yarn with RS facing.
Cont in garter st until border, when slightly stretched,
fits up left front opening edge, ending with a WS row.
Cast (bind) off.
Slipstitch border in place.
Mark positions for 9 buttons on this border, the first
to come level with top of garter st hem border, the
last to come 1.5cm (⅝in) below neck shaping and
rem
7 buttons evenly spaced between.

BUTTONHOLE BORDER

Work to match button border, rejoining yarn with
WS facing and with the addition of 9 buttonholes
worked to correspond with positions marked for
buttons as folls:
BUTTONHOLE ROW (RS): K4, yfwd (to make a
buttonhole), K2tog, K3.

COLLAR

Cast on 133 sts using 2¾mm (US 2) needles and yarn A.
Knit 2 rows.
ROW 3 (DEC): K14, sl1, K2tog, psso, K to last 17 sts,
sl1, K2tog, psso, K14. *129 sts*
Knit 1 row.
ROW 5: K13, sl1, K2tog, psso, K to last 16 sts, sl1,
K2tog, psso, K13. *125 sts*
Cont in this way, dec on every foll alt row and
working 1 less st before and after decreases, until the
following row has been worked:
NEXT ROW: Sl1, K2tog, psso, K to last 3 sts, sl1,
K2tog, psso.
Knit 1 row. Cast (bind) off.
Sew cast-off edge of collar to neck edge, positioning
ends of collar midway across top of borders.
See information page for finishing instructions.

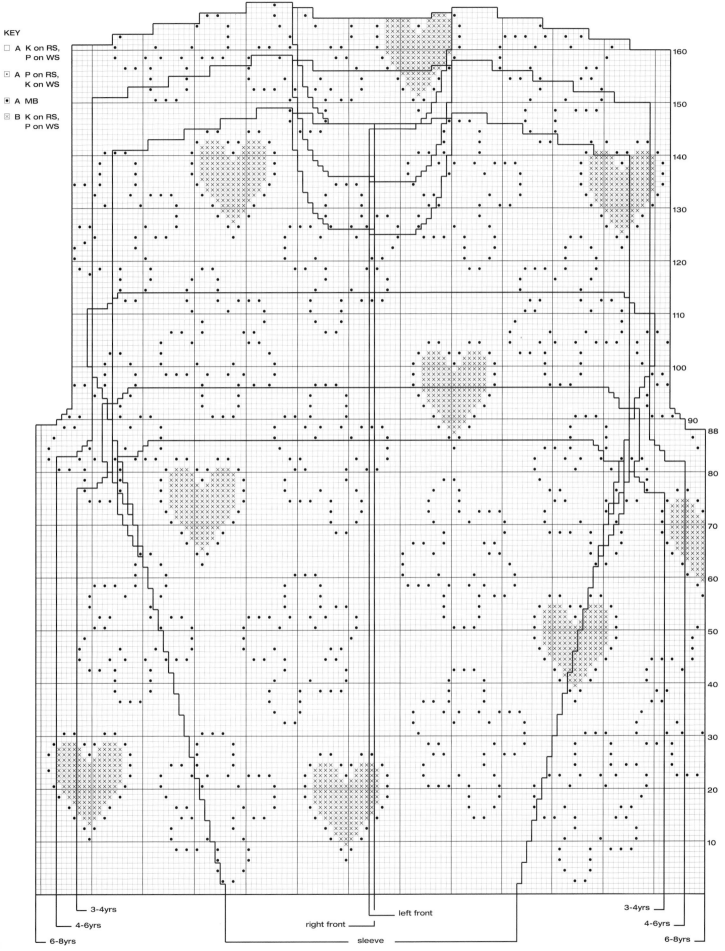

KEY

☐ A K on RS,
P on WS

⊡ A P on RS,
K on WS

▣ A MB

☒ B K on RS,
P on WS

160

150

140

130

120

110

100

90

88

80

70

60

50

40

30

20

10

3-4yrs

4-6yrs

6-8yrs

right front

left front

sleeve

3-4yrs

4-6yrs

6-8yrs

RIGHT AND LEFT FRONTS, BACK AND SLEEVE

millais by Sharon Peake

SIZES

	S	M	
To fit bust	81–86	86–91	cm
	32–34	34–36	in
Actual width	43	47	cm
	17	18½	in
Length	51	56	cm
	20	22	in
Sleeve length	46	48	cm
	18	19	in

YARNS

Rowan True 4-ply Botany 50gm (1¾oz) balls:

		S	M
A	Conker 555	7	7
B	Marino 380	1	1
C	Avocado 559	1	1
D	Redwood 549	1	1
E	Camouflage 562	1	1
F	Sloe 548	1	1
G	Plum 547	1	1

NEEDLES

1 pair 3mm (US 2) needles
1 pair 3¼mm (US 3) needles

BUTTONS

7

TENSION (GAUGE)

27 sts and 34 rows to 10cm (4in) measured over patterned stocking (stockinette) stitch using 3¼mm (US 3) needles

back

Cast on 112 (124) sts using 3¼mm (US 3) needles and yarn A.
Work 8 rows in garter st (knit every row).
Starting with chart row 7 for small size or row 1 for medium size and using the intarsia technique described on the information page, cont in patt from chart for back until row 58 (60) is complete and AT THE SAME TIME shape sides by dec as indicated on chart. *94 (104) sts*
Cont in patt from chart until row 110 (116) is complete and AT THE SAME TIME shape side edges by inc as indicated on chart to 116 (126) sts, ending with a WS row.

SHAPE ARMHOLE

Cast (bind) off 5 (6) sts at beg of next 2 rows.
Dec 1 st at each end of next row and 4 foll alt rows
96 (104) sts

Cont until chart row 172 (182) is complete, ending with a WS row.

SHAPE BACK NECK

Patt 35 (39) sts, turn and leave rem sts on a holder.
Work each side of neck separately.
Cast (bind) off 4 sts, patt to end.
Dec 1 st at neck edge on next 2 rows.
Cast (bind) off rem *29 (33) sts*
With RS facing, rejoin yarn to rem sts, cast (bind) off center 26 (26) sts, patt to end.
Complete to match first side, rev shaping.

left front

CENTER PANEL

Cast on 28 sts using 3¼ (US 3) needles and yarn A.
Work 7 rows in garter st, ending with a RS row.
NEXT ROW (WS): K6 and leave these 6 sts on a holder for front band, K to end. *22 sts*
Starting with the appropriate row, work from chart for left front center panel until chart row 40 is complete, ending with a WS row.
Leave sts on a spare needle.

SIDE PANEL

Cast on 29 (35) sts using 3¼ (US 3) needles and yarn A.
Work 8 rows in garter st, ending with a WS row.
Starting with the appropriate row, work from chart for left front side panel until row 40 is complete, shaping side edge by dec as given for back as indicated on chart and AT THE SAME TIME shape inside edge by inc 1 st at end of 3rd (9th) row and 3 foll 8th rows as shown. *25 (30) sts* *

JOIN PANELS

NEXT ROW (RS): Keeping side dec correct, patt to last st, inc in last st, patt across 22 sts of center panel. *48 (52) sts*
Keeping dec correct cont until chart row 58 (60) is complete, ending with a WS row. *47 (52) sts*
Cont until chart row 110 (116) is complete and AT THE SAME TIME shape side edge by inc as indicated on chart to 58 (63) sts, ending with a WS row.

SHAPE ARMHOLE

Cast (bind) off 5 (6) sts, patt to end. Work 1 row.
Dec 1 st at beg next row and 4 foll alt rows. *48 (52) sts*
Cont until chart row 130 (134) is complete, ending with a WS row.
Dec 1 st at neck edge on next 13 rows and 6 foll 4th rows. *29 (33) sts*
Cont without further shaping until chart row 176 (186) is complete, ending with a WS row.
Cast (bind) off.

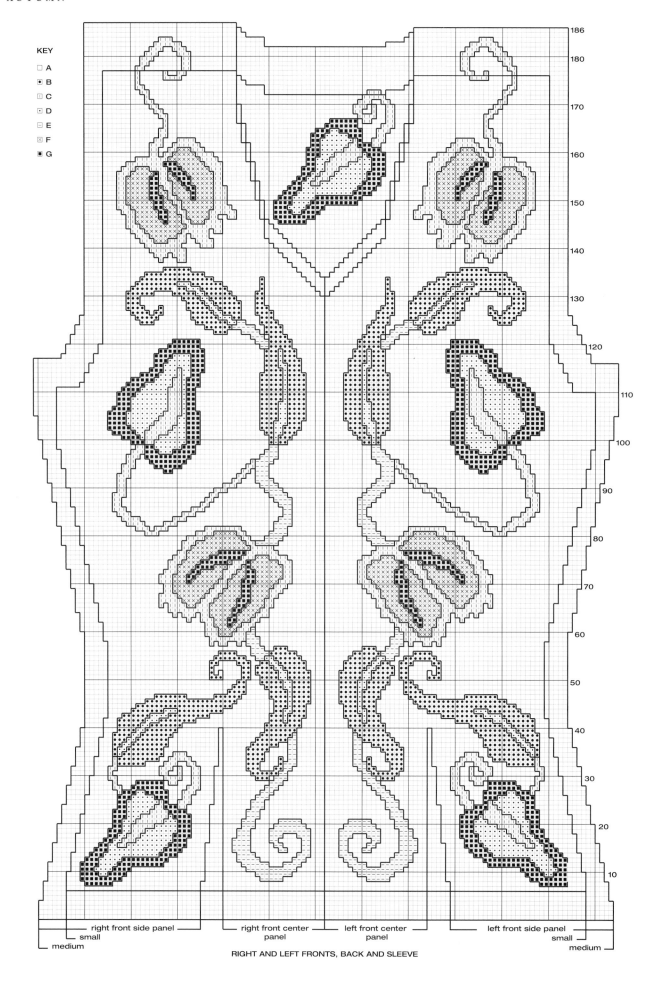

KEY

□ A
◉ B
▦ C
⊡ D
⊟ E
⊠ F
■ G

186
180
170
160
150
140
130
120
110
100
90
80
70
60
50
40
30
20
10

right front side panel — small — medium

right front center panel

left front center panel

left front side panel — small — medium

RIGHT AND LEFT FRONTS, BACK AND SLEEVE

right front

SIDE PANEL

Cast on 29 (35) sts using 3¼mm (US 3) needles and yarn A.

Work 8 rows in garter st, ending with a WS row. Starting with appropriate row and following chart for right front side panel, work as given for left front side panel to *. 25 (30) sts

Leave sts on a spare needle.

CENTER PANEL

Cast on 28 sts using 3¼mm (US 3) needles and yarn A. Work 7 rows in garter st, ending with a RS row.

NEXT ROW (WS): Knit to last 6 sts, turn and leave these 6 sts on a holder for front band. 22 sts

Starting with the appropiate row, work from chart for right front panel until chart row 40 is complete, ending with a WS row.

JOIN PANELS

NEXT ROW (RS): Patt to last st of center panel, inc in last st, patt across 25 (30) sts of side panel keeping side dec correct. 48 (52) sts

Keeping dec correct, cont until chart row 58 (60) is complete, ending with a WS row. 47 (52) sts

Complete as given for left front, rev patt and shaping.

sleeves (both alike)

Cast on 58 sts using 3mm (US 2) needles and yarn A. Work 6cm (2½in) in KI, P1 rib, inc 1 st at end of last row, ending with a WS row. 59 sts

Change to 3¼mm (US 3) needles, join yarns C and B and, using the intarsia technique as described on the information page, cont in patt from chart for sleeve, rep the 16-row patt throughout and AT THE SAME TIME shape sides by inc 1 st at each end of 3rd row and every foll 6th row to 97 (91) sts, and then every foll 4th row to 103 (109) sts.

Cont without further shaping until work measures 46 (48)cm [18¾ (18¾]in) from cast-on edge, ending with a WS row.

SHAPE SLEEVE HEAD

Cast (bind) off 5 (6) sts at beg of next 2 rows.

Dec 1 st at each end of next row and every foll alt row to 63 (67) sts, ending with a WS row.

Cast (bind) off loosely and evenly.

finishing

Press all pieces as described on the information page. Join both shoulder seams using back stitch.

BUTTON BAND

With RS facing, slip 6 sts from holder on left front onto a 3mm (US 2) needle and cont in garter st until band fits up front to beg of neck shaping.

Slipstitch into place.

Cast (bind) off.

Mark the positions of 7 buttons, the first to come opposite row 14 (22), the last 1cm (½in) below cast-(bound-) off edge and the rem spaced evenly between.

BUTTONHOLE BAND

Work as given for button band, with the addition of 7 buttonholes worked to correspond with markers as foll:

BUTTONHOLE ROW (RS): K2, yon, K2tog, K2.

COMPLETE FRONT VENTS (BOTH ALIKE)

With RS of front facing and using 3¼mm (US 3) needles and yarn A, pick up and knit 58 (68) sts along full length of edge of vent when vent is opened out.

Work 3 rows in garter st.

Cast (bind) off loosely and evenly.

COLLAR

Cast on 114 (122) sts using 3¼mm (US 3) needles and yarn A.

Work 4 rows in garter st.

ROW 1 (RS) (INC): K3 using yarn A; join yarns C and B and work 19 sts of row 1 of lace panel on sleeve chart; using yarn A, K1, M1, K to last 23 sts; M1, K1; join yarns C and B and work 19 sts of row 1 of lace panel; K3 using yarn A. 116 (124) sts

ROW 2: K3 using yarn A; work 19 sts of row 2 of lace panel; using yarn A, P to last 22 sts; work 19 sts of row 2 of lace panel; K3 using yarn A.

ROW 3 (INC): K3 using yarn A, work 19 sts of row 3 of lace panel; using yarn A, K1, M1, K to last 23 sts, M1, K1; work 19 sts of row 3 of lace panel, K3 using yarn A.

Cont working on sts as set until 16 rows of lace panel are complete, and AT THE SAME TIME inc as given above on every RS row. Then keeping inc correct and starting again at row 1, cont in patt until work measures 6 (7)cm [2½ (2¾)in] from cast-on edge, ending with a WS row.

SHAPE COLLAR

NEXT ROW (RS): Patt 50 (60) sts, wrap next st (sl1 st, bring yarn to front of work, put sl st back onto LH needle), turn and work on these 50 (60) sts only, patt to end.

NEXT ROW: Patt 42 (52) sts, wrap next st, turn, patt to end.

NEXT ROW: Patt 34 (44) sts, wrap next st, turn, patt to end. Cont in this way, working 8 sts fewer on every row until 10 (12) sts rem.

NEXT ROW (RS): Work in patt across sts.

NEXT ROW (WS): Patt 50 (60) sts, wrap next st, turn and work on these 50 (60) sts only, patt to end.

Complete to match first side, ending at side edge.

Purl 1 row using yarn A across all sts.

Work 6 rows in garter st using yarn A. Cast (bind) off.

Sew cast-on edge of collar neatly into place around neck edging, starting and ending halfway across front bands and matching center of collar with center back neck.

Sew on buttons.

See information page for finishing instructions.

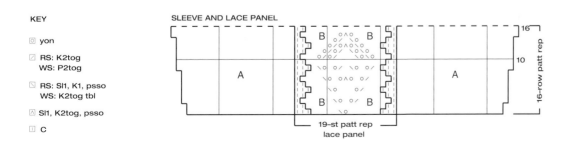

KEY

▣ yon

▨ RS: K2tog
WS: P2tog

◹ RS: Sl1, K1, psso
WS: K2tog tbl

◮ Sl1, K2tog, psso

☐ C

SLEEVE AND LACE PANEL

B   B

A   A

B   B

19-st patt rep
lace panel

16

10

16-row patt rep

flourish by Kim Hargreaves

SIZES

	XS	S	M	L	XL	
To fit bust	81	86	91	97	102	cm
	32	34	36	38	40	in
Actual width	46.5	49	51.5	54.5	57	cm
	18½	19½	20½	21½	22½	in
Length	55	56	57	58	59	cm
	21½	22	22½	23	23	in
Long sleeve length	41	41	42	42	43	cm
	16	16	16½	16½	17	in
Short sleeve length	9	9	9	9	9	cm
	3½	3½	3½	3½	3½	in

YARN

Rowan Cotton Glacé 50gm (1¾oz) balls:
Multi-colored cardigan

	XS	S	M	L	XL
A Oyster 730	10	11	11	12	12
B Butter 795	1	1	1	1	1
C Terracotta 786	2	2	2	2	2
D Blood Orange 445	2	2	3	3	3
E Black 727	1	1	1	1	1
One-color cardigan					
	8	8	9	9	10

NEEDLES

1 pair 2¾mm (US 2) needles
1 pair 3¼mm (US 3) needles

BUTTONS

5

TENSION (GAUGE)

23 sts and 32 rows to 10cm (4in) measured over patterned stocking (stockinette) stitch using 3¼mm (US 3) needles

multi-colored cardigan
back

Cast on 107 (113: 119: 125: 131) sts using 2¾mm (US 2) needles and yarn C.
Break yarn C and join yarn A.
Knit 3 rows.
ROW 4 (WS): P1 (0: 1: 0: 1), *K1, P1, rep from * to last 0 (1: 0: 1: 0) st, K0 (1: 0: 1: 0).
ROW 5: As row 4.
These 2 rows form moss (seed) st. Work another 15 rows in moss (seed) st. Change to 3¼mm (US 3) needles.
Using the intarsia technique described on the information page and starting and ending rows as indicated, cont in patt, foll chart for back, which is worked entirely in st st, as folls:
Work 2 rows.
Place markers on 26th (29th: 32nd: 35th: 38th) st from each end of row.
ROW 3 (DEC) (RS): K2tog, patt to within 1 st of marked st, K3tog tbl, patt to within 1 st of 2nd marked st, K3tog, patt to last 2 sts, K2tog.
Work 7 rows.
Rep last 8 rows twice more and then row 3 (the dec row) again. *83 (89: 95: 101: 107) sts*
Work 15 rows, ending with chart row 42.
ROW 43 (INC) (RS): Inc in first st, *patt to marked st, M1, K marked st, M1, rep from * once more, patt to last st, inc in last st.
Work 11 rows.
Rep last 12 rows twice more and then row 43 (the inc row) again. *107 (113: 119: 125: 131) sts*
Work 13 (17: 17: 21: 21) rows, ending with chart row 92 (96: 96: 100: 100).
Work measures 35 (36: 36: 37: 37)cm (13¾ [14¼: 14¼: 14½: 14½]in).
SHAPE ARMHOLES
Keeping chart correct, cast (bind) off 3 (4: 4: 5: 5) sts at beg of next 2 rows. *101 (105: 111: 115: 121) sts*
Dec 1 st at each end of next 5 (5: 7: 7: 9) rows, then on foll 6 (7: 7: 8: 8) alt rows. *79 (81: 83: 85: 87) sts*
Cont straight until chart row 156 (160: 164: 168: 170) has been completed, ending with a WS row. Armhole measures 20 (20: 21: 21: 22)cm (7¾ [7¾: 8¼: 8¼: 8½]in).
SHAPE SHOULDERS AND BACK NECK
Cast (bind) off 8 sts at beg of next 2 rows.
63 (65: 67: 69: 71) sts
NEXT ROW (RS): Cast (bind) off 8 sts, patt until there are 11 (11: 12: 12: 13) sts on right needle and turn, leaving rem sts on a holder.
Work each side of neck separately.
Cast (bind) off 4 sts at beg of next row.
Cast (bind) off rem 7 (7: 8: 8: 9) sts.
With RS facing, rejoin yarn to rem sts, cast (bind) off center 25 (27: 27: 29: 29) sts, patt to end.
Work to match first side, rev shaping.

left front

Cast on 28 sts using 2¾mm (US 2) needles and yarn C.
Break yarn C and join yarn A.
Knit 3 rows.
ROW 4 (WS): *K1, P1, rep from * to end.
This row sets position of moss (seed) st.
ROW 5: P1, K1, pick up loop lying between needles and P then K into back of this loop, moss (seed) st to end.

Work 5 rows.
Rep last 6 rows once more. *32 sts*
Break yarn and leave sts on a holder.

SIDE PANEL
Cast on 21 (24: 27: 30: 33) sts using 2¾mm (US 2)
needles and yarn C.
Break yarn C and join yarn A.
Knit 3 rows.
ROW 4 (WS): *P1, K1, rep from * to last 1 (0: 1: 0: 1)
st, P1 (0: 1: 0: 1).
This row sets position of moss (seed) st.
ROW 5: Moss (seed) st to last 2 sts, pick up loop lying
between needles and K then P into back of this loop,
K1, P1.
Work 5 rows.
Rep last 6 rows once more. *25 (28: 31: 34: 37) sts*

JOIN PANELS
ROW 17 (RS): Moss (seed) st across first 24 (27: 30: 33:
36) sts of side panel, (P1, K1) into next st, then moss
(seed) st across 32 sts of center front panel.
58 (61: 64: 67: 70) sts
Work 2 rows.
ROW 20 (WS): Moss (seed) st 6 sts and slip these sts onto
a holder for button band, M1, moss (seed) st to end.
53 (56: 59: 62: 65) sts
Change to 3¼mm (US 3) needles.
Cont in patt, foll chart for fronts as folls:
Work 2 rows.
Place marker on 26th (29th: 32nd: 35th: 38th) st from
side seam.
ROW 3 (DEC) (RS): K2tog, patt to within 1 st of marked
st, K3tog tbl, patt to end.
Work 7 rows.
Rep last 8 rows twice more and then row 3 (dec row)
again. *41 (44: 47: 50: 53) sts*
Work 15 rows, ending with chart row 42.
ROW 43 (INC) (RS): Inc in first st, patt to marked st, M1,
K marked st, M1, patt to end.
Work 11 rows.
Rep last 12 rows twice more and then row 43 (inc
row) again. *53 (56: 59: 62: 65) sts*
Work 13 (17: 17: 21: 21) rows, ending with chart row
92 (96: 96: 100: 100). (Front matches back to beg of
armhole shaping.)

SHAPE ARMHOLE
Keeping chart correct, cast (bind) off 3 (4: 4: 5: 5) sts
at beg of next row. *50 (52: 55: 57: 60) sts*
Work 1 row.
Dec 1 st at armhole edge of next 5 (5: 7: 7: 8) rows,
then on foll 5 (3: 2: 0: 0) alt rows. *40 (44: 46: 50: 52) sts*
Work 1 (1: 1: 1: 0) row, ending with chart row 110.

SHAPE FRONT SLOPE
Dec 1 st at armhole edge of next and foll 0 (3: 4: 7: 8)
alt rows and AT THE SAME TIME dec 1 st at neck
edge on next and every foll 6th row. *38 (38: 39: 39:
40) sts*
Dec 1 st at neck edge on every foll 6th row from
previous dec until 35 (35: 36: 36: 37) sts rem.
Work 6 (4: 8: 4: 6) rows, ending with chart row 135
(139: 143: 145: 147).

SHAPE NECK
Cast (bind) off 3 sts at beg of next row.
32 (32: 33: 33: 34) sts
Dec 1 st at neck edge of next 5 (5: 5: 3: 3) rows, then
on foll 3 (3: 3: 5: 5) alt rows, then on foll 4th row.
23 (23: 24: 24: 25) sts
Work 5 rows, ending with chart row 156 (160: 164:
168: 170).

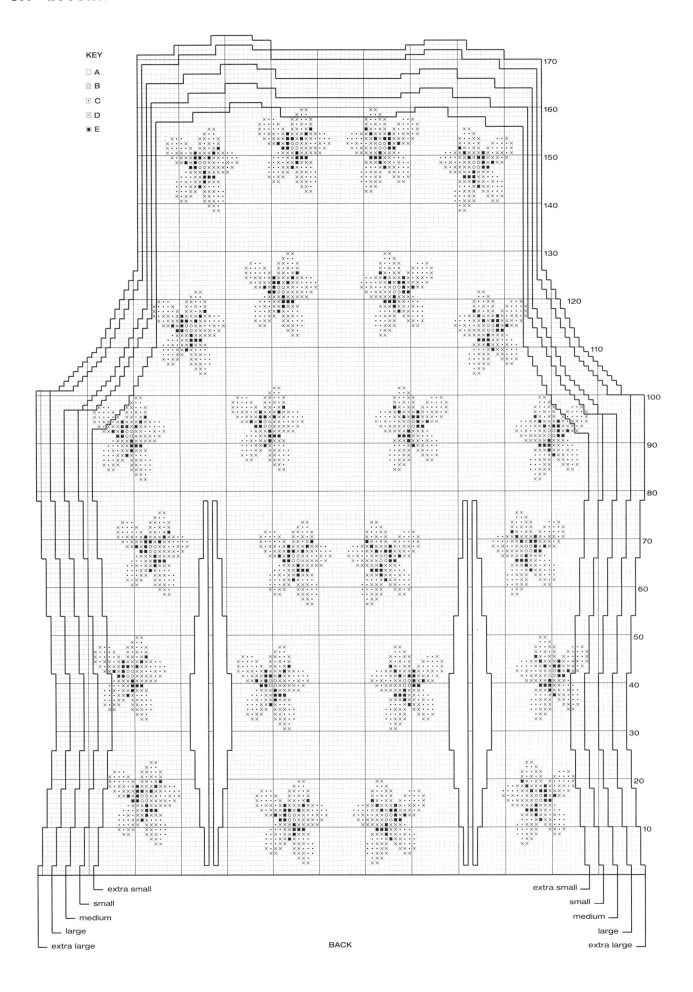

KEY

☐ A
◙ B
⊡ C
☒ D
■ E

170
160
150
140
130
120
110
100
90
80
70
60
50
40
30
20
10

extra small
small
medium
large
extra large

extra small
small
medium
large
extra large

BACK

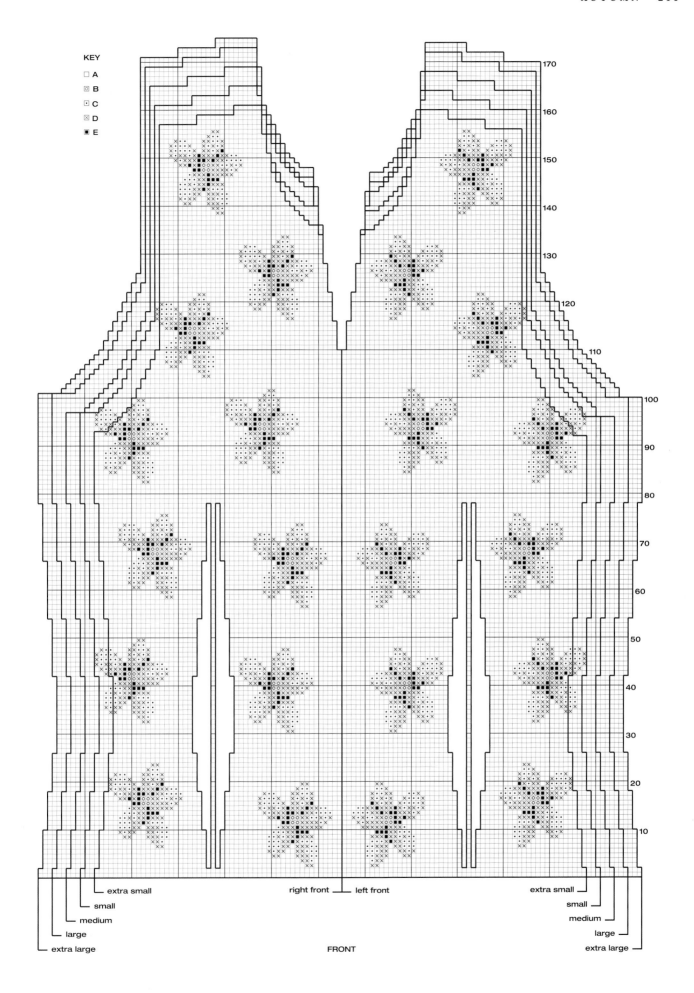

KEY

☐ A
⊡ B
⊡ C
⊠ D
■ E

170

160

150

140

130

120

110

100

90

80

70

60

50

40

30

20

10

extra small

small

medium

large

extra large

right front — left front

extra small

small

medium

large

extra large

FRONT

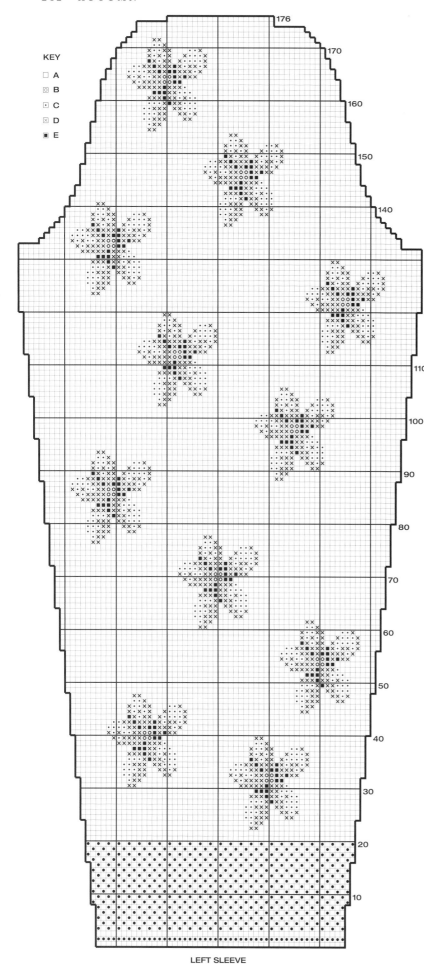

KEY
☐ A
⊡ B
⊡ C
☒ D
■ E

176
170
160
150
140
130
120
110
100
90
80
70
60
50
40
30
20
10

LEFT SLEEVE

SHAPE SHOULDER
Cast (bind) off 8 sts at beg of next and foll alt row.
Work 1 row. Cast (bind) off rem 7 (7: 8: 8: 9) sts.

right front
SIDE PANEL
Cast on 21 (24: 27: 30: 33) sts using 2¾mm (US 2)
needles and yarn C.
Break yarn C and join yarn A.
Knit 3 rows.
ROW 4 (WS): P1 (0: 1: 0: 1), *K1, P1, rep from * to end.
This row sets position of moss (seed) st.
ROW 5: P1, K1, pick up loop lying between needles and
P then K into back of this loop, moss (seed) st to end.
Work 5 rows.
Rep last 6 rows once more. *25 (28: 31: 34: 37) sts*
Break yarn and leave sts on a holder.
CENTER FRONT PANEL
Cast on 28 sts using 2¾mm (US 2) needles and yarn C.
Break yarn C and join yarn A. Knit 3 rows.
ROW 4 (WS): *P1, K1, rep from * to end.
This row sets position of moss (seed) st.
ROW 5: Moss (seed) st to last 2 sts, pick up loop lying
between needles and K then P into back of this loop,
K1, P1.
Work 5 rows. Rep last 6 rows once more. *32 sts.*
JOIN PANELS
ROW 17 (RS): Moss (seed) st across first 31 sts of center front
panel, (P1, K1) into next st, then moss (seed) st across
25 (28: 31: 34: 37) sts of side panel. *58 (61: 64: 67: 70) sts*
Work 2 rows.
ROW 20 (WS): Moss (seed) st to last 6 sts, M1 and turn,
leaving rem 6 sts on a holder for buttonhole band.
53 (56: 59: 62: 65) sts
Change to 3¼mm (US 3) needles. Cont in patt, foll
chart for fronts as folls: Work 2 rows.
Place marker on 26th (29th: 32nd: 35th: 38th) st in
from side seam.
ROW 3 (DEC) (RS): Patt to within 1 st of marked st,
K3tog, patt to last 2 sts, K2tog.
Complete to match left front, rev shaping.

left sleeve
Cast on 49 (49: 49: 53: 53) sts using 2¾mm (US 2)
needles and yarn C.
Break yarn C and join yarn A. Knit 3 rows.
Work 17 rows in moss (seed) st, inc 1 st at each end
of 6th and foll 8th row. *53 (53: 53: 57: 57) sts*
Change to 3¼mm (US 3) needles.
Cont in patt, foll chart for sleeve as folls:
Work 4 rows.
Inc 1 st at each end of next and every foll 8th row until
there are 77 (79: 81: 83: 85) sts, taking inc sts into patt.
Cont straight until chart row 112 (112: 116: 116: 118)
has been completed, ending with a WS row.
SHAPE TOP
Keeping chart correct, cast (bind) off 3 (4: 4: 5: 5) sts
at beg of next 2 rows.
71 (71: 73: 73: 75) sts
Dec 1 st at each end of next 5 rows, then on foll 3 alt
rows, then on every foll 4th row until 45 (45: 47: 47:
49) sts rem.
Work 1 row.
Dec 1 st at each end of next and foll 2 (2: 3: 3: 4) alt
rows, then on foll 3 rows. *33 sts*
Cast (bind) off 6 sts at beg of next 2 rows, ending
with chart row 156 (156: 162: 162: 166).
Cast (bind) off rem 21 sts.

right sleeve

Work as given for left sleeve but rev chart by reading odd-numbered K rows from left to right, and even-numbered P rows from right to left.

one-color cardigan
back and fronts

Work as given for multi-colored cardigan but use same color throughout.

sleeves

Cast on 71 (73: 75: 77: 79) sts using 2¾mm (US 2) needles. Knit 3 rows.
Work 17 rows in moss (seed) st, inc 1 st at each end of 4th and every foll 6th row. 77 *(79: 81: 83: 85) sts*
Change to 3¼mm (US 3) needles.
Beg with a K row, cont in st st until sleeve measures 9cm (3½in), ending with a WS row.

SHAPE TOP

Cast (bind) off 3 (4: 4: 5: 5) sts at beg of next 2 rows. *71 (71: 73: 73: 75) sts*
Dec 1 st at each end of next 5 rows, then on foll 3 alt rows, then on every foll 4th row until 45 (45: 47: 47: 49) sts rem. Work 1 row.
Dec 1 st at each end of next and foll 2 (2: 3: 3: 4) alt rows, then on foll 3 rows, ending with a WS row. *33 sts*
Cast (bind) off 6 sts at beg of next 2 rows.
Cast (bind) off rem 21 sts.

finishing

Press all pieces as described on the information page.
Multi-colored cardigan
Join shoulder seams using back stitch or mattress stitch if preferred.

BUTTON BAND

Slip the 6 sts from holder for button band onto 2¾mm (US 2) needles and rejoin yarn A with RS facing.
Cont in moss (seed) st as set until band, when slightly stretched, fits up left front opening edge to start of neck shaping, ending with a WS row.
Break yarn and leave sts on a holder.
Slipstitch band in place.
Mark positions for 5 buttons on this band, the lowest button level with beg of chart, the top button 2cm (¾in) below start of front slope shaping and the rem 3 buttons evenly spaced between.

BUTTONHOLE BAND

Work as given for button band, rejoining yarn with WS facing and with the addition of 5 buttonholes to correspond with positions marked for buttons worked as folls:
BUTTONHOLE ROW (RS): Moss (seed) st 2 sts, yrn (to make a buttonhole), work 2 tog, moss (seed) st 2 sts.
When band is complete, ending with a WS row, do NOT break off yarn.
Slipstitch band in place.

NECKBAND

With RS facing, using 2¾mm (US 2) needles and yarn A, moss (seed) st across 6 sts of buttonhole band, pick up and knit 29 (29: 29: 31: 31) sts up right side of neck, 33 (35: 35: 37: 37) sts from back and 29 (29: 29: 31: 31) sts down left side of neck, then moss (seed) st across 6 sts of button band. *103 (105: 105: 111: 111) sts*
Work in moss (seed) st as set by front bands for 5 rows.
Cast (bind) off in moss (seed) st.
See information page for finishing instructions, setting in sleeves using the set-in method.

brocade by Kaffe Fassett

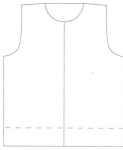

SIZE	XS	S	M	L	XL	
To fit bust	81	86	91	97	102	cm
	32	34	36	38	40	in
Actual width	48	50.5	53	55	57.5	cm
	19	20	21	21½	22½	in
Length	51	52	53	54	55	cm
	20	20½	21	21½	21½	in
Sleeve length	41	41	42	42	43	cm
	16	16	16½	16½	17	in

YARN

Rowan Wool Cotton 50gm (1¾oz) balls:

A Rich 911	8	9	9	9	10
B Pinky 902	4	5	5	5	5
C Amazon 905	1	1	1	1	1
D Deepest Olive 907	2	2	2	2	2

NEEDLES

1 pair 3¼mm (US 3) needles
1 pair 3¾mm (US 5) needles
1 pair 4mm (US 6) needles

BUTTONS

7

TENSION (GAUGE)

25 sts and 29 rows to 10cm (4in) measured over patterned stocking (stockinette) stitch using 4mm (US 6) needles.

back

Cast on 120 (126: 132: 138: 144) sts using 3¼mm. (US 3) needles and yarn D.
Purl 4 rows.
Change to 3¾mm (US 5) needles.
Using the Fair Isle technique described on the information page and starting and ending rows as indicated, cont in patt, foll lower section of body chart, which is worked entirely in st st, as folls:
ROW 1 (RS): Using yarn D, P4; work next 112 (118: 124: 130: 136) sts as given for row 1 of chart; using yarn D, P4.
ROW 2: Using yarn D, P4; work next 112 (118 124: 130: 136) sts as given for row 2 of chart; using yarn D, P4.
These 2 rows set the sts.
Keeping sts correct as set, work another 10 rows, ending with chart row 12.
Change to 4mm (US 6) needles.
Using the intarsia technique described on the information page and starting and ending rows as

indicated, cont in patt, foll main section of body chart, which is worked entirely in st st, as folls:
Work 76 (78: 78: 80: 80) rows.

SHAPE ARMHOLES

Keeping chart correct, cast (bind) off 3 (4: 4: 5: 5) sts at beg of next 2 rows. *114 (118: 124: 128: 134) sts*
Dec 1 st at each end of next 5 (5: 7: 7: 9) rows, then on foll 3 (4: 4: 5: 5) alt rows, then on every foll 4th row until 94 (96: 98: 100: 102) sts rem.
Cont straight until chart row 134 (136: 140: 142: 144) has been completed, ending with a WS row.

SHAPE SHOULDERS AND BACK NECK

Cast (bind) off 9 sts at beg of next 2 rows.
76 (78: 80: 82: 84) sts
NEXT ROW (RS): Cast (bind) off 9 sts, patt until there are 12 (12: 13: 13: 14) sts on right needle and turn, leaving rem sts on a holder.
Work each side of neck separately.
Cast (bind) off 4 sts at beg of next row.
Cast (bind) off rem 8 (8: 9: 9: 10) sts.
With RS facing, rejoin yarn to rem sts, cast (bind) off center 34 (36: 36: 38: 38) sts, patt to end.
Work to match first side, rev shaping.

left front

Cast on 60 (63: 66: 69: 72) sts using 3¼mm (US 3) needles and yarn D.
Purl 4 rows.
Change to 3¾mm (US 5) needles.
Cont in patt, foll lower section of body chart as folls:
ROW 1 (RS): Using yarn D, P4; work next 52 (55: 58: 61: 64) sts as given for row 1 of chart; using yarn D, P4.
ROW 2: Using yarn D, P4; work next 52 (55: 58: 61: 64) sts as given for row 2 of chart; using yarn D, P4.
These 2 rows set the sts.
Keeping sts correct as set, work another 10 rows, ending with chart row 12.
Change to 4mm (US 6) needles.
Cont in patt foll main section of body chart as folls:
Work 76 (78: 78: 80: 80) rows.

SHAPE ARMHOLE

Keeping chart correct, cast (bind) off 3 (4: 4: 5: 5) sts at beg of next row.
57 (59: 62: 64: 67) sts
Work 1 row.
Dec 1 st at armhole edge of next 5 (5: 7: 7: 9) rows, then on foll 3 (4: 4: 5: 5) alt rows, then on every foll 4th row until 47 (48: 49: 50: 51) sts rem.
Cont straight until chart row 115 (117: 121: 121: 123) has been completed, ending with a RS tow.

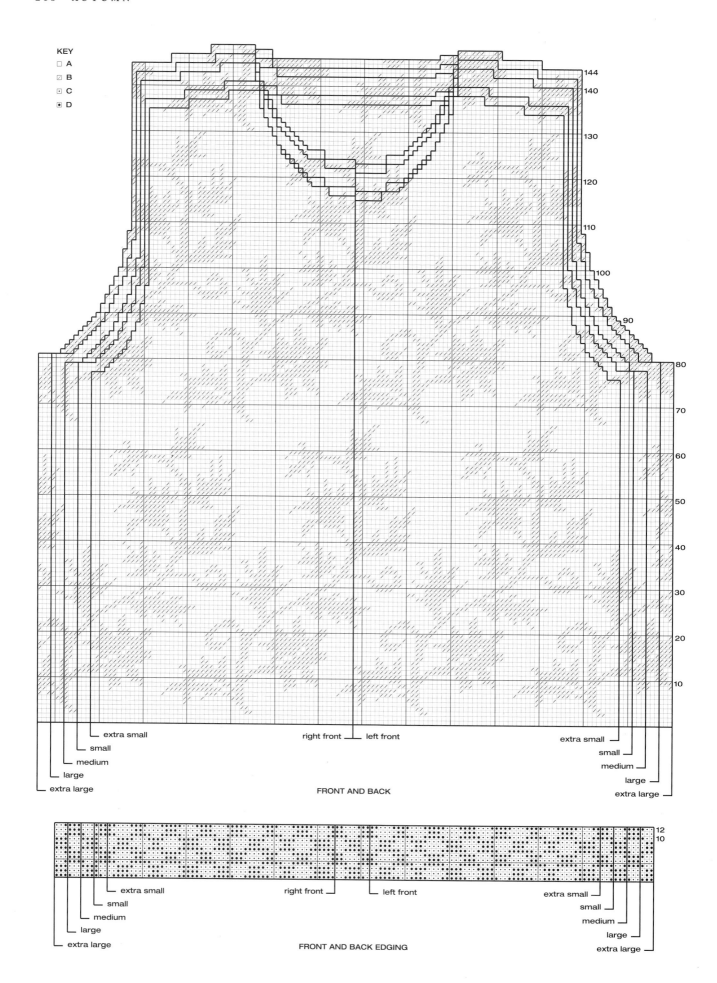

KEY
- ☐ A
- ☒ B
- ⊡ C
- ▣ D

144
140
130
120
110
100
90
80
70
60
50
40
30
20
10

— extra small
— small
— medium
— large
— extra large

right front — left front

extra small —
small —
medium —
large —
extra large —

FRONT AND BACK

12
10

— extra small
— small
— medium
— large
— extra large

right front — left front

extra small —
small —
medium —
large —
extra large —

FRONT AND BACK EDGING

SHAPE NECK

Keeping chart correct, cast (bind) off 6 (7: 7: 7: 7) sts
at beg of next row and 4 sts at beg of foll alt row.
37 (37: 38: 39: 40) sts
Dec 1 st at neck edge of next 7 rows, then on foll
4 (4: 4: 5: 5) alt rows. *26 (26: 27: 27: 28) sts*
Work 1 row, ending with chart row 134 (136: 140:
142: 144).

SHAPE SHOULDER

Cast (bind) off 9 sts at bg of next and foll alt row.
Work 1 row.
Cast (bind) off rem 8 (8: 9: 9: 10) sts.

right front

Work as given for left front, rev shaping.

sleeves (both alike)

Cast on 54 (54: 54: 58: 58) sts using 3¼mm (US 3)
needles and yarn D. Purl 4 rows.
Change to 3¾mm (US 5) needles.
Cont in patt, foll chart for sleeves as folls:
Work 12 rows.
Change to 4mm (US 6) needles.
Inc 1 st at each end of 3rd and every foll 6th row
until there are 84 (86: 88: 90: 92) sts, taking inc sts
into patt.
Cont straight until chart row 116 (116: 118: 118: 122)
has been completed, ending with a WS row.

SHAPE TOP

Keeping chart correct, cast (bind) off 3 (4: 4: 5: 5) sts
at beg of next 2 rows. *78 (78: 80: 80: 82) sts*
Dec 1 st at each end of next 5 rows, then on foll
3 alt rows, then on every foll 4th row until 56 (56:
58: 58: 60) sts rem. Work 1 row.
Dec 1 st at each end of next and foll 4 (4: 5: 5: 6) alt
rows, then on foll 7 rows. *32 sts*
Cast (bind) off 4 sts at beg of next 2 rows, ending
with chart row 160 (160: 164: 164: 170).
Cast (bind) off rem 24 sts.

finishing

Press all pieces as described on the information page.
Join shoulder seams using back stitch or mattress
stitch if preferred.

BUTTON BAND

With RS facing, using 3¼ mm (US 3) needles and
yarn A, pick up and knit 97 (97: 103: 103: 103) sts
along left front opening edge between neck shaping
and top of lower-edge border.
ROW 1 (WS): K1, *Pl, KI, rep from * to end.
ROW 2: As row 1.
These 2 rows form moss (seed) st.
Work another 2 rows in moss (seed) st.
Cast (bind) off in moss (seed) st.

BUTTONHOLE BAND

Work as given for button band, with the addition of 7
buttonholes worked in row 2 as folls:
BUTTONHOLE ROW (RS): Moss (seed) st 3 sts, *yrn (to
make a buttonhole), work 2 tog, moss (seed) st 13
(13: 14: 14: 14) sts, rep from * to last 4 sts, yrn (to
make 7th buttonhole), work 2 tog, moss (seed) st 2
sts.

COLLAR

Cast on 109 (113: 113: 121: 121) sts 3¼mm (US 3)
needles and yarn A.
Work in moss (seed) st as given for button band for

8cm (3¼in). Cast (bind) off in moss (seed) st.
Sew cast-on edge of collar to neck edge, positioning
ends of collar halfway across top of bands.
See information page for finishing instructions, setting
in sleeves using the set-in method.

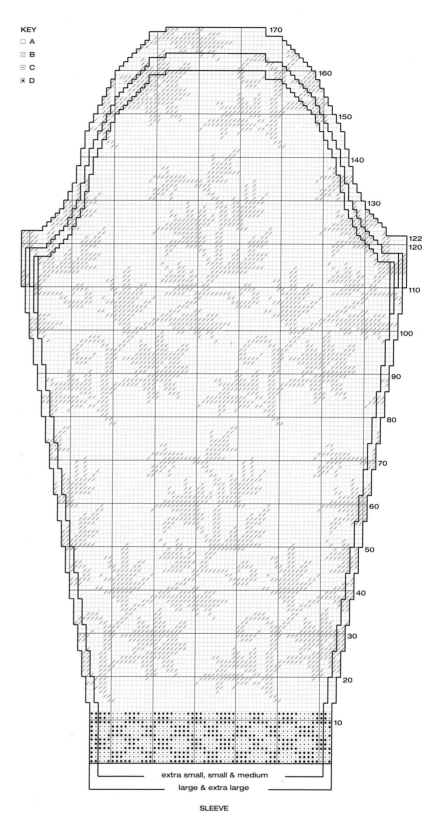

KEY
□ A
☑ B
⊡ C
▣ D

extra small, small & medium
large & extra large

SLEEVE

winter

These chunky pullovers and long stylish cardigans are guaranteed to keep all the family snug in even the coldest winter weather.

joss by Rowan Design Studio

SIZES	1ST	2ND	3RD	4TH	5TH	6TH	7TH	8TH	9TH	
	6MTHS	9MTHS	1-2YRS	2-3YRS	3-4YRS	4-6YRS	6-8YRS	8-9YRS	9-10YRS	
Actual width	29	32	35	38	41	44	47	51	55	cm
	11½	12½	13¾	15	16	17¼	18½	20	21½	in
Length	30.5	33	38	42	45	49.5	53.5	57	61	cm
	12	13	15	16½	17¾	19½	21	22½	24	in
Sleeve length	19	20	23	25	28	30.5	35.5	38	40.5	cm
	7½	8	9	10	11	12	14	15	16	in

YARN

Rowan Handknit DK Cotton 50gm (1¾oz) balls

A Ecru	251	4	5	5	7	9	11	12	13	14	
B Navy	224	1	1	1	1	2	2	2	3	4	

NEEDLES

1 pair 3¼mm (US 3) needles
1 pair 4mm (US 6) needles

BUTTONS

4 buttons (first 4 sizes only)

TENSION (GAUGE)

20 sts and 28 rows to 10cm (4in) measured over stocking (stockinette) stitch using 4mm (US 6) needles

back

Cast on 58 (64: 70: 76: 82: 88: 94: 102: 110) sts using 3¼mm (US 3) needles and yarn A and work 6 (6: 8: 8: 8: 8: 10: 10: 10) rows in garter stitch (knit every row). Change to 4mm (US 6) needles.
NEXT ROW: K4 (5: 6: 5: 6: 5: 6: 6: 6) sts, K2, *P2, K2, rep from * to last 4 (5: 6: 5: 6: 5: 6: 6: 6) sts, K4 (5: 6: 5: 6: 5: 6: 6: 6).
NEXT ROW: K4 (5: 6: 5: 6: 5: 6: 6: 6) sts, P2, *K2, P2, rep from * to last 4 (5: 6: 5: 6: 5: 6: 6: 6) sts, K4 (5: 6: 5: 6: 5: 6: 6: 6).
Rep these 2 rows 1 (1: 2: 2: 2: 2: 3: 3: 3) times more. Cont in st st, beg with a K row, until work measures 15.5 (17.5: 21: 23.5: 24.5: 28: 30.5: 33: 35.5)cm (6 [6¾: 8¼: 9¼: 9¾: 11¼: 12: 13: 14]in) from cast-on edge, ending with a WS row.

WORK STRIPED YOKE

ROW 1 (RS): Purl using A.
ROW 2: Knit using A.
ROW 3: Knit using B.
ROW 4: Purl using B.
ROW 5 AND 6: Knit using A.
ROW 7: Purl using A.
Place markers at each end of last row for armhole.

ROW 8: Purl using B.
ROW 9: Knit using B.
ROW 10: Purl using A. **
Rep these 10 rows until work measures 30.5 (33: 38: 42: 45: 49.5: 53.5: 57: 61)cm (12 [13: 15: 16½: 17¾: 19½: 21: 22½: 24]in) from cast-on edge, ending with a WS row.

SHAPE SHOULDER AND BACK NECK

Keeping color sequence correct, cast (bind) off 18 (20: 22: 24: 26: 29: 30: 33: 37) sts, work 22 (24: 26: 28: 30: 30: 34: 36: 36) sts and leave these on a holder. Work to end.

1st, 2nd, 3rd & 4th sizes only

Work 2 more rows in st st using yarn A to form band for shoulder buttons.

All sizes

Cast (bind) off.

front

Work as for back to **
Rep these 10 rows until front is 12 (12: 14: 14: 16: 16: 18: 18: 18) rows shorter than back to shoulder shaping, ending with a WS row.

SHAPE FRONT NECK

NEXT ROW: Work 26 (28: 30: 32: 34: 37: 40: 44: 48) sts, turn, leaving rem sts on a holder, and work each side separately.
Dec 1 st at neck edge on next 8 (8: 8: 8: 8: 8: 10: 11: 11) rows. *18 (20: 22: 24: 26: 29: 30: 33: 37) sts*
Cont without further shaping until front matches back to shoulder, ending with a WS row. ***

1st, 2nd, 3rd & 4th sizes only

Work buttonhole band for shoulder fastening using yarn A.

Knit 2 rows.

BUTTONHOLE ROW (RS) : K2, [yon, K2tog, K3 (4: 5: 5)] twice, yon, K2tog, K4 (4: 4: 6).

Knit 1 row.

All sizes

Cast (bind) off.

Return to stitches on holder and with RS facing slip center 6 (8: 10: 12: 14: 14: 14: 14: 14) sts onto a holder, rejoin correct yarn and work to end.

Work as for first side to ***.

Cast (bind) off.

sleeves (both alike)

Cast on 28 (28: 32: 32: 38: 38: 42: 42: 42) sts using 3¼mm (US 3) needles and yarn A. Work 6 (6: 8: 8: 8: 8: 10: 10: 10) rows in garter st.

Change to 4mm (US 6) needles and cont in st st, shaping sides by inc as folls:

NEXT ROW (INC) : K2, M1, K to last 2 sts, M1, K2.

Work 3 rows.

Rep these 4 rows until there are 50 (52: 58: 64: 72: 76: 82: 86: 92) sts on needle.

Cont without further shaping until work measures 17 (18: 21: 23: 26: 28.5: 33.5: 36: 38.5)cm, (6½ [7: 8¼: 9: 10¼: 11¼: 13: 14¼: 15¼]in) or length required from cast-on edge, ending with a WS row.

Work first 7 rows of striped patt as for back.

Purl 1 row using A.

Cast (bind) off loosely and evenly using A.

finishing

Press all pieces except ribbing on wrong side using a warm iron over a damp cloth.

Join right shoulder seam using back stitch.

NECK BAND

With RS facing, using 3¼mm (US 3) needles, yarn A and beg at left shoulder, on first 4 sizes only pick up and knit 2 sts across buttonhole band. Then on all sizes pick up and knit 12 (12: 13: 14: 16: 16: 18: 18: 18) sts down left front neck, 6 (8: 10: 12: 14: 14: 14: 14: 14) sts from holder at center front, 12 (12: 13: 14: 16: 16: 18: 18: 18) sts up right front neck and 22 (24: 26: 28: 30: 30: 34: 36: 36) sts from holder at back neck. On first 4 sizes only pick up and knit 2 sts from button band.

56 (60: 66: 72: 76: 76: 84: 86: 86) sts

1st, 2nd, 3rd & 4th sizes only

Knit 2 rows.

NEXT ROW (BUTTONHOLE) (WS) : Knit to last 4 sts, K2tog, yon, K2.

Knit 1 row.

Cast (bind) off loosely and evenly.

Join back and front at left shoulder edge, overlapping front onto back.

Sew on buttons.

5th, 6th, 7th, 8th & 9th sizes only

Work 4 (4: 6: 6: 6) rows in garter st.

Cast (bind) off loosely and evenly.

Join left shoulder and neckband seam.

See information page for finishing instructions.

pumpkin by Kim Hargreaves

SIZES	1ST	2ND	3RD	4TH	5TH	6TH	7TH	8TH	9TH	
	0-6MTHS	6-12MTHS	1-2YRS	2-3YRS	3-4YRS	4-5YRS	6-7YRS	8-9YRS	9-10YRS	
Chest size	41	46	51	56	58	61	66	71	76	cm
	16	18	20	22	23	24	26	28	30	in
Actual width	26	29.5	33	37	40.5	43	46	50.5	56	cm
	10	11½	13	14½	16	17	18	20	22	in
Length	23	28	33	38	43	47	50.5	57	61	cm
	9	11	13	15	17	18.5	20	22.5	24	in
Sleeve length	12.5	16.5	18	21.5	23	26	30.5	33	35.5	cm
	5	6½	7	8½	9	10	12	13	14	in

YARN

Rowan Wool Cotton 50gm (1¾oz) balls:

Rich 911	3	4	5	6	7	9	10	12	13

NEEDLES

1 pair 3¼mm (US 3) needles
1 pair 4mm (US 6) needles

BUTTONS

2

TENSION (GAUGE)

22 sts and 30 rows to 10cm (4in) measured over stocking (stockinette) stitch using 4mm (US 6) needles

back

Cast on 57 (65: 73: 81: 89: 95: 101: 111: 123) sts using 3¼mm (US 3) needles.
Knit 3 rows.
ROW 4 (WS) : K1, *P1, K1, rep from * to end.
ROW 5: As row 4.
Rows 4 and 5 form moss (seed) st.
Work another 3 (3: 3: 5: 5: 5: 7: 7: 7) rows in moss (seed) st, ending with a WS row.
Change to 4mm (US 6) needles and, beg with a K row, cont in st st as folls:
Work straight until back measures 11.5 (15: 18: 21.5: 25.5: 28: 30.5: 35.5: 38)cm (4½ [6: 7: 8½: 10: 11¼: 12: 14: 15]in), ending with a WS row.

SHAPE ARMHOLES

Cast (bind) off 4 (4: 4: 5: 5: 5: 6: 6: 6) sts at beg of next 2 rows. *49 (57: 65: 71: 79: 85: 89: 99: 111) sts*
Cont straight until armhole measures 11.5 (13: 15: 16.5: 17.5: 19: 20: 21.5: 23)cm (4½ [5: 6: 6½: 6¾: 7½: 7¾: 8½: 9]in), ending with a WS row.

SHAPE SHOULDERS AND BACK NECK

Cast (bind) off 4 (5: 6: 6: 8: 8: 9: 10: 12) sts at beg of next 2 rows. *41 (47: 53: 59: 63: 69: 71: 79: 87) sts*

NEXT ROW (RS): Cast (bind) off 4 (5: 6: 6: 8: 8: 9: 10: 12) sts, K until there are 7 (8: 9: 11: 11: 13: 12: 14: 15) sts on right needle and turn, leaving rem sts on a holder.
Work each side of neck separately.
Cast (bind) off 4 sts at beg of next row.
Cast (bind) off rem 3 (4: 5: 7: 7: 9: 8: 10: 11) sts.
With RS facing, rejoin yarn to rem sts, cast (bind) off center 19 (21: 23: 25: 25: 27: 29: 31: 33) sts, K to end.
Work to match first side, rev shaping.

front

Work as for back until armhole measures 3.5 (4: 6: 6.5: 7.5: 8: 9: 9.5: 11)cm, (1¼ [1½: 2½: 2¾: 3: 3¼: 3½: 3¾: 4¼]in), ending with a WS row.

DIVIDE FOR FRONT OPENING

NEXT ROW (RS) : K22 (26: 30: 33: 37: 39: 41: 46: 52), [K1, P1] 2 (2: 2: 2: 2: 3: 3: 3: 3) times, K1 and turn, leaving rem sts on a holder.
Work each side of neck separately.
NEXT ROW (WS) : [K1, P1] 2 (2: 2: 2: 2: 3: 3: 3: 3) times, K1, P to end. *27 (31: 35: 38: 42: 46: 48: 53: 59) sts.*
This row sets 5 (5: 5: 5: 5: 7: 7: 7: 7) front-opening edge sts now worked in moss (seed) st.
Keeping border correct as set, cont straight until front matches back to start of shoulder shaping, ending with a WS row.

SHAPE SHOULDER

Cast (bind) off 4 (5: 6: 6: 8: 8: 9: 10: 12) sts at beg of next and foll alt row, then 3 (4: 5: 7: 7: 9: 8: 10: 11) sts at beg of foll alt row.
Work 1 row on rem 16 (17: 18: 19: 19: 21: 22: 23: 24) sts.
Break yarn and leave sts on a holder.

With RS facing, rejoin yarn to rem sts, cast on
5 (5: 5: 5: 5: 7: 7: 7: 7) sts, [K1, P1] 2 (2: 2: 2: 2: 3:
3: 3: 3) times, K1 across these 5 (5: 5: 5: 5: 7: 7:
7: 7) sts, then K to end.
27 (31: 35: 38: 42: 46: 48: 53: 59) sts

NEXT ROW (WS) : P to last 5 (5: 5: 5: 5: 7: 7: 7: 7) sts,
[K1, P1] 2 (2: 2: 2: 2: 3: 3: 3: 3) times, K1.
This row sets 5 (5: 5: 5: 5: 7: 7: 7: 7) front-opening
edge sts now worked in moss (seed) st.
Keeping border correct as set, cont straight until front
matches back to start of shoulder shaping, ending
with a RS row.

SHAPE SHOULDER
Cast (bind) off 4 (5: 6: 6: 8: 8: 9: 10: 12) sts at beg of
next and foll alt row, then 3 (4: 5: 7: 7: 9: 8: 10: 11) sts
at beg of foll alt row.
Do NOT break yarn.
Leave rem 16 (17: 18: 19: 19: 21: 22: 23: 24) sts on a
holder and set aside ball of yarn; it will be used for
hood.

sleeves (both alike)
Cast on 33 (37: 39: 41: 45: 47: 51: 53: 55) sts using
3¼mm (US 3) needles.
Knit 3 rows.
Work 3 (3: 3: 5: 5: 5: 7: 7: 7) rows in moss (seed) st as
given for back, ending with a WS row.
Change to 4mm (US 6) needles and, beg with a K
row, cont in st st, inc 1 st at each end of next and
every foll alt (4th: alt: alt: alt: 4th: 4th: 4th: 4th) row to
39 (53: 49: 49: 49: 81: 79: 87: 93) sts, then on every
foll 4th (6th: 4th: 4th: 4th: 6th: 6th: 6th: 6th) row until
there are 51 (57: 67: 73: 77: 83: 89: 95: 101) sts.
Cont straight until sleeve measures 14.5 (18.5: 20: 24:
25.5: 28.5: 33.5: 36: 38.5)cm, (5¾ [7¼: 7¾: 9½: 10:
11¼: 13: 14¼: 15¼]in), ending with a WS row.
Cast (bind) off loosely.

finishing
Press all pieces as described on the information page.
Join shoulder seams using back stitch.
HOOD
With RS facing, using the ball of yarn from front
neck edge and 4mm (US 6) needles, patt across 16
(17: 18: 19: 19: 21: 22: 23: 24) sts of right front as folls:
[K1, P1] to last 0 (1: 0: 1: 1: 1: 0: 1: 0) st, K0 (1: 0: 1:
1: 1: 0: 1: 0), pick up and knit 27 (29: 31: 33: 33: 35:
37: 39: 41) sts across back neck, placing marker on
center st, then patt across 16 (17: 18: 19: 19: 21: 22: 23:
24) sts of left front as folls: K0 (1: 0: 1: 1: 1: 0: 1: 0),
[P1, K1] to end. *59 (63: 67: 71: 71: 77: 81: 85: 89) sts*
Working all sts in moss (seed) st as set by front neck
sts, cont as folls:
Work 7 rows.
NEXT ROW (RS) (INC): Moss (seed) st to marked st, M1,
K1, M1, moss (seed) st to end.
Rep last 8 rows once more.
63 (67: 71: 75: 75: 81: 85: 89: 93) sts
Cont straight until hood measures 19 (20: 21: 22: 23:
24: 25: 26: 27)cm, (7½ [7¾: 8¼: 8½: 9: 9½: 9¾: 10¼:
10¾]in), ending with a WS row.
NEXT ROW (RS) (DEC): Moss st to within 2 sts of
marked st, work 2 tog, K1, work 2 tog tbl, moss (seed)
st to end.
Work 1 row.
Rep last 2 rows twice more, dec 1 st at center of last
row. *56 (60: 64: 68: 68: 74: 78: 82: 86) sts*
NEXT ROW (RS): Patt 28 (30: 32: 34: 34: 37: 39: 41: 43)
sts and turn.
Fold hood in half with WS facing and, using a spare
needle, cast (bind) off sts from each needle tog to
form hood seam.
BUTTON LOOPS (MAKE 2)
Cast on 14 sts using 3¼mm (US 3) needles.
Cast (bind) off.
Lay one front border over the other and sew cast-on
edge in place on inside. Fold button loops in half and
sew to inside of front-opening edge as in photograph.
Attach buttons to correspond with button loops.
See information page for finishing instructions, setting
in sleeves using the square set-in method.

jack flash by Kim Hargreaves

SIZES	1ST 0-6MTHS	2ND 6-9MTHS	3RD 1-2YRS	4TH 2-3YRS	5TH 3-4YRS	6TH 4-5YRS	7TH 6-7YRS	8TH 8-9YRS	9TH 9-10YRS	
Chest size	29.5	32.5	35.5	38.5	41.5	44.5	47.5	51.5	55.5	cm
	11½	12½	14	15½	16½	17½	18½	20½	22	in
Length	29	32	35	38	41	44	47	51	55	cm
	11½	12½	13½	15	16½	17½	18½	20	21½	in
Sleeve length	19	20	23	25	28	30.5	35.5	38	40.5	cm
	7½	8	9	9½	11	12	14	15	16	in

YARN

Rowan Handknit DK Cotton 50gm (1¾oz) balls

A Ecru	251	2	2	3	3	3	4	5	5	5
B Black	252	2	2	3	3	3	3	4	4	4
C Diana	287	3	3	4	4	4	5	5	6	6

NEEDLES

1 pair 3¼mm (US 3) needles
1 pair 4mm (US 6) needles

BUTTONS

6 (6: 6: 6: 7: 7: 7: 8: 8)

TENSION (GAUGE)

20 sts and 28 rows to 10cm (4in) measured over stocking (stockinette) stitch using 4mm (US 6) needles

back

Cast on 51 (57: 63: 69: 75: 81: 87: 93: 101) sts using 3¼mm (US 3) needles and yarn A.
Work in moss (seed) stitch as folls:
ROW 1: *K1, P1, rep from * to last st, K1.
Rep this row 5 (5: 5: 5: 5: 5: 7: 7: 7) times more.
Change to 4mm (US 6) needles and cont in st st in stripe sequence as folls:
ROW 1 (RS): K using A.
ROW 2: P using A.
ROW 3: K using B.
ROW 4: P using B.
These 4 rows form the patt and are repeated throughout the back.
Keeping patt correct, inc 1 st at each end of next row and 3 (3: 3: 3: 3: 3: 3: 4: 4) foll 10th rows.
59 (65: 71: 77: 83: 89: 95: 103: 111) sts
Cont without further shaping until work measures 29 (32: 35: 38: 41: 44: 47: 51: 55)cm (11½ [12½: 13¾: 15: 16¼: 17¼: 18½: 20: 21½]in) from cast-on edge, ending with a WS row.

SHAPE SHOULDERS AND BACK NECK

Keeping color sequence correct, cast (bind) off 6 (7: 8: 9: 10: 10: 11: 12: 13) sts at beg of next 2 rows.
Cast (bind) off 6 (7: 8: 9: 10: 10: 11: 12: 13) sts, K 11 (12: 12: 13: 13: 15: 15: 16: 17) and turn, leaving rem sts on a holder.
Work each side of neck separately.
Cast (bind) off 4 sts, work to end.
Cast (bind) off rem 7 (8: 8: 9: 9: 11: 11: 12: 13) sts.
With RS facing, rejoin correct yarn, cast (bind) off center 13 (13: 15: 15: 17: 19: 21: 23: 25) sts and work to end.
Complete to match first side, rev shaping.

right front

Cast on 30 (33: 36: 39: 42: 45: 48: 51: 55) sts using 3¼mm (US 3) needles and yarn C.
Girl's jacket
Work 5 (5: 5: 5: 5: 5: 7: 7: 7) rows in moss (seed) st.
Boy's jacket
Work 2 (2: 2: 2: 2: 2: 4: 4: 4) rows in moss (seed) st.
NEXT ROW (BUTTONHOLE ROW) (RS): Work in moss (seed) st to last 5 sts, K2tog, yrn twice, K2tog, K1.
NEXT ROW: Moss (seed) st to end, working into back of loops made on previous row.
Work 1 row in moss (seed) st.
Both girl's and boy's jacket
ROW 6 (6: 6: 6: 6: 6: 8: 8: 8) (WS): Work 5 sts in moss (seed) st, leave these sts on a holder, patt to end.
25 (28: 31: 34: 37: 40: 43: 46: 50) sts
Change to 4mm (US 6) needles and work 4 rows in st st, beg with a K row and ending with a WS row.
Inc 1 st at beg of next row and 3 (3: 3: 3: 3: 3: 3: 4: 4) foll 10th rows. *29 (32: 35: 38: 41: 44: 48: 51: 55) sts*

Cont without shaping until work is 9 (9: 9: 9: 11: 11: 11: 13: 13) rows shorter than back to shoulder, ending with a RS row.

SHAPE FRONT NECK

Cast (bind) off 3 (3: 3: 3: 3: 4: 4: 4: 4) sts at beg of next row and foll alt row.

Dec 1 st at neck edge on next 4 (4: 5: 5: 6: 5: 7: 7: 8) rows. *19 (22: 24: 27: 29: 31: 33: 36: 39) sts*

Cont without further shaping until front matches back to shoulder shaping, ending with a WS row.

SHAPE SHOULDER

Cast (bind) off 6 (7: 8: 9: 10: 10: 11: 12: 13) sts at beg of next row and foll alt row.

Work 1 row.

Cast (bind) off rem 7 (8: 8: 9: 9: 11: 11: 12: 13) sts.

right front

Cast on 30 (33: 36: 39: 42: 45: 48: 51: 55) sts using 3¼mm (US 3) needles and yarn C.

Girl's jacket

Work 2 (2: 2: 2: 2: 2: 4: 4: 4) rows in moss (seed) st.

NEXT ROW (BUTTONHOLE ROW) (RS): Patt 1, K2tog, yrn twice, K2tog, patt to end.

NEXT ROW: Moss (seed) st to end, working into back of loops made on previous row.

Work 1 row in moss (seed) st.

Boy's jacket

Work 5 (5: 5: 5: 5: 5: 7: 7: 7) rows in moss (seed) st.

Both girl's and boy's jacket

ROW 6 (6: 6: 6: 6: 6: 8: 8: 8) (WS): Work in moss (seed) st to last 5 sts and turn, leaving rem sts on a holder. *25 (28: 31: 34: 37: 40: 43: 46: 50) sts*

Change to 4mm (US 6) needles and complete as given for left front, rev all shaping.

sleeves (both alike)

Cast on 29 (29: 33: 33: 37: 37: 43: 43: 43) sts using 3¼mm (US 3) needles and yarn A.

Work 6 (6: 6: 6: 6: 6: 8: 8: 8) rows in moss (seed) st as given for back.

Change to 4mm (US 6) needles and cont in st st, beg with a knit row. Work in the color sequence as given for back and AT THE SAME TIME shape sides by inc 1 st at each end of 3rd row and every foll 4th row to 51 (53: 59: 65: 73: 77: 83: 87: 93) sts.

Cont without further shaping until sleeve measures 19 (20: 23: 25: 28: 30.5: 35.5: 38: 40.5)cm, (7½ [7¾: 9: 9¾: 11¼: 12: 14: 15: 16]in) or length required from cast-on edge, ending with a WS row.

Cast (bind) off loosely and evenly.

finishing

Press all pieces as described on the information page.

Join both shoulder seams using back stitch.

BUTTON BAND

Right front boy's, left front girl's

Using 3¼mm (US 3) needles, slip sts from holder onto LH needle, join in yarn C and, keeping patt correct, cont in moss (seed) st until band fits up front to neck shaping when slightly stretched. Slipstitch into place. Cast (bind) off.

Mark position of 6 (6: 6: 6: 7: 7: 7: 8: 8) buttons, the first to match buttonhole in band of opposite front the last to come 1.5cm (¾in) from neck edge and the remaining spaced evenly between.

BUTTONHOLE BAND

Work as for button hand with the addition of 5 (5: 5: 5: 6: 6: 6: 7: 7) buttonholes worked as before to correspond with markers.

COLLAR

Cast on 59 (59: 61: 61: 67: 69: 71: 77: 79) sts using 3¼mm (US 3) needles and yarn C.

ROW 1 (RS) : K2, moss (seed) st to last 2 sts, K2.

ROW 2: Rep row 1 again.

NEXT ROW (INC): K2, M1, moss (seed) st to last 2 sts, M1, K2.

Cont as set, inc as before on every foll 3rd row until collar measures 6 (6: 7: 7: 8: 8: 9: 9: 10)cm, (2½ [2½: 2¾: 2¾: 3¼: 3¼: 3½: 3½: 4]in) from cast-on edge.

Cast (bind) off in patt.

PATCH POCKETS

Cast on 17 (17: 19: 19: 21: 23: 23: 25: 25) sts using 3¼mm (US 3) needles and yarn C.

Work in moss (seed) st until work measures 7.5 (8: 8.5: 9: 9.5: 10: 11: 12: 13)cm (3 [3¼: 3½: 3½: 3¾: 4: 4¼: 4¾: 5]in) from cast-on edge, ending with a WS row.

Dec 1 st at each end of next 4 (4: 4: 4: 5: 5: 5: 6: 6) rows. *9 (9: 11: 11: 11: 13: 13: 13: 13) sts*

Cast (bind) off in moss (seed) stitch.

Sew pockets into place.

Sew cast-on edge of collar into place, starting and ending halfway across front bands and matching center of collar with center back neck.

See information page for finishing instructions, leaving moss (seed) st border at bottom side edges open to form side vents. Press all seams.

thorn by Kim Hargreaves

SIZES	S	M	L	
To fit bust	86	91	97	cm
	34	36	38	in
Actual width	58.5	61	63	cm
	23	24	25	in
Length	71	73.5	76	cm
	28	29	30	in
Sleeve length	43	43	43	cm
	17	17	17	in

YARN

Rowan Magpie Aran 100gm (3½oz) balls:
Chutney 319   8   9   9

NEEDLES

1 pair 4mm (US 6) needles
1 pair 4½mm (US 7) needles
1 pair 5mm (US 8) needles

TENSION (GAUGE)

18 sts and 23 rows to 10cm (4in) over stocking (stockinette) stitch using 5mm (US 8) needles

back

Cast on 105 (109: 113) sts using 4½mm (US 7) needles.
ROW 1 (RS) : K0 (1: 3), P2 (3: 3), *K5, P3, rep from * to last 7 (9: 11) sts, K5, P2 (3: 3), K0 (1: 3).
ROW 2: P0 (1: 3), K2 (3: 3), *P5, K3, rep from * to last 7 (9: 11) sts, P5, K2 (3: 3), P0 (1: 3).
Rep these 2 rows until 12 rows in all are complete, ending with a WS row.
Change to 5mm (US 8) needles and work in st st, beg with a K row until work measures 48 (50.5: 53)cm (18¾ [20: 21]in) from cast-on edge, ending with a WS row.
SHAPE ARMHOLE AND WORK FULLY FASHIONED SHAPING AS FOLLS:
Cast (bind) off 4 sts at beg of next 2 rows.
NEXT ROW (RS) (DEC): K3, K3tog, K to last 6 sts, K3tog tbl, K3.
Work 1 row.
Dec 2 sts as in dec row at each end of next row, 1 foll alt row and 3 foll 4th rows.
73 (77: 81) sts
Cont without shaping until work measures 23cm (9in) from beg armhole shaping, ending with a WS row.
SHAPE SHOULDERS AND BACK NECK
Cast (bind) off 7 (8: 9) sts at beg of next 2 rows.
Cast (bind) off 8 (8: 9) sts, K12 (13: 13), turn and leave rem st on a holder. Work each side of neck separately.
Cast (bind) off 4 sts, P to end.

Cast (bind) off rem 8 (9: 9) sts. With RS facing, rejoin yarn to rem sts, cast (bind) off center 19 sts, K to end.
Complete to match first side, rev shaping.

pocket lining (work 2)

Cast on 20 sts using 5mm (US 8) needles and work 20 rows in st st, beg with a K row.
Leave sts on a holder.

front

Work as given for back until 20 rows in st st are complete, ending with a WS row.
DIVIDE FOR POCKET
NEXT ROW (RS): K14 (16: 18), leave rem sts on a holder, K across 20 sts from first pocket lining.
34 (36: 38) sts
Work 26 rows in st st, ending at inside edge.
Leave on a spare needle.
POCKET FRONT
With RS facing, rejoin yarn to rem sts, K77 sts, turn and leave rem sts on a holder.
Dec 1 st at each end of next 2 rows. *73 sts*
Work 1 row.
Rep these last 3 rows until 41 sts rem.
Work 1 row. Leave sts on a holder.
With RS facing, rejoin yarn and knit across 20 sts of second pocket lining, knit across 14 (16: 18) rem sts of front. *34 (36: 38) sts*
Work 26 rows in st st, ending at side edge.
JOIN PIECES
NEXT ROW (WS): P32 (34: 36), now with needles parallel, place side piece in front of pocket front,
* purl next st and first st of pocket front tog at the same time, rep from *once, P across pocket front until 2 sts rem, *purl next st and first st of side piece tog at the same time, rep from *once, P to end. *105 (109: 113) sts*
Cont working as given for back until front is 16 rows shorter than back to shoulder shaping, ending with a WS row.
SHAPE FRONT NECK
NEXT ROW (RS) : K31 (33: 35), turn and leave rem sts on a holder.
Work each side of neck separately.
Work 1 row.
NEXT ROW (RS) (DEC): K to last 6 sts, K3tog tbl, K3.
Work 1 row.
Dec as in dec row, 1 foll alt row and 1 foll 4th row.
23 (25: 27) sts
Cont without further shaping until front matches back to shoulder shaping, ending with a WS row.

SHAPE SHOULDER

Cast (bind) off 7 (8: 9) sts at beg of next row and
8 (8: 9) sts at beg of foll alt row.
Work 1 row. Cast (bind) off rem 8 (9: 9) sts.
With RS facing, rejoin yarn to rem sts, cast (bind) off
center 11 sts, K to end.
Complete to match first side, rev shaping.

sleeves (both alike)

Cast on 45 sts using 4½mm (US 7) needles.
ROW 1 (RS): K1*P3, K5, rep from * to last 4 sts, P3,
K1.
ROW 2: P1, *K3, P5, rep from * to last 4 sts, K3, P1.
Rep these 2 rows until 12 rows in all are complete,
ending with a WS row.
Keeping patt correct, inc 1 st at each end of next row.
Work 5 more rows in rib.
Change to 5mm (US 8) needles and work in st st, beg
with a K row, inc 1 st at each end of 5th row and
every foll 10th row to 63 sts.
Cont without shaping until sleeve measures 43cm
(17in) from cast-on edge, ending with a WS row.

SHAPE SLEEVEHEAD

Cast (bind) off 4 sts at beg of next 2 rows.
NEXT ROW (RS) (DEC): K3, K3tog, K to last 6 sts, K3tog
tbl, K3.
Work 3 rows.
Dec 5 in dec row on next row, 1 foll 4th row and
4 foll 6th rows. *27 sts*
Work 3 rows.
Dec as before on next row and 1 foll alt row. *19 sts*
Work 1 row. Cast (bind) off 4 sts at beg of next 2
rows.
Cast (bind) off rem 11 sts.

finishing

Press pieces as described on the information page.
Join right shoulder seam using back stitch.

NECKBAND

With RS facing and using 4mm (US 6) needles, pick
up and knit 20 sts down left front neck, 11 sts across
front neck, 20 sts up right front neck and 29 sts across
back neck. *80 sts*
Work 13cm (5in) in K5, P3 rib. Cast (bind) off in rib.

POCKET EDGINGS (BOTH ALIKE)

With RS facing and using 4mm (US 6) needles, pick
up and knit 23 sts across pocket edge.
ROW 1 (WS): K1, (P5, K3) twice, P5, K1.
ROW 2: K6, (P3, K5) twice, K1.
Rep these 2 rows twice more.
Cast (bind) off loosely and evenly in rib.
Slipstitch edgings into place on front.
Sew pocket linings to WS of front.
See information page for finishing instructions.

trellis by Kim Hargreaves

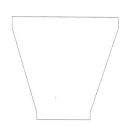

SIZES

			CHILDREN'S					ADULTS'			
	1	**2**	**3**	**4**	**5**	**6**	**7**	**8**	**9**	**10**	
To fit year/size	1	2	4	6	8	9	10	S	M	L	
To fit bust	–	–	–	–	–	–	–	86	91	97	cm
	–	–	–	–	–	–	–	34	36	38	in
Actual width	33	37.5	39.5	41.5	44	46.5	48.5	54	56.5	59.5	cm
	13	14¾	15½	16½	17¼	18¼	19	21¼	22¼	23½	in
Length	31	35	40	45	50	55	60	68	71	73	cm
	12¼	13¾	15¾	17¾	19¾	21¾	23¾	26¾	28	28¾	in
Sleeve length	17	21	26	31	36	41	46	48	48	48	cm
	6¾	8¼	10¼	12¼	14¼	16¼	18¼	19	19	19	in

YARN

Rowan Designer DK or Tweed DK 50gm (1¾oz) balls:

Trellis

DDK	4	5	6	7	8	9	10	11	12	13
Tweed Seal 852	5	6	7	8	9	10	11	12	13	14

Bobble

DDK	5	6	7	8	9	10	11	12	13	14
Tweed	6	7	8	9	10	11	12	13	14	15

NEEDLES
1 pair 3¼mm (US 3) needles
1 pair 4mm (US 6) needles

BUTTONS
(on sizes 1, 2 and 3 only)
3 buttons for polo-collar version
4 buttons for garter-stitch neckband

TENSION (GAUGE)
22 sts and 30 rows to 10cm (4in) measured over stocking (stockinette) stitch using 4mm (US 6) needles. When using the Fox Tweed DK, you may find that you will need to use a 3¾mm (US 5) needle to obtain the correct tension (gauge).

PATTERN NOTE
The three smallest sizes have front openings and either a polo collar or a garter stitch neckband; the other sizes have either a turtle neck or a polo neck with bobbles.

STITCH NOTE
This pattern can be knitted as either a trellis or bobble stitch. For the trellis version, treat the dot on the chart as a purl stitch on the RS. For the bobble-stitch version, treat the dot on the pattern as a bobble;

this is made by knitting into the front, back, front and back of the stitch indicated by the dot, pass the first 3 of these stitches, one at a time, over the fourth stitch (bobble made), then purl the next stitch (not indicated on chart). Continue pattern from chart.

back
Cast on 73 (83: 87: 91: 97: 103: 107: 119: 125: 131) sts using 3¼mm (US 3) needles and work 8 (10: 10: 12: 12: 14: 14: 16: 16: 16) rows in garter st (knit every row). Change to 4mm (US 6) needles.
1st, 2nd, 3rd, 4th, & 5th sizes only (no side vents)
CHART ROW 1 (RS): Work in patt from chart, working between markers for correct size and working the trellis or bobble pattern as described above.
CHART ROW 2: Purl. *
6th, 7th, 8th, 9th & 10th sizes only (with side vents)
CHART ROW 1 (RS): Work in patt from chart, working between markers for correct size, working the trellis or bobble pattern as described in stitch note but on these larger sizes knit the first 6 and last 6 sts to form side vents, even if the chart indicates otherwise.
CHART ROW 2: K6 to form side vents, purl across row to last 6 sts, K6.

Cont in patt from chart, keeping 6 edge sts correct as set and work 20-row patt rep until work measures 15 (15: 20: 20: 20)cm (6 [6: 7¾: 7¾: 7¾]in) from cast-on edge, ending with a WS row.
This completes the side vents.
NEXT ROW: Foll chart for appropriate row and, working between markers for correct size, work in patt across all sts.
NEXT ROW: Purl. *

All sizes
Cont in patt, working 20-row patt rep until work measures 31 (35: 40: 45: 50: 55: 60: 68: 71: 73)cm (12¼ [13¾: 15¾: 17¾: 19¾: 21¾: 23½: 26¾: 28: 28¾]in), from cast-on edge, ending with a WS row.

SHAPE SHOULDER AND BACK NECK
Cast (bind) off 8 (9: 10: 10: 11: 12: 12: 13: 14: 15) sts at beg of next row, patt 21 (24: 25: 25: 27: 28: 30: 32: 34: 36) sts, turn, and leave rem sts on a holder.
Work each side of neck separately.
Cast (bind) off 4 sts, patt to end.
Cast (bind) off 8 (10: 10: 10: 11: 12: 13: 14: 15: 16) sts, patt to end.
Work 1 row.
Cast (bind) off rem 9 (10: 11: 11: 12: 12: 13: 14: 15: 16) sts.
With RS facing, rejoin yarn to rem sts, cast (bind) off center 15 (17: 17: 21: 21: 23: 23: 29: 29: 29) sts, patt to end.
Complete to match first side, rev shaping.

front
All sizes
Work as for back to *.
1st, 2nd & 3rd sizes only
Work until front measures 17 (21: 26)cm (6½ [8¼: 10¼ in]) from cast-on edge, ending with a WS row.

DIVIDE FOR FRONT NECK
Work 34 (39: 41) sts, turn and leave rem sts on a holder.
Work each side of neck separately.
Keeping patt correct, work another 9cm (3½in), ending at neck edge.

SHAPE FRONT NECK
NEXT ROW (WS): Cast (bind) off 3 sts, patt to end.
Dec 1 st at neck edge on next 6 (7: 7) rows.
25 (29: 31) sts
Cont without further shaping until front matches back to shoulder, ending with a WS row.

SHAPE SHOULDER
Cast (bind) off 8 (9: 10) sts at beg of next row and 8 (10: 10) sts at beg of foll alt row.
Work 1 row.
Cast (bind) off rem 9 (10: 11) sts.
With RS facing, place center 5 sts on a holder, rejoin yarn to rem sts and patt to end.
Complete to match first side, rev shaping.

4th, 5th, 6th, 7th, 8th, 9th & 10th sizes only
Work until front measures 40 (45: 50: 55: 61: 64: 66)cm (15¾ [17¾: 19¾: 21¾: 24: 25¼: 26]in), from cast-on edge, ending with a WS row.

SHAPE FRONT NECK
Patt 39 (42: 45: 47: 52: 55: 58) sts, turn and leave rem sts on a holder.
Dec 1 st at neck edge on next 8 (8: 9: 9: 11: 11: 11) rows. *31 (34: 36: 38: 41: 44: 47) sts*
Cont without further shaping until front matches back to shoulder shaping, ending with WS row.

SHAPE SHOULDER

Cast (bind) off 10 (11: 12: 12: 13: 14: 15) sts at beg of next row. Work 1 row.
Cast (bind) off 10 (11: 12: 13: 14: 15: 16) sts at beg of next row. Work 1 row.
Cast (bind) off rem 11 (12: 12: 13: 14: 15: 16) sts.
With RS facing, rejoin yarn to rem sts, cast (bind) off center 13 (13: 13: 13: 15: 15: 15) sts, patt to end.
Complete to match first side, rev shaping.

sleeves (both alike)

Cast on 28 (32: 34: 36: 38: 40: 42: 46: 46: 46) sts using 3¼mm (US 3) needles and work 8 (10: 10: 12: 12: 14: 14: 16: 16: 16) rows in either garter st or, if preferred, K2, P2 rib. Inc 1 st at end of last row. *29 (33: 35: 37: 39: 41: 43: 47: 47: 47) sts*
Change to 4mm (US 6) needles and cont in pattern, shaping sides by inc as folls:
CHART ROW 1 (RS): Cont from chart for sleeve, working between markers for correct size.
CHART ROW 2: Purl.
Keeping patt correct and working extra sts into patt, inc 1 at each end of next row and every foll 2nd (2nd: 3rd: 4th: 4th: 4th: 4th: 4th: 4th) row to 55 (59: 73: 77: 83: 89: 83: 105: 105: 105) sts.

1st, 2nd & 7th sizes only

Inc 1 st at each end of every 4th (4th: 6th) row to 59 (69: 95) sts.

All sizes

Cont without further shaping until work measures 17 (21: 26: 31: 36: 41: 46: 48: 48: 48)cm (6½ [8¼: 10¼: 12¼: 14¼: 16¼: 18: 18¾: 18¾: 18¾]in) or length required from cast-on edge.
Cast (bind) off loosely and evenly.

finishing

Press all pieces as described on the information page.
1st, 2nd & 3rd sizes only
Join shoulder seams.
BUTTON BAND
Place a marker through 5 sts at center front.
With RS facing and using 3¼mm (US 3) needles, rejoin yarn to 5 sts at center front.
Cont in garter st until band fits, when slightly stretched, to beg of neck shaping, ending with a WS row.
Leave sts on holder for garter-st neckband or cast (bind) off for polo-collar version.
Slipstitch band into place on right side for boys and left side for girls.
Mark position of 3 buttons, the first to come 1.5cm (¾in) up from marker, the 3rd to come 1.5cm (¾in) down from neck shaping, the other in the center.
BUTTONHOLE BAND
With RS facing, rejoin yarn to same sts with marker and work as given for button band, working button holes to correspond with button position as foll:
BUTTONHOLE ROW (RS): K2, yrn twice, K2tog, K1.
NEXT ROW: K, dropping one of the loops made on previous row.
Slip st onto opposite side of neck opening.
Polo collar
Cast on 68 (72: 76) sts using 3¼mm (US 3) needles.
ROW 1 (RS): K3, *P2, K2, rep from * to last 5 sts, P2, K3.
ROW 2: K1, P2, *K2, P2, rep from * to last st, K1.
NEXT ROW (RS) (INC): K3, M1, work in rib to last 3 sts, M1, K3.

Keeping rib correct, work 7cm (2¾in) in rib, inc as before on every RS row and working extra sts in rib. Cast (bind) off evenly in rib.
Slipstitch cast-on edge of collar into place, matching center of collar with center back neck and placing ends of collar at center of button bands.

Garter-st neckband

With right side facing and using 3¼mm (US 3) needles, rejoin yarn and K across 5 sts at top of right band, pick up and K 18 (20: 20) sts evenly up right side of front neck, 23 (25: 25) sts across back neck, 18 (20: 20) sts down left side of front neck and 5 sts at top of left band.
69 (75: 75) sts
Work 5 rows in garter st, working buttonhole as before on 2nd row, in line with previous buttonholes.
Cast (bind) off evenly.

Turtle neck and Polo neck with bobbles

Join right shoulder seam.
With RS facing and using 3¼mm (US 3) needles, rejoin yarn and pick up and K 20 (20: 20: 20: 25: 25: 25) sts evenly down left side of front neck, 13 (13: 13: 13: 15: 15: 15) sts across center front, 20 (20: 20: 20: 25: 25: 25) sts evenly up right side of front neck and 29 (29: 33: 33: 37: 37: 37) sts across back neck.
82 (82: 86: 86: 102: 102: 102) sts
ROW 1 (WS): K2, *P2, K2, rep from * to end.
ROW 2: P2, *P2, K2, rep from * to end.

Turtle neck

Rep last 2 rows for 5 (5: 5: 5: 8: 8: 8)cm (2 [2: 2: 2: 3¼: 3¼: 3¼]in), ending with a WS row.
Cast (bind) off evenly in rib.
Join left shoulder and neckband seam.

Polo neck with bobbles

Rep last 2 rows until work measures 12cm (4¾in), from beg, ending with a RS row.
NEXT ROW (WS): K1, make bobble, *P2, K1, make bobble, rep from *to end.
Keeping rib correct, cont until work measures 14cm (5½in) from beg, ending with a RS row.
Cast (bind) off evenly in rib.
Join left shoulder and neckband seam.
See information page for finishing instructions.

EMBROIDERY (OPTIONAL)

Using 2 strands of yarn, embroider flowers in Lazy daisy stitch with center French knot. See diagram. Position at random.

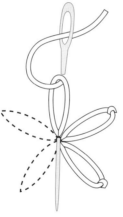

KEY

☐ K on RS
P on WS

Trellis Stitch
⊡ Purl on RS

Bobble stitch
⊡ Knit into front, back, front and back of st, pass the first 3 of these sts one at a time over the 4th st (bobble made) then purl the next stitch (not indicated on chart)

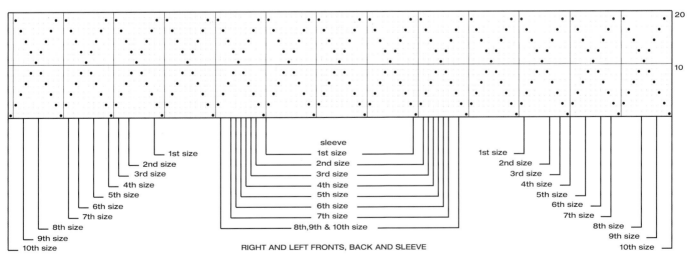

RIGHT AND LEFT FRONTS, BACK AND SLEEVE

men's shawl collar by Kim Hargreaves

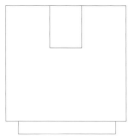

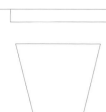

SIZE

One size to fit	xx	cm
	38–42	in
Actual width	68.5	cm
	27	in
Length	72.5	cm
	28½	in
Sleeve length	48	cm
	19	in

YARN

Designer DK Tweed 50gm (1¾oz) balls:
Charcoal 869   15

NEEDLES

1 pair 3¼ mm (US 3)
1 pair 4mm (US 6)
Circular needle 3¼mm (no 10) (US 3), 60cm
    (24in) long
Cable needle

TENSION (GAUGE)

22 sts and 30 rows to 10cm (4in) measured over
stocking (stockinette) stitch using 4mm (US 6) needles

back

Cast on 126 sts using 3¼mm (US 3) needles.
Work 8cm (3¼in) in K2, P2 rib ending with a RS row.
NEXT ROW (INC): Rib 15, (M1, rib 4) 24 times, MI, rib
15. *151 sts*
Change to 4mm (US 6) needles and cont in patt as folls:
ROW 1: *K1, P1, rep from * to last st, K1.
ROW 2: Work as row 1.
ROW 3: K3, *P1, K1, P1 K1, P1, K3, P1, K1, P1, K3,
rep from * to last 8 sts, (P1, K1) twice, P1, K3.
ROW 4: P4, *K1, P1, K1, P5, K1, P5, rep from * to
last 7 sts, K1, P1, K1, P4.
ROW 5: K5, *P1, K13, rep from * to last 6 sts, P1, K5.
ROW 6: Purl.
ROWS 7–102: Rep rows 5 and 6.
Now work rows 103–120 in patt from chart A, rep 14
patt sts 10 times across row and working last 11 sts on
RS rows and first 11 sts on WS rows as indicated.
ROW 121: Purl (mark each end of this row with
colored thread for sleeve position).**
ROW 122: *P10, K1, P1, K into front and back of next
4 sts, P1, K1, P15, KI, P1, K into front and back of
next 4 sts, P1, K1, P11, K1, P1,* K into front and
back of next 4 sts, K1, K into front and back of next
4 sts, P1, K1, P21, K1, PI, K into front and back of

next 4 sts, K1, K into front and back of next 4 sts,
*** P1, K1, P11, K1, P1, K into front and back of
next 4 sts, P1, K1, P15, K1, P1, K into front and back
of next 4 sts, P1, KI, P10. *** *183 sts*
Now work rows 123–194 in patt from chart B.

SHAPE SHOULDERS

Keeping patt correct (rows 195–196 of chart B), cast
(bind) off 63 sts at beg of next 2 rows.
Cast (bind) off rem 57 sts.

front

Work as given for back to **.

SHAPE FRONT NECK

ROW 122: Work as given for row 122 of back from
* to *, P1, cast (bind) off next 41 sts, P1, then work
rem sts as given for row 122 of back from *** to ***.
Now work first 63 sts in patt from chart B (left front),
leaving rem sts on a holder and working neck edge
st in st st. Cont in patt until 194 patt rows have been
completed. Cast (bind) off.
With RS facing, rejoin yarn to rem sts and complete
to match first side, rev all shaping.

sleeves (both alike)

Cast on 46 sts using 3¼mm (US 3) needles and work
7.5cm (3in) in K2, P2 rib, ending with a RS row.
NEXT ROW (INC): Rib 2, (M1, rib 3) 14 times,
M1, rib 2. *61 sts*

CHART A

☐ K on RS, P on WS

◉ P on RS, K on WS

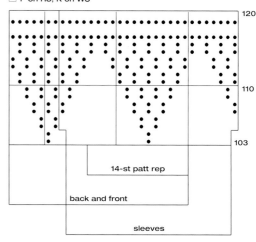

Change to 4mm (US 6) needles and patt as folls:

ROW 1: *P1, K1, rep from * to last st, P1.

ROW 2: Work as row 1.

ROW 3: K into front and back of first st, K1, P1, K1, P1, * K3, P1, K1, P1, K3, P1, K1, P1, K1, P1; rep from *, ending last rep by working into front and back of last st. *63 sts*

ROW 4: P2, *K1, P1, K1, P5, K1, P5, rep from * to last 5 sts, K1, P1, K1, P2.

ROW 5: K3, *P1, K13,, rep from * to last 4 sts, P1, K3.

ROW 6: Purl.

ROWS 7–102: Rep rows 5 and 6 and AT THE SAME TIME, shape sides by inc 1 st at each end of next row and every foll 4th row until there are 99 sts, then every foll 6th row until there are 107 sts. Take extra sts into patt as they occur.

Now work rows 103–120 in patt from chart A, rep 14 patt sts 7 times across row. Work first 6 sts and last 3 sts on RS rows, and first 3 sts and last 6 sts on WS rows as indicated AT THE SAME TIME, shape sides by inc 1 st at each end of 3rd row, taking extra sts into patt. *109 sts*

ROW 121: Purl.

Cast (bind) off loosely and evenly.

finishing

Press all pieces (except ribbing) on WS using a warm iron over a damp cloth.

Join both shoulder seams using back stitch.

COLLAR

With RS facing and 3¼mm (US 3) circular needle, pick up and K 60 sts up right front neck, 40 sts across back neck and 60 sts down left front neck. *160 sts*

Working backward and forward and not in rounds, cont K2, P2 rib until collar measures 15cm (6in).

Cast (bind) off loosely and evenly.

Sew side edges of collar to cast-(bound)-off sts at center front so that they overlap left over right to within 2.5cm (1in) of seam at either sideof front neck.

Sew sleeve top into position between markers.

Join side and sleeve seams.

Press seams.

CHART B KEY

☐ K on RS, P on WS

▣ P on RS, K on WS

⟩⟨ C8F = slip the next 4 sts onto a cable needle and hold at front of work, K4 then K4 from cable needle

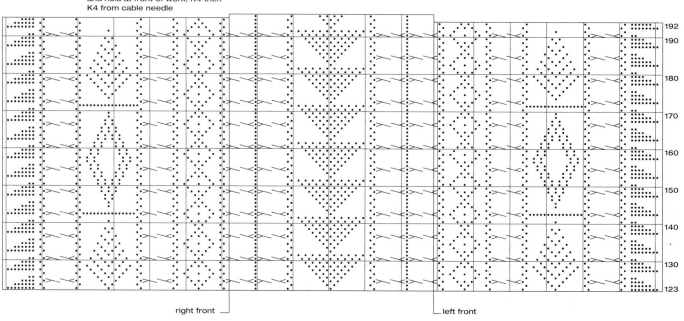

right front ⌐   ⌐ left front

RIGHT AND LEFT FRONTS AND BACK

polar by Kim Hargreaves

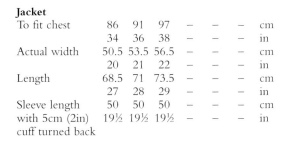

SIZES	LADIES'			MEN'S		
	S	M	L	M	L	XL
Pullover						
To fit chest	86	91	97	**97**	**102**	**107**	cm
	34	36	38	**38**	**40**	**42**	in
Actual width	58	60.5	63.5	**63.5**	**66.5**	**69.5**	cm
	23	24	25	**25**	**26**	**27½**	in
Length	68.5	71	73.5	**68.5**	**71**	**73.5**	cm
	27	28	29	**27**	**28**	**29**	in
Sleeve length	47	47	47	**52**	**52**	**52**	cm
with 5cm (2in)	18½	18½	18½	**20½**	**20½**	**20½**	in
cuff turned back						

	S	M	L	M	L	XL
Jacket						
To fit chest	86	91	97	–	–	–	cm
	34	36	38	–	–	–	in
Actual width	50.5	53.5	56.5	–	–	–	cm
	20	21	22	–	–	–	in
Length	68.5	71	73.5	–	–	–	cm
	27	28	29	–	–	–	in
Sleeve length	50	50	50	–	–	–	cm
with 5cm (2in)	19½	19½	19½	–	–	–	in
cuff turned back						

YARNS

Rowan Chunky Tweed 100gm (3½oz) balls:
Pullover

	S	M	L	M	L	XL
Polar 879	11	11	12	**12**	**12**	**13**

Jacket

	S	M	L
Bliss 816	10	10	11

(Shade no longer available)

NEEDLES

1 pair 5½mm (US 9) needles
1 pair 6mm (US 10) needles

TENSION (GAUGE)

14 sts and 20 rows to 10cm (4in) measured over patt
using 6mm (US 10) needles

PATTERN NOTE

The pattern is written for the three ladies' sizes,
followed by the men's sizes in bold.

Pullover
back

Cast on 81 (85: 89: **89: 93: 97**) sts using 5½mm
(US 9) needles.
ROW 1 (RS): [K1, P1] 0 (1: 2: **2: 0: 1**) times, *K3, P1,
K1, P1, rep from * to last 3 (5: **7: 7: 3: 5**) sts, K3, [P1,
K1] 0 (1: 2: **2: 0: 1**) times.
ROW 2: K0 (1: 0: **0: 0: 1**), P4 (5: 2: **2: 4: 5**), *K1, P5, rep
from * to last 5 (1: 3: **3: 5: 1**) sts, K1, P4 (0: 2: **2: 4: 0**).
These 2 rows form patt.
Patt another 8 rows, thus ending with a WS row.
Change to 6mm (US 10) needles and cont in patt until
back measures 43.5 (46: 48.5: **43.5: 46: 48.5**)cm, (17
[18: 19: **17: 18: 19**]in), ending with a WS row.
SHAPE ARMHOLES
Keeping patt correct, cast (bind) off 4 sts at beg of next
2 rows. *73 (77: 81: 81: 85: 89) sts*
Dec 1 st at each end of next 6 rows.
61 (65: 69: 69: 73: 77) sts
Cont straight until armholes measure 25cm (9¾in),
ending with a WS row.
SHAPE SHOULDERS AND BACK NECK
Cast (bind) off 5 (6: 7: **7: 7: 8**) sts at beg of next
2 rows. *51 (53: 55: 55: 59: 61) sts*
NEXT ROW (RS): Cast (bind) off 5 (6: 7: **7: 7: 8**) sts, patt
until there are 10 (10: 10: **10: 12: 12**) sts on right
needle and turn, leaving rem sts on a holder.
Work each side of neck separately.
Cast (bind) off 4 sts at beg of next row.
Cast (bind) off rem 6 (6: 6: **6: 8: 8**) sts.
With RS facing, rejoin yarn to rem sts, cast (bind) off
center 21 sts, patt to end.
Work to match first side, rev shaping.

front

Work as given for back until there are 16 rows fewer
than on back to start of shoulder shaping, thus ending
with a WS row.
SHAPE NECK
NEXT ROW (RS): Patt 26 (28: 30: **30: 32: 34**) sts and
turn, leaving rem sts on a holder.
Work each side of neck separately.
Keeping patt correct, cast (bind) off 4 sts at beg of
next row. *22 (24: 26: 26: 28: 30) sts*
Dec 1 st at neck edge on next 3 rows, then on foll
2 alt rows. *17 (19: 21: 21: 23: 25) sts.*
Work 3 rows.
Dec 1 st at neck edge on next row.
16 (18: 20: 20: 22: 24) sts
Work 3 rows, thus ending with a WS row.

SHAPE SHOULDER

Cast (bind) off 5 (6: 7: **7: 7: 8**) sts at beg of next and foll alt row.

Work 1 row.

Cast (bind) off rem 6 (6: 6: **6: 8: 8**) sts.

With RS facing, rejoin yarn to rem sts, cast (bind) off center 9 sts, patt to end.

Work to match first side, rev shaping.

sleeves (both alike)

Cast on 49 sts using 6mm (US 10) needles.

ROW 1 (RS): K1, *P1, K3, P1, K1, rep from * to end.

ROW 2: K1, *P5, K1, rep from * to end.

These 2 rows form patt.

Cont in patt, inc 1 st at each end of 21st row (from beg of patt) and every foll 6th (6th: 6th: **8th: 8th: 8th**) row to 57 (57: 57: **67: 67: 67**) sts, then on every foll 8th (8th: 8th: **10th: 10th: 10th**) row until there are 71 sts, taking inc sts into patt.

Cont without further shaping until sleeve measures 52 (52: 52: **57: 57: 57**)cm (20½ [20½: 20½: 22½: 22½: 22½]in), ending with a WS row.

SHAPE TOP

Keeping patt correct, cast (bind) off 4 sts at beg of next 2 rows. *63 sts*

Dec 1 st at each end of next 6 rows.

Cast (bind) off rem 51 sts.

jacket

Ladies' sizes only
back

Cast on 71 (75: 79) sts using 5½mm (US 9) needles.

ROW 1 (RS): [P1, K1] 1 (2: 0) times, K2, *P1, K1, P1, K3, rep from * to last 1 (3: 5) sts, P1, [K1, P1] 0 (1: 1) times, K0 (0: 2).

ROW 2: P0 (1: 3), K0 (1: 1), *P5, K1, rep from * to last 5 (1: 3) sts, P5 (1: 3).

These 2 rows form patt.

Patt another 8 rows, thus ending with a WS row. Change to 6mm (US 10) needles and cont in patt until back measures 48.5 (51: 53.5)cm (19 [20: 21]in), ending with a WS row.

SHAPE ARMHOLES

Keeping patt correct, cast (bind) off 3 sts at beg of next 2 rows. *65 (69: 73) sts*

Dec 1 st at each end of next 7 rows. *51 (55: 59) sts*

Cont straight until armholes measure 20cm (7¾in), ending with a WS row.

SHAPE SHOULDERS AND BACK NECK

Cast (bind) off 4 (5: 6) sts at beg of next 2 rows. *43 (45: 47) sts*

NEXT ROW (RS): Cast (bind) off 4 (5: 6) sts, patt until there are 9 sts on right needle and turn, leaving rem sts on a holder.

Work each side of neck separately.

Cast (bind) off 4 sts at beg of next row.

Cast (bind) off rem 5 sts.

With RS facing, rejoin yarn to rem sts, cast (bind) off center 17 sts, patt to end.

Work to match first side, rev shaping.

left front

Cast on 43 (45: 47) sts using 5½mm (US 9) needles.

ROW 1 (RS): [P1, K1] 1 (2: 0) times, K2, *P1, K1, P1, K3, rep from * to last 3 sts, P1, K1, P1.

ROW 2: P1, K1, *P5, K1, rep from * to last 5 (1: 3) sts, P5 (1: 3).

These 2 rows form patt.

Patt another 8 rows, thus ending with a WS row.

Change to 6mm (US 10) needles and cont in patt until there are 18 rows fewer worked than on back to start of armhole shaping, thus ending with a WS row.

REVERSE PATT FOR LAPEL

NEXT ROW (RS): Patt to last 4 sts, P1, patt to end.

NEXT ROW: Patt 3 sts, K1, patt to end.

Rep last 2 rows once more.

NEXT ROW: Patt to last 5 sts, P2, patt to end.

NEXT ROW: Patt 3 sts, K2, patt to end.

Rep last 2 rows once more.

NEXT ROW: Patt to last 6 sts, P3, patt to end.

NEXT ROW: Patt 3 sts, K3, patt to end.

Rep last 2 rows 4 times more.

SHAPE ARMHOLES

Keeping patt correct as now set, cast (bind) off 3 sts at beg of next row. *40 (42: 44) sts*

Work 1 row.

Dec 1 st at armhole edge on next 4 rows.
36 (38: 40) sts

NEXT ROW (RS): Work 2 tog, patt to last 10 sts, P1, patt to end.

NEXT ROW: Patt 9 sts, K1, patt to last 2 sts, work 2 tog.

NEXT ROW: Work 2 tog, patt to last 10 sts, P1, patt to end. *33 (35: 37) sts*

NEXT ROW: Patt 9 sts, K1, patt to end.

NEXT ROW (RS): Patt to last 11 sts, P2, patt to end.

NEXT ROW: Patt 9 sts, K2, patt to end.

Rep last 2 rows once more.

NEXT ROW (RS): Patt to last 12 sts, P3, patt to end.

NEXT ROW: Patt 9 sts, K3, patt to end.

Last 2 rows now form patt.

Cont straight until there are 15 rows fewer than on back to start of shoulder shaping, thus ending with a RS row.

SHAPE NECK

Cast (bind) off 15 sts at beg of next row.
18 (20: 22) sts

Dec 1 st at neck edge on next and foll 3 alt rows, then on foll 4th row. *13 (15: 17) sts*

Work 3 rows, thus ending with a WS row.

SHAPE SHOULDER

Cast (bind) off 4 (5: 6) sts at beg of next and foll alt row.

Work 1 row. Cast (bind) off rem 5 sts.

right front

Cast on 43 (45: 47) sts using 5½mm (US 9) needles.

ROW 1 (RS): *P1, K1, P1, K3, rep from * to last 1 (3: 5) sts, P1, [K1, P1] 0 (1: 1) times, K0 (0: 2).

ROW 2: P0 (1: 3), K0 (1: 1), *P5, K1, rep from * to last st, P1.

These 2 rows form patt.

Complete to match left front, rev shaping.

sleeves (both alike)

Cast on 39 sts using 6mm (US 10) needles.

ROW 1 (RS): P1, *K1, P1, rep from * to end.

This row forms moss (seed) st.

Work a further 25 rows in moss (seed) st, inc 1 st at each end of 21st row (from beg of moss (seed) st) and thus ending with a WS row. *41 sts*

NEXT ROW (RS): [K1, P1] twice, *K3, P1, K1, P1, rep from * to last st, K1.

NEXT ROW: P2, *K1, P5, rep from * to last 3 sts, K1, P2.

Last 2 rows form patt.

Cont in patt, inc 1 st at each end of every foll 10th

row (from previous inc) until there are 57 sts, taking inc sts into patt. Cont without further shaping until sleeve measures 55cm (21½in), ending with a WS row.

SHAPE TOP
Keeping patt correct, cast (bind) off 3 sts at beg of next 2 rows. *51 sts.*
Dec 1 st at each end of next 6 rows.
Cast (bind) off rem 39 sts.

finishing
Press all pieces as described on the information page.
Pullover
Join right shoulder seam using back stitch.
NECK BORDER
With RS facing and using 6mm (US 10) needles, pick up and knit 23 sts down left front neck, 9 sts across front neck, 23 sts up right front neck and 29 sts across back neck. *84 sts*
ROW 1 (WS OF BODY, RS OF COLLAR): *K3, P1, K1, P1, rep from * to end.
ROW 2: *P1, K1, P4, rep from * to end.
Rep last 2 rows for 15cm (6in).
Cast (bind) off loosely and evenly in patt.
See information page for finishing instructions.
Jacket
Join both shoulder seams using back stitch.
COLLAR
Cast on 71 sts using 5½mm (US 9) needles.
Work in moss (seed) st as for sleeves, inc 1 st at each end of 3rd and every foll 4th row until there are 81 sts, taking inc sts into moss (seed) st. Place markers at both ends of last row. Cont straight until collar measures 12.5cm (5in). Cast (bind) off loosely and evenly in moss (seed) st.
Sew collar to neck edge as folls: position markers on collar 6 sts from front opening edges, match shaped row-end edges of collar to rem 9 cast- (bound-) off sts, then sew cast- (bound-) on edge of collar to rem neck edge.
POCKETS (MAKE TWO)
Cast on 21 sts using 6mm (US 10) needles.
ROW 1 (RS): P1, K1, P1, *K3, P1, K1, P1, rep from * to end.
ROW 2: P1, *K1, P5, rep from * to last 2 sts, K1, P1.
These 2 rows form patt.
Cont in patt until pocket measures 14cm (5½in), ending with a WS row. Cast (bind) off in patt.
Sew pockets onto fronts, matching patt and positioning lower edge of pocket 5cm (2in) above cast-on edge of front.
BELT
Cast on 7 sts using 5½mm (US 9) needles.
Work in moss (seed) st as for sleeves for 150cm (59in).
Cast (bind) off.
See information page for finishing instructions.

odd job by Kim Hargreaves

SIZES	1ST	2ND	3RD	4TH	5TH	6TH	7TH	8TH	9TH	
	6MTHS	9MTHS	1–2YRS	2–3YRS	3–4YRS	4–5YRS	6–7YRS	8–9YRS	9–10YRS	
Actual width	29.5	31.5	35	38	40.5	44	47	50.5	55	cm
	11½	12½	13½	15	16	17½	18½	20	21½	in
Length	30.5	33	38	42	45	49.5	53.5	57	61	cm
	12	13	15	16½	17½	19½	21	22½	24	in
Sleeve length	19	20	23	25	28	30.5	35.5	38	40.5	cm
	7½	8	9	10	11	12	14	15	16	in

YARN

Rowan Magpie Aran 100gm (3½oz) balls:

A	Raven	62	2	3	3	4	4	5	5	6	7
B	Dapple	450	1	1	1	1	1	1	1	1	1

NEEDLES

1 pair 4mm (US 6) needles
1 pair 5mm (US 8) needles

BUTTONS

5

TENSION (GAUGE)

18 sts and 23 rows to 10cm (4in) measured over stocking (stockinette) stitch using 5mm (US 8) needles

pullover
back

Cast on 52 (56: 62: 68: 72: 78: 84: 90: 98) sts using 4mm (US 6) needles and yarn A, then work in two-color rib as folls:

ROW 1 (RS): P0 (0: 2: 0: 0: 2: 0: 2: 2) in A (K2 in B, P2 in A) to end.

ROW 2: (K2 in A, P2 in B) to last 0 (0: 2: 0: 0: 2: 0: 2: 2) sts, K0 (0: 2: 0: 0: 2: 0: 2: 2) in A.

Rep these 2 rows twice more, inc 1 st at end of last row. *53 (57: 63: 69: 73: 79: 85: 91: 99) sts*
Change to 5mm (US 8) needles.

* Working between markers for appropriate size and using the Fair Isle technique as described on the information page, cont in patt from chart until chart row 38 is complete.

Using yarn A only, cont in st st until work measures 30.5 (33: 38: 42: 45: 49.5: 53.5: 57: 61)cm (12 [13: 15: 16½: 17¾: 19½: 21: 22½: 24]in) from cast-on edge, ending with a WS row. **

SHAPE SHOULDERS AND BACK NECK

Cast (bind) off 5 (6: 6: 7: 7: 8: 9: 10: 11) sts at beg of next 2 rows.

Cast (bind) off 6 (6: 7: 7: 8: 9: 9: 10: 11) sts, K10 (10: 11: 12: 12: 13: 14: 14: 16) and turn, leaving rem sts on a holder.

Work each side of neck separately.

Cast (bind) off 4 sts, patt to end.

Cast (bind) off rem 6 (6: 7: 8: 8: 9: 10: 10: 12) sts.

With RS facing, slip center 11 (13: 15: 17: 19: 19: 21: 23: 23) sts onto a holder for back neck, rejoin yarn to rem sts, patt to end.

Complete to match first side, rev shaping.

front

Work as for back until front is 10 (10: 10: 12: 12: 12: 12: 14: 14) rows shorter than back to shoulder shaping, ending with a WS row.

SHAPE FRONT NECK

Knit 23 (25: 27: 30: 32: 35: 38: 40: 44) and turn, leaving rem sts on a holder.

Work each side of neck separately.

Cast (bind) off 3 sts, P to end.

Dec 1 st at neck edge on next 3 (4: 4: 5: 5: 5: 5: 5: 5) rows and 0 (0: 0: 0: 1: 1: 2: 2: 2) alt rows.
17 (18: 20: 22: 23: 26: 28: 30: 34) sts

Cont without further shaping until front matches back to shoulder shaping, ending with a WS row.

SHAPE SHOULDER

Cast (bind) off 5 (6: 6: 7: 7: 8: 9: 10: 11) sts at beg of next row and 6 (6: 7: 7: 8: 9: 9: 10: 11) sts at beg of foll alt row. Work 1 row.

Cast (bind) off rem 6 (6: 7: 8: 8: 9: 10: 10: 12) sts.

With RS facing slip center 7 (7: 9: 9: 9: 9: 9: 11: 11) sts onto a holder for front neck, K to end.

Complete as for first side, rev all shaping.

sleeves (both alike)

Cast on 24 (24: 28: 28: 32: 32: 38: 38: 38) sts using 4mm (US 6) needles and yarn A.

Work 6 rows in two-color rib as folls:

ROW 1 (RS): P0 (0: 0: 0: 0: 0: 2: 2: 2) in A, (K2 in B, P2 in A) to end.

ROW 2: (K2 in A, P2 in B) to last 0 (0: 0: 0: 0: 0: 2: 2: 2) sts, K0 (0: 0: 0: 0: 0: 2: 2: 2) in A.

Rep these 2 rows twice more, inc 1 st at end of last row. *25 (25: 29: 29: 33: 33: 39: 39: 39) sts*

*Change to 5mm (US 8) needles and, working between appropriate markers, work 12 rows in patt from chart and AT THE SAME TIME shape sides by inc 1 st at each end of 3rd row and 3 foll 3rd rows.

1st, 2nd, 3rd, 4th, 5th & 6th sizes only
Using yarn A, work in st st, inc every foll 3rd row to 45 (47: 53: 57: 65: 69) sts.

7th, 8th & 9th sizes only
Using yarn A, work in st st, inc every foll 3rd row to 49 (49: 61) sts and then every foll 4th row to 73 (77: 83) sts.

All sizes
Cont without further shaping until work measures 19 (20: 23: 25: 28: 30.5: 35.5: 38: 40.5)cm (7½ [7¾: 9: 9¾: 11¼: 12: 14: 15: 16]in), from cast-on edge, ending with a WS row.

Cast (bind) off loosely and evenly.

cardigan
back

Cast on 53 (57: 63: 69: 73: 79: 85: 91: 99) sts using 4mm (US 6) needles and yarn A and work in moss (seed) st as folls:

ROW 1 (RS): K1, *P1, K1, rep from * to end.

ROW 2: Work as given for row 1.

Rep these 2 rows twice more.

Change to 5mm (US 8) needles and, joining yarn B, work as given for pullover back from * to **.

SHAPE SHOULDERS AND BACK NECK

Cast (bind) off 6 (6: 7: 8: 8: 9: 10: 10: 12) sts at beg of next 2 rows.

Cast (bind) off 6 (7: 7: 8: 8: 9: 10: 11: 12) sts, K11 (11: 12: 12: 13: 14: 14: 15: 16) turn, leaving rem sts on a holder.

Work each side of neck separately.

Cast (bind) off 4 sts, patt to end.

Cast (bind) off rem 7 (7: 8: 8: 9: 10: 10: 11: 12) sts.

With RS facing, rejoin yarn to rem sts, cast (bind) off center 7 (9: 11: 13: 15: 15: 17: 19: 19) sts, K to end.

Complete to match first side, rev shaping.

sleeves

Cast on 25 (25: 29: 29: 33: 33: 39: 39: 39) sts using 4mm (US 6) needles and yarn A.

Work 6 rows in moss (seed) st as given for back.

Complete as given for pullover sleeve from *.

pocket linings (make 2)
4 larger sizes only

Cast on 19 (21: 23: 23) sts using 5mm (US 8) needles and yarn A.

Work 30 (34: 38: 38) rows in st st, beg with a K row.

Leave sts on a holder.

right front

Cast on 30 (32: 35: 38: 40: 43: 46: 49: 53) sts using 4mm (US 6) needles and yarn A.

Girls' cardigan
Work 5 rows in moss (seed) st.

Boys' cardigan
Work 2 rows in moss (seed) st.

NEXT ROW (BUTTONHOLE ROW) (RS): Work in moss (seed) st to last 4 sts, K2tog, yon, moss (seed) st 2.

NEXT ROW: Work in moss (seed) st to end, working into back of loop made on previous row.

Work 1 row.

KEY
☐ A
☒ B

```
38

30

20

10

12-row
patt
sleeve
```

| 1st |
| 2nd |
| 3rd |
| 4th |
| 5th |
| 6th |
| 7th |
| 8th |
| 9th |

right front ⌐ left front
sleeve 1st & 2nd sizes
sleeve 3rd & 4th sizes
sleeve 5th & 6th sizes
sleeve 7th, 8th & 9th sizes

1st
2nd
3rd
4th
5th
6th
7th
8th
9th

RIGHT AND LEFT FRONTS, BACK AND SLEEVE

Girls' and boys' cardigans

NEXT ROW (WS): Moss (seed) st 4, leave these sts on a holder for front band, moss (seed) st to end.
26 (28: 31: 34: 36: 39: 42: 45: 49) sts
Change to 5mm (US 8) needles.

1st, 2nd, 3rd, 4th & 5th sizes only
Work 38 rows in patt from chart for left front, ending with a WS row.

6th, 7th, 8th & 9th sizes only
Work 30 (34: 38: 38) rows in patt from chart, ending with a WS row.

PLACE POCKETS
NEXT ROW (RS): Using yarn A, K10 (11: 12: 14), slip next 19 (21: 23: 23) sts onto a holder and K across sts from first pocket lining, patt to end.

6th & 7th sizes only
Cont in patt until chart row 38 is complete.

All sizes
Cont in st st using yarn A until work measures 19 (21.5: 25: 27: 28.5: 33: 35.5: 40: 43.5)cm (7½ [8½: 9¾: 10¾: 11¼: 13: 14: 15¾: 17]in), from cast-on edge.

SHAPE FRONT NECK
Dec 1 st at neck edge on next row and every foll 3rd

row to 19 (20: 22: 24: 25: 28: 30: 32: 36) sts.
Cont without further shaping until front matches back to shoulder shaping, ending with a WS row.

SHAPE SHOULDERS
Cast (bind) off 6 (6: 7: 8: 8: 9: 10: 10: 12) sts at beg of next row and 6 (7: 7: 8: 8: 9: 10: 11: 12) sts at beg of foll alt row.
Work 1 row.
Cast (bind) off rem 7 (7: 8: 8: 9: 10: 10: 11: 12) sts.

right front

Cast on 30 (32: 35: 38: 40: 43: 46: 49: 53) sts using 4mm (US 6) needles and yarn A.

Boys' cardigan
Work 5 rows in moss (seed) st.

Girls' cardigan
Work 2 rows in moss (seed) st.
NEXT ROW (BUTTONHOLE ROW) (RS): Moss (seed) st 2, yon, K2tog, moss (seed) st to end.
NEXT ROW: Work in moss (seed) st to end, working into back of loop made on previous row.
Work 1 row.

Girls' and boys' cardigans
NEXT ROW (WS): Moss (seed) st to last 4 sts, turn and leave these 4 sts on a holder for front band.
26 (28: 31: 34: 36: 39: 42: 45: 49) sts
Change to 5mm (US 8) needles and complete as for left front, rev all shaping and placing pockets on larger sizes.

finishing

Press all pieces as described on the information page.

Pullover
Join right shoulder seam using back stitch.

NECK BAND
With RS facing, using 4mm (US 6) needles and yarn A and beg at left shoulder, pick up and knit 16 (16: 16: 18: 18: 18: 20: 20) sts down left front neck, 7 (7: 9: 9: 9: 9: 9: 11: 11) sts from holder, 16 (16: 16: 18: 18: 18: 18: 20: 20) sts up right front neck, 4 sts down back neck, 11 (13: 15: 17: 19: 19: 21: 23: 23) sts from holder and 4 sts up back neck.
58 (60: 64: 70: 72: 72: 74: 82: 82) sts
Work 4 rows in two-color rib.
Cast (bind) off in rib using yarn A.

Cardigan
Join both shoulder seams using back stitch.

BUTTONBAND
(RIGHT FRONT BOYS, LEFT FRONT GIRLS)
Using 4mm (US 6) needles, slip sts from holder onto LH needle, join yarn A and, keeping patt correct, cont in moss (seed) stitch until band fits up front to shoulder and across to center back when slightly stretched. Slip stitch into place. Cast (bind) off.
Mark positions of 5 buttons, the first to match buttonhole in band on oposite front, the last to come 1.5cm (¾in) from front neck shaping and the rem spaced evenly between.

BUTTONHOLE BAND
Work as for button band with the addition of buttonholes worked as before to correspond with markers.

POCKET TOPS
Slip sts from holder onto a 4mm (US 6) needle and work 4 rows in moss (seed) st.
Cast (bind) off in moss (seed) st.
See information page for finishing instructions.

highlander by Kim Hargreaves

SIZES

	1ST 2-3YRS	2ND 3-4YRS	3RD 4-6YRS	4TH 6-8YRS	5TH 8-9YRS	6TH 9-10YRS	
Actual width	38	40.5	44	47	51.5	55	cm
	15	16	17	18½	20	21½	in
Length	39	41	44	48	51	55.5	cm
	15½	16½	17½	19	20	22	in
Sleeve length	25	28	30.5	35.5	38	40.5	cm
	10	11	12	14	15	16	in

YARN

Rowan Magpie Tweed 100gm (3½oz) balls and Rowanspun DK 50gm (1¾oz) balls

1st colorway

A	Magpie	Berry	684	3	3	4	5	7	7
B	DK Spun*	Jade	735	2	3	3	3	4	4
C	DK Spun*	Grass	686	1	1	2	2	2:	2
D	DK Spun*	Purple	687	1	1	2	2	2	2
E	DK Spun*	Blue	696	2	2	3	3	4	4

2nd colorway

A	Magpie	Black	62	3	3	4	5	7	7
B	DK Spun*	Pink	694	2	3	3	3	4	4
C	DK Spun*	Cream	649	1	1	2	2	2	2
D	DK Spun*	Pea	664	1	1	2	2	2	2
E	DK Spun*	Blue	665	2	2	3	3	4	4

*used double throughout

NEEDLES

1 pair 4mm (US 6) needles
1 pair 5mm (US 8) needles

BUTTONS

4 (4: 5: 5: 6: 6)

TENSION (GAUGE)

18 sts and 23 rows to 10cm (4in) measured over patterned stocking (stockinette) stitch using 5mm (US 8) needles

back

Cast on 69 (73: 79: 85: 93: 99) sts using 5mm (US 8) needles and yarn A.

Joining and breaking colors as required, cont in patt from chart for back using the intarsia technique described on the information page. Work until chart row 90 (94: 102: 110: 118: 128) is complete, ending with a WS row.

SHAPE SHOULDERS AND BACK NECK

Cast (bind) off 8 (9: 9: 10: 11: 12) sts at beg of next 2 rows.
Cast (bind) off 8 (9: 10: 11: 11: 12) sts, patt 13 (13: 14: 15: 16: 17) and turn, leaving rem sts on a holder.
Work each side of neck separately.
Cast (bind) off 4 sts, patt to end.
Cast (bind) off rem 9 (9: 10: 11: 12: 13) sts.
With RS facing, rejoin correct yarn, cast (bind) off center 11 (11: 13: 13: 17: 17) sts, patt to end.
Complete to match first side, rev all shaping.

KEY

☐ A
◉ B
☒ C
◼ D
⊡ E

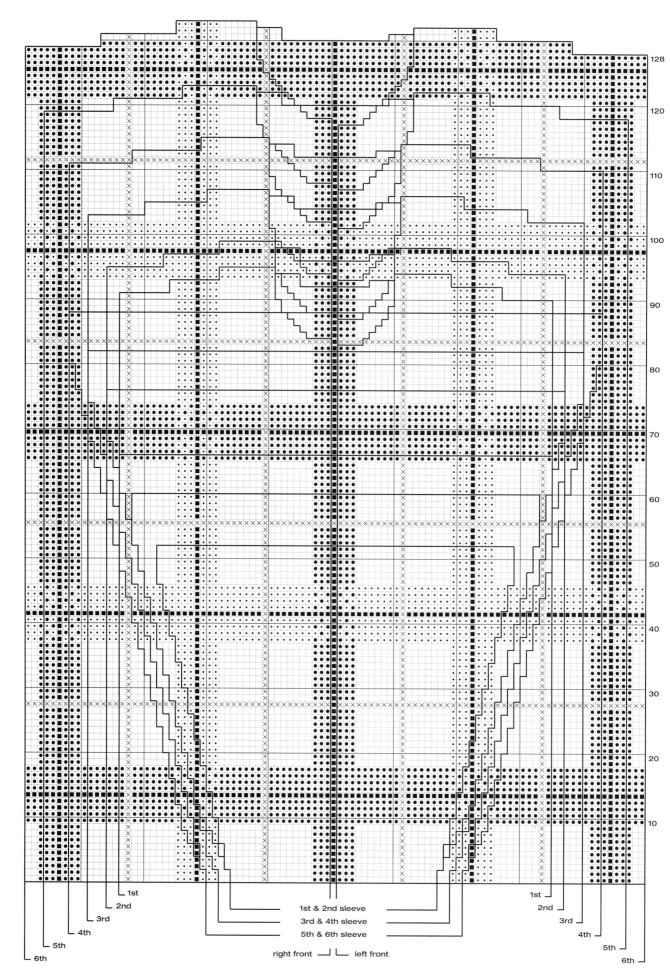

1st
2nd
3rd
4th
5th
6th

1st & 2nd sleeve
3rd & 4th sleeve
5th & 6th sleeve

1st
2nd
3rd
4th
5th
6th

right front ⌐ ⌐ left front

RIGHT AND LEFT FRONTS, BACK AND SLEEVE

left front

Cast on 34 (36: 39: 42: 46: 49) sts using 5mm (US 8) needles and yarn A.

Joining and breaking colors as required, cont in patt from chart for left front until chart row 83 (87: 93: 101: 107: 117) is complete, ending with a RS row.

SHAPE FRONT NECK

Cast (bind) off 4 sts at beg of next row.

Dec 1 st at neck edge on next 4 (4: 5: 5: 7: 7) rows and 1 foll alt row. *25 (27: 29: 32: 34: 37) sts*

Cont without further shaping until front matches back to shoulder shaping, ending with a WS row.

SHAPE SHOULDER

Keeping patt correct, cast (bind) off 8 (9: 9: 10: 11: 12) sts at beg of next row and 8 (9: 10: 11: 11: 12) sts at beg of foll alt row.

Work 1 row. Cast (bind) off rem 9 (9: 10: 11: 12: 13) sts.

right front

Work as for left front, rev all shaping and following chart for right front.

sleeves (both alike)

Cast on 33 (33: 37: 37: 41: 41) sts using 4mm (US 6) needles and yarn A. Work 6 rows in moss (seed) st.

Change to 5mm (US 8) needles and, working between markers for appropriate size, cont in patt from chart for sleeve until chart row 52 (60: 66: 76: 82: 88) is complete. AT THE SAME TIME shape sides by inc 1 st at each end of 3rd row and 0 (5: 1: 1: 0: 3) foll alt rows and then every foll 4th row to 57 (65: 69: 73: 79: 85) sts, ending with a WS row.

Cast (bind) off loosely and evenly.

finishing

Press all pieces as described on the information page. Join both shoulder seams using back stitch.

BUTTON BAND

(Left side girl, right side boy)

Cast on 5 sts using 4mm (US 6) needles and work in moss (seed) st until band fits neatly up front edge to beg neck shaping, ending with a WS row. Slipstitch into place. Cast (bind) off.

Mark position of 4 (4: 5: 5: 6: 6) buttons, the first to come 1.5cm (¾in) from cast-on edge, the last 1.5cm (¾in) from neck edge and the others spaced evenly between.

BUTTONHOLE BAND

Work as for button band with the addition of 4 (4: 5: 5: 6: 6) buttonholes, worked to correspond with button markers as folls:

BUTTONHOLE ROW (RS): Patt 2, yon twice, patt 2 tog, patt 1.

NEXT ROW: Work across row in patt, dropping one of loops made on previous row.

COLLAR

Cast on 53 (53: 59: 59: 67: 67) sts using 4mm (US 6) needles.

ROW 1: K2, moss (seed) st to last 2 sts, K2.

ROW 2: Work as given for row 1.

ROW 3: K2, M1, moss (seed) st to last 2 sts, M1, K2.

Rep these 3 rows until collar measures 6 (6: 7: 8: 9: 10)cm (2½ [2½: 2¾: 3¼: 3½: 4]in), from cast-on edge.

Cast (bind) off in moss (seed) st.

See information page for finishing instructions.

Make a fringe along bottom edge of garment. Use 4 lengths of yarn, each 18cm (7in) long, and knot through every 2nd st.

shark by Brandon Mably

SIZES	S	M	L	XL	
To fit chest	97	102	107	112	cm
	38	40	42	44	in
Actual width	63	66	68.5	71.5	cm
	25	26	27	28	in
Length	68	69	70	71	cm
	27	27	27½	28	in
Sleeve length	49	49	50	50	cm
	19½	19½	19½	19½	in

YARN

Rowan Wool Cotton 50gm (1¾oz) balls:

First colorway

A French Navy	909	15	15	16	16
B Rich	911	1	1	1	1

Second colorway

A Inky	908	15	15	16	16
B Beechnut	938	1	1	1	1

NEEDLES

1 pair 3¼mm (US 3) needles
1 pair 4mm (US 6) needles

TENSION (GAUGE)

22 sts and 30 rows to 10cm (4in) measured over patterned stocking (stockinette) stitch using 4mm (US 6) needles

back

Cast on 139 (145: 151: 157) sts using 3¼mm (US 3) needles and yarn A.
ROW 1 (RS): P2, *K3, P3, rep from * to last 5 sts, K3, P2.
ROW 2: K2, *P3, K3, rep from * to last 5 sts, P3, K2.
These 2 rows form rib.
Work another 14 rows in rib.
Change to 4mm (US 6) needles.
Beg with a K row, cont in st st until back measures 40 (41: 41: 42)cm (15¾ [16¼: 16¼: 16½]in), ending with a WS row.

SHAPE ARMHOLES

Cast (bind) off 4 sts at beg of next 2 rows.
131 (137: 143: 149) sts.
Dec 1 st at each end of next 7 rows.
117 (123 129: 135) sts
Cont straight until armhole measures 28 (28: 29: 29)cm (11¼ [11¼: 11½: 11½]in), ending with a WS row.

SHAPE SHOULDERS AND BACK NECK

Cast (bind) off 12 (13: 14: 15) sts at beg of next 2 rows.
93 (97: 101: 105) sts

NEXT ROW (RS): Cast (bind) off 12 (13: 14: 15) sts, K until there are 16 (17: 18: 19) sts on right needle and turn, leaving rem sts on a holder.
Work each side of neck separately.
Cast (bind) off 4 sts at beg of next row.
Cast (bind) off rem 12 (13: 14: 15) sts.
With RS facing, rejoin yarn to rem sts, cast (bind) off center 37 sts, K to end.
Work to match first side, rev shaping.

front

Work as for back until front measures 22cm (8½in) from cast-on edge, ending with a WS row.
Join yarn B and place chart as folls:
NEXT ROW: K16 (19: 22: 25), starting with chart row 1 and using the intarsia method as described on the information page, work 107 sts from chart, K16 (19: 22: 25).
NEXT ROW: P16 (19: 22: 25), work across row 2 from chart, P16 (19: 22: 25).
Cont working from chart until row 98 has been completed. Then cont in st st using yarn A only and AT THE SAME TIME work as for back until there are 22 rows fewer than on back to start of shoulder shaping, ending with a WS row.

SHAPE NECK

NEXT ROW (RS): K50 (53: 56: 59) and turn, leaving rem sts on a holder.
Work each side of neck separately.
Cast (bind) off 4 sts at beg of next row. *46 (49: 52: 55) sts*
Dec 1 st at neck edge on next 5 rows, then on foll 4 alt rows, then on foll 4th row. *36 (39: 42: 45) sts*
Work 3 rows, ending with a WS row.

SHAPE SHOULDER

Cast (bind) off 12 (13: 14: 15) sts at beg of next and foll alt row.
Work 1 row. Cast (bind) off rem 12 (13: 14: 15) sts.
With RS facing, rejoin yarn to rem sts, cast (bind) off center 17 sts, K to end.
Work to match first side, rev shaping.

sleeves (both alike)

Cast on 67 (67: 69: 69) sts using 3¼mm (US 3) needles and yarn A.
ROW 1 (RS): K2 (2: 3: 3), P3, *K3, P3, rep from * to last 2 (2: 3: 3) sts, K2 (2: 3: 3).
ROW 2: P2 (2: 3: 3), K3, *P3, K3, rep from * to last 2 (2: 3: 3) sts, P2 (2: 3: 3).
These 2 rows form rib. Work another 14 rows in rib.
Change to 4mm (US 6) needles. Beg with a K row, cont

until there are 73 (73: 75: 7 5) sts, then on every foll 6th row until there are 123 (123: 127: 127) sts.
Cont straight until sleeve measures 49 (49: 50: 50)cm (19½ [19½: 19¾: 19¾]in), from cast-on edge, ending with a WS row.

SHAPE TOP
Cast (bind) off 4 sts at beg of next 2 rows.
115 (115: 119: 119) sts.
Dec 1 st at each end of next and foll 4 alt rows.
Work 1 row, ending with a WS row.
Cast (bind) off rem 105 (105: 109: 109) sts.

finishing

Press all pieces as described on the info page.
Join right shoulder seam using back stitch.

Crew neck version only
NECKBAND
With RS facing, 3¼mm (US 3) needles and yarn A, pick up and knit 29 sts down left side of neck, 17 sts from front, 29 sts up right side of neck and 45 sts from back. *120 sts*
ROW 1 (WS): *K3, P3, rep from * to end.
Rep row until neckband measures 5cm (2in).

High-neck version
NECKBAND
With RS facing, 4mm (US 6) needles and yarn A, pick up and knit 29 sts down left side of neck, 17 sts from front, 29 sts up right side of neck, and 45 sts from back. *120 sts*
ROW 1 (WS): *K3, P3, rep from * to end.
Rep last row until neckband measures 10cm (4in).

Both versions
Cast (bind) off in rib.
See information page for finishing instructions, setting in sleeves using the set-in method.

KEY
☐ A
⊡ B

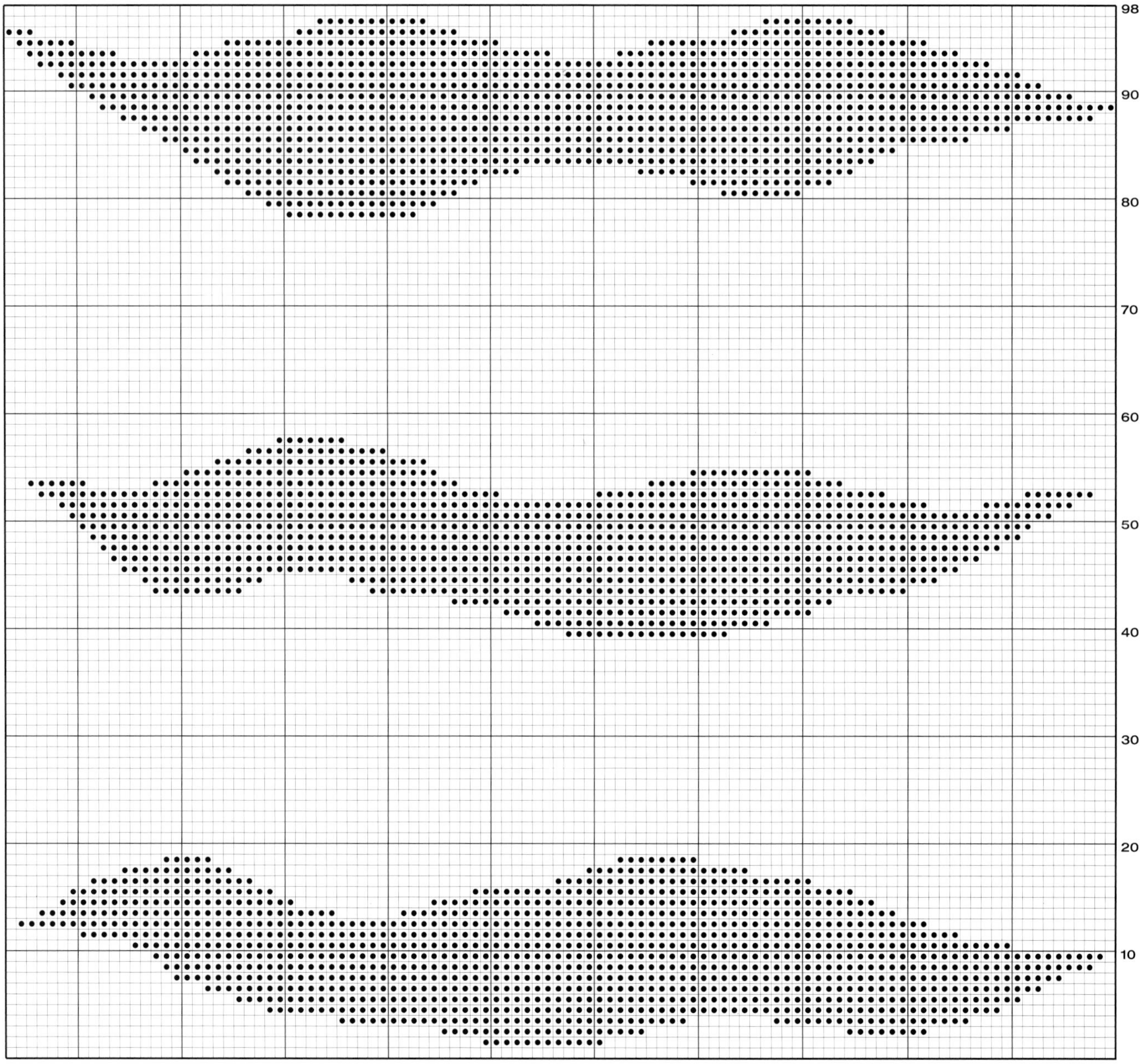

FRONT MOTIF

zebra by Kim Hargreaves

SIZE				
	S	**M**	**L**	
To fit bust	86	91	97	cm
	34	36	38	in
Actual width	53	55.5	59.5	cm
	21	22	23½	in
Length	73.5	76.5	80	cm
	29	30	31½	in
Sleeve length	43.5	43.5	43.5	cm
	17	17	17	in

YARN

Rowan Chunky Chenille 100gm (3½oz) balls

Two-color version

A Parchment	383	6	6	6
B Black	367	5	5	5

One-color version

Lush	382	11	11	11

NEEDLES

1 pair 4mm (US 6) needles
1 pair 4½mm (US 7) needles

BUTTONS

6

TENSION (GAUGE)

16 sts and 24 rows to 10cm (4in) measured over stocking (stockinette) stitch using 4½mm (US 7) needles

two-color version
back

Cast on 85 (89: 95) sts using 4mm (US 6) needles and yarn A.
Work in garter st (knit every row) for 2.5cm (1in), ending with a WS row.
Change to 4½mm (US 7) needles.
Beg and ending rows as indicated and using the intarsia technique described on the information page, work 16 (20: 24) rows in patt from body chart, which is worked entirely in st st, beg with a K row and ending with a WS row.
Keeping chart correct, shape side seams by dec 1 st at each end of next and every foll 6th row until 69 (73: 79) sts rem.
Cont without further shaping until chart row 76 (80: 86) has been worked, thus ending with a WS row.
Inc 1 st at each end of next and every foll 4th row

until there are 85 (89: 95) sts.
Cont without further shaping until chart row 114 (122: 130) has been worked, thus ending with a WS row.
SHAPE ARMHOLES
Keeping chart correct, cast (bind) off 4 sts at beg of next 2 rows. *77 (81: 87) sts*
Dec 1 st at each end of next 5 rows, then on every foll alt row until 61 (65: 71) sts rem.
Cont without further shaping until chart row 170 (178: 186) has been worked, thus ending with a WS row.
SHAPE BACK NECK AND SHOULDERS
Cast (bind) off 6 (6: 7) sts at beg of next 2 rows. *49 (53: 57) sts*
NEXT ROW (RS): Cast (bind) off 6 (7: 8) sts, patt until there are 10 (11: 12) sts on right needle and turn, leaving rem sts on a holder.
Work each side of neck separately.
Cast (bind) off 4 sts at beg of next row.
Cast (bind) off rem 6 (7: 8) sts.
With RS facing, rejoin yarn to rem sts, cast (bind) off center 17 sts, patt to end.
Work to match first side, rev shaping.

pocket linings (make 2)

Cast on 20 sts using 4½mm (US 7) needles and yarn A.
Beg with a K row, work 36 (38: 40) rows in st st.
Break yarn and leave sts on a holder.

left front

Cast on 43 (45: 48) sts using 4mm (US 6) needles and yarn A.
Work in garter st for 2.5cm (1in), ending with a WS row.
Change to 4½mm (US 7) needles.
Beg and ending rows as indicated, work 16 (20: 24) rows in patt from body chart, thus ending with a WS row.
Keeping chart correct, shape side seam by dec 1 st at beg of next and every foll 6th row until 39 (42: 45) sts rem.
Work 1 (5: 3) rows, thus ending with a WS row.
PLACE POCKET
NEXT ROW (RS): [Patt 2 tog] 0 (1: 0) times, patt 7 (7: 11) sts, slip next 20 sts onto a holder, patt across 20 sts of first pocket lining, patt 12 (13: 14) sts. *39 (41: 45) sts*
Cont foll chart, dec 1 st at beg of every foll 6th row from previous dec until 35 (37: 40) sts rem.
Cont without further shaping until chart row 76 (80: 86) has been worked, thus ending with a WS row.
Inc 1 st at beg of next and every foll 4th row until there are 43 (45: 48) sts.

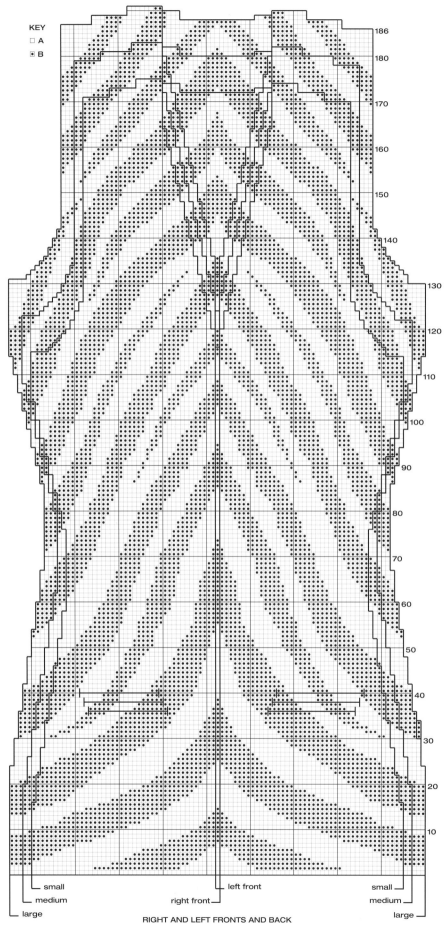

KEY

☐ A

▣ B

small
medium
large

left front
right front

small
medium
large

RIGHT AND LEFT FRONTS AND BACK

Cont without shaping until chart row 114 (122: 130) has been worked, thus ending with a WS row.

SHAPE ARMHOLE

Keeping chart correct, cast (bind) off 4 sts at beg of next row. *39 (41: 44) sts*

Work 1 row, thus ending with a WS row.

SHAPE FRONT SLOPE

Place marker at beg of last row to denote start of front slope shaping.

Dec 1 st at armhole edge on next 5 rows, then on foll 3 alt rows and AT THE SAME TIME dec 1 st at front slope edge on next and every foll 4th row. *28 (30: 33) sts* Dec 1 st at front slope edge only on every foll 4th row from previous dec until 18 (20: 23) sts rem.

Work 5 rows, thus ending with chart row 170 (178: 186) and a WS row.

SHAPE SHOULDER

Cast (bind) off 6 (6: 7) sts at beg of next row, then 6 (7: 8) sts at beg of foll alt row.

Work 1 row.

Cast (bind) off rem 6 (7: 8) sts.

right front

Work as for left front, rev all shapins and placing pocket as folls:

PLACE POCKET

NEXT ROW (RS): Patt 12 (13: 14) sts, slip next 20 sts on a holder, patt across 20 sts of second pocket lining, patt 7 (7: 11) sts, [patt 2 tog] 0 (1: 0) times. *39 (41: 45) sts*

sleeves (both alike)

Cast on 33 sts using 4½mm (US 7) needles and yarn A. Beg with a K row, work in patt from sleeve chart, shaping sides by inc 1 st at each end of 21st and every foll 8th row until there are 49 sts, then on every foll 10th row until there are 53 sts, taking inc sts into patt. Cont without further shaping until chart row 104 has been worked, ending with a WS row.

SHAPE TOP

Keeping chart correct, cast (bind) off 4 sts at beg of next 2 rows. *45 sts*

Dec 1 st at each end of next and foll 2 alt rows, then on every foll 4th row until 31 sts rem.

Work 1 row, thus ending with a WS row.

Dec 1 st at each end of next and foll 2 alt rows. *25 sts*

Dec 1 st at each end of next 5 rows, thus ending with a WS row.

Cast (bind) off rem 15 sts.

one-color version

Work as for two-color version but using one color throughout.

finishing

Press all pieces as described on the information page. Join both shoulder seams using back stitch.

BUTTON BAND

With RS facing, using 4mm (US 6) needles and yarn A, pick up and knit 77 (82: 87) sts evenly along left front opening edge between start of front slope shaping and cast-on edge. K 2 rows.

Cast (bind) off knitwise.

BUTTONHOLE BAND

With RS facing, using 4mm (US 6) needles and yarn A, pick up and knit 77 (82: 87) sts evenly along right front opening edge between cast-on edge and start of front slope shaping.

K1 row.

NEXT ROW (RS) (BUTTONHOLE ROW): K2, *K2tog, yfwd
twice to make a buttonhole (drop extra loop on next
row), K12 (13: 14), rep from * 4 times more, K2tog,
yfwd twice to make a buttonhole (drop extra loop on
next row), K3.

Cast (bind) off knitwise.

LEFT COLLAR

Cast on 3 sts using 4½mm (US 7) needles and yarn A.
K 4 rows, inc 1 st at end of 3rd of these rows. *4 sts*
Now work in fringe patt as folls:

ROW 1 (RS): Cast on 4 sts and then cast (bind) off same
4 sts (now termed "fringe 1"), K1, fringe 1, K1.

ROW 2: Inc in first st, K1, P1, K1. *5 sts*

ROWS 3 & 4: Knit.

ROW 5: (K1, fringe 1) twice, inc in last st. *6 sts*

ROW 6: P2, (K1, P1) twice.

ROW 7: Knit.

ROW 8: Inc in first st, K to end. *7 sts*

ROW 9: (Fringe 1, K1) 3 times, K2.

ROW 10: P1, (P1, K1) 3 times.

ROW 11: K to last st, inc in last st. *8 sts*

ROW 12: Knit.

ROW 13: (K1, fringe 1) 3 times, K2.

ROW 14: Inc in first st, P1, (K1, P1) 3 times. *9 sts*

ROWS 15 & 16: Knit.

ROW 17: (Fringe 1, K1) 4 times, inc in last st. *10 sts*

ROW 18: P3, K1, (P1, K1) 3 times.

ROW 19: Knit.

ROW 20: Inc in first st, K to end. *11 sts*

ROW 21: (K1, fringe 1) 5 times, K1.

ROW 22: P1, (K1, P1) 5 times.

These 22 rows set position of patt and start to shape
inner edge. Keeping patt correct as now set, inc 1 st at
end of next row and at the same edge on every foll
3rd row until there are 26 sts, taking inc sts into patt.
Patt another 21 rows, thus ending after a WS row that
is after a fringe row.

Cast (bind) off.

RIGHT COLLAR

Cast on 3 sts using 4½mm (US 7) needles and yarn A.
K 4 rows, inc 1 st at beg of 3rd of these rows. *4 sts*
Now work in fringe patt as folls:

ROW 1 (RS): (K1, fringe 1) twice.

ROW 2: K1, P1, K1, inc in last st. *5 sts*

ROWS 3 & 4: Knit.

ROW 5: Inc in first st, (fringe 1, K1) twice. *6 sts*

ROW 6: (P1, K1) twice, P2.

ROW 7: Knit.

ROW 8: K5, inc in last st. *7 sts*

ROW 9: K1, (K1, fringe 1) 3 times.

ROW 10: (K1, P1) 3 times, P1.

ROW 11: Inc in first st, K6. *8 sts*

ROW 12: Knit.

ROW 13: K2, (fringe 1, K1) 3 times.

ROW 14: (P1, K1) 3 times, P1, inc in last st. *9 sts*

ROWS 15 & 16: Knit.

ROW 17: Inc in first st, (K1, fringe 1) 4 times. *10 sts*

ROW 18: (K1, P1) 3 times, K1, P3.

ROW 19: Knit.

ROW 20: K9, inc in last st. *11 sts*

ROW 21: (K1, fringe 1) 5 times, K1.

ROW 22: P1, (K1, P1) 5 times.

Complete to match left collar, rev shaping. Join cast-
(bound-) off edges of collar pieces. Sew collar to neck
edge, matching cast-on edges to top of button, and
buttonhole bands and collar seam to center back neck.

POCKET TOPS

Slip 20 pocket sts onto 4mm (US 6) needles and
rejoin yarn A with RS facing. K 3 rows, ending with
a RS row.
Cast (bind) off knitwise.

BELT

Cast on 230 sts using 4mm (US 6) needles and yarn A.
K 10 rows
Cast (bind) off loosely and evenly knitwise.

CUFFS

Cast on 33 sts using 4½mm (US 7) needles and yarn A.
K 4 rows.
Now work in fringe patt as folls:
ROW 1 (RS): *K1, fringe 1, rep from * to last st, K1.
ROW 2: P1, *K1, P1, rep from to * end.
ROWS 3 & 4: Knit.
ROW 5: K2, *fringe 1, K1, rep from * to last st, K1.
ROW 6: P2, *K1, P1, rep from * to last st, P1.
ROW 7 & 8: Knit.
Rep the last 8 rows twice more.
K 2 rows.
Cast (bind) off knitways.
Join row ends of cuff to form ring. With RS of cuff
to WS of sleeve, sew cuff to sleeve cast-on edge.
Fold cuff back to RS.
See information page for finishing instructions.

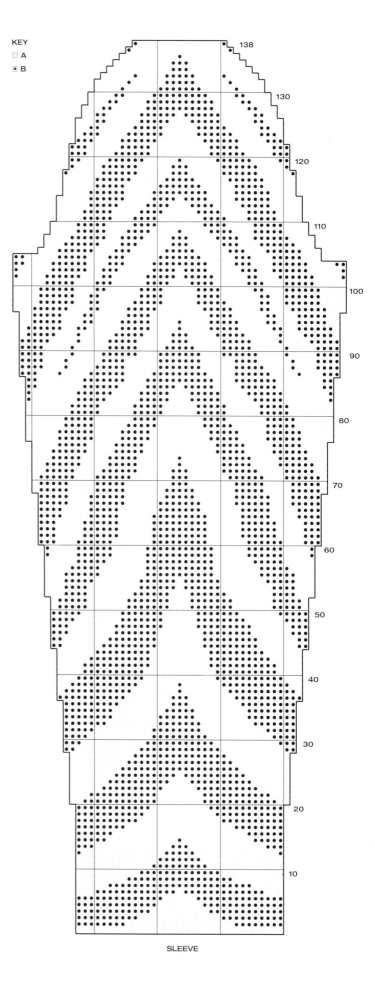

KEY
☐ A
▣ B

138
130
120
110
100
90
80
70
60
50
40
30
20
10

SLEEVE

block pullover by Kim Hargreaves

SIZES

	1ST	2ND	3RD	4TH	5TH	
To fit bust	81	86	91	97	102	cm
	32	34	36	38	40	in
Actual width	59	61	63.5	65.6	68	cm
	23	24	25	26	27	in
Length	72	73	74	75	76	cm
	28½	28½	29	29½	30	in
Sleeve length	46	46	46	46	46	cm
	18	18	18	18	18	in

YARNS

Rowan Magpie Aran 100gm (3½oz) balls:

		1ST	2ND	3RD	4TH	5TH
A Charcoal	625	4	4	4	5	5
B Mulled	315	2	2	2	3	3
C Steam	316	2	3	3	3	3
D Shakespear	317	3	3	3	3	3
E Raven	062	2	3	3	3	3

NEEDLES

1 pair 4mm (US 6) needles
1 pair 5mm (US 8) needles
Short 4mm (US 6) 18in circular needle

TENSION (GAUGE)

18 sts and 23 rows to 10cm (4in) measured over patterned stocking (stockinette) stitch using 5mm (US 8) needles

back and front (both alike)

Cast on 106 (110: 114: 118: 122) sts using 4mm (US 6) needles and yarn A.
Knit 8 rows.
Change to 5mm (US 8) needles.
Using the intarsia technique described on the information page, joining and breaking colors as required and beg with a K row, work in patt from body chart, which is worked entirely in st st, as follows:
Cont in patt from chart until row 104 (106: 108: 110: 112) is complete, thus ending with a WS row.

SHAPE ARMHOLES

Keeping chart correct, cast (bind) off 5 sts at beg of next 2 rows. *96 (100: 104: 108: 112) sts*
Cont straight until chart row 162 (164: 166: 168: 170) is complete, thus ending with a WS row.

SHAPE SHOULDERS

Keeping chart correct, cast (bind) off 8 (8: 9: 9: 10) sts at beg of next 4 rows, then 8 (9: 9: 10: 10) sts at beg of foll 2 rows.
Leave rem 48 (50: 50: 52: 52) sts on a holder.

KEY
A
B
C
D
E

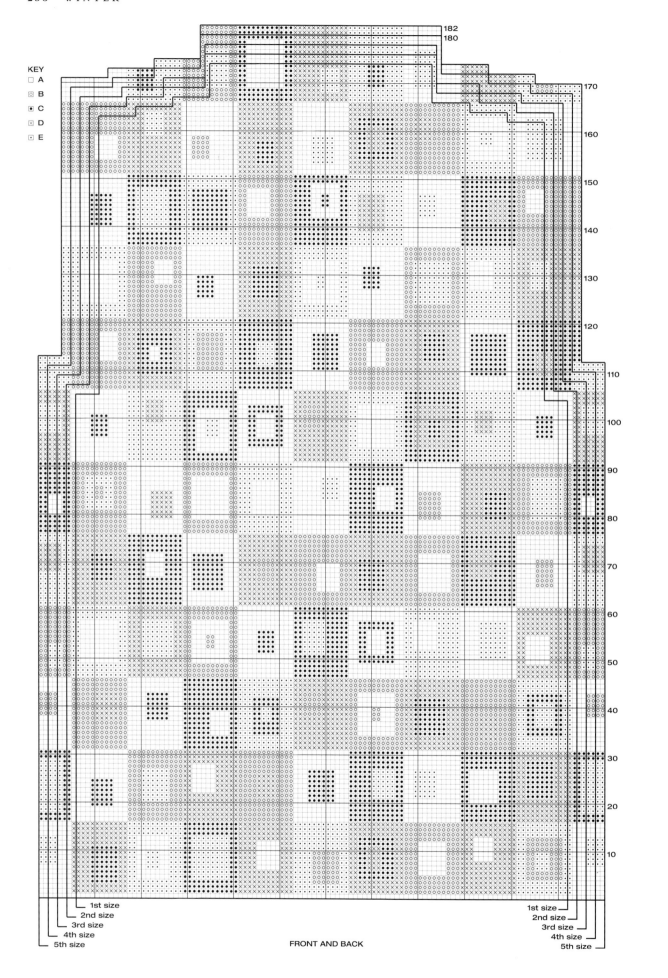

182
180
170
160
150
140
130
120
110
100
90
80
70
60
50
40
30
20
10

1st size
2nd size
3rd size
4th size
5th size

1st size
2nd size
3rd size
4th size
5th size

FRONT AND BACK

sleeves (both alike)

Cast on 54 sts using 4mm (US 6) needles and yarn A.
Knit 8 rows.

Change to 5mm (US 8) needles and work in patt
from sleeve chart as follows:

Inc 1 st at each end of chart row 3 and every foll 6th
row to 72 sts, then on every foll 4th row until there
are 90 sts, taking inc sts into patt.

Cont without further shaping until chart row 100 is
complete, thus ending with a WS row.

Cast (bind) off.

finishing

Press all pieces as described on the information page.
Join shoulder seams using back stitch.

NECK BORDER

Slip sts from front and back holders onto 4mm
(US 6) circular needle and rejoin yarns with RS
facing.

Working in rows, proceed as follows:

Work another 6 rows in patt, foll chart, thus ending
with chart row 174 (176: 178: 180: 182).

Then work in rounds as follows:

NEXT ROUND: Using yarn A, knit.

NEXT ROUND: Using yarn A, purl.

NEXT ROUND: Using yarn A, knit.

Cast (bind) off purlways using yarn A.

See information page for finishing instructions.

KEY
☐ A
▨ B
▣ C
▨ D
▫ E

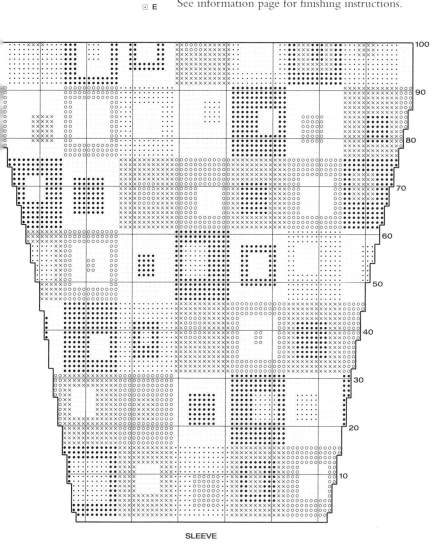

SLEEVE

shawl-collared coat by Kim Hargreaves

SIZE

One size to fit up to	97	cm
	38	in
Actual width	71.5	cm
	28¼	in
Length	109	cm
	43	in
Sleeve length	46.5	cm
	18¼	in

YARN
Rowan Aran 100gm (3½oz) balls and
Rowan Fine Cotton Chenille–50gm (1¾oz) balls:
A Aran Misty   314   10
B Cotton Chenille Black   367* 17
*yarn used double throughout

NEEDLES
1 pair 4mm (US 6) needles
1 pair 5mm (US 8) needles

BUTTONS
5

TENSION (GAUGE)
18 sts and 22 rows to 10cm (4in) measured over
patterned stocking (stockinette) stitch using 5mm
(US 8) needles

back
Cast on 109 sts using 4mm (US 6) needles and yarn B.
* Work 11 rows in st st, beg with a K row.
NEXT ROW (WS FACING): Knit to form hemline. *
Change to 5mm (US 8) needles and join yarn A. Work
168 rows in patt from chart for back, which is worked
entirely in st st, beg with a K row. AT THE SAME
TIME shape sides by inc 1 st at each end of 15th row
and every foll 14th row until there are 129 sts.
PATTERN NOTE
It is advisable not to take the contrast yarn across
entire row, but to use separate balls or lengths of yarn
B for each motif that makes up the pattern.
SHAPE ARMHOLES
Cast (bind) off 5 sts at beg of next 2 rows. *119 sts*
Work another 70 rows in patt.
SHAPE SHOULDERS
Cast (bind) off 11 sts at beg of next 6 rows.
Cast (bind) off 12 sts at beg of next 2 rows.
Cast (bind) off rem 29 sts.

pocket linings (make 2)
Cast on 30 sts using 5mm (US 8) needles
and yarn A.
Work 40 rows in st st, beg with a K row.
Leave sts on a holder.

left front
Cast on 57 sts using 4mm (US 6) needles and yarn B.
Work as given for back from * to *.
Change to 5mm (US 8) needles and joining in yarn
A. Work 120 rows in patt from chart for left front, and
AT THE SAME TIME shape sides by inc 1 st at beg
of 15th row and at same edge on every foll 14th row
until there are 65 sts.
PLACE POCKET LINING
Patt 12 sts, slip next 30 sts onto a holder and, in place of
these, patt across 30 sts of first pocket lining, patt to end.
Work 5 rows, then inc 1 st at side edge on next row
and foll 14th row. *67 sts*
Work another 23 rows in patt, ending with a
WS row.
SHAPE FRONT NECK AND ARMHOLE
NEXT ROW: Patt to last 2 sts, K2 tog.
Cont to dec 1 st at neck edge on every foll 4th row

until there are 45 sts. AT THE SAME TIME shape armhole by casting off 5 sts at beg of chart row 169.

Cont without further shaping until front matches back to start of shoulder shaping.

SHAPE SHOULDER

Cast (bind) off 11 sts at beg of next row and foll 2 alt rows.

Work 1 row.

Cast (bind) off rem 12 sts.

right front

Work as given for left front, rev all shaping and position of pocket and foll chart for right front. AT THE SAME TIME. Work 5 buttonholes in the following manner on rows 81, 101, 121, 141 and 161.

BUTTONHOLE ROW: Patt 3 sts, cast (bind) off 3 sts, patt to end.

NEXT ROW: Patt across row, casting on 3 sts in place of those cast (bound) off on previous row.

sleeves (both alike)

Cast on 61 sts using 4mm (US 6) needles and yarn B.
Work as given for back from * to *.

Change to 5mm (US 8) needles and join yarn A.
Work 102 rows in patt from chart for sleeves. AT THE SAME TIME shape sides by inc 1 st at each end of 11th row and every foll 3rd row until there are 117 sts.

Cast (bind) off loosely and evenly.

finishing

Press all pieces on WS using a warm iron over a damp cloth.

LEFT FRONT FACING

With RS facing, 4mm (US 6) needles and yarn B, pick up and K 123 sts (3 sts for every 4 rows of knitting) evenly down left front, starting at beg of neck shaping and ending at hemline.

Knit 1 row to form hemline.

Work 9 rows in st st beg with a K row.

Cast (bind) off loosely and evenly.

RIGHT FRONT FACING

With RS facing, 4mm (US 6) needles and yarn B, pick up and knit 123 sts evenly up the front, starting at hemline and ending at start of neck shaping.

Knit 1 row to form hemline.

Work 4 rows in st st, beg with a K row.

NEXT ROW (RS FACING): K 60 sts, turn and work 3 rows st st on these 60 sts, beg with a P row. Leave these sts on a holder.

** Return to rem sts and K across next 15 sts, turn and work 3 rows st st on these 15 sts, beg with a P row. Leave these sts on holder. * *

Repeat from * * to * * 3 more times, making 5 buttonholes in all.

Return to rem 3 sts and work 4 rows st st across these 3 sts, beg with a K row.

Rejoin yarn B to sts left on holder and K across all 123 sts.

Cast (bind) off loosely and evenly.

POCKET TOPS

With RS facing, 4mm (US 6) needles and yarn B, slip sts left on holder onto LH needle and knit 2 rows to form hemline.

Work 7 rows in st st, beg with a K row. Cast (bind) off.
Sew pocket linings to WS, and pocket tops to RS.
Join both shoulder seams using back stitch.

Sew sleeve top into armhole using back stitch.
Join side and sleeve seams.
Fold all edgings to WS at hemline and slipstitch into place.

LEFT SIDE COLLAR

Cast on 2 sts using 4mm (US 6) needles and yarn B.
Work in moss (seed) st as folls:

ROW 1: K1, P1.

ROW 2: P1, K1.

Keeping moss (seed) stitch correct, shape collar by inc 1 st at end (inside edge) of next row and 3 foll alt rows.
Work 3 rows without shaping.
Inc 1 st at end of next row and 19 foll 4th rows. *26 sts*
Work 15 rows without further shaping.
Leave sts on a holder.

RIGHT SIDE COLLAR

Work as for left side collar, rev all shaping (inc at beg of rows instead of end) and work rows 1 and 2 as foll

ROW 1: P1, K1.

ROW 2: P1, K1.

Rejoin yarn to sts of left side collar, patt across these in moss (seed) stitch, cast on 23 sts, patt across sts of right side collar in moss (seed) stitch. *75 sts*
Work 9 rows without shaping.
Then shape outer edge of collar by dec 1 st at each end of next row and 2 foll 6th rows.
Work 3 rows without shaping.
Dec 1 st at each end of next row and foll 4th row.
Work 1 row, then dec 1 st at each end of the next row and every foll alt row until 57 sts rem.

Dec 1 st at each end of every row until there are 49 sts.
Cast (bind) off 4 sts at beg of next 2 rows and 6 sts at
beg of foll 2 rows.
Cast (bind) off rem 29 sts.

COLLAR EDGING
With RS facing, 4mm (US 6) needles and yarn B,
pick up and K 220 sts evenly around outer edge of
collar.
Work 4 rows in K1, P1 rib.
Cast (bind) off evenly in rib.
Stitch collar into place evenly round neck edge,
matching center of collar to center back neck.
Sew on buttons to correspond with buttonholes.
See information page for finishing instructions.

percy by Kim Hargreaves

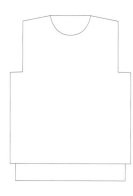

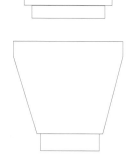

SIZES

	10YRS	MED	LARGE	
To fit chest	–	86–91	97–102	cm
	–	34–36	38–40	in
Actual width	55	63.5	66	cm
	21½	25	26	in
Length	60	71	71	cm
	23½	28	28	in
Sleeve length	40	52	52	cm
	15½	20½	20½	in

YARN
Rowan Chunky Tweed or Recycled Chunky Tweed 100gm (3½oz) balls:

Polar	879	9	13	14
Whale	880	9	13	14

NEEDLES
1 pair 5mm (US 8) needles
1 pair 6mm (US 10) needles
Cable needle

TENSION (GAUGE)
16 sts and 20 rows to 10cm (4in) measured over stocking (stockinette) stitch using 6mm (US 10) needles

PATTERN NOTE
The pattern is written for the child's size followed by the adults' medium and large.

back
Cast on 88 (100: 104) sts using 5mm (US 8) needles and work 5 (6: 6)cm (2 [2½: 2½]in), in K2, P2 rib, ending with a RS row.
NEXT ROW (WS) INC: Rib 10 (16: 18), (M1, rib 1, M1, rib 5, M1, rib 1, M1, rib 7) twice, (M1, rib 1) 3 times, M1, rib 5 sts, (M1, rib 1) 3 times, (M1, rib 7, M1, rib 1, M1, rib 5, M1, rib 1) twice, M1, rib 11 (17: 19). *112 (124: 128) sts*
Change to 6mm (US 10) needles and cont in patt from chart for back, working between appropriate markers and rep the 24-row patt rep until work measures 60 (46: 46)cm (23½ [18: 18]in), from cast-on edge, ending with a WS row.
Adults' only
SHAPE ARMHOLE
Cast (bind) off 5 sts at beg of next 2 rows.
(114 (118) sts
Cont in patt until work measures 25cm (9¾in) from beg of armhole shaping, ending with a WS row.

All sizes
SHAPE SHOULDER AND BACK NECK
Cast (bind) off 12 (12: 13) sts at beg of next 2 rows.
Cast (bind) off 12 (12: 13) sts, patt 16 (17: 17), turn and leave rem sts on a holder.
Work each side of neck separately.
Cast (bind) off 4 sts at beg of next row.
Cast (bind) off rem 12 (13: 13) sts.
With RS facing, rejoin yarn to rem sts, cast (bind) off center 32 sts, patt to end.
Complete to match first side, rev shaping.

front
Work as given for back until front is 10 (12: 12) rows shorter than back to shoulder, ending with a WS row.
SHAPE FRONT NECK
Patt 45 (48: 50) sts, turn and leave rem sts on holder.
Work each side of neck separately.
Cast (bind) off 4 sts, patt to end.
Dec 1 st at neck edge on next 3 (5: 5) rows and 2 foll alt rows. *36 (37: 39) sts*
Cont without further shaping until front matches back to shoulder shaping, ending with a WS row.
SHAPE SHOULDER
Cast (bind) off 12 (12: 13) sts at beg of next row and foll alt row.

Work 1 row. Cast (bind) off rem 12 (13: 13) sts.
With RS facing, rejoin yarn to rem sts, cast (bind) off center 22 (18: 18) sts, patt to end.
Complete to match first side, rev shaping.

sleeves (both alike)

Cast on 36 (42: 42) sts using 5mm (US 8) needles and work 5 (6: 6)cm (2 [2½: 2½]in) in K2, P2 rib, ending with a RS row.

NEXT ROW (WS) INC: Rib 7 (10: 10), M1, rib 1, M1, rib 5, M1, rib 1, M1, rib 7, M1, rib 1, M1, rib 5, M1, rib 1, M1, rib 8 (11: 11). *44 (50: 50) sts*

Change to 6mm (US 10) needles and cont in patt from chart for sleeve, working between markers for appropriate size, rep the 24-row patt throughout and AT THE SAME TIME inc 1 st at each end of 3rd row and every foll alt (4th: 4th) row to 58 (80: 80) sts and then every foll 4th (6th: 6th) row to 82 (88: 88) sts, taking extra sts into double moss (seed) st patt.
Keeping patt correct, cont without shaping until work measures 40 (52: 52)cm (15¾ [20½: 20½]in), or length required from cast-on edge, ending with a WS row.
Cast (bind) off in pattern.

finishing

Press all pieces as described on the information page.
Join right shoulder seam using back stitch.

NECKBAND

With RS facing and using 5mm (US 8) needles, pick up and knit 18 (28: 28), down left front to center front neck, 18 (28: 28) sts up right front neck to shoulder and 28 (36: 36) sts across back neck.
64 (92: 92) sts

Child's only

Work 4 rows in K2, P2 rib.
Work 4 rows in st st, beg with a P row.
Cast (bind) off loosely purlwise.

Adults' only

Work 16cm (6¼in) in K2, P2 rib. Cast (bind) off in rib.
See information page for finishing instructions.

KEY

□ P on the RS, K on the WS

▫ K on the RS, P on the WS

⟋ slip next 2 sts onto cable needle, hold at back, K2, K2 from cable needle

⟍ slip next 2 sts onto cable needle, hold at front, K2, K2 from cable needle

⟋ slip next 4 sts onto cable needle, hold at back, K4, K4 from cable needle

⟍ slip next 4 sts onto cable needle, hold at front, K4, K4 from cable needle

⟋ Slip 1st onto cable needle hold at back, K4, K1 from cable needle

⟍ Slip next 4 sts onto cable needle, hold at front, K1, k4 from cable needle

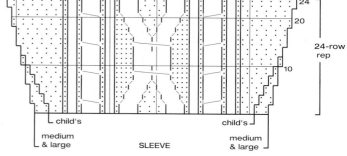

SLEEVE

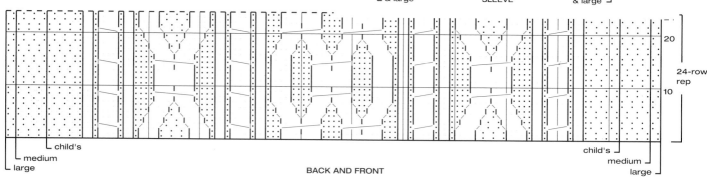

BACK AND FRONT

pam by Debbie Bliss

SIZES

		XS	S	M	L	XL	
To fit bust		81	86	91	97	102	cm
		32	34	36	38	40	in
Actual width		45.5	48	52	54.5	58	cm
		18	19	20½	21½	23	in
Length		50	51	52	53	54	cm
		19½	20	20½	21	21½	in
Sleeve length		42	42	43	43	43	cm
		16½	16½	17	17	17	in

YARN

Rowan Wool Cotton 50gm (1¾oz) balls:

Spark	947	11	11	12	12	13

NEEDLES

1 pair 3¾mm (US 5) needles
1 pair 4mm (US 6) needles
Cable needle

BUTTONS

6

TENSION (GAUGE)

22 sts and 30 rows to 10cm (4in) measured over stocking (stockinette) stitch using 4mm (US 6) needles

SPECIAL ABBREVIATIONS

C3F = Cable 3 front: Slip next 2 sts onto cable needle and leave at front of work, K1, then K2 from cable needle.

C3B = Cable 3 back: Slip next st onto cable needle and leave at back of work, K2, then K1 from cable needle.

C4F = Cable 4 front: Slip next 2 sts onto cable needle and leave at front of work, K2, then K2 from cable needle.

C4B = Cable 4 back: Slip next 2 sts onto cable needle and leave at back of work, K2, then K2 from cable needle.

CR3L = Cross 3 left: Slip next 2 sts onto cable needle and leave at front of work, P1, then K2 from cable needle.

CR3R = Cross 3 right: Slip next st onto cable needle and leave at back of work, K2, then P1 from cable needle.

C5B = Cable 5 back: Slip next 3 sts onto cable needle and leave at back of work, K2, then K3 from cable needle.

back

Cast on 102 (106: 114: 118: 126) sts using 3¾mm (US 5) needles.

ROW 1 (RS): K2, *P2, K2, rep from * to end.
ROW 2: P2, *K2, P2, rep from * to end.
These 2 rows form rib.
Cont in rib, dec 1 st at each end of 13th and every foll 6th row until 92 (96: 104: 108: 116) sts rem.
Cont straight until back measures 15cm (6in), ending with a RS row.
NEXT ROW (WS): Rib 6 (4: 8: 6: 10), *M1 purlwise, rib 4, rep from * to last 6 (4: 8: 6: 10) sts, M1 purlwise, rib 6 (4: 8: 6: 10). *113 (119: 127: 133: 141) sts*
Change to 4mm (US 6) needles.
Starting and ending rows as indicated, working rows 1 and 2 once only and then rep the 16-row rep throughout, cont in patt, foll chart for back as folls:
Work 6 rows.
Inc 1 st at each end of next and every foll 6th row until there are 123 (129: 137: 143: 151) sts, taking inc sts into patt.
Cont straight until back measures 30 (31: 31: 32: 32)cm (12 [12¼: 12¼: 12½: 12½]in), ending with a WS row.

SHAPE ARMHOLES

Keeping patt correct, cast (bind) off 5 sts at beg of next 2 rows. *113 (119: 127: 133: 141) sts*
Dec 1 st at each end of next 5 rows.
103 (109: 117: 123: 131) sts
Cont straight until armhole measures 20 (20: 21: 21: 22)cm (7¾ [7¾: 8¼: 8¼: 8½]in), ending with a WS row.

SHAPE SHOULDERS AND BACK NECK

Keeping patt correct, cast (bind) off 10 (11: 12: 13: 14) sts at beg of next 2 rows. *83 (87: 93: 97: 103) sts*
NEXT ROW (RS): Cast (bind) off 10 (11: 12: 13: 14) sts, patt until there are 15 (15: 17: 17: 19) sts on right needle and turn, leaving rem sts on a holder.
Work each side of neck separately.
Cast (bind) off 4 sts at beg of next row.
Cast (bind) off rem 11 (11: 13: 13: 15) sts.
With RS facing, rejoin yarn to rem sts, cast (bind) off center 33 (35: 35: 37: 37) sts, patt to end.
Work to match first side, rev shaping.

left front

Cast on 50 (54: 58: 62: 66) sts using 3¾mm (US 5) needles.
Work in rib as given for back, dec 1 st at beg of 15th and every foll 6th row until 45 (49: 53: 57: 61) sts rem.

Cont straight until left front measures 15cm (6in), ending with a RS row.

NEXT ROW (WS): Rib 6 (4: 1: 1: 3), *M1 purlwise, rib 3 (4: 5: 6: 6), rep from * to last 6 (5: 2: 2: 4) sts, M1 purlwise, rib 6 (5: 2: 2: 4). *57 (60: 64: 67: 71) sts*
Change to 4mm (US 6) needles.
Starting and ending rows as indicated, working rows 1 and 2 once only and then rep the 16-row repeat throughout, cont in patt, foll chart for fronts as folls:
Work 6 rows.
Inc 1 st at beg of next and every foll 6th row until there are 62 (65: 69: 72: 76) sts, taking inc sts into patt.
Cont straight until left front matches back to beg of armhole shaping, ending with a WS row.

SHAPE ARMHOLE
Keeping patt correct, cast (bind) off 5 sts at beg of next row. *57 (60: 64: 67: 71) sts*
Work 1 row.
Dec 1 st at armhole edge of next 5 rows.
52 (55: 59: 62: 66) sts
Work 5 rows, ending with a WS row.

SHAPE NECK
Keeping patt correct, dec 1 st at end of next and every foll alt row until 31 (33: 37: 39: 43) sts rem.
Cont straight until left front matches back to start of shoulder shaping, ending with a WS row.

SHAPE SHOULDER
Keeping patt correct, cast (bind) off 10 (11: 12: 13: 14) sts at beg of next and foll alt row.
Work 1 row.
Cast (bind) off rem 11 (11: 13: 13: 15) sts.

right front
Cast on 50 (54: 58: 62: 66) sts using 3¾mm (US 5) needles.
Work in rib as given for back, dec 1 st at end of 15th and every foll 6th row until 45 (49: 53: 57: 61) sts rem.
Complete to match left front, rev shaping.

sleeves (both alike)
Cast on 50 (50: 54: 54: 54) sts using 3¾mm (US 5) needles.
Work in rib as given for back for 10cm (4in), ending with a RS row.

KEY

☐ K on RS, P on WS

▣ P on RS, K on WS

C4F

C4B

C3B

C3F

Cr3R

Cr3L

C5B

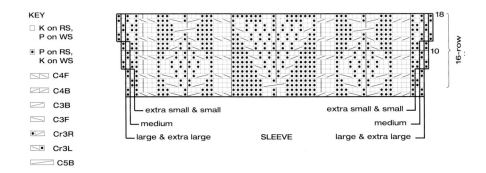

SLEEVE

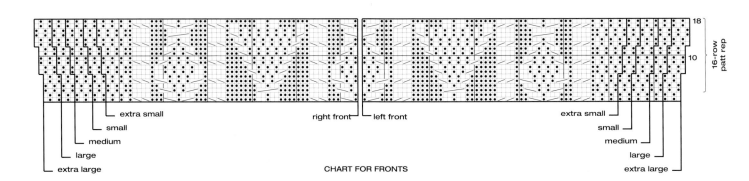

CHART FOR FRONTS

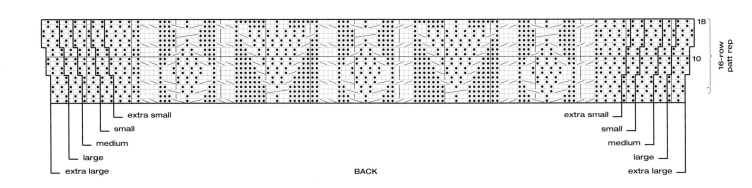

BACK

NEXT ROW (WS): Rib 1 (1: 7: 3: 3), *M1 purlwise, rib 4, rep from * to last 1 (1: 7: 3: 3) sts, M1 purlwise, rib 1 (1: 7: 3: 3). *63 (63: 65: 67: 67) sts*

Change to 4mm (US 6) needles.

Starting and ending rows as indicated, working rows 1 and 2 once only and then rep the 16-row rep throughout, cont in patt, foll chart for sleeves as folls:

Work 6 rows.

Inc 1 st at each end of next and every foll 6th row to 83 (83: 83: 89: 81) sts, then on every foll 4th row until there are 103 (103: 107: 107: 111) sts, taking inc sts into patt.

Cont straight until sleeve measures 47 (47: 48: 48: 48)cm (18½ [18½: 18¾: 18¾: 18¾]in) from cast-on edge, ending with a WS row.

SHAPE TOP

Cast (bind) off 5 sts at beg of next 2 rows. *93 (93: 97: 97: 101) sts*

Dec 1 st at each end of next and foll 3 alt rows.

Work 1 row, ending with a WS row.

Cast (bind) off rem 85 (85: 89: 89: 93) sts.

finishing

Press all pieces as described on the information page. Join shoulder seams using back stitch or mattress stitch if preferred.

LEFT BORDER AND COLLAR

Cast on 154 (158: 162: 166: 170) sts using 3¾mm (US 5) needles.

Work in rib as given for back for 10 rows, ending with a WS row.

Cast (bind) off 82 (86: 86: 90: 90) sts at beg of next row. *72 (72: 76: 76: 80) sts*

Work 1 row.

Cast (bind) off 3 sts at beg of next and foll 10 alt rows, then 5 sts at beg of foll 3 alt rows.

Work 1 row.

Cast (bind) off rem 24 (24: 28: 28: 32) sts.

RIGHT BORDER AND COLLAR

Cast on 154 (158: 162: 166: 170) sts using 3¾mm (US 5) needles.

Work in rib as given for back for 4 rows, ending with a WS row.

NEXT ROW (RS) (BUTTONHOLE ROW): Rib 75 (74: 78: 77: 81), *yrn (to make a buttonhole), work 2 tog, rib 13 (14: 14: 15: 15), rep from * to last 4 sts, yrn (to make 6th buttonhole), work 2 tog, rib 2.

Work in rib for another 5 rows, ending with a WS row.

NEXT ROW (RS): Rib 72 (72: 76: 76: 80), cast (bind) off rem 82 (86: 86: 90: 90) sts.

Rejoin yarn with WS facing and cont as folls:

Cast (bind) off 3 sts at beg of next and foll 10 alt rows, then 5 sts at beg of foll 3 alt rows.

Work 1 row.

Cast (bind) off rem 24 (24: 28: 28: 32) sts.

Sew border and collar pieces to neck and front opening edges, joining row ends of collar sections at center back.

See information page for finishing instructions, setting in sleeves using the shallow set-in method.

trinity by Kim Hargreaves

SIZES

	CHILDREN'S				LADIES'			
	6-8YRS	8-9YRS	9-11YRS	12-14YRS	S	M	L	
To fit chest	–	–	–	–	81–86	86–91	97–102	cm
	–	–	–	–	32–34	34–36	38–40	cm
Actual width	38	40.5	43	45.5	48.5	51.5	53.5	cm
	15	16	17	18	19	20½	21	in
Length	35.5	38	40.5	43	43	45.5	48.5	cm
	14	15	16	17	17	18	19	in
Sleeve length	43	45.5	48.5	50.5	43	43	43	cm
	17	18	19	20	17	17	17	in

YARN

Rowan Denim 50gm (1¾oz) balls:

	13	14	15	16	**16**	**16**	**17**

(Children's cardigan photographed in Ecru 324, ladies' pullover in Nashville 225)

NEEDLES
1 pair 3¼mm (US 3) needles
1 pair 4mm (US 6) needles
Cable needle

BUTTONS
9 for cardigan

TENSION (GAUGE) BEFORE WASHING
20 sts and 28 rows to 10cm (4in) measured over
stocking (stockinette) stitch using 4mm (US 6) needles

PATTERN NOTE
Denim will shrink in length when washed for the
first time. Allowances have been made in this pattern
for shrinkage.
The pattern is written for the four children's sizes,
followed by the ladies' sizes in bold.

SPECIAL ABBREVIATIONS
MB = Make bobble: (K1, P1, K1, P1, K1) into next st,
turn, K5, turn, K5, then slip 2nd, 3rd, 4th and 5th sts
over first.
C4F = Cable 4 front: Slip next 2 sts onto cable needle
and hold at front, K2, then K2 from cable needle.
C4B = Cable 4 back: Slip next 2 sts onto cable needle
and hold at back, K2, then K2 from cable needle.

cardigan
back
Cast on 77 (81: 87: 91: **91: 97: 101**) sts using 3¼mm
(US 3) needles.
NEXT ROW (WS) (INC): K10 (12: 15: 17: **17: 20: 22),
(P1, M1) 3 times, P1, (rib 2, M1) 6 times, rib 25,
(M1, rib 2) 6 times, (P1, M1) 3 times, P1, K10 (12:
15: 17: **17: 20: 22**).
95 (99: 105: 109: 109: 115: 119) sts
Change to 4mm (US 6) needles and, foll chart for
body, work in patt as folls:
ROW 1 (RS): P9 (11: 14: 16: **16: 19: 21**), work next 77
sts as chart row 1, P9 (11: 14: 16: **16: 19: 21**).
ROW 2: K1 (3: 2: 0: **0: 3: 1**), * (K1, P1, K1) into next
st, P3tog*, rep from * to * 1 (1: 2: 3: **3: 3: 4**) times
more, work next 77 sts as chart row 2, rep from * to
* 2 (2: 3: 4: **4: 4: 5**) times more, K1 (3: 2: 0: **0:
3: 1**).
ROW 3: P9 (11: 14: 16: **16: 19: 21**), work next 77 sts as
chart row 3, P9 (11: 14: 16: **16: 19: 21**).
ROW 4: K1 (3: 2: 0: **0: 3: 1**), *P3tog, (K1, P1, K1) into
next st *, rep from * to * 1 (1: 2: 3: **3: 3: 4**) times
more, work next 77 sts as chart row 4, rep from * to
* 2 (2: 3: 4: **4: 4: 5**) times more, K1 (3: 2: 0: **0: 3: 1**).
These 4 rows form blackberry st at sides and set the
position of the chart.
(**Note:** chart shows first full rep of each section. When
rep chart, rep the number of rows within each section
as indicated above section.)
Ladies' sizes only
Keeping chart correct and taking inc sts into
blackberry st, cont in patt as now set, shaping side
seams by inc 1 st at each end of 15th row (from beg

of patt) and every foll 14th row until there are (**115: 121: 125**) sts.

All sizes

Cont in patt as now set until back measures 18.5 (21.5: 24.5: 27.5: **28: 30.5: 34**)cm (7¼ [8½: 9¾: 11: **11¼: 12: 13½**]in), ending with a WS row.

SHAPE ARMHOLES

Cast (bind) off 4 sts at beg of next 2 rows.

Dec 1 st at each end on next 6 (6: 6: 6: **5: 5: 5**) rows.
75 (79: 85: 89: 97: 103: 107) sts

Ladies' sizes only

Now dec 1 st at each end of every foll alt row (from previous dec) until (**85: 91: 95**) sts rem.

All sizes

Cont without further shaping until armhole measures 24cm (9½in), ending with a WS row.

SHAPE SHOULDERS AND BACK NECK

Cast (bind) off 8 (9: 9: 10: **9: 10: 11**) sts at beg of next 2 rows.

NEXT ROW (RS): Cast (bind) off first 8 (9: 9: 10: **9: 10: 11**) sts, patt until there are 12 (12: 14: 14: **13: 14: 14**) sts on right needle and turn, leaving rem sts on a holder.

Work each side of neck separately.

Cast (bind) off 4 sts at beg of next row.

Cast (bind) off rem 8 (8: 10: 10: **9: 10: 10**) sts.

With RS facing rejoin yarn to rem sts, cast (bind) off center 19 (19: 21: 21: **23: 23: 23**) sts, patt to end.

Complete to match first side, rev shaping.

left front

Cast on 39 (41: 44: 46: **46: 49: 51**) sts using 3¼mm (US 3) needles.

NEXT ROW (WS) (INC): Rib 13, (M1, rib 2) 6 times, (P1, M1) 3 times, P1, K10 (12: 15: 17: **17: 20: 22**).
48 (50: 53: 55: 55: 58: 60) sts

Change to 4mm (US 6) needles and, foll chart for body, work in patt as folls:

ROW 1 (RS): P9 (11: 14: 16: **16: 19: 21**), work last 39 sts as chart row 1, ending at point indicated.

ROW 2: Beg at point indicated, work first 39 sts as chart row 2, *(K1, P1, K1) into next st, P3tog,*rep from * to * 1 (1: 2: 3: **3: 3: 4**) times more, K1 (3: 2: 0: **0: 3: 1**).

ROW 3: P9 (11: 14: 16: **16: 19: 21**), work last 39 sts as chart row 3, ending at point indicated.

ROW 4: Beg at point indicated, work first 39 sts as chart row 4, *P3tog, (K1, P1, K1) into next st*, rep from * to * 1 (1: 2: 3: **3: 3: 4**) times more, K1 (3: 2: 0: **0: 3: 1**).

These 4 rows form blackberry st at side and place chart.

(**Note:** Omit bobble shown on chart that falls on center front opening edge st)

Ladies' sizes only

Keeping chart correct and taking inc sts into blackberry st, cont in patt as now set, shaping side seams by inc 1 st at beg of 15th row (from beg of patt) and every foll 14th row until there are (58: 61: 63) sts.

All sizes

Cont in patt as now set until left front matches back to start of armhole shaping, ending with a WS row.

SHAPE ARMHOLE

Cast (bind) off 4 sts at beg of next row.

Work 1 row.

Dec 1 st at armhole edge on next 6 (6: 6: 6: **5: 5: 5**) rows. *38 (40: 43: 45: 49: 52: 54) sts*

Children's sizes only

Work 4 rows, thus ending with a WS row.

SHAPE FRONT SLOPE

Dec 1 st at front opening edge on next and every foll 3rd row until 24 (26: 28: 30) sts rem.

Ladies' sizes only

Now dec 1 st at armhole edge of every foll alt row (from previous dec) until (**47: 50: 52**) sts rem.

Work 1 row, thus ending with a WS row.

KEY

☐ K on RS, P on WS

▣ P on RS, K on WS

◉ yfwd

■ MB

◪ K2tog

◩ Sl1, K1, psso

◻ C4F

◻ C4B

◻ Slip next 2 sts onto CN, hold at front, P1, K2 from CN

◻ Slip next st onto CN, hold at back, K2, P1 from CN

◻ Slip next 3 sts onto CN, hold at front, K2, slip last st on CN back onto left needle, P1, K2 from CN

◻ Slip next 3 sts onto CN, hold at back, K2, slip last st on CN back onto left needle, P1, K2 from CN.

◻ Slip next 3 sts onto CN, hold at front, K4, K3 from CN

◻ Slip next 4 sts onto CN, hold at back, K3, K4 from CN

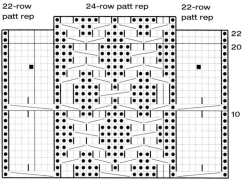

SLEEVE

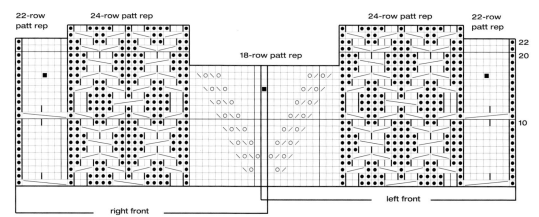

RIGHT AND LEFT FRONTS AND BACK

SHAPE FRONT SLOPE

Dec 1 st at front opening edge on next and every foll 3rd row and AT THE SAME TIME dec 1 st at armhole edge on next and foll 3 alt rows.
(40: 43: 45) sts.
Dec 1 st at front opening edge only on every foll 3rd row (from previous dec) until (**27: 30: 32**) sts rem.

All sizes

Cont without further shaping until left front matches back to start of shoulder shaping, ending with a WS row.

SHAPE SHOULDER

Cast (bind) off 8 (9: 9: 10: **9: 10: 11**) sts at beg of next and foll alt row.
Work 1 row.
Cast (bind) off rem 8 (8: 10: 10: **9: 10: 10**) sts.

right front

Cast on 39 (41: 44: 46: **46: 49: 51**) sts using 3¼mm (US 3) needles.
NEXT ROW (WS) (INC): K10 (12: 15: 17: **17: 20: 22**), (P1, M1) 3 times, P1, (rib 2, M1) 6 times, rib 13.
48 (50: 53: 55: 55: 58: 60) sts
Change to 4mm (US 6) needles and, foll chart for body, work in patt as folls:
ROW 1 (RS): Beg at point indicated, work first 39 sts as chart row 1, P9 (11: 14: 16: **16: 19: 21**).
ROW 2: K1 (3: 2: 0: **0: 3: 1**), *(K1, P1, K1) into next st, P3tog*, rep from * to * 1 (1: 2: 3: **3: 3: 4**) times more, work last 39 sts as chart row 2, ending at point indicated.
ROW 3: Beg at point indicated, work first 39 sts as chart row 3, P9 (11: 14: 16: **16: 19: 21**).
ROW 4: K1 (3: 2: 0: **0: 3: 1**), *P3tog, (K1, P1, K1) into next st*, rep from * to * 1 (1: 2: 3: **3: 3: 4**) times more, work last 39 sts as chart row 4, ending at point indicated.
These 4 rows form blackberry st at sides and place chart.
Complete to match left front, rev shaping.

sleeves (both alike)

Cast on 42 (46: 46: 46: **46: 46: 46**) sts using 3¼mm (US 3) needles.
ROW 1 (RS): K2, *P2, K2, rep from * to end.
ROW 2: P2, *K2, P2, rep from * to end.
Rep these 2 rows for 6cm (2½in), ending with a RS row.
NEXT ROW (WS) (INC): Inc in first st, K10 (12: 12: 12: **12: 12: 12**), (P1, M1) 3 times, rib 3, (M1, rib 2) 5 times, rib 1, (P1, M1) 3 times, K10 (12: 12: 12: **12: 12: 12**), inc in last st. *55 (59: 59: 59: 59: 59: 59) sts*
Change to 4mm (US 6) needles and, foll chart for sleeve, work in patt as folls:
ROW 1 (RS): P10 (12: 12: 12: **12: 12: 12**), work next 35 sts as chart row 1, P10 (12: 12: 12: **12: 12: 12**).
ROW 2: K2 (0: 0: 0: **0: 0: 0**), *(K1, P1, K1) into next st, P3tog*, rep from * to * 1 (2: 2: 2: **2: 2: 2**) times more, work next 35 sts as chart row 2, rep from * to * 2 (3: 3: 3: **3: 3: 3**) times more, K2 (0: 0: 0: **0: 0: 0**).
ROW 3: P10 (12: 12: 12: **12: 12: 12**), work next 35 sts as chart row 3, P10 (12: 12: 12: **12: 12: 12**).
ROW 4: K2 (0: 0: 0: **0: 0: 0**), *P3tog, (K1, P1, K1) into next st*, rep from * to * 1 (2: 2: 2: **2: 2: 2**) times more, work next 35 sts as chart row 4, rep from * to * 2 (3: 3: 3: **3: 3: 3**) times more, K2 (0: 0: 0: **0: 0: 0**).
These 4 rows form blackberry st at sides and place chart.

Note: Chart shows first full rep of each section. When rep chart, rep the number of rows within each section as indicated above section.
Cont in patt as set, shaping sides by inc 1 st at each end on 7th (7th: 9th: 9th: **13th: 13th: 13th**) row (from beg of chart) and every foll 6th (6th: 8th: 8th: **12th: 12th: 12th**) row until there are 83 (63: 85: 77: **67: 67: 67**) sts, taking inc sts into blackberry st.
Now inc 1 st at each end on every foll 8th (8th: 10th: 10th: **14th: 14th: 14th**) row (from previous inc) until there are 91 (91: 91: 91: **77: 77: 77**) sts.

Cont without further shaping until sleeve measures 51.5 (54.5: 58: 60.5: **52: 52: 52**)cm (20¼ [21½: 22¾: 23¾: 20½: 20½: 20½]in), ending with a WS row.

SHAPE TOP

Cast (bind) off 4 sts at beg of next 2 rows.

Children's sizes only

Dec 1 st at each end on next 6 rows.

Cast (bind) off rem 71 sts loosely and evenly.

Ladies' sizes only

Dec 1 st at each end on next 5 rows, then on every foll alt row until 55 sts rem.

Dec 1 st at each end on every foll 4th row (from previous dec) until 45 sts rem.

Work 1 row, thus ending with a WS row.

Now dec 1 st at each end on next and foll 4 alt rows. *35 sts*

Dec 1 st at each end on next 5 rows, thus ending with a WS row. *25 sts*

Cast (bind) off 4 sts at beg of next 2 rows.

Cast (bind) off rem 17 sts.

pullover
Ladies' sizes only
back

Cast on (**90: 98: 102**) sts using 3¼mm (US 3) needles.

ROW 1 (RS): K2, *P2, K2, rep from * to end.

ROW 2: P2, *K2, P2, rep from * to end.

Rep these 2 rows for 6cm, ending with a RS row and (**inc: dec: dec**) 1 st at center of last row.

(**91: 97: 101**) *sts*

Complete as for back of cardigan from **.

front

Work as given for back until there are 26 rows fewer than on back to shoulder, thus ending with a WS row.

SHAPE NECK

NEXT ROW (RS): Patt (**39: 42: 44**) and turn, leaving rem sts on a holder.

Work each side of neck separately.

Cast (bind) off 4 sts at beg of next row.

Dec 1 st at neck edge on next 3 rows, then on every foll alt row until (**30: 33: 35**) sts rem.

Now dec 1 st at neck edge on every foll 4th row (from previous dec) until (**27: 30: 32**) sts rem.

Patt 5 rows, thus ending with a WS row.

SHAPE SHOULDER

Cast (bind) off (**9: 10: 11**) sts at beg of next and foll alt row.

Work 1 row.

Cast (bind) off rem (**9: 10: 10**) sts.

With RS facing rejoin yarn to rem sts, cast (bind) off center 7 sts, patt to end.

Complete to match first side, rev shaping.

sleeves (both alike)

Work as for sleeves of cardigan.

finishing

DO NOT PRESS.

Cardigan

Join shoulder seams using back stitch.

FRONT BAND

Cast on 5 sts using 3¼mm (US 3) needles.

Cont in garter st (knit every row) until band, when slightly stretched, fits along left front opening edge, starting at a point 2.5cm (1in) below cast-on edge, up left front slope, across back neck and down right front slope to start of front slope shaping, sewing in place as you go along.

Mark positions for 9 buttons on first section of band, the first to be 1cm (½in) above cast-on edge, the last to be level with start of front slope shaping and the rem evenly spaced between.

Cont in garter st down right front opening edge, with the addition of 9 buttonholes to correspond with positions marked for buttons, ending band 2.5cm (1in) below right front cast-on edge.

TO MAKE A BUTTONHOLE (RS): K2, yfwd, K2tog, K1.

When band is complete, cast (bind) off.

Sew rem section of band in place.

HEM EDGING

Cast on 5 sts using 4mm (US 6) needles.

ROW 1 (RS): K2, yfwd, K3.

ROW 2 & ALL WS ROWS: Knit.

ROW 3: K2, yfwd, K4.

ROW 5: K2, yfwd, K5.

ROW 7: K2, yfwd, K6.

ROW 9: K2, yfwd, K7.

ROW 11: K2, yfwd, K8.

ROW 12: Cast (bind) off first 6 sts, K to end. *5 sts*

Rep these 12 rows until strip measures about 92.5 (97: 104.5: 109: **109: 116.5: 121**)cm (36½ [38: 41¼: 43: **43: 45¾: 47¾**]in), ending with row 12.

Cast (bind) off.

Machine wash all pieces tog before sewing together (see ball band for washing instructions).

Join side seams. Sew straight edge of hem edging to lower edge, matching ends to free row-end edges of front band. See information page for finishing instructions.

Pullover

Join right shoulder seam using back stitch.

NECK BAND

Ladies' sizes only

With RS facing and 3¼mm (US 3) needles, pick up and knit 28 sts down left front neck, 7 sts across center front, 28 sts up right front neck, 4 sts down right back neck, 23 sts across center back and 4 sts up left back neck. *94 sts*

Beg with row 1, work 9cm (3½in) in K2, P2 rib as for back.

Cast (bind) off loosely and evenly.

Machine wash all pieces tog before sewing tog (see ball band for washing instructions).

See information page for finishing instructions.

jack by Kim Hargreaves

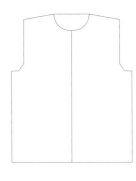

SIZES

	LADIES'			MEN'S			
	S	**M**	**L**	**M**	**L**	**XL**	
To fit chest	86	91	97	**97**	**102**	**107**	cm
	34	36	38	**38**	**40**	**42**	in
Actual width	58.5	61	63.5	**63.5**	**66**	**68.5**	cm
	23	24	25	**25**	**26**	**27**	in
Length	68.5	71	73.5	**68.5**	**71**	**73.5**	cm
	27	28	29	**27**	**28**	**29**	in
Sleeve length	48	48	48	**53**	**53**	**53**	cm
	19	19	19	**21**	**21**	**21**	in

YARNS

Rowan Chunky Tweed 100gm (3½oz) balls

Polar 871	13	13	14	14	14	15

NEEDLES

1 pair 5½mm (US 9) needles
1 pair 6½mm (US 10½) needles
Cable needle

TENSION (GAUGE)

14 sts and 19 rows to 10cm (4in) measured over stocking (stockinette) stitch using 6½mm (US 10½) needles.

PATTERN NOTE

The pattern is written for the three ladies' sizes, followed by the men's sizes in bold.

SPECIAL ABBREVIATIONS

CR4R = Slip next st onto cable needle and leave at back of work, K3, then P1 from cable needle.
CR4L = Slip next 3 sts onto cable needle and leave at front of work, P1, then K3 from cable needle.
C4B = Slip next 2 sts onto cable needle and leave at back of work, K2, then K2 from cable needle.
C4F = Slip next 2 sts onto cable needle and leave at front of work, K2, then K2 from cable needle.
C6B = Slip next 3 sts onto cable needle and leave at back of work, K3, then K3 from cable needle.
C6F = Slip next 3 sts onto cable needle and leave at front of work, K3, then K3 from cable needle.

back

Cast on 94 (98: 102: **102: 106: 110**) sts using 5½mm (US 9) needles.
ROW 1 (RS): P0 (1: 0: **0: 1: 0**), K1 (2: 1: **1: 2: 1**), [P2, K2] 1 (1: 2: **2: 2: 3**) times, [P1, K2] 4 times, P2, K2, P3, K2, P2, [K2, P1] 4 times, [K2, P2] 3 times, K2,

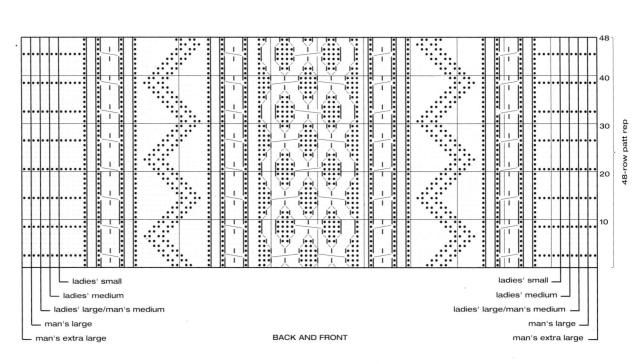

KEY

- ☐ K on RS
  P on WS
- ▣ P on RS,
  K on WS

- ▱ C4F
- ▱ C4B
- ▱ C6F
- ▱ C6B
- ▥ C4L
- ▥ C4R

— ladies' small
— ladies' medium
— ladies' large/man's medium
— man's large
— man's extra large

BACK AND FRONT

ladies' small —
ladies' medium —
ladies' large/man's medium —
man's large —
man's extra large —

48-row patt rep

48
40
30
20
10

[P1, K2] 4 times, P2, K2, P3, K2, P2, [K2, P1] 4 times, [K2, P2] 1 (1: 2: **2: 2: 3**) times, K1 (2: 1: **1: 2: 1**), P0 (1: 0: **0: 1: 0**).

ROW 2: K0 (1: 0: **0: 1: 0**), P1 (2: 1: **1: 2: 1**), [K2, P2] 1 (1: 2: **2: 2: 3**) times, [K1, P2] 4 times, K2, P2, K3, P2, K2, [P2, K1] 4 times, [P2, K2] 3 times, P2, [K1, P2] 4 times, K2, P2, K3, P2, K2, [P2, K1] 4 times, [P2, K2] 1 (1: 2: **2: 2: 3**) times, P1 (2: 1: **1: 2: 1**), K0 (1: 0: **0: 1: 0**). Rep last 2 rows 5 times more and then row 1 again, thus ending with a RS row.

ROW 14 (INC) (WS): Rib 9 (11: 13: **13: 15: 17**), M1, rib 2, M1, rib 23, M1, rib 2, M1, rib 4, M1, rib 1, [M1, rib 4] 3 times, M1, rib 1, M1, rib 4, M1, rib 2, M1, rib 23, M1, rib 2, M1, rib 9 (11: 13: **13: 15: 17**). *108 (112: 116: 116: 120: 124) sts*
Change to 6½mm (US 10½) needles.
Beg and ending rows as indicated, now work foll back and front chart, rep the 48-row patt, until back measures 43.5 (46: 48.5: **43.5: 46: 48.5**)cm (17 [18: 19: **17: 18: 19**]in), ending with a WS row.

SHAPE ARMHOLES
Keeping patt correct, cast (bind) off 4 sts at beg of next 2 rows. *100 (104: 108: 108: 112: 116) sts*
Dec 1 st at each end of next 4 rows.
92 (96: 100: 100: 104: 108) sts.
Cont straight until armhole measures 25cm (9¾in), ending with a WS row.

SHAPE SHOULDERS AND BACK NECK
Cast (bind) off 8 (9: 9: **9: 10: 11**) sts at beg of next 2 rows. *76 (78: 82: 82: 84: 86) sts*
NEXT ROW (RS): Cast (bind) off 8 (9: 9: **9: 10: 11**) sts, patt until there are 12 (12: 14: **14: 14: 14**) sts on right needle and turn, leaving rem sts on a holder.
Work each side of neck separately.
Cast (bind) off 4 sts at beg of next row.
Cast (bind) off rem 8 (8: 10: **10: 10: 10**) sts.
With RS facing, rejoin yarn to rem sts, cast (bind) off center 36 sts, patt to end.
Work to match first side, rev shaping.

KEY

☐ K on RS
  P on WS

⊡ P on RS,
  K on WS

▱ C4F

▱ C4B

▭ C6F

▭ C6B

▱ C4L

▱ C4R

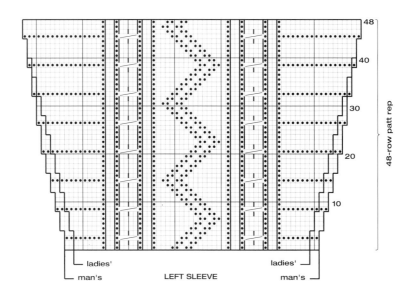

LEFT SLEEVE

ladies'
man's
ladies'
man's

48-row patt rep

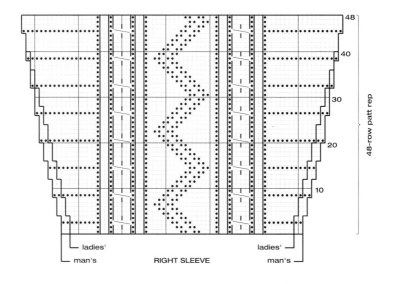

RIGHT SLEEVE

ladies'
man's
ladies'
man's

48-row patt rep

front

Work as given for back until there are 14 rows fewer than on back to start of shoulder shaping, thus ending with a WS row.

SHAPE NECK

NEXT ROW (RS): Patt 35 (37: 39: **39: 41: 43**) sts and turn, leaving rem sts on a holder.

Work each side of neck separately.

Keeping patt correct, cast (bind) off 6 sts at beg of next row. *29 (31: 33: 33: 35: 37) sts*

Dec 1 st at neck edge on next and foll 3 alt rows, then on foll 4th row.

24 (26: 28: 28: 30: 32) sts

Work 1 row, thus ending with a WS row.

SHAPE SHOULDER

Cast (bind) off 8 (9: 9: **9: 10: 11**) sts at beg of next and foll alt row. Work 1 row. Cast (bind) off rem 8 (8: 10: **10: 10: 10**) sts. With RS facing, rejoin yarn to rem sts, cast (bind) off center 22 sts, patt to end.

Work to match first side, rev shaping.

left sleeve

Cast on 45 (45: 45: **49: 49: 49**) sts using 5½mm (US 9) needles.

ROW 1 (RS): P0 (0: 0: **1: 1: 1**), K1 (1: 1: **2: 2: 2**), P2, K2, [P1, K2] 4 times, P2, K2, P3, K2, P2, [K2, P1] 4 times, K2, P2, K1 (1: 1: **2: 2: 2**), P0 (0: 0: **1: 1: 1**).

ROW 2: K0 (0: 0: **1: 1: 1**), P1 (1: 1: **2: 2: 2**), K2, P2, [K1, P2] 4 times, K2, P2, K3, P2, K2, [P2, K1] 4 times, P2, K2, P1 (1: 1: **2: 2: 2**), K0 (0: 0: **1: 1: 1**).

Rep last 2 rows 5 times more and then row 1 again, thus ending with a RS row.

ROW 14 (INC) (WS): Rib 9 (9: 9: **11: 11: 11**), M1, rib 2, M1, rib 23, M1, rib 2, M1, rib 9 (9: 9: **11: 11: 11**).

49 (49: 49: 53: 53: 53) sts

Change to 6½mm (US 10½) needles.

Beg and ending rows as indicated, work left sleeve chart, rep the 48-row patt, as folls:

Inc 1 st at each end of next and every foll 4th row to 83 (83: 83: **65: 65: 65**) sts, then on every foll 6th row until there are 85 sts, taking inc sts into patt. Cont without further shaping until sleeve measures 48 (48: 48: **53: 53: 53**)cm (18¾ [18¾: 18¾: **21: 21: 21**]in), ending with a WS row.

SHAPE TOP

Keeping patt correct, cast (bind) off 4 sts at beg of next 2 rows. *77 sts*

Dec 1 st at each end of next 4 rows.

Cast (bind) off rem 69 sts.

right sleeve

Work as for left sleeve but foll chart for right sleeve.

finishing

Press all pieces as described on the information page.

Join right shoulder seam using back stitch.

NECK BORDER

With RS facing and using 6½mm (US 10½) needles, pick up and knit 21 sts down left front neck, 16 sts across front neck, 21 sts up right front neck and 38 sts across back neck. *96 sts*

ROW 1 (WS): *K2, P2, rep from * to end.

Rep last row for 15cm (6in).

Cast (bind) off loosely and evenly in rib.

See information page for finishing instructions.

spencer by Louisa Harding

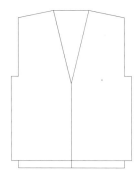

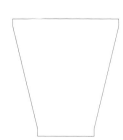

SIZES

One size to fit up to	97	cm
	38	in
Actual width	56.5	cm
	22½	in
Length	60.5	cm
	24	in
Sleeve length	45.5	cm
	18	in

YARNS
Wool Cotton and Rowanspun DK
50gm (1¾oz) balls:

A	DK Spun	Seal	852	8
B	Wool Cot	Skye	858	2
C	DK Spun	Swallow	859	2
D	Wool Cot	Pink	694	2
E	Wool Cot	Wren	850	1
F	DK Spun	Purple	628	2
G	Wool Cot	Blue	642	2

NEEDLES
1 pair 3¼mm (US 3) needles
1 pair 4mm (US 6) needles

BUTTONS
7

TENSION (GAUGE)
22 sts and 28 rows to 10cm (4in) measured over patterned stocking (stockinette) stitch using 4mm (US 6) needles

back
Cast on 134 sts using 3¼mm (US 3) needles and yarn A.
ROW 1 (RS): *K2, P2, rep from * to last 2 sts, K2.
ROW 2: P2, *K2, P2, rep from * to end.
Rep these 2 rows until work measures 2.5cm (1in) from cast-on edge, ending with a WS row.
Change to 4mm (US 6) needles, joining and breaking colors as required and using the intarsia technique described on the information page, work from chart for back as folls:
Working between appropriate markers, starting at chart row 1 for cardigan until chart row 94 is complete, ending with a WS row.
SHAPE ARMHOLES
Cast (bind) off 6 sts at beg of next 2 rows. *122 sts*
Cont without further shaping until chart row 164 is complete, ending with a WS row.

SHAPE SHOULDERS AND BACK NECK
Cast (bind) off 14 sts at beg of next 2 rows.
Cast (bind) off 14 sts, patt 19 sts, turn and leave rem sts on a holder.
Work each side of neck separately.
Cast (bind) off 4 sts, patt to end. Cast (bind) off rem 15 sts.
With RS facing, rejoin yarn to rem sts, cast (bind) off center 28 sts, patt to end.
Complete to match first side, rev shaping.

left front
Cast on 66 sts using 3¼mm (US 3) needles and yarn A.
Work 2.5cm (1in) in rib as given for back, ending with a WS row and inc 1 st at end of last row. *67 sts*
Change to 4mm (US 6) needles and, beg with chart row 1, work 94 rows in patt from chart for left front, ending with a WS row.
SHAPE ARMHOLE
Cast (bind) off 6 sts at beg of next row. *61 sts*
Cont without further shaping until chart row 104 is complete, ending with a WS row.
SHAPE FRONT NECK
Dec 1 st at neck edge on next row and every foll 3rd row to 43 sts.
Work without shaping until chart row 164 is complete, ending with a WS row.
SHAPE SHOULDER
Cast (bind) off 14 sts at beg of next row and foll alt row.
Work 1 row. Cast (bind) off rem 15 sts.

right front
Work as given for left front working from chart for right front and rev shaping.

sleeves (both alike)
Cast on 54 sts using 3¼mm (US 3) needles and yarn A.
ROW 1 (RS): *K2, P2, rep from * to last 2 sts, K2.
ROW 2: P2, *K2, P2 rep from * to end.
Rep these 2 rows until work measures 2.5cm, (1in) from cast-on edge, ending with a WS row.
Change to 4mm (US 6) needles.
Work 120 rows in patt from chart for sleeve, inc 1 st at each end of 3rd row and 4 foll alt rows and then every foll 4th row to 110 sts. Cast (bind) off loosely and evenly.

finishing
Press all pieces as described on the information page.
BUTTONHOLE BAND AND COLLAR
With RS of right front facing, using 3¼mm (US 3) needles and yarn A, pick up and knit 88 sts from

KEY
A
B
C
D
E
F
G

back

right front — left front

back

RIGHT AND LEFT FRONTS AND BACK

cast-on edge to beg of neck shaping, 48 sts to shoulder and 20 sts to center back neck. *156 sts*

NEXT ROW (WS): *K2, P2, rep from * to end.

NEXT ROW: Work as previous row.

NEXT ROW (WS) (BUTTONHOLE ROW): Rib 77 sts, (K2tog, yon twice, K2tog, patt 8) 6 times, K2tog, (yon) twice, K2tog, patt 3.

Work 4 more rows in rib.

NEXT ROW (RS): Cast (bind) off 77 sts, rib to end. *79 sts*

SHAPE COLLAR

Note: The wrong side of the band now becomes the RS of collar.

NEXT ROW (RS) (DEC): Rib to last 4 sts, K2tog, K2. *78 sts*

NEXT ROW: K1, P2, rib to end.

Rep these 2 rows 5 times ending at center back neck. *73 sts*

NEXT ROW (RS) (DEC): Rib to last 4 sts, K2tog, K2.

NEXT ROW (DEC): K1, P1, P2tog, rib to end.

Rep these 2 rows until 58 sts rem, ending with a RS row. Work collar edging as folls:

NEXT 2 ROWS (WS): K1, P1, P2tog, wrap next st (see information page), turn, K3.

These 2 rows form the edging, rep until only 3 edge sts rem. Cast (bind) off.

BUTTON BAND AND COLLAR

With RS of left front facing, using 3¼mm (US 3) needles and yarn A, pick up and knit 20 sts from center back neck to shoulder, 48 sts from shoulder to beg of front neck shaping and 88 sts to cast-on edge. *156 sts*

NEXT ROW (WS): *P2, K2, rep from * to end.

NEXT ROW: Work as previous row.

Rep these 2 rows until 7 rows in all are complete ending with a WS row.

NEXT ROW (RS): Rib 79 sts, cast (bind) off 77 sts. *79 sts*

SHAPE COLLAR

Note: The wrong side of the band now becomes the RS of collar.

NEXT ROW (DEC): Rejoin yarn to rem sts, K2, K2tog, rib to end. *78 sts*

NEXT ROW: Rib to last 3 sts, P2, K1.

Rep these 2 rows 5 times more. *73 sts*

NEXT ROW (RS) (DEC): K2, K2tog, rib to end.

NEXT ROW (DEC): Rib to last 4 sts, P2tog, P1, K1. Rep these 2 rows until 58 sts rem, ending with a WS row.

NEXT 2 ROWS (RS): K2, K2tog, wrap next st, turn P2, K1. These 2 rows form the edging, rep until only 3 edge sts rem. Cast (bind) off.

See information page for finishing instructions.

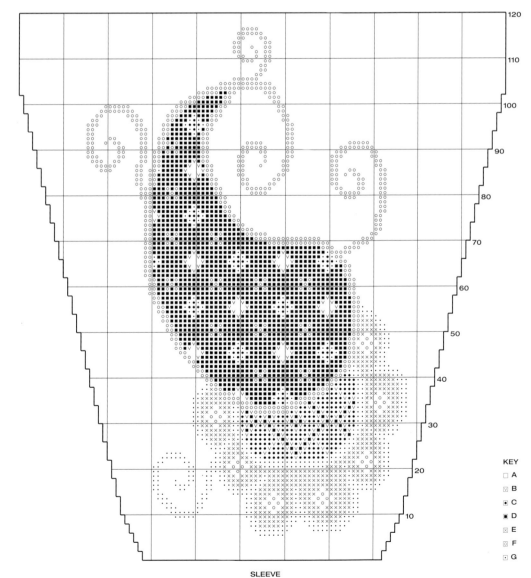

SLEEVE

KEY

☐ A
☑ B
⊡ C
■ D
☒ E
◉ F
⊡ G

information page

Below you will find some useful information about knitting and simple guidelines to help ensure that your garment turns out perfectly every time.

tension (gauge)

Obtaining the correct tension (gauge) is perhaps the single factor, which can make the difference between a successful garment and a disastrous one. It controls both the shape and size of an article, so any variation, however slight, can distort the look of the finished garment.

Different designers feature in our books and it is their tension, (gauge) given at the start of each pattern, which you must match. We recommend that you knit a square in pattern and/or stocking (stockinette) stitch (depending on the pattern instructions) of perhaps 5–10 more stitches and 5–10 more rows than those given in the tension note. Press the finished square under damp cloth and mark out the central 10cm (4in) square with pins. If you have too many stitches to 10cm (4in) try again using thicker needles, if you have too few stitches to 10cm (4in) try again using finer needles. Once you have achieved the correct tension (gauge) your garment will be knitted to the measurements indicated in the size diagram shown at the end of the pattern.

sizing and size diagram note

The instructions are given for the smallest size. Where they vary; work the figures in brackets for the larger sizes. One set of figures refers to all sizes.

Included with every pattern is a "size diagram" or sketch of the finished garment and its actual dimensions are given at the beginning of the pattern. The purpose of this is to enable you to accurately achieve a perfect-fitting garment without the need for worry during knitting. The measurement for the actual width gives the finished width of the garment at the under-arm point, and it is this measurement that the knitter should choose first; a useful tip is to measure one of your own garments which is a comfortable fit. Having chosen a size based on width, look at the corresponding length for that size; if you are not happy with the total length which we recommend, adjust your own garment before beginning your armhole shaping. Any adjustment after this point will mean that your sleeve will not fit into your garment easily. Don't forget to take your adjustment into account if there is any side seam shaping. Finally, look at the sleeve length, which gives the finished sleeve measurement, taking into account any top-arm insertion length. Measure your body between the center of your neck and your wrist, this measurement should correspond to half the garment width plus the sleeve length. Again, your sleeve length may be adjusted, but remember to take into consideration your sleeve increases. If you do adjust the length you must increase more frequently than the pattern states to shorten your sleeve, less frequently to lengthen it.

HEADING

Easy, straightforward knitting

Suitable for average knitter

For the more experienced knitter

chart note

Many of the patterns in the book are worked from charts. Each square on a chart represents a stitch and each line of squares a row of knitting. Each color used is given a different symbol or letter and these are shown in the materials section, or in the key alongside the chart of each pattern.

When working from the charts, read odd rows (K) from right to left and even rows (P) from left to right, unless otherwise stated.

knitting with color

There are two main methods of working color into a knitted fabric: Intarsia and Fair Isle techniques. The first method produces a single thickness of fabric and is usually used where a color is only required in a particular area of a row and does not form a repeating pattern across the row, as in the Fair Isle technique.

Intarsia

The simplest way to do this is to cut short lengths of yarn for each motif or block of color used in a row. Then joining in the various colors at the appropriate point on the row, link one color to the next by twisting them around each other where they meet on the wrong side. All ends can then either be darned along the color join lines, as each motif is completed or then can be "knitted-in" to the fabric of the knitting as each color is worked into the pattern. This is done in much the same way as "weaving-in" yarns when working the Fair Isle technique and does save time darning-in ends. It is essential that the tension is noted for Intarsia as this may vary from the stocking (stockinnette) stitch if both are used in the same pattern.

Fair Isle type knitting

When two or three colors are worked repeatedly across a row, strand the yarn not in use loosely behind the stitches being worked. If you are working with more than two colors, treat the "floating" yarns as if they were one yarn and always spread the stitches to their correct width to keep them elastic. It is advisable not to carry the stranded or "floating" yarns over more than three stitches at a time, but to weave them under and over the color you are working. The "floating" yarns are therefore caught at the back of the work.

All ribs should be knitted to a firm tension, for some knitters it may be necessary to use a smaller needle. In order to prevent sagging in cuffs and welts we suggest you use a "knitting-in" elastic.

finishing instructions

After working for hours knitting a garment, it seems a great pity that many garments are spoiled because such little care is taken in the pressing and finishing process. Follow the following tips for a truly professional-looking garment.

Pressing

Darn in all ends neatly along the selvage edge or a color join, as appropriate. Block out each piece of knitting using pins and gently press each piece, omitting the ribs, using a warm iron over a damp cloth.

Tip: Take special care to press the edges, as this will make sewing up both easier and neater.

Stitching

When stitching the pieces together, remember to match areas of color and texture very carefully where they meet. Use a seam stitch such as back stitch or mattress stitch for main knitting seams and join all ribs and neckband with a flat seam, unless otherwise stated.

Construction

Having completed the pattern instructions, join left shoulder and neckband seams as detailed above.

Sew the top of the sleeve to the body of the garment using the method detailed in the pattern, referring to the appropriate guide:

STRAIGHT CAST-OFF SLEEVES
Place center of cast-off edge of sleeve to shoulder seam. Sew top of sleeve to body, using markers as guidelines where applicable.

SQUARE SET-IN SLEEVES
Set sleeve head into armhole, the straight sides at top of sleeve to form a neat right-angle to cast-off sts at armhole on back and front.

SHALLOW SET-IN SLEEVES
Join cast-off sts, at beg of armhole shaping to cast-off sts at start of sleeve-head shaping. Sew sleeve head into armhole, easing in shaping.

SET-IN SLEEVES
Set in sleeve, easing sleeve head into armhole.

Join side and sleeve seams. Slipstitch pocket edgings and linings into place. Sew on buttons to correspond with buttonholes. After sewing up, press seams and hems. Ribbed welts and neckbands and any areas of gaiter stitch should not be pressed.

abbreviations

K	knit
P	purl
st(S)	stitch(es)
inc	increas(e)(ing)
dec	decreas (e) (ing)
St St	stocking stitch (1 row K, 1 row P)
garter st	garter stitch (K every row)
beg	begin(ning)
foll	following
rem	remain(ing)
revers (e) (ing)	reverse
rep	repeat
alt	alternate
cont	continue
patt	pattern
tog	together
mm	millimetres
cm	centimetres
in(s)	inch(es)
RS	right side
WS	wrong side
Sl1	slip one stitch
PSSO	pass slipped stitch over
p2sso	pass 2 slipped stitches over
tbl	through back of loop
M1	make one stitch by picking up horizontal loop before next stitch and knitting into back of it
yfwd	yarn forward
yrn	yarn round needle
yon	yarn over needle
cn	cable needle

CONVERSIONS
Needle sizes
Knitting needle are sized according to a standard sizing system, whatever material they are made from. There are three different systems: a metric system used in Europe and the UK; a US system and an old UK and Canadian system.

Old UK & Canadian size	Metric size	US size
000	10	15
00	9	13
0	8	11
1	7½	11
2	7	10½
3	6½	10½
4	6	10
5	5½	9
6	5	8
7	4½	7
8	4	6
9	3¾	5
10	3¼	4
11	3	2/3
12	2¾	2
13	2¼	1
14	2	0

Converting weights and lengths

oz = g x 0.0352
g = oz x 28.35
in = cm x 0.3937
cm = in x 2.54
yds = m x 0.9144
m = yds x 1.0936

yarn information

ALL SEASONS COTTON
60% cotton/40% acrylic/microfibre
Approximately 90m (98yds) per 50g

CHUNKY COTTON CHENILLE
Chunky-weight chenille yarn (US bulky-weight) 100% cotton
Approximately 140m (153yds) per 100g (3½oz) ball

CHUNKY TWEED
Chunky-weight wool yarn
(US bulky-weight)
100% pure new wool
Approximately 100m (109yds) per 100g (3½oz) hank

COTTON GLACÉ
Lightweight cotton yarn
100% cotton
Approximately 115m (125yds) per 50g (1¾oz) ball

DK TWEED
Double-knitting weight wool yarn (between US sport and worsted)
100% wool
Approximately 110m (120yds) per 50g (1¾oz) hank

FINE COTTON CHENILLE
Lightweight chenille yarn
89% cotton/11%polyester
Approximately 160m (175yds) per 50g (1¾oz) ball

4-PLY COTTON
Very lightweight cotton yarn (US fingering)
100% cotton
Approximately 170m (185yds) per 50g (1¾oz) ball

HANDKNIT DK COTTON
Medium-weight cotton yarn
100% cotton
Approximately 85m (92yds) per 50g (1¾oz) ball

MAGPIE ARAN
Aran-weight wool yarn
100% wool
Approximately 140m (153yds) per 100g (3¾oz) hank

MAGPIE TWEED
Aran-weight wool yarn
100% wool
Approximately 170m (185yds) per 100g (3¾oz) hank

ROWAN DENIM
Note: the denim shrinks in length when it is washed. This
must be taken into account if using a different yarn.
Medium-weight cotton yarn
100% cotton
Approximately 93m (101yds) per 50g (1¾oz) ball

ROWANSPUN DK
100% pure new wool
Approximately 200m (219yds) per 50g

TRUE 4-PLY BOTANY
4-ply-weight yarn
(US fingering)
100% pure new wool
Approximately 170m (185yds) per 50g (1¾oz) ball

WOOL COTTON
Double-knitting weight wool and cotton yarn (between
US sport and worsted)
50% merino wool/50% cotton
Approximately 113m (123yds) per 50g (1¾oz) ball

suppliers

Rowan Yarns are widely available. For a stockist near you or mail-order details, telephone Rowan Yarns direct on 01484 681 881 or visit their website on www.knitrowan.com.

For more information on suppliers outside the UK, contact the Rowan & Jaeger Handknits distributor listed for your country below:

BELGIUM: Pavan, Koningin Astridlaan 78, B9000 Gent. Tel: (32) 9 221 8591

CANADA: Canada: Diamond Yarn, 9697 St. Laurent, Montreal, Quebec, H3L 2N1. Tel: (514) 388-6188, www.diamondyarn.com.

Diamond Yarn (Toronto), 155 Martin Ross, Unit 3, Toronto, Ontario, M3J 2L9. Tel: (416) 736-6111.

FRANCE: Elle Tricot, 8 Rue du Coq, 67000 Strasbourg. Tel: (33) 3 88 23 03 13

GERMANY: Wolle & Design, Wolfshovener Strasse 76, 52428 Julich-Stetternich. Tel: (49) 2461 54735

HOLLAND: de Afstap, Oude Leliestraat 12, 1015 AW Amsterdam. Tel: (31) 20 6231445

HONG KONG: East Unity Co. Ltd, Unit B2, 7/F, Block B, Kailey Industrial Centre, 12 Fung Yip Street, Chai Wan. Tel: (852) 2869 7110

ICELAND: Storkurinn, Kjorgardi, Laugavegi 59, Reykjavik. Tel: (354) 551 82 58

JAPAN: DiaKeito Co. Ltd, 2-3-11 Senba-Higashi, Minoh City, Osaka. Tel: (81) 727 27 6604

SWEDEN: Wincent, Norrtulsgaten 65, 11345 Stockholm. Tel: (46) 8 673 70 60

USA: USA: Rowan USA, 4 Townsend West, Suite 8, Nashua, NH 03064. Tel: (603) 886-5041

index